CHRISTER BE

Arnhem 1944 – An Epic Battle Revisited
1: Tanks and Paratroopers

VAKTEL FÖRLAG

Some previous books by Christer Bergström

Luftwaffe Fighter Aircraft in Profile, 1997
Deutsche Jagdflugzeuge, 1999
Black Cross/Red Star: The Air War over the Eastern Front, vol. 1, 2000
Black Cross/Red Star: The Air War over the Eastern Front, vol. 2, 2001
More Luftwaffe Fighter Aircraft in Profile, 2002
Graf & Grislawski: A Pair of Aces, 2003
Jagdwaffe: Barbarossa – The Invasion of Russia, 2003
Jagdwaffe: The War in Russia January–October 1942, 2003
Jagdwaffe: The War in Russia November 1942–December 1943, 2004
Jagdwaffe: War in the East 1944–1945, 2005
Black Cross/Red Star: The Air War over the Eastern Front, vol. 3, 2006
Barbarossa: The Air Battle, 2007
Stalingrad: The Air Battle, 2007
Kursk: The Air Battle, 2008
Hans-Ekkehard Bob, 2008
Max-Hellmuth Ostermann, 2008
Bagration to Berlin, 2008
The Ardennes 1944–1945: Hitler's Winter Offensive, 2014
The Battle of Britain – An Epic Battle Revisited, 2015
Berömda flygaress, 2015
Black Cross/Red Star: The Air War over the Eastern Front, vol. 4, 2019

Vaktel
förlag

Vaktel förlag
Box 3027
630 03 Eskilstuna
vaktelforlag.se
forlag@vaktelforlag.se

This edition of Arnhem 1944 – An Epic Battle Revisited, Volume 1: Tanks and Paratroopers
first published 2019.
First published in Swedish by Vaktel Förlag 2017.
Original Swedish edition: Arnhem 1944 – Slaget om Holland. 1: Pansar och fallskärmsjägare
© 2017 and 2019 Christer Bergström.
English translation: Jonathan Newton.
Cover design: Fredrik Gustafson.
Insert layout: Fredrik Gustafson fredrikgustafsondesign@gmail.com
Maps: Samuel Svärd info@samuelsvard.se
ISBN 978-91-88441-48-5

CONTENTS

In memory of Cornelius Ryan

GLOSSARY AND GUIDE TO ABBREVIATIONS

Ia, German operational officer.
Ic, German intelligence officer.
1st Airlanding Light Regiment, British airborne artillery regiment.
1st Royal Dragoon, the 1st battalion of The Royal Dragoons.
2nd South Staffords, the 2nd battalion of South Staffordshire Regiment.
2nd Tactical Air Force, British tactical air corps, based in Belgium and France.
2nd TAF, abbreviation of the British 2nd Tactical Air Force.
7th KOSB, the 7th battalion of the British King's Own Scottish Borderers.
7th (Galloway) Battalion The King's Own Scottish Borderers, the 7th battalion (with local designation) of the British King's Own Scottish Borderers.
8th Air Force, American strategic air corps, based in England.
9th Air Force, American tactical air corps, based in Belgium and France.
IX Troop Carrier Command, American air transportation force on the Western Front 1944–1945.
43rd (Wessex) Infantry Division, British infantry division with local designation.
50th (Northumbrian) Infantry Division, British infantry division with local designation.
52nd (Lowland) Division, British infantry division with local designation.
86th (East Anglian) (Herts Yeo) Field Regiment, British artillery regiment with local designation.
88 mm gun, common name for a German anti-aircraft gun or anti-tank gun with a caliber of 88 mm.
A 4 (Aggregat 4), German ballistic missile, also called V 2.
Abteilung, battalion of the cavalry, panzer troops, anti-tank troops, artillery, and communications troops within the German

Army and within the Waffen-SS.
Acting Captain, see WS (British).
Air Vice Marshal, military rank within the British air force, the equivalent of a German Generalleutnant.
All American, honorary name for the U.S. 82nd Airborne Division.
Armee, army (German).
Armeegruppe, army group (German).
Armeekorps, army corps (German).
Armeeoberkommando, (Army Supreme Command), the staff of a German army.
Armoured Division, British tank division with a nominal strength in December 1944 of 343 tanks.
Army, military unit consisting of two or more corps, or the military ground troops of a country.
Army Group, military unit consisting of two or more armies.
Artillerie, artillery (German).
Assault gun, armoured tracked combat vehicle, whose mission it is to support infantry with a large-calibre gun firing high-explosive shells. The German assault gun StuG III combined that role with the role of being an anti-tank assault gun.
Aufklärungs-Abteilung, German reconnaissance battalion.
Ausf. (Ausführung), mark, model, or type (German).
B-17 Flying Fortress, (Bomber-17), American four-engined heavy bomber aircraft made by Boeing.
B-24 Liberator, (Bomber-24), American four-engined heavy bomber aircraft made by Consolidated.
B-25 Mitchell, (Bomber-25), American twin-engined heavy bomber aircraft made by North American.
B-26 Marauder, (Bomber-26), American twin-engined medium bomber aircraft made by Martin.

Bailey Bridge, Allied field bridge system consisting of prefabricated framework.

Bar, Medal Bar, a small medal bar attached to a medal's ribbon and which among the Western Allied forces indicated that a decoration had been bestowed once (or multiple times), e.g. DSO and two bars.

Bataillon, battalion (German).

Battalion, military unit, a subdivision to a brigade or a regiment, with a nominal force of 860 men in both the German and the American infantry in December 1944.

Batterle, battery (German); the equivalent within the German artillery of the infantry's companies, with a nominal strength of four guns.

Battery, the equivalent within the American artillery of the infantry's companies, with a nominal strength of mostly four guns.

Bazooka, American anti-tank rocket launcher.

Bf, (Bayerische Flugzeugwerke), alternative name for early constructions of German Messerschmitt aircraft.

Bletchley Park, the site outside London where the British during the Second World War deciphered German messages transmitted using the Enigma code machine.

Bomb Division, American air unit consisting of several Bomb Groups.

Bomber Command, the British strategic bomber aviation.

Bomb Group, aka Bombardment Group, American aviation unit, consisting of Heavy Bomb Groups with nominally 72 heavy bomber aircraft, or Medium Bomb Groups or Light Bomb Groups, consisting of 96 bomber aircraft.

Bomb Squadron, American air unit; three Bomb Squadrons formed a Bomb Group.

Border Regiment, a specific British military unit.

Brigade, military unit, usually consisting of two or more battalions or regiments, less than one division.

Brigade, British unit consisting of a number of battalions, or German military unit of varying size, however, less than one division.

Bronze Star, the fifth highest American decoration for acts ov valour in combat.

C-47, (Carrier-47), American twin-engined transportation aircraft made by Douglas.

Cavalry, British or American mechanised and armoured forces.

CCS, (Combined Chiefs of Staff), the supreme Allied military command.

Char, tank (French).

Close air support, air strike against enemy positions on the ground at the front in direct support of own ground troops.

Club Route, the Allied name for the XXX Corp's route of advance in "Market Garden".

Coldstream Guards, British regiment, originally organised in Coldstream, Scotland.

Company, military unit, subdivision of a battalion, with a nominal strength of about 200 men.

Corps, military unit, consisting of two or more divisions.

Delaying action, a tactical procedure intended to delay the opponent's advancement.

Dingo, British armoured scout car made by Daimler.

Direct Fire, firing with a direct aim against a target visible from the place of firing.

Distinguished Service Cross, the second highest U.S. decoration for gallantry.

Distinguished Service Order, one of the most prominent British military decorations. Usually only awarded officers with the rank of major or higher.

Division, military unit, the basic unit in both the German and the American armies, usually consisting of three regiments with auxiliary units and with a strength of between 10,000 and 20,000 men.

Douglas Boston, British name for American-made twin-engined bomber aircraft made by Douglas.

DSO, see Distinguished Service Order.

Engineer troops, also known as pioneer troops, a branch of the army mainly intended for work such as building bridges

6

and roads, as well as destruction work such as blasting, blocking, and mining, but also for battle using such weapons as flame-throwers.

Ersatz, (replacement) German (reserve) replacement unit, intended to replace casualties at other units.

Ersatzheer, (the replacement army) German military organisation for the training of troops and the replacement of casualties in the regular frontline units.

Fallschirmjäger, paratrooper (German).

Fallschirm-Ersatz- und Ausbildungs-Regiment, (para[trooper] replacement and training regiment), German replacement unit.

Fallschirm-Panzer-Ersatz- und Ausbildungs-Regiment, (para[trooper] [and] panzer replacement and training regiment), German replacement unit.

Field artillery, mobile artillery intended to support army units.

Field Marshal, the highest British military rank.

Fife and Forfarshire Yeomanry, a specific British military unit, originally a reserve unit. A Yeoman was originally a farmer, and Fife and Forfarshire are places in Scotland.

Fighter-bomber/fighter-bomber aircraft, fighter aircraft attacking targets on the ground with machine guns, automatic cannon, and bombs or high-explosive rockets.

Fighter Group, here: American air unit consisting of three American Fighter Squadrons with a total of 111-126 fighter/fighter-bomber aircraft.

Fighter Squadron, here: British fighter division usually with 12 aircraft.

FK, (Feldkanone), field cannon (German).

Flak (Fliegerabwehrkanone), anti-aircraft cannon (German).

Flieger-Division, (air division) German air unit, consisting of a non-defined number of Geschwader.

Flieger-Regiment, (air regiment) a unit where recruits in the German air force had their basic infantry training.

Focke Wulf 190, German single-engined fighter aircraft.

"Frundsberg", the honorary name of the German 10th SS Panzer Division, after Georg von Frundsberg, a German knight (1473–1528).

Field Gendarmes, uniformed police units of the Wehrmacht.

Field gun, cannon within the field artillery firing with a flat trajectory, i.e. with the barrel set to an angle less than 45°.

Field howitzer, an artillery gun able to fire with a muzzle angle larger and smaller than 45°.

"Garden", the codename for the ground operation within Operation Market Garden.

General der Artillerie, German general within the artillery.

General der Infanterie, German general within the infantry.

General der Panzertruppen, German general within the panzer troops.

Gepanzerte, armoured (German).

Glider Field Artillery Battalion, American artillery battalion landed by gliders.

Glider Infantry Regiment, American airborne regiment intended to be landed by glider.

Grenadier Guards, a specific British regiment.

Grenadier-Regiment, German infantry regiment.

Group, American Group: See Bomb Group and Fighter Group; British Group: the equivalent of the American air force's Wings, with a non-defined strength, however between 200 and 400 aircraft.

Gruppe, (group) German air unit consisting of (in December, 1944) four Staffels with, nominally, 16 aircraft in each, and a staff Schwarm with 4 aircraft within attack aviation and three Staffel with nominally 12 aircraft each and one staff Kette with 3 aircraft within bomber aviation.

Guards, British military units.

Half-track, vehicle combining wheel and track propulsion.

Halifax, British four-engined heavy bomber made by Handley-Page.

Hamilcar, British military transportation glider.

Hanomag, German Sonderkraftfahrzeug 251-type half-track, anti-tank vehicle.
HCR, abbreviation of Household Cavalry Regiment.
Heeres-Flak-Abteilung, army anti-aircraft battalion (German).
Heeresgruppe, army group (German).
Hetzer, German Panzerjäger 38(t)-type tracked tank destroyer.
Hohenstaufen, honorary name for the 9th German SS-Panzer division, named after a German medieval royal house, which, amongst others, included the crusader Frederick of Barbarossa.
Home Guard, military reserve units consisting of volunteers, during wartime of an age unfit for military service.
Hoog, (high [elevated]), Dutch.
Horsa, British military transportation glider.
Household Cavalry Regiment, a special British armoured reconnaissance unit. The name refers to the royal household.
Howitzer, artillery gun capable of firing at both higher and lower angles than 45°.
I.D., infantry division.
Indirect fire, arc firing against targets situated at such a large distance or hidden behind blocking terrain that they cannot be seen from the firing site.
Infanterie-Division, (infantry division), German.
Intelligence Officer, officer at a military staff, responsible for information about the opponent.
Irish Guards, a specific British regiment.
Jabo, (Jagdbomber), fighter-bomber (German).
Jagd-Division, (fighter squadron) German air unit consisting of an undefined number of Jagdgeschwader, however, smaller than a Luftflotte.
Jagdgeschwader, (fighter group) German fighter aircraft unit usually (in September, 1944) consisting of three Gruppe with 40 fighter aircraft and one staff Staffel of 12 fighter aircraft in each.
Jagdkorps, (fighter corps) German fighter aircraft unit consisting of a non-defined

number of Jagdgeschwaders, however, smaller than a Luftflotte.
Jagdpanther, German tracked tank destroyer.
Jagdpanzer, anti-tank assault gun (German).
Jagdpanzer IV, German tracked tank destroyer.
Jagdpanzer 38(t) Hetzer, German tracked tank destroyer.
JG (Jagdgeschwader), German fighter air unit, see Jagdgeschwader.
Junkers Ju 88, German twin-engined medium bomber made by Junkers.
Junkers Ju 188, German twin-engined medium bomber made by Junkers.
Kampfgeschwader, (combat group) German bomber air unit usually consisting of three Gruppen with 40 bombers and one staff Staffel with 12 bombers each.
Kampfgruppe, (battle group) within the German ground troops, an ad hoc battle group of non-defined size varying between slightly smaller than a regiment and generally slightly larger than a battalion; within the German air force, an air bomber unit consisting of three Staffel with 12 bombers and one staff Kette with three bombers each.
Kavallerie-Division, (cavalry division) German.
KG (Kampfgeschwader), German bomber air unit, see Kampfgeschwader.
King's Own Scottish Borders, a specific British regiment.
Knight's Cross, Ritterkreutz, Germany's highest decoration for valour in combat during the Second World War. The Knight's Cross had three additional levels: with oak leaves (Ritterkreuz mit Eichenlaub), with oak leaves and swords (Ritterkreuz mit Eichenlaub und Schwertern), and with oak leaves, swords, and diamonds (Ritterkreuz mit Eichenlaub, Schwertern und Brillanten).
Kompanie, company (German).
Korps, corps (German).
Kübelwagen, car model from Volkswagen, a German small military terrain vehicle.

KwK (Kampfwagen-Kanone), tank gun (German).
L, indicates the relation between the calibre and the length of the bore of a cannon; for example, L/71 indicates that the length of the bore is 71 times the calibre.
Laag, (low, lower), Dutch.
Lancaster, British four-engined heavy bomber made by Avro.
Landesschütze, (land shot) German Home Guard unit.
Lehrgeschwader, (learning group) in reality (in December 1944) a German bomber air unit, synonymous with Kampfgeschwader.
LFH 18/40 (leichte Feldhaubitze 18/40), German light field howitzer.
Light infantry company, German company with nothing else than small-bore arms (rifles, submachine-guns, machine guns).
Lightning, American Lockheed P-38-type twin-engined fighter/fighter-bomber.
Long Tom, the name of the American 155 millimetre field gun M1.
Luftflotte, (air fleet) the largest German air unit, consisting of two or more Korps or Divisions.
Luftflotte Reich, (air fleet of the Reich) the German air force's leadership organisation at home in Germany.
Luftwaffe, (air force) the German air force.
Luftwaffen-Feld-Division, (air force field division) ground unit formed by staff from the German air force.
Luftwaffenkommando West, the German air force's leadership organisation on the Western front.
M4 Sherman, American medium tank.
M5 Stuart, American light tank.
M10, American 3-inch Gun Motor Carriage M10-type tracked tank destroyer.
M18 Hellcat, American 76 mm Gun Motor Carriage (GMC) M18-type tracked tank destroyer.
M20, American six wheel-drive armoured car.
M24 Chaffee, American light tank.
M36 Jackson, American 90 mm Gun Motor Carriage M36-type tracked tank destroyer.

Marauder, American Martin B-26-type twin-engined medium bomber.
"Market", code name for the airborne operation within Operation "Market Garden".
Marschbataillon, (marching battalion) German replacement battalion.
Medal of Honor, the highest American decoration for valour in combat.
Mechanised, mechanised infantry is infantry equipped with armoured combat vehicles.
Messerschmitt Me 109, German single-engined fighter made by Messerschmitt.
Messerschmitt Me 262, German twin-engined fighter and fighter-bomber jet made by Messerschmitt.
MEW (Microwave Early Warning), Allied ground radar for combat control of aircraft.
MG 42 (Maschinengewehr 42), German machine gun.
Military Cross, the third highest military decoration for officers in the British and Commonwealth armed forces.
Mine roadblock, a string of mines tied together with a rope so that they could be pulled out in front of e.g. a vehicle.
Mortar, simple (usually muzzle-loaded) infantry support weapon firing grenades at angles exceeding 45°.
Mosquito, British twin-engined bomber, reconnaissance aicraft, and night fighter made by de Havilland.
Mustang, American North American P-51-type single-engined fighter.
Nachschub, (supplies) German military supply unit.
Nachtjagdgeschwader, (night fighter group) German night fighter wing consisting of two to four Gruppen with a nominal strength of 40 night fighters each.
Nachrichten-, German signal (corps).
Nebelwerfer, (smoke mortar), German rocket-propelled artillery.
Nottinghamshire Yeomanry (Sherwood Rangers), British tank regiment with local designation, originally a reserve unit. A Yeoman was originally a farmer, and Nottinghamshire and Sherwood are geographical places.

NJG, (Nachtjagdgeschwader), German fighter unit, see Nachtjagdgeschwader.
Oberbefehlshaber West, (Supreme Commander West) the German military Supreme Commander on the Western front.
Oberst der Polizei, (police colonel), German.
OB West, abbreviation for Oberbefehlshaber West.
OKW (Oberkommando der Wehrmacht), (the Supreme Command of the Armed Forces) the German armed forces' supreme command.
Operations Officer, staff officer responsible for any unit's planning of military operations and exercises as well as the development of tactics.
Ordnance QF, Quick-Firing British gun made by Ordnance.
OT (Organisation Todt), a militarily organised construction and engineering organisation in Germany.
P (Pursuit), American name for fighters.
P-38 Lightning, American twin-engined fighter/fighter-bomber made by Lockheed.
P-47 Thunderbolt, American single-engined fighter/fighter-bomber made by Republic.
P-51 Mustang, American single-engined fighter made by North American.
Pak (Panzerabwehr-Kanone), anti-tank gun (German).
Pak40 auf 38H Selbstfahrlaffete, (38H-type tracked tank destroyer), a German tracked tank destroyer.
Panther, German Panzerkampwagen V–type medium tank.
Panzerarmee, Panzer army (German).
Panzer-Artillerie-Regiment, (Panzer artillery regiment) artillery regiment in a German Panzer division.
Panzer-Aufklärungs-Abteilung, Panzer reconnaissance battalion (German).
Panzer-Division, Panzer division (German).
Panzerfaust, (Panzer fist) German anti-tank rocket launcher.
Panzer-Füsilier, (Armoured Fusiliers) German anti-tank and reconnaissance troops.
Panzer Grenadier, mechanised infantry, that is, equipped with armoured combat vehicles.

Panzer Grenadier vehicle, armoured combat vehicle intended for transportation of infantry soldiers.
Panzer IV, German Panzerkampwagen IV–type medium tank.
Panzer reconnaissance battalion, battalion for battle reconnaissance for a Panzer division.
Panzerjäger-Abteilung, anti-tank battalion (German).
Panzerkorps, Panzer Corps (German).
Panzer-Pionier-Bataillon, pioneer battalion in the German Panzer units.
Panzer-Regiment, Panzer Regiment (German).
Panzerschreck, (tank's fright) German Raketenpanzerbüchse 54-type anti-tank rocket launcher.
Para, abbreviation for Parachute or Paratroop.
Parachute Battalions, British or American parachute units.
Parachute Brigade, British unit, normally consisting of three Parachute Battalions.
Parachute Field Artillery Battalion, field artillery battalion in the British and American parachute units.
Parachute Infantry Regiment, British parachute infantry unit.
Pathfinder, British and American special parachute units deployed ahead of the main forces so as to mark the landing zone with radio beam guides, smoke signals, colour panels, etc.
PIAT, Projector, Infantry, Anti Tank, a British one-man anti-tank rocket launcher for close combat.
Pionier-Bataillon, German military engineer battalion.
PIR, abbreviation of Parachute Infantry Regiment.
PK, see Propagandakompanie.
Platoon, military unit, subdivision of a company. The German infantry companies consisted of three platoons, the American infantry companies consisted of four platoons. The nominal strength of a platoon was 48-50 men in the German infantry and 41 men in the American infantry.

Platoon Sergeant, the platoon leader's second in command in an American platoon.

Polish Independent Parachute Brigade Group, Polish parachute unit.

Propagandakompanie, (propaganda company) German military unit with the task of raising morale, for instance by reporting from the front.

PzDiv, abbreviation of Panzer-Division.

RAF (Royal Air Force), see Royal Air Force.

Red Army, (krasnaja armija) the Soviet army during the Second World War.

The Red Devils, name for British paratroopers.

Regiment, military unit, subdivision of a division, with a nominal strength of about 3,000 men.

Rijksweg, (national highway) Dutch.

Royal Air Force, the British air force.

Royal Artillery, the British artillery.

Royal Army Service Corps (RASC), a British military organisation for distributing supplies to the armed forces.

Royal Dragoons, a British tank regiment.

Royal Tank Regiment, British tank regiment.

SA, (Sturmabteilung) German Nazi paramilitary force.

Sanität, (healthcare) German medical unit.

SAS (Special Air Service), British military special forces for intelligence and operations behind enemy lines.

SA-Standarte, (SA standard) regional SA force.

Self-propelled artillery, artillery gun mounted on tracked vehicle.

Schiffstamm-Abteilung, (ship regular battalion) German battalion of seamen who were currently not at sea.

Schlachtgeschwader, (battle group) German ground-attack aviation group.

Schwere Heeres-Panzerjäger-Abteilung, heavy army tank destroyer battalion (German).

Schwere Panzer-Abteilung, heavy Panzer battalion (German).

Schwere Panzerjäger-Abteilung, heavy tank destroyer battalion (German).

Screaming Eagles, honorary name for the American 101st Airborne Division.

Sd.Kfz. (Sonderkraftfahrzeug), see Sonderkraftfahrzeug.

SdKfz 10, German open, lightly armoured cross-country military half-track (tank destroyer) intended for troop transportation and as a traction vehicle.

SdKfz 222, German open, four-wheel Panzer reconnaissance vehicle.

Sdkfz 233, German open, eight-wheel Panzer reconnaissance vehicle, usually with a 75mm gun.

Sdkfz 234 Puma, German eight-wheel Panzer reconnaissance vehicle with a 50mm gun in a revolving turret.

SdKfz 250, German open, lightly armoured cross-country military half-track (tank destroyer) mainly intended for troop transportation.

Serjeant, (sergeant). The British and New Zealand armies (but not the air forces) spelled this military rank with a "j" instead of a "g" until 1953.

sFH 18, (schwere Feldhaubitze 18) German heavy field howitzer.

SHAEF (Supreme Headquarters Allied Expeditionary Force) see Supreme Headquarters Allied Expeditionary Force.

Sherman, American M4-type medium tank.

Signal Corps, military unit handling radio liaison.

Signals, Signal (Corps).

Silver Star, the third highest American decoration for valour in combat.

Sonderkraftfahrzeug, (special vehicle) collective name for German Panzer vehicles.

The South Staffordshire Regiment, British infantry and parachute regiment with local designation.

Spitfire, British single-engined fighter made by Vickers Supermarine.

Squad, group (U.S. Army).

Squadron, British tank company consisting of four Troops (platoons and one HQ Troop (staff platoon) with four tanks each. Also Air Squadron, 12 fighters.

SS (Schutzstaffel), (protection unit) the German Nazi Party's paramilitary and also purely military force.

SS-Reichsführer, (national leader of the SS) the title of the leader of the SS, Heinrich Himmler.

Staffel, (squadron) in the German air force with a nominal strength of 12–16 aircraft.

Stuart, American M5-type light tank.

StuG III (Sturmgeschütz III), see Sturmgeschütz III.

StuK (Sturmkanone), see Sturmkanone.

Sturmgeschütz III, German tracked assault gun.

Sturmgeschütz-Brigade, assault gun brigade (German).

Sturmkanone, German assault gun.

Sturm-Zug, (storm platoon) the head platoon in a German infantry or paratrooper battalion.

Supreme Headquarters Allied Expeditionary Force, the headquarters of the Supreme Commander of the Allied forces in Western Europe, General Eisenhower.

Tank destroyer, armoured combat vehicle intended to combat tanks.

TAC (Tactical Air Command), see Tactical Air Command.

Tactical Air Command, the command for the tactical air support for a given American army. A Tactical Air Command of the 9th Air Force consisted in December 1944 of four to six Fighter Groups and one Squadron each, with reconnaissance aircraft (24 aircraft) and night fighters (18 aircraft).

Thunderbolt, American Republic P-47-type single-engined fighter.

Tiger I, German heavy Panzerkampfwagen VI-type tank.

Tiger II, German heavy Panzerkampfwagen VI Ausf. B Königstiger-type tank.

Troop, the approximate equivalent of a platoon in British tank units, four tanks.

Troop Carrier Group, American air transport unit, nominally consisting of 80–110 transportation aircraft.

Troop Carrier Squadron, American air transport unit; each Troop Carrier Group consisted of three Troop Carrier Squadrons.

Troop Carrier Wing, American air transport unit, consisting of two to five Troop Carrier Groups.

Typhoon, British single-engined ground attack aircraft made by Hawker.

Ultra, code for the British decryption of German messages that had been coded with the Enigma code machine.

USAAF (United States Army Air Force), the American army air force: during the Second World War, the American military air force was divided between the Army Air Force, the Navy Air Force, and the Marine Corps Aviation.

U.S. Strategic Air Forces in Europe, the supreme command for the American strategic air force in Europe.

V 1 (Vergeltungswaffe 1), (retaliation weapon 1) German rocket-propelled Fieseler 103-type robot bomb.

V 2 (Vergeltungswaffe 2), (retaliation weapon 2) German ballistic bomb, also known as A4.

Verschleiung, (concealing) German name for a military operation to conceal, mislead, and keep thing secret from the opponent.

V weapons, German V1, V2, and V3-type retaliation weapons.

Waco, American military transportation glider.

Wachbataillon, (guard battalion) German.

Waffen-SS, (the armed SS), the exclusively military troops of the SS.

Wehrkreis, (defence area) part of Germany's military territorial division, corresponding to Military Districts or Military Command Areas. For instance, Wehrkreis VI, which included Westphalia, the northern Rhineland, and eastern Belgium.

Wehrmacht, (the defence force) the German armed forces.

Wehrmachtbefehlshaber Niederlande, (the Supreme Commander of the armed forces in the Netherlands) the Supreme Command for the German armed forces in the occupied Netherlands.

Wehrmachtsbericht, (the armed forces' report) the German armed forces' daily news reports, broadcast by radio.

West Wall, the German fortification line along Germany's western border.

Wing, an American Wing: an American

air unit consisting of two or more Groups;
usually, two Wings were included in an
American air division. British Wing: the
equivalent of the U.S. Air Force's Group.
Wirtschafts-Bataillon, (science battalion)
German army service battalion, that is,
cooking units.
WS, (War Substantive) temporary wartime
(higher) military rank (British).
z.b.V., (zur besonderen Verwendung) for
special use (German).
Zug, German platoon.

MILITARY RANKS

WEHRMACHT	WAFFEN-SS	BRITISH ARMY	U.S. ARMY
Generals			
Reichsmarschall*	(no equivalence)	(no equivalence)	(no equivalence)
Generalfeldmarschall	Reichsführer SS	Field Marshal	General of the Army
Generaloberst	SS-Oberstgruppenführer	General	General
General	SS-Obergruppenführer	Lieutenant-General	Lieutenant General
Generalleutnant	SS-Gruppenführer	Major-General	Major General
Generalmajor	SS-Brigadeführer	Brigadier	Brigadier General
Officers			
(no equivalence)	SS-Oberführer	(no equivalence)	(no equivalence)
Oberst	SS-Standartenführer	Colonel	Colonel
Oberstleutnant	SS-Obersturmbannführer	Lieutenant-Colonel	Lieutenant Colonel
Major	SS-Sturmbannführer	Major	Major
Hauptmann	SS-Hauptsturmführer	Captain	Captain
Oberleutnant	SS-Obersturmführer	Lieutenant	First Lieutenant (1/Lt)
Leutnant	SS-Untersturmführer	Second Lieutenant	Second Lieutenant (2/Lt)
Non-commissioned officers			
Stabsfeldwebel	SS-Sturmscharführer	Regimental Serjeant-Major	Sergeant Major
Oberfeldwebel	SS-Hauptscharführer	Battalion Serjeant-Major	Master Sergeant
Feldwebel	SS-Oberscharführer	Company Serjeant-Major	Sergeant First Class
Unterfeldwebel	SS-Scharführer	Platoon Serjeant-Major	Staff Sergeant
Unteroffizier	SS-Unterscharführer	Serjeant	Sergeant
Junior non-commissioned officers & privates			
Stabsgefreiter	(no equivalence)	(no equivalence)	(no equivalence)
Obergefreiter	SS-Rottenführer	Corporal	Corporal
Gefreiter	SS-Sturmmann	Lance Corporal	(no equivalence)
Oberschütze	SS-Oberschütze	(no equivalence)	Private First Class (PFC)
Soldat/Schütze/	SS-Schütze	Private	Private
Grenadier			

* Only one person held this highest military rank, Hermann Göring.

Apart from this, the U.S. Army had non-commissioned and junior non-commissioned ranks for so-called technical specialists. These had the following equivalents: First Sergeant – Master Sergeant, Technical Sergeant – (no equivalence), Technician Third Grade [T/3] – Staff Sergeant, Technician fourth Grade [T/4] – Sergeant, Technician Fifth Grade [T/5] – Corporal

TIMELINE

1939	1 September	Germany attacks Poland
	3 September	The United Kingdom and France declares war on Germany
1940	10 May	Germany launches full-scale attack in the West
	25 June	France surrenders to Germany
1941	22 June	Germany invades the Soviet Union
	11 December	Germany declares war on the United States
1944	6 June	The Allies land in Normandy
	1 August	The Allies break through the frontline in Normandy
	7–21 August	Most of the German Western army perishes in the Falaise pocket
	1 September	General Eisenhower takes over the command of the Allied ground forces in the West from Montgomery
	3 September	The British army liberates Brussels
	4 September	The German First Parachute Army is formed in the Netherlands and northern Belgium
	8 September	German bombing of London with V2 rockets begins from The Hague
	10 September	The outline of Operation "Market Garden" is established
	17 September	Operation "Market Garden" commences
1945	8 May	Germany surrenders

DRAMATIS PERSONAE

GERMANY

von Allwörden, SS-Hauptsturmführer Klaus, commander of SS-Jagdpanzer-Abteilung 9/Kampfgruppe Allwörden.

Bittrich, Obergruppenführer Wilhelm, commander of II. SS-Panzerkorps.

Brinkmann, SS-Sturmbannführer Heinrich, commander of SS-Panzer-Aufklärungs-Abteilung 10.

Chill, Generalleutnant Kurt, commander of Kampfgruppe Chill.

Christiansen, General Friedrich, Wehrmachtbefehlshaber Niederlande.

Euling, SS-Hauptsturmführer Karl-Heinrich, commander of I. Bataillon/SS-Panzergrenadier-Regiment 22/SS-Kampfgruppe Euling.

Feldt, General Kurt, commander of "Korps Feldt".

Gräbner, SS-Hauptsturmführer Viktor, commander of SS-Panzer-Aufklärungs-Abteilung 9/SS-Kampfgruppe Gräbner.

Harmel, SS-Oberführer Heinrich, commander of 10. SS-Panzer-Division "Frundsberg".

Harzer, SS-Obersturmbannführer Walter, acting commander of 9. SS-Panzer-Division "Hohenstaufen".

Helle, SS-Standartenführer Paul, commander of SS-Wachbataillon 3.

Hencke, Oberst Fritz, commander of Fallschirm-Lehrstab 1/Kampfgruppe Hencke.

von der Heydte, Oberstleutnant Friedrich August Freiherr, commander of Fallschirmjäger-Regiment 6/ Kampfgruppe von der Heydte.

Knaust, Major Hans-Peter, commander of Kampfgruppe Knaust.

Krafft, SS-Sturmbannführer Josef "Sepp", commander of SS-Panzergrenadier-Ausbildungs- und Ersatz-Bataillon 16/SS-Kampfgruppe Krafft.

Kussin, General Friedrich, field commander in Arnhem.

Lippert, SS-Standartenführer Michael, commander of SS Unterführerschule Arnheim.

Meindl, General Eugen, commander of II. Fallschirmkorps.

Model, Generalfeldmarschall Walter, commander of Heeresgruppe B.

Möller, SS-Hauptsturmführer Hans, commander of SS-Panzer-Pionier-Bataillon 9/Kampfgruppe Möller.

Paetsch, SS-Obersturmbannführer Otto, deputy division commander of 10. SS-Panzer-Division "Frundsberg" 17 September 1944.

Rauter, SS-Obergruppenführer Hanns Albin, the highest SS and police commander in the Netherlands.

Reinhard, General Hans Wolfgang, commander of LXXXVIII. Armeekorps.

Reinhold, SS-Sturmbannführer Leo, commander of II. Abteilung/SS-Panzer-Regiment 10.

von Rundstedt, Generalfeldmarschall Gerd, Oberbefehlshaber West.

Scherbenning, Generalleutnant Walter, commander of Division z.b.V. 406.

Schwappacher, SS-Sturmbannführer Oskar, commander of V. Abteilung/SS-Artillerie-Ausbildungs-und-Ersatz-Regiment.

Sonnenstuhl, Sturmbannführer Hans-Georg, commander of SS-Panzer-Artillerie-Regiment 10.

Student, Generaloberst Kurt, commander of 1. Fallschirmarmee.

von Tettau, Generalleutnant Hans, commander of Division Tettau.

Walther, Oberst Erich, commander of Kampfgruppe Walther.

BRITAIN

Adair, Major-General Allan, commander of Guards Armoured Division.
Browning, Lieutenant-General Frederick, commander of I Airborne Corps.
Dempsey, Lieutenant-General Miles, commander of British Second Army.
Frost, Lieutenant-Colonel John, commander of 2nd Battalion, 1st Parachute Brigade.
Goulburn, Lieutenant-Colonel Edward, "Eddie". commander of 1st (Motor) Battalion, Grenadier Guards.
Gwatkin, Brigadier Norman, commander of 5th Guards Armoured Brigade.
Hackett, Brigadier John, commander of 4th Parachute Battalion.
Hicks, Brigadier Philip, commander of 1st Air Landing Brigade.
Horrocks, Lieutenant-General Brian, commander of XXX Corps.
Lathbury, Brigadier Gerald, commander of 1st Parachute Brigade.
Montgomery, Field Marshal Bernard Law, commander of British-Canadian 1st Army Group.
O'Connor, Lieutenant-General Sir Richard, commander of VIII Corps.
Payton-Reid, Lieutenant-Colonel Robert, commander of 7th KOSB, 1st Air Landing Brigade.
Ritchie, Lieutenant-General Neil, commander of XII Corps.
Vandeleur, Lieutenant-Colonel John Ormsby Evelyn, "Colonel Joe", commander of Irish Guards.
Urquhart, Major-General Robert Elliott, "Roy", commander of 1st Airborne Division.

UNITED STATES

Bradley, Lieutenant General Omar, commander of 12th Army Group.
Brereton, Lieutenant General Lewis H., commander of First Allied Airborne Army.
Eisenhower, General Dwight D., the Allied Supreme Commander in the West.
Ekman, Colonel William, commander of the 505th Parachute Infantry Regiment.
Gavin, Brigadier General James, commander of U.S. 82nd Airborne Division.
Hodges, Lieutenant General Courtney, commander of U.S. First Army.
Lindquist, Colonel Roy, commander of 508th Parachute Infantry Regiment.
Patton, Lieutenant General George S., commander of U.S. Third Army.
Sink, Colonel Robert F., commander of 506th Parachute Infantry Regiment.
Taylor, Major General Maxwell, commander of U.S. 101st Airborne Division.
Tucker, Colonel Reuben H., commander of 504th Parachute Infantry Regiment.
Vandervoort, Lieutenant Colonel Benjamin, "Vandy", commander of 2nd Battalion, 505th Parachute Infantry Regiment.
Williams, Major General Paul L., commander of IX Troop Carrier Command.

Author's Preface

I had the impulse to write this book many years ago, when I was browsing through material about "Market Garden" when visiting archives to research other chapters of the Second World War, and, by sheer coincidence, stumbled across previously unpublished material that definitely killed the myth that the British paratroopers "landed in the middle of accumulations of German tanks" in Arnhem. The assumption I made then – that this could not be the only material of this kind, unknown first-hand material that showed that the common image of "Market Garden" is not correct – has been confirmed to an even larger extent than I could imagine at the time.

Even though it has soon been 75 years since the Second World War, the historiography of this largest armed conflict in human history is still marred by a number of errors and misunderstandings. Myths that have more or less been fabricated still live on.

The major part of the archive material on the Second World War in official collections has now been made accessible, but this has obviously not helped – for several reasons. To begin with, we have the fact that the German side destroyed most of its remaining military documents at the end of the war. Even if Germany's Bundesarchiv has an impressive collection of documents from the Second World War at its disposal, it only constitutes a small part of the German military documents that were produced during the war. This is especially true for the last years of the war. In order to get as good an image as possible from the German side, I have during the last few decades had access to large quantities of first-hand material (documents from the war) from private collections – veterans, veterans' associations, collectors, etc. The typical fate of such material that is not present at the

Bundesarchiv, is that a clerk saved a war diary or something similar from being burned, and instead buried it in a leather briefcase next to a certain tree. After the fall of the Berlin Wall, many such briefcases have been unearthed, and the documents have been saved for posterity. However, the veterans that have dug them up again have, to a remarkably low extent, been interested in handing the material over to the Bundesarchiv.

But even when using first-hand sources, you will be facing large challenges, which every historian knows. Documents are, after all, written by human beings of flesh and blood, who often have reason to embellish their own or their commanders' actions before superiors, and so on.

Military documents are not enough by themselves. It takes genuine previous knowledge in order to critically examine what is reasonable and the importance of the event that the report deals with. At the time of the creation of these reports, the report writers often had no knowledge of how significant the events that are being discussed in the report were. This affects what they chose to include in the report, and what was omitted.

The cultural context in which the documents were created also plays a role that is not insignificant. Without making any assessment of it, it is obvious, when studying military reports from the war, notice how different military traditions and writing traditions were affecting the way in which these documents were written. German and British internal military reports, for example, are usually written in quite a cold and objective tone. Reports from the U.S. Army, however, are often characterised by the report writer's subjectivity, so that these reports become more of "literature". American reports, therefore, often have higher legibility, at the expense of certain, as the Americans put it, "hard facts".

Cross-referencing documents from both sides is absolutely crucial to form an image that is as close to the actual events as possible. To take an example from the contents in this book, a German unit's report at one occasion gives the image of a German tactical withdrawal from a certain sector on a certain day. If one studies the American unit's report of the same incident, an image instead emerges of the German unit's defence collapsing as most of the soldiers threw their weapons and gave up, after which only scattered remnants were forced into a headlong retreat.

The war veterans' own stories play an important part in all of my books. When treating these subjective accounts, it is indeed of greatest importance to have a strictly critical attitude to the sources. A personal account in and by itself could be very valuable, but it could also give a completely erroneous image of the real events. This is a well-known phenomenon within, for example, witness psychology. Here, too, genuine previous knowledge is a prerequisite in order to assess how well a recollection that is 60, 70, or 75 years old reflects the actual events. But often the veterans' accounts serve as a crucial complement to the official military reports. In the above case with two versions of the German retreat, I have had the opportunity to speak to veterans who participated themselves in this battle. Then, it turns out that voices from both sides, both Germans and Americans, generally confirm the American report in the example above, why you can conclude that the German description of a "tactical withdrawal" in reality is an euphemism of an unplanned outright flight.

Apart from the large number of veterans (and their relatives) whom I have met and interviewed or corresponded with, or have asked questions by proxy during the last four decades, there has been, notably in the case with Operation "Market Garden", yet another unique goldmine of veterans' own accounts, and that is the property left by Irish-American war correspondent and author Cornelius Ryan.

Cornelius Ryan astounded the world with *The Longest Day* – his highly detailed book about the invasion of Normandy, which in those days (1959) was quite unique with its accounts from both of the warring sides. A few years later, Ryan published his book about the Battle of Berlin, but he has earned his greatest fame for his last magnum opus from the Second World War, *A Bridge Too Far*, about Operation "Market Garden". Before this book was published in 1974, Operation "Market Garden" was not particularly well known in the prevailing historiography, and, to whatever extent the subject was treated, the accounts were characterised by the victor's perspective.

It is quite obvious that it was Ryan's ambition to rectify both these factors, and he spent enormous work on penetrating deeply into the available material – on both sides.

Cornelius Ryan's passionate writing of his book took part in a neck-and-neck race with the fatal disease that had got a grip on him. Perhaps this led him to publish it before he was actually finished with his work. When the book was published in January 1974, Ryan had ten months left to live.

Ryan bequeathed the property he left, as basic research for this book, to the Ohio University, USA. This collection – The Cornelius Ryan Collection of World War II Papers and the Mahn Center for Archives and Special Collections, Ohio University Libraries – shows the immense and very careful research work that Ryan spent ahead of this book. The collection consists of an impressing amount of typed interviews or correspondence with veterans, reports that had been written both during and after the war, military studies, various other documents, etc., systematically gathered in about 1,500 folders and 148 boxes.

Even if I myself have been spending many years and numerous travels on basic research ahead of this book of my own about Operation "Market Garden", my research material cannot be measured in any way by extent with Cornelius Ryan's. I doubt that there is any other writer about the Second World War who has amassed such extensive basic material about one and the same chapter. Ryan's material was gathered by him himself already during the war, and after that, during the entire period until his decease. The last document, a correspondence between Ryan and British paratroop veteran John Frost, is dated 7 November 1974 – sixteen days before Ryan's premature decease (at age 54).

The fact that Ryan continued his research work about "Market Garden", even after the book had been published, indicates that he himself might have believed that he was not really finished, that his first book was only a sort of preliminary edition. How it was with that we will likely never know, but even a cursory study of the Cornelius Ryan Collection shows that there are large amounts of material that Ryan had not included in his book. Unless the book had been published during the author's own race against his own fatal disease, one would have been tempted to believe that Ryan simply was unable to survey his own immense material. The fact is that diving genuinely deeply into this material shows that not only was there very much that Ryan did not use in his book, but that a large amount of this refutes some of the theses that Ryan himself is pursuing in his book. We can probably rest assured that if Ryan had been spared this tragic disease, he would have spent yet a few more years on the work with his book about "Market Garden", and that it would thus have supplied us with quite a number of other conclusions than what is now the case.

The fact that Cornelius Ryan donated his rich material to public access at the Ohio University in the hope that others would take over where he left off, and, with the help of the material indicates that he probably did not have time to include in his book, that others would complete his own work. A careful study of the property Ryan left and of the accessible literature on the subject, however, shows that this quite obviously has been the case.

A torrent of new books about "Market Garden" has been published since 1974, and many of its authors have done meritorious work in producing new research. But it appears quite obvious that nobody has previously tried to go through the Cornelius Ryan Collection in its entirety in order to publish the important pieces of the jigsaw puzzle that Ryan produced but was never able to use in his book. This is even more remarkable considering how easily accessible this material is, and how very helpful the staff handling the collection is. I would especially like to emphasise the very kind courtesy shown by Sara Harrington, Head of Arts and Archives at Ohio University Libraries.

This book of mine is not an academic thesis – I have, to a larger extent than in any of my previous books (with the exception of outright biographies) let individual personal accounts and people's own experiences on a "ground level" characterise the story – but, in one respect, I have had the ambition of an academic thesis: It has been my ambition to study as much of the available first-hand material about "Market Garden" as possible. Even if this is virtually impossible – considering the abundance of minor veterans' associations, military unit archives, local folklore archives that contain some relevant material, and personal belongings – I think I can say that the material for this book is based on the absolute majority of the official archives, including some minor archives. Volume 1 of *Arnhem 1944* is mainly based on material from some twenty official archives, and primary documents from private archives. In that way, my first suspicion that all was not right with the common image of "Market Garden" has been increasingly confirmed.

This book thus presents what is largely a completely new image of Operation "Market Garden", but I would like to repeat that this material is based on both my own research and the previously unused research of others that I have been allowed to take part of.

There are individual human accounts here, and actions by individuals that played a decisive role, but which have sunk into oblivion or, for various reasons, have been kept secret when writing history; accounts of great mistakes on both sides that unnecessarily cost many human lives but which have previously been swept under the carpet, and where scapegoats have been made. One of the more conspicuous examples of the latter is a pointless bloodbath of young Americans, which in the prevalent historiography has been exalted into a successful military operation. On the other side, a German officer has been undeservedly blamed for a virtual suicidal attack. These are just a few examples.

In general, there is, as mentioned, a large number of human stories and eyewitness accounts in the book. My ambition here is to keep the balance so that both sides get equal space; as many Germans as Allies get to express themselves, and Dutch civilians also share their experiences.

This book differs from most of my previous books partly through the smaller, more "usual" format, and partly because it is more of a "text book" with the text gathered and the images mostly concentrated to specific pages of images. One exception has been made for photographs that illustrate specific events in the text: descriptions of certain events in the text are being illustrated by, for example, an image of the place where it all took place, the way it looked by that time.

I have also included a large amount of QR codes to illustrate what is being described in the text. In Volume 1 alone, 41 QR codes have been included. There you can see newsreels from the time, or veterans talking about what is being described, etc. Film clips indicated in the QR codes could perhaps be removed from the web site (which is being controlled by somebody else) in the future. Please contact me at the e-mail address below in such case, and we will surely be able to solve this.

Clear and comprehensive maps are indispensable for books of this kind. The masterly military history cartographer Samuel Svärd has contributed maps for this book. .

No human product is possible without the support and help in various ways from many other people. This is true not least for the writing of a book such as this.

First of all, great and warm thanks to my family, Maria, Bambi, Caroline, Albin, Benjamin, and Bianca. Without their understanding and support, this book could never have been realised. I would also like to extend many thanks to my mother, Britta Lindberg, for her constant support and encouragement. My thanks also to Hans Östensson, "Mr Hans", who has been working as a sounding board and "the devil's advocate".

The following people have also been assisting me with large and small things for the creation of this book:

James W. Alexander, Frans Ammerlaan, Francis J. Anderson, Joseph E. Atkins, Gerhard Baeker, Günther Bahr, Mirko Bayerl, Ben Beck, Salvatore Bellavia – Archives Assistant King's College London Archives and Liddell Hart Centre for Military Archives, Holger Benecke, Helmut Berendes, Mario Van den Berg – Gemeentearchiv Ede, Dag Berggren, Lennart Berns, Björn Bertilsson, Peter Björk, Irene Chr. Blasczyk – Geldersarchief Arnhem, Gordon Blume, Jessica Borge – Archives Assistant King's College London Archives, Jan van den Born, Dr. Jan Brouwer, Richard H. Byers, Thomas Caesar, Toni Canfora, Niall Cherry, Jeff Clements, Mats Drugge, Olve Dybvig, Joseph S. Evans Jr., Lisbeth och Peter Figur, Anders Frankson, Adolf Galland, Robert Garlich, Wendy George – Ast. Curator Airborne Assault Archive, Baron Hugh Griffiths, Fred Gordon, Alfred Grislawski, Fredrik Gustafson, Lars Gyllenhaal, Rense Havinga – Conservator archief Bevrijdingsmuseum Groesbeek, Martin Hoffmann, Jonathan Holt – Archive and Library Officer The Tank Museum Bovington, Wilhelm Huber, Werner Hohenberg, Michael Holm, Bengt Högberg, Miel Jacobs – Geldersarchief Arnhem, Per Åke Jansson, Morten Jessen, Daniel Johansson, Seppo Juttula, Rolf Kant, Michael Kenny, Lisa van Kessel – Research and Projects Archief Bevrijdingsmuseum Groesbeek, Kenneth Kik, Petter Kjellander, Friedrich Lademann, Pär Lagerqvist, Donald D. Lassen, Ola Laveson, Johannes Lange, Eric "Rony" Lemoine, William J. Leonard, William Lyons, Bruce Maki, Rosemarie Martin, Friedrich Meyer, Helga Meyer, William S. Meyer, Martin Månsson, John M. Nolan, Hans-J. Oehler, Per Erik Olsen – Militærhistorie, Roger Pedersen – the City Library of Eskilstuna, Roland Pfeiffer, Peter Pferdekämper, Robert Powell, Scott Revell, Matti Salonen, Heinrich Scheibe, Anneluise Schreier, Horst Schmidt, Klaus Schröder, Ralf Anton Schäfer, Niclas Sennerteg, Stefan Sjöberg, John Sliz, Marco Smedberg, Willem Smit – Nederlands Instituut voor Militaire Historie, Ben Soisson, Vince Speranza, Ronald Stassen, Ivan Steenkiste, Åke Steinwall, Dieter Stenger, Tim Streefkerk – Airborne Museum Hartenstein Archives Oosterbeek, Samuel Svärd, Hans E. Söder, Max Thimmig, M. Kathleen Thompson, Stephen Thompson, Dariusz Tyminski, Jan Waernberg, Jan Warßischek – Bundesarchiv, Abt. Militärarchiv, Lennart Wennergrund, Lennart Westberg, Dieter Woratz, Maarten Vossen, Peter Wouters – Geldersarchief Arnhem, Manfred Wägenbaur.

If I have happened to forget any person who has been of assistance with this book, it is entirely unintentional and pure coincidence; please regard this as my implied gratitude.

Christer Bergström, Eskilstuna, 17 September 2017
forlag@vaktelforlag.se

QR codes

QR codes (Quick Response) are codes for optical scanning reminiscent of common bar codes. It is easy to download software that scans QR codes on your smartphone or tablet computer. After that, it is sufficient to hold your telephone with that software running above a QR code in order for the web page with the video clip in question to be opened.

There are many free QR scanner apps that you can download onto your smartphone or tablet computer. They can be downloaded from, for example, Apple's App Store or the Android Market, depending on which type of smartphone or tablet computer you are using.

Below, you will find the QR codes for Vaktel Book's homepage and my own author's page on the Internet. On the latter, you will find links for all QR codes and many other things. That page will be updated regularly.

 VAKTEL FÖRLAG

 BERGSTRÖM BOOKS

The combat area during "Market Garden"

●●●●● "Club Route"   0   10   20 km

N

Amsterdam
Zuiderzee
Nunspeet
Harderwijk
Hilversum
Apeldoorn
Zutphen
Utrecht
Ede
Deelen
IJssel
Wolfheze
Heelsum
Oosterbeek
Arnhem
Rhine
Renkum
Driel
Heteren
Opheusden
Elst
Betuwe
Heuvel
Valburg
Bemmel
Oosterhout
Lent
Fort Beneden
Waal
THE NETHERLANDS
Nijmegen
Beek
Waal
Wyler
Kranenburg
Kleve
Hatert
Groesbeek
Ridge
Maas
Malden
Oss
Groesbeek
GERMANY
Grave
Velp
Overasselt
Mook
Maas
Heesch
Reichswald
's-Hertogenbosch
Heeswijk
Uden
Boxmeer
Maas
Vught
Schijndel
Eerde
Veghel
Boekel
Boxtel
Koeveringen
Sint-Oedenrode
Overloon
Tilburg
Best
Son
Venray
Nederwetten
Helmond
Wilhelmina Canal
Nuenen
Aa
Eindhoven
Dommel
Venlo
Aalst
Asten
Heeze
Turnhout
Valkenswaard
Leende
Zuid-Willemsvaart Canal
Bergeijk
Maas
Rethy
Budel
Lommel
Hamont
Weert
Ten Aard
Neerpelt
Sint-Huibrechts-Lille
Maas-Scheldt Canal
Eksel
Roermond
Geel
Bree
Leopoldsburg
Hechtel
Juliana Canal
Heppen
BELGIUM
Beeringen
Helchteren
Asch
Sittard
Albert Canal
Hasselt

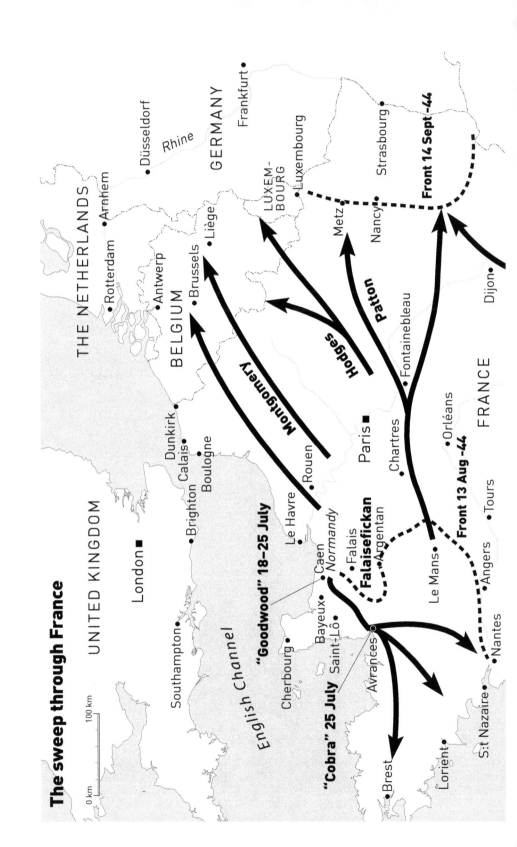

The sweep through France

UNITED KINGDOM

London ■

Southampton ●

Brighton ●

English Channel

0 km   100 km

THE NETHERLANDS

Rotterdam ●
Arnhem ●

Antwerp ●

Dunkirk ●
Calais ●
Boulogne ●

Düsseldorf ●

Rhine

GERMANY

Frankfurt ●

BELGIUM

Brussels ●
Liège ●

LUXEM-
BOURG

Luxembourg ●

Strasbourg ●

Front 14 Sept -44

Metz ●
Nancy ●

Montgomery

Hodges

Patton

Fontainebleau ●

Cherbourg ●

Bayeux ●
Saint-Lô ●

Caen ●
Normandy

"Goodwood" 18–25 July

Le Havre ●

Rouen ●

Paris ■

Chartres ●

Orléans ●

Dijon ●

FRANCE

Falaise ●
Argentan

Falaisefickan

Front 13 Aug -44

Le Mans ●

Tours ●

Angers ●

"Cobra" 25 July

Avranches ○

Brest ●

Lorient ●

Nantes ●

S:t Nazaire ●

I.

German Collapse in the West

"Our headquarters exists no longer, only Weinhopel, Mittermaier and I are left... Our Combat HQ was set up in a house, the English broke through, surrounded the house and shot everything up with tanks and machine-guns. We don't know who escaped alive, I mean by that who is dead or a prisoner. I don't know what will happen to us or whether we shall be pulled out, as even our regimental commander was captured. My dear Liani, the fighting here is so fearfully hard I cannot even begin to describe it. The English are trying with their whole might to end the war with all the material that they have."
– *Obergefreiter Heinrich Roos, II. Battalion, Grenadier Regiment 987/ German 276. infantry division. Letter on 13 August 1944.*[1]

"Passing through the Falaise Gap after the battle was not a pleasant experience. Men horses, vehicles and guns lay sprawled along the roads and in the ditches, mute evidence of the vastly superior fire power of the attacking forces. We were noticeably quiet as we passed through the area where the worst destruction had been wrought. It was spread out in front of us, beside us and behind us, limbless corpses, headless corpses, corpses foubled up in painful attitudes, corpses with their insides spewing out, who were grinning sickeningly, and corpses which might have been weeping. It was a relief to hurry on and forget what we'd seen. Even so, many of us must have wondered who was going to clear up the human wreckage. There was no need of P.O.W. cages for them; only graves. Their battle had been fought and lost. Ours was still going on."
– *Lieutenant David Holdsworth, 2nd Battalion, British Devonshire Regiment.*[2]

The German attempts to turn the reverse in the battle for Normandy through a last desperate counterattack ended with disaster. After six weeks of bloody static warfare following the invasion of Normandy on 6 June 1944, the Allied managed to outwit, or, rather, outmanoeuvre, the Germans in a series of coordinated attacks. The plan for this had been hammered out by General Montgomery, the renowned victor at el-Alamein in North Africa in 1942, and doubtlessly one of the most skilled military commanders of the Allies during the Second World War. "Monty" Montgomery was now the commander of the Allied ground troops in France, which had been organised into the 1st Army Group. The operation commenced on 18 July with Operation "Goodwood", which meant that Montgomery's British-Canadian forces attacked the German eastern flank, at Caen. At Normandy, about 380,000 German soldiers were facing 1.5 million men on the Allied side, but the Germans had concentrated 645 of their more than 800 tanks to the eastern flank.[3] When "Goodwood" was discontinued a few days later without any real territorial gains having been made, while the 1st Army Group had lost more than a quarter of its tanks, Montgomery was subject to a barrage of criticism. But the purpose of "Goodwood" had not been primarily to break through the strong and deep German defence lines, but to draw the attention of the Germans to this sector. In reality, the main attack would be set in by U.S. First Army under Brigadier General Omar Bradley on the western flank, the weakest sector of the German lines. This operation plan, under the codename "Cobra", had been produced in collaboration between Montgomery and Bradley.

In spite of the American attack not beginning until 25 July, four days after Montgomery had been forced to withdraw his armoured forces in the east to save it from even worse losses, the Germans were taken completely by surprise. After one of the war's most concentrated air attacks, the Americans, enjoying total air supremacy and a 17 to 1 supremacy in tanks, managed to break up the German defence.

On 30 July, Montgomery made his next move: Operation "Bluecoat", an attack by the British VIII and XXX Army Corps just east of the Americans, but still far west of Caen. In that way, the Germans definitely were led to believe that the Allies had moved the entire emphasis of their strategy to the west. When the Americans then punched a hole through the German lines and streamed south through the so-called "Avranches Gap" on the west coast of the Cotentin Peninsula, Hitler gave the order to send in eight of the nine Panzer divisions in Normandy in a counterattack against Avranches, with the purpose of cutting off the American forces in the south. This took place in spite of an overwhelming Allied air superiority – by that time, the Luftwaffe, the German Air Force, only had little more than 300 fighter aircraft left in France against nearly 10,000 Allied fighters and bombers, and the once-efficient German bomber and dive-bomber forces had been chased out of the sky. It also was the Allied air superiority that became decisive.

After new massive air bombing, this time aimed at the Falaise area on the eastern flank, south of Caen, Montgomery put in an attack at Caen on 8 August, the day after the Germans had moved their armoured forces to the west and launched the attack against Avranches. While the Allied aviation practically paralysed all German troop movements in the area between the Avranches sector and Falaise, the American forces in the southwest turned first towards the east and then towards the north.

The American units had now been reorganised into two armies – the new Third Army under Lieutenant General George S. Patton and the First Army, which was put under the command of Lieutenant General Courtney Hodges as Bradley was elevated to commander of the new 12th Army Group, taking command of both of these armies. It was the thick-skinned Lieutenant General Patton's forces that turned northbound in order to cut off, in collaboration with Montgomery, the entire German army in Normandy. Only far too late did the Germans realise what a trap they had gone into. A fifty-kilometre stretch west

QR1: VIDEO
Authentic footage from
the Falaise Pocket.

of Falaise turned into killing fields, where Allied aircraft, and eventually also artillery, virtually obliterated the German Seventh Army (7. Armee).

Now, two German armies did indeed remain in northern France, but the Falaise disaster had caused a morale breakdown on the German side – especially as this followed immediately after an almost complete collapse of the German Eastern Front. The Fifth Panzer Army (5. Panzerarmee) had mainly made it out of the Falaise pocket, but was hit by serious losses when it was attacked by Allied aircraft during the retreat across River Seine. SS-Hauptscharführer* (Battalion Sergeant-Major) Willy Fey recounts: "At the river crossing, we are met with terrible chaos, stemming from the previous day's bomb attack. Everywhere, vehicle wrecks are still smouldering, and among them, dead and injured soldiers, who had been left to themselves without any help." [4] SS-Oberst-Gruppenführer** Josef "Sepp" Dietrich reported: "From the point of view of equipment abandoned, the Seine crossing was almost as great a disaster as the Falaise Pocket." [5]

It was hardly an army that made it over the Seine, but demoralised groups of soldiers fleeing at an increasing degree of disorder towards the German border. On 25 August, the same day as the German garrison in Paris surrendered, the 5. Panzerarmee had no more than 17,980 men left – that is, about the equivalent of the strength of one division – with 42 tanks and assault guns. [6] The breakdown was followed by a crisis of leadership. Field Marshal Günther von Kluge, who had replaced the ousted Generalfeldmarschall Gerd von Rundstedt as the Supreme Commander West (Oberbefehlshaber West) the previous month, was fired from his post on 17 August and committed suicide. He was succeeded by Generalfeldmarschall Walter Model, who came directly from the Eastern Front and discovered a chaos that he accounted for in a report, "Columns which have been routed, which have broken from the front and which for the moment have no firm destination push on backwards. With them travel idle talk, rumours, haste, inconsiderateness, unnecessary disorder and short-sighted selfishness. They

---

* The SS had its own military ranks. An SS-Hauptscharführer corresponded to the armed forces' (Wehrmacht) Oberfeldwebel.
** Corresponding to the Wehrmacht's Generaloberst.

may bring this feeling into the rear areas and into the fully intact bodies, so the fighting troops must be prevented at this moment of tension with the severest measures."[7]

Out of the German armoured forces in Normandy, no more than between 100 and 120 tanks made it across the Seine. The five SS Panzer divisions (1., 2., 9., 10., and 12.) were unable to take more than a total of 45 tanks with them. The 2nd and 9th SS-Panzer Divisions reported strengths of 450 and 460 men respectively on 21 August.[8] The 116th Panzer Division reported a strength of 20 tanks.[9] The 3rd and 5th Paratroop Divisions (Fallschirmjäger-Division) had lost between 95 and 99 per cent of their frontline soldiers.[10] These Panzer and paratroop units, which were responsible for most of the Allied losses during the Battle of Normandy, no longer constituted any threats. The road towards Germany lay open for the Allies, especially as the last remaining army in northern France, which also was the weakest, 15. Armee, was pinned down in the French harbour towns in the Pas de Calais area.

By the end of August 1944, Montgomery gave the order for a Blitz offensive from the Seine and up towards Belgium to take advantage of the situation. This would be carried out by British Second Army under Lieutenant-General Miles Dempsey, while Canadian First Army would work its way up the Channel coast.

The only problem was that the Allies did not yet have any other harbours at their disposal with which to supply their armies in northern France than the ones in Normandy, and their capacity was insufficient to maintain a general offensive of four full armies. But Montgomery decided to keep one of Dempsey's three corps, VIII Corps, and most of his artillery, at the Seine, and let the XII and XXX Corps carry out the offensive.

QR2: VIDEO
07:58: Film clip of German veterans
(e.g. Werner Krüger and Karl Heinz Henschel,
both from 9. SS-Pz-Div) about the retreat from
France (in German and Dutch).

The advance began on 29 August 1944 and proceeded at break-neck speed, without encountering more than weak and uncoordinated resistance. Lieutenant-Colonel Edward Roderick Hill, a battalion commander in the British Guards Armoured Division, recalls that there were German soldiers in every grove and behind bushes and hedges, hopelessly disorganised and very keen to surrender.[11] In a single day, British 11th Armoured Division swept forward 60 kilometres. The next day, Corporal Joseph Byrne, commander of a Sherman tank in 2nd Battalion, The Fife and Forfarshire Yeomanry, took the commander of German 5. Panzerarmee, General Heinrich Eberbach, captive. The German general was unceremoniously hauled up on the rear of the tank, which then trundled off at top speed to deliver the important booty.[12] Lieutenant William Steel Brownlie of the 11th Armoured Division recounts 1 September, "Off we went again, via Villers-Boxage (where there were 88s but the crews surrendered), then Talmas, Beauquesne, Halloy, Grande-Rullecourt, Savy and Estrée. It was a hectic dash and mostly cross country, map reading not easy. [Major David] Voller and I competed (as so often) as to who could go faster."[13] Everywhere, the British were received by cheering French people.

On 1 September, the 11th Armoured Division advanced another 80 kilometres. On 2 September, the British crossed the border into Belgium. Here, they received an even more enthusiastic reception than in France. Major Frank Clark of the Guards Armoured Division remembers that the Belgian villages and towns were decorated in a festive way with large amounts of Belgian and Allied flags. Across the streets, large banners hung, sporting phrases such as "Welcome Liberators", and orchestras stood along the road playing for them. The civilian population received them with completely hysterical joy. When the British had come only a few kilometres inside of the Belgian border, their combat vehicles were almost completely hidden under enormous amounts of flowers, and every time they made a stop, the soldiers were inundated with fruit and wine. All day, they were munching cake, cookies, fruit, and wine.

The tendencies of dissolving increased at the same pace on the German side. "Civilians state that all day on Saturday [2 September]

SS troops were shooting up the Wehrmacht, who were throwing away their arms and clamouring to surrender", the 7th Armoured Division reported. "All reports speak of the enemy as completely exhausted."[14]

"Enemy Information - one word, chaos. Our intention: the Irish Group will dine in Brussels tomorrow night!" That was the Order of the Day that was issued on 2 September by the colourful commander of the Irish Guards regiment, Lieutenant-Colonel John Ormsby Evelyn Vandeleur, better known as "Colonel Joe" because of his initials. And "Colonel Joe's" words would come true. The next day, the Guards Armoured Division's tanks rolled into the Belgian capital, 350 kilometres from the starting point five days previously. Lieutenant Dav Holdsworth of the 2nd Battalion, The Devonshire Regiment, remem bers, "Champagne, flowers, flags, cheering crowds, British soldie dancing in the streets, Belgians sitting and standing on every military vehicle; hands waving, hands shaking; tears, laughter, and bottles of wine passing from mouth to mouth. That was Brussels."[15] The same day, the following was noted in the war diary of the 7th Armoured Division: "3 September 1944: Enemy inactive."[16] That evening, "Colonel Joe" and his officers had their dinner at one of the nicer restaurants at Grote Markt in Brussels.

South and southeast of Brussels, the remnants of the German 9. and 10. SS-Panzer divisions – which had now been reorganised from divisions into so-called battle groups (Kampfgruppen) – were in full flight from Wavre towards Maastricht. SS-Oberführer Heinz Harmel, commander of the latter division, noted on 4 September, "Accumulation of vehicles between Wavre and Tirlemont, which were almost ceaselessly attacked by low-flying enemy aircraft".[17]

This 4 September, the British 11th Armoured Division, in collaboration with the Belgian resistance, took the port city of Antwerp.

QR3: VIDEO
Documentary from the
liberation of Brussels.

This had large consequences. A false radio message that the Allies had entered the Netherlands led to the so-called Dolle Dinsdag ("the Mad Tuesday) in the Netherlands on 5 September: all over the country, cheering Dutchmen went out into the streets, waving flags, celebrating that liberation was near. The resistance appeared, taking Dutch Nazis captive in several places. The Germans were too confused and terrified to act.*

GERMAN COUNTERMEASURES

The news of the fall of Antwerp – which also led to the German 15. Armee being isolated in the Pas de Calais area in north-eastern France – triggered a powerful reaction in Hitler's headquarters Wolfsschanze (the Wolf's Lair) near Rastenburg in East Prussia. Generaloberst Kurt Student, the commander of the German airborne forces (which were part of the Luftwaffe, the air force), was at his headquarters in Berlin-Wannsee on the afternoon of 4 September 1944, when he received an order by telephone directly from the Führer's headquarters: he was to set up a defence line along the Albert Canal, which runs to the north-west in northern Belgium.[18]

The Commander of the Luftwaffe, Reichsmarschall Hermann Göring, had promised Hitler to close the gap in the German lines in the Netherlands with paratroopers. With the greatest difficulty, he managed to scrape together 10,000 men by taking in wounded convalescents, supply and staff personnel, superfluous personnel from the Luftwaffe, and recruits who were not yet fully trained. (We have already seen that the 3. and 5. Fallschirmjäger-Divisions had lost between 95 and 99 % of their frontline soldiers in Normandy.) The unit

*QR4: VIDEO
Authentic wartime footage of
Dolle Dinsdag.

commanders were usually exceedingly experienced, but most of the men left much to be desired.

Oberstleutnant (Lieutenant-Colonel) Friedrich August Freiherr von der Heydte, the commander of Fallschirmjäger-Regiment 6, reported the condition in his own regiment in September 1944: "The young replacements, comprising roughly 75 percent of the entire regiment, had received very little or no training – hundreds of the men in the regiment had never yet touched a rifle and fired their first shot during their first battle; many of the officers were unable to meet the demands made upon an officer."[19] A British intelligence report concluded that "it was admittedly a scratch unit, and nothing whatever to do with the original 6 Para Regt that fought against the Americans at St Lô." [20]

Freiherr von der Heydte was even more negative in his judgment of the I. Bataillon of Fallschirmjäger-Regiment 2, which, together with Fallschirmjäger-Regiment 6 formed the battle group Kampfgruppe von der Heydte: he considered this battalion to be even of poorer quality than those of his own regiment, with abysmal officers, without the capacity of maintaining discipline, and soldiers who indulged in arbitrary punitive measures against the civilian population, looting, and other abuse of civilians.[21] In order to form this battalion, they had collected men from, amongst other places, the Nazi paramilitary organisation SA ("the Brown Shirts"). In the chronicles of Fallschirmjäger-Regiment 2, Willi Kammann describes the composition of the unit, "The number of veteran paratroopers in the new battalion amounts to only about 10 per cent. The replacements are coming mainly from the Fallschirm-Ersatz- und Ausbildungsregiment 1 (Cdr. Oberst Udo von Kummer) and from the SA-Standarte 'Feldherrnhalle'. They are mostly 17- to 18-year-old soldiers. In addition, 26 officer candidates and non-commissioned officers are coming from the Air Sector (Luftgau) and from the Reich Air Transport Ministry; almost all of them without any frontline experience. A few weeks' intensive training will have to suffice to make the newly-formed battalion ready for action." [22]

On 4 September, paratroop units all over Germany were alerted, mobilised, and sent with so-called "Blitz transports" by rail to Belgium and the Albert Canal.[23] Ten thousand paratroopers ended up forming the core of German First Parachute Army (1. Fallschirm-Armee) under Student's command. The 88th Army Corps (LXXXVIII. Armeekorps), which had commanded the coastal defence of the Netherlands, was also added to this. The coastal defence division 719. Infanterie-Division also came along, consisting of more than 7,000 men without any combat experience, and lacking both artillery and anti-tank weapons and even modern machine guns.[24]

Moreover, Student was also given the newly-formed Division 176, which had hastily been formed as a so-called "division of invalids".[25] In the absence of accessible reserves, the Germans now called up second-class soldiers, men who were normally considered unfit for service. These were divided into special so-called *Magen Batail-*

German 1. Fallschirmarmee in mid-September 1944

KAMPFGRUPPE VON DER HEYDTE
- I. Bataillon/ Fallschirmjäger-Regiment 2
- Fallschirmjäger-Regiment 6
Total strength about 1,000 men

FALLSCHIRMJÄGER-REGIMENT 18
about 900 men

FALLSCHIRMJÄGER-DIVISION ERDMANN
about 2,000 men

FALLSCHIRM-ERSATZ-UND AUSBILDUNGS-REGIMENT 1*
about 2,500 men

FALLSCHIRM-PANZER-ERSATZ- UND AUSBILDUNGS-REGIMENT
"HERMANN GÖRING"
about 2,400 men

3. FALLSCHIRMJÄGER-DIVISION**
about 850 men

5. FALLSCHIRMJÄGER-DIVISION**
about 300 men

* In the rear area.
** Did not arrive until 18–19 September 1944.

lon ("stomach batallions") and *Ohren Bataillon* ("ear battalions"); in the former units, men with chronic stomach diseases were placed and were given special food, in the latter, men with severe hearing damage were placed, and the tasks they were assigned were adapted accordingly. In that way, between 70,000 and 80,000 men could be mobilised for the defence of the German western borders.[26] Ten thousand of these were grouped into Division 176.

Student also received 20 heavy, medium, and light anti-aircraft batteries from Germany's Air Defence Forces (Luftflotte Reich) as well as the anti-tank battalion schwere Heeres-Panzerjäger-Abteilung 559, and took operative command of all rear units in the Netherlands.[27] Schwere Heeres-Panzerjäger-Abteilung 559, equipped with 18 Jagdpanthers and 28 Sturmgeschütz IIIs, was without doubt the best among these units. After losing 46 tank destroyers against 78 reportedly destroyed Soviet tanks, this battalion had been withdrawn from the Eastern Front in January 1944. Since then, it had been held in reserve, and now mustered a large number of well-trained soldiers, many of them also with much combat experience. With a very high morale, the battalion stood out considerably among most of the German military units at this time. Moreover, it was one of the first units to be equipped with the mighty tank destroyer Jagdpanther. This 45-ton beast was armed with an 88 mm PaK 43/1 L/71 – perhaps the best anti-tank gun of the Second World War, without any equivalence on the Allied side – mounted on top of the chassis of a Panzerkampfwagen V Panther, which is also considered one of the war's best tanks. The commander of the battalion, 30-year-old Major Erich Sattler, had combat experience as a company and battalion commander for various tank destroyer units ever since the war broke out, and had seen action on the Western Front in 1940 and the Eastern Front in 1941–1944.

What was completely surprising to Student was the appearance of a "ghost unit" that nobody had expected at the Geel sector, 40 kilometres north-east of Brussels. Here, Generalleutnant Kurt Chill, the commander of a battle group (Kampfgruppe) which bore his name, had halted on his own responsibility.*

---

* Kampfgruppe Chill was formed in August 1944 out of the remains of the 84., 85., and 89. Infanterie-Division.

Actually, Chill was the commander of the 85. Infanterie-Division, which had been smashed to smithereens by Montgomery in France. The OKW gave the order that the remains of the division should be withdrawn to Germany in order to regroup, but Chill decided to defy this order and instead use the resources he had to form a blocking line at the Albert Canal. This line was not primarily aimed against the Allies, but against German soldiers who, individually and in small groups, were in retreat to escape the British steamroller. Chill caught a motley collection of soldiers from all kinds of supply units, staffs, and torn-up frontline units, and inserted them into Kampfgruppe Chill, which reached a strength of about 6,500 men. After that, he went to the headquarters of LXXX-VIII. Armeekorps and informed them that he had a new battle group – a new division – under his command. In fact, Kampfgruppe Chill would form the backbone around which Student could create his 1. Fallschirmarmee.

In total, 1. Fallschirmarmee reached a frontline strength of about 34,000 men, with extremely weak artillery support and (with the exception of schwere Heeres-Panzerjäger-Abteilung 559) anti-tank weapons. Everything bore the mark of hasty improvisation. Even within Student's headquarters, there were large shortcomings. Above all, there was no chief of staff, which placed an extra burden on Student personally. However, since new units were to be squeezed out of a stone, there was a lack of good unit commanders, and therefore, Student had assigned his chief of staff, Generalleutant Wolfgang Erdmann, with the task of taking command of a newly-formed division with his own name (Division Erdmann). Student would not get any new chief of staff until mid-September 1944.[28]

Student's closest colleagues were three other commanders – Feldmarschall Walter Model, the commander of army group Heeresgruppe B and thus his closest superior; furthermore, General Friedrich Christiansen, who since 1940 was serving as Wehrmachtbefehlshaber Niederlande, the commander of all the armed forces in the Netherlands and thus also of Student; and, finally, General Hans Wolfgang Reinhard, the commander of the LXXXVIII. Armeekorps.

While Christiansen, together with the Reichskommissar in the Netherlands, Arthur Seyss-Inquart, and SS-Obergruppenführer Hanns Albin Rauter, the highest SS and police commander in the Netherlands,* cracked down on the enraptured Dutch with terrible force on 6 September, the day after Dolle Dinsdag, the paratroopers were immediately sent in to the front.

Student recounted that they often received their weapons only as they alighted the trains at the destinations, and after that, they immediately marched out to the front.[29]

On 7 September, Generalfeldmarschall Wilhelm Keitel, the commander of the German Wehrmacht's Supreme Command, gave the order to stage a new operation plan, called "Herbststurm" (Autumn Storm).[30] This was aimed against withdrawing German units, with the objective of stopping the retreat. With the 719. Infanterie-Division on the western flank, Kampfgruppe Chill and the paratroop units at the centre, and Division 176 to the east, Student was to hold the Albert Canal along almost 100 kilometres between Maastricht to the east and the Antwerp sector to the west.

"ALL ORGANISED GERMAN RESISTANCE WILL GRADUALLY DISINTEGRATE"

In the prevalent historiography – which has the advantage of hinsight – Montgomery's failure to order his units to continue the advance to the north, past Antwerp, is usually condemned vehemently. It is concluded, absolutely correctly, that if he had done so, he would probably both have been able to stop the German 15. Armee from evacuating across the Scheldt Estuary, and also have been able to open the great harbour of Antwerp for supply traffic much earlier. As was now the case, Montgomery's omission led to the 15. Armee being able to evacuate more than 82,000 men, 530 artillery guns, 4,600 motor vehicles and 4,000 horses, as well as a large number of other equipment during the month of September 1944, so that these could be sent in

* Höherer SS- und Polizeiführer (HSSPF).

41

during the battle of the Netherlands and – above all – cling on to the islands in the Scheldt Estuary long enough for the approach to the Antwerp harbour to remain blocked for two months.[31]

But, of course, Montgomery's actions must be judged from the perspectives of that time. On 4-6 September 1944, when he according to these modern-day writers ought to have given this order, the situation was as follows:

- The German Western Army was basically annihilated and the remaining troops showed strong signs of demoralisation and war fatigue. The resistance was weak and disorganised almost everywhere.
- On the Eastern Front, the entire German Eastern Army was in a similar state.
- There had been no reports of any real German replacements for losses for several weeks, which clearly showed that the Wehrmacht was destitute.
- After the remains of the German 5. Panzerarmee had been surrounded and annihilated at Mons in southern Belgium on 2–4 September (when 25,000 prisoners were taken, the remains of twenty different divisions), there was a 100-kilometre gap in the German defences east of Brussels.
- The extremely rapid advance from the Seine had meant great strains on the Allied armies' logistics, great enough for Dempsey to find himself obliged to halt the advance on 4 September and order his Second Army to pause and wait for more supplies to be brought forward.

It looked as though the entire war would end any day. "The enemy has no coherent order of battle", the Intelligence Committee of the new Supreme Headquarters for the Allied forces in Western Europe (SHAEF) had reported on 2 September. "His armies have been reduced to a number of fugitive battle groups, disorganised and demoralised, short of equipment and arms."[32]

The British Government's Joint Intelligence Committee (JIC) drew the conclusion on 5 September that the end of the war was nigh. They wrote, "Germany has suffered further catastrophic disasters. The process of final military defeat leading to the cessation of organised resistance has begun in the West. [...] Whatever action Hitler may now take it will be too late to affect the issue in the West where organised German resistance will gradually disintegrate under our attack."[33] The following day, General John Kennedy, assistant chief of staff at the The Imperial General Staff in London, predicted that "if we continue to advance at the same pace as that of recent weeks we should be in Berlin on 28 September."

An American intelligence report even drew the conclusion that Germany was on the brink of a revolution, just as at the end of the First World War. "The psychological breaking point of the German people must be close. It is believed that Southern Germany under the influence of the leadership of the Catholic Church, will be the first to refuse to follow the Fuehrer on the path of national suicide. This will probably take the form of a general strike, combined with a political revolution. The exact time of such a rising in relation to the date of our arrival at the West Wall is impossible to predict, but it is believed it may well occur within 30 to 60 days of our investiture of Festung Deutschland."[34]

Among ordinary soldiers – on both sides – the same opinion prevailed. "Everybody thought that all was ending when we were staggering back from France, cut down to size and at a loss as to what to do", Friedrich Lademann, one of the surviving paratroopers of 5. Fallschirmjäger-Division, recalled. Lieutenant William "Hugh" Griffiths of the British Guards Armoured Division told of how he was able to relax with golf on the large golf course at Waterloo, and how he and his companions found an enormous German cache of champagne bottles; they loaded all of it up onto three trucks and took it for themselves. "Now remember, this isn't looting at all, this is organised liberation", said one of the participating officers.

The German Wehrmachtbefehlshaber Niederlande, General Christiansen, estimated that he did not have enough troops to resist Montgomery's attack, and asked on 6 September the new Supreme Commander in the West, Feldmarschall von Rundstedt, for permission to destroy the Dutch harbour docks – a request that, however, was denied.[35]

"It was my view that the end of the war in Europe was most certainly 'within reach'. What was now needed were quick decisions", Montgomery wrote in his memoirs.[36] Taking advantage in that situation of the 100-kilometre gap in the German defence lines east of Brussels corresponded to the theory of "the indirect approach" which had been put forward by the British military theorist Basil Liddell Hart in 1941, and was also completely in line with the German commander Erich Ludendorff's tactics during the First World War to circumvent strongly defended sectors and instead hit the enemy where he was at his weakest. Montgomery had gained notoriety by winning the battle of el-Alamein through the opposite strategy, Clausewitz's so-called strategy of annihilation, where the idea was to hit and wear down the enemy where he was at his strongest. Montgomery was considered by the Germans to be a "cautious general" who methodically built up sufficient strength for success to be guaranteed before he attacked. In reality, this method had its origins in Montgomery's realistic assessment of the combat value of the British units, which were not always very motivated. But now, he was able to take advantage of the Germans' prejudice of him by surprisingly dealing a blow straight into the German "gap". Had he not done that, one could conclude that history's judgement had been even harsher of him; as we shall see, he had all opportunities for his intents to succeed.

In order not to become unnecessarily delayed, Montgomery chose to circumvent the West Wall (the "Siegfried Line" in Allied language), the German fortified line that ran along the country's western border from the border against Switzerland in the south and up towards the area east of Nijmegen in the north. Instead of going east, he planned to strike northward in order to turn east, in towards the Ruhr area, the German industry's heartland, north of Nijmegen – more precisely, at Arnhem. "I consider that we have now reached a stage where one really powerful and full-blooded thrust towards Berlin is likely to get there and thus end the German war", he said on 4 September.[37]

Perhaps it was no coincidence that this operation was in full accord in style with the way that his main opponent in North Africa, "the Desert Fox" Rommel, had achieved his astonishing successes. But Montgomery would learn from his enemy in more than one way. One

First Allied Airborne Army, 1 September 1944
Commander: Lieutenant-General Lewis H. Brereton

BRITISH I AIRBORNE CORPS
Lieutenant-General Frederick Browning
- 1st Airborne Division (British)
- 6th Airborne Division (British)

U.S. XVIII AIRBORNE CORPS
Major General Matthew B. Ridgway
- 17th U.S. Airborne Division
- 82nd U.S. Airborne Division
- 101st U.S. Airborne Division

1ST POLISH INDEPENDENT PARACHUTE BRIGADE GROUP
Major-General Stanisław Sosabowski

U.S. IX TROOP CARRIER COMMAND
Major General Paul L. Williams
Troop carriers

of his most important opponents in the Netherlands was now, as we have seen, Generaloberst Kurt Student. More than four years previously, he had been the brain behind the German invasion from the air of the Netherlands. By a combination of surprising airdrop attacks against strategic points in the deep and Panzer troops that advanced towards these points, the Germans conquered the Netherlands in only five days in May 1940.

In the evening of 3 September 1944, Montgomery got in touch with the headquarters of Allied First Airborne Army. In spite of this having been formed as late as one month previously, it had already previously been preparing a major effort in the West – that, too, on Montgomery's initiative.*

On 25 August, Montgomery and his chief of staff, Major-General Francis "Freddy" de Guingand, had proposed an operation by air-

* During August 1944, several other airborne operations had been planned to support advancements in the West – under the codenames "Transfigure", "Axehead" and "Boxer" – but they had all been cancelled for different reasons.

borne forces towards the area between Lille and Arras in north-eastern France with the purpose of cutting off the German armies' line of retreat. The plan was called "Linnet" and was intended to involve three of the army's divisions – the American 82nd and 101st and the British 1st Airborne Divisions – and the Polish independent parachute brigade. The British 6th Airborne Division and the American 17th Airborne Division would not be sent in – the former because it was completely worn out after two months of fighting in Normandy, and the latter because it had just arrived in the U.K. from the United States and was considered much too "fresh".

But the German collapse in the West forestalled "Linnet". On 2 September, the French resistance was able to liberate Lille as the Germans abandoned the city. A certain level of frustration arose within the airborne army, which lay idle in England.. The the army's C.O., American Lieutenant General Lewis H. Brereton, was eager to let his units take part in the final battle. Brereton was used to being in the middle of events: he had led the U.S. Far East Air Force during the Japanese attacks in 1941–1942, the American air units in Egypt in 1942, and, after that, the U.S. Ninth Air Force with 5,000 aircraft during the softening attacks ahead of the Normandy landing and in tactical support of the American ground troops in Normandy.

Brereton was pressing on for another operation by his airborne units, proposing on 2 September what he called "Linnet II", an airdrop aiming at securing the river crossings across the Maas (Meuse) river north of Liège in eastern Belgium. Brereton's eagerness is evident not least by him wanting to carry out this operation only two days later, without both proper maps of the area or photographs by air reconnaissance. His assistant commander and commander of the British I Airborne Corps, Lieutenant-General Frederick "Boy" Browning, was so upset by this that he threatened to resign, which led to a conflict between the two. The discord did not cease, but the immediate reason disappeared as Montgomery on 3 September instead asked them to prepare an airdrop of British 1st Airborne Division and the Polish Parachute Brigade aimed at taking control of the bridges across the Rhine between Arnhem and Wesel ahead of British Second Army's expected advance to the north. The operation was given the codename "Comet".

But this time, it became, contrary to what had been the case with "Linnet", the unexpectedly slow advance of the British ground forces that crossed the plan.

THE DRAINING OF STUDENT'S ARMY

Postwar historiography has pointed at the stiffening German resistance after the first week of September 1944, hinting that this ought to have made the British commanders realize that the time when they could expect a swift victory had come and gone. The decision to let the Second Army pause to await supplies is not infrequently called "Montgomery's second big mistake". But the supplies for the great offensive aimed at conquering the German Ruhr area were far from secured, which we shall see later. On 6 September, two days after the pause that Dempsey had ordered with Montgomery's consent, Lieutenant-General Brian Horrocks, the commander of the XXX Corps, was ordered to cross the Albert Canal and advance into the Netherlands.

The fact that the British now met considerably harder resistance than previously is something that Montgomery has been reproached for in the history books; it has been suggested that the offensive should immediately have continued on 4 September, and that the XXX Corps actually had fuel for another 100 kilometres. Indeed so, but 100 kilometres is less than the distance from Brussels to the Dutch border. If the advance had continued immediately, it is likely that the British would have made it across the Albert Canal and reached the Maas-Scheldt Canal*, located slightly further to the north, at Neerpelt on 6 September.

In that case, the XXX Corps would have encountered even stronger resistance that what was now the case – for the simple reason that the Germans would then have been closer to their base area – and, on top of everything else, new supply problems. As we shall see further

* Currently named the Bocholt-Herentals Canal. See map page 27.

on in this volume, neither is it likely that the British would have been able to make it across the Maas-Scheldt Canal during such a scenario, and this would have jeopardised Operation "Market Garden". Instead, Montgomery's and Dempsey's pause in Brussels resulted in Student transferring large parts of his new units across the sandy terrain between the two canals, where they would be heavily drained during one week of fighting – which, of course, benefitted the British, who by this received the best possible conditions for the continued offensive into the Netherlands.

It is of course natural that the British met stronger resistance when the new units in Student's 1. Fallschirmarmee reached the front – anything else would have been strange in comparison with the totally demoralised and harrowed remains of military units that were fleeing rather than retreating. One of the soldiers in Student's army recounted the sight that met his units when it was approaching the front: "Wild flight along the rail and roads, Luftwaffe and Marine! Thousands of officers are trying to save their lives. Complete disorder. We have to protect the retreat of these cowardly bastards!"[38]

The new German troops were, so far, unaffected by the epidemic collapse of fighting spirits in the German Western Army – but this was soon to change. In any event, they were far too weak to be able to resist Lieutenant-General Dempsey's Second Army. On both sides, the men were well aware that these German troops only constituted a thin "shell" which, once cracked, did not have much that could back it up in the rear.

Generalleutenant Chill had divided his battle group into three "sub-battle groups", which, according to the prevailing norm, were given their designations from their commanders: Kampfgruppen Buchholz, Seidel, and Dreyer. The latter, under Oberstleutnant Georg Dreyer, was the strongest and could count in 3,500 men, positioned on the north side of the Albert Canal south of Geel, northeast of Brussels. It was of utmost importance that Dreyer was supported by some of the mighty tank destroyers of schwere Heeres-Panzerjäger-Abteilung 559.

Horrocks's XXX Corps had more than three divisions at its disposal for the push towards the north, the Guards Armoured Division, and the 43rd (Wessex) and 50th (Northumbrian) Infantry divisions. The soldiers of the former were completely unaware that they would meet stubborn resistance from Dreyer's newly-arrived units, especially the Jagdpanther tank destroyers. The mood within the division was characterised by euphoria, and an expectation that the war would soon be over. Lieutenant Geoffrey Picot recounts that there were wild rumours: The war was over, Hitler had fled to Spain. "Most of the Hampshire [Regiment] believed the war was over. 'It's on the wireless, isn't it'."

Bitter fighting took place at Geel between 6 and 12 September, before the British got the situation under control, and sent in the 15th (Scottish) Infantry Division from the XII Corps instead of the 50th (Northumbrian). After that, the Scots were able to advance to the Maas-Scheldt Canal about five kilometres north of the Albert Canal, but became stuck in a very small bridgehead at Ten Aard on the northern side. Here, two battalions from the Scottish division's 44th Brigade found themselves in new and very bloody fighting. Seen from this horizon, a turning point had entered, where the German resistance was much harder in an enduring way. But a close study of the German side gives a completely different image.

The power of the defence at Geel has been overrated in the historiography. This is clearly evident by the report from the headquarters of the LXXXVIII. Armeecorps on not only Kampfgruppe Dreyer, but on the entire Kampfgruppe Chill on 8 September, "People that are untrained as infantry, having little ammunition. [...] Our own troops are, especially in the sector 85.I.D., in great disarray, many combat-fatigued splinter units among the older age groups from all parts of the Werhrmacht, the young men from the Luftwaffe units are mostly recruits, still inexperienced in battle. We are lacking leaders able to take action, especially non-commissioned officers. Often, a shortage of ammunition occurs due to insufficient transport capacity. We are lacking anti-tank weapons and especially anti-tank weapons for close combat, and this makes the troops lose their self-confidence".[39] The fact is that the Germans lost more than 2,000 men, one third of Kampfgruppe Chill, at Geel, and on 14 September, the number of operational Jagdpanthers in schwere Heeres-Panzerjäger-Abteilung

559 had been reduced to exactly two.[40] Nevertheless, two battalions from Fallschirm-Panzer-Ersatz- und Ausbildungs-Regiment "Hermann Göring", with a total of 1,600 men, were hurriedly assigned to Kampfgruppe Chill and positioned against the bridgehead at Ten Aard. Moreover, all of Kampfgruppe Chill's artillery was sent in against the Scots.

As the Germans were driven away from Geel, the paratroop units east of Kampfgruppe Chill had been firmly beaten, this too after a few days of fighting. The main part of the Guards Armoured Division marched off from Brussels on 6 September towards the Albert Canal at Beringen, some 15 kilometres southeast of Geel. From there, they were to turn northwards towards Eindhoven on the small highway (which today has been expanded into the N 715) that crossed the Maas-Scheldt Canal on one of the two bridges that the Germans still had not demolished, but had kept to move reinforcements forward towards the Albert Canal. The eighty kilometres to Beringen were quickly covered. "Virtually no opposition was encountered in our advance from Brussels to the Albert canal", the War Diary of the 32nd Guards Brigade noted.[41] They found the bridge to be blown up by the Germans, and were met here by fire from the other side of the canal, which, however, ceased soon. German Kampfgruppe Vehrenkamp under Oberst Otto Vehrenkamp – a scrambled-together force consisting of coastal defence soldiers, a couple of Dutch SS home guard battalions, and apparently also Hitlerjugend youth – had been assigned to hold this part of the Albert Canal, but fled as soon as the British arrived.[42] A furious Generalleutnant Chill reported that Oberst Vehrenkamp, and his entire unit, had "deserted".[43] A group of German soldiers that did not manage to flee is described in the chronicle of the Welsh Guards, "About 70 of them, some no more than 15 years old, crying of shame, gave themselves up."[44]

This was the beginning of a whole series of clashes between the Guards Armoured Division and various German units, which were dispatched to the front as they arrived. (One of these battalions came on bicycle all the way from the Rhine.[45]) Soon after the British had arrived at the canal, two battalions of German paratroopers and two battalions from Flieger-Regiment 22 (consisting of superannuated personnel from the German Air Force) arrived at the other side of the canal. But the Welsh Guards 1st Battalion* crossed the canal in storm boats and drove these Germans away as well. The following night was spent building a Bailey bridge.**

Generaloberst Student was at his headquarters together with Chill when the report came that the British had crossed the Albert Canal at Beringen. "This news had the effect of a bombshell", Student recounted, "I immediately assigned Generalleutnant Chill to the command of this crucial sector and instructed him to carry out a counterattack." [46]

Meanwhile, the paratroop units were arriving. Fallschirm-jäger-Regiment 6, with four battalions, and I. Bataillon of Fallschirm-jäger-Regiment 2 were rushed by lorry to Baelen, north of Beeringen. After having had weapons handed out to them, the soldiers of the new Fallschirmjäger-Division Erdmann set off on a quick march from the northeast. Moreover, schwere Heeres-Panzerjäger-Abteilung 559 was sent in.

On 7 September, the British attacked from the bridgehead at Beringen. Now, they had also been able to transfer their tanks from the 2nd Battalion, The Welsh Guards (2il Fataliwn Gwarchodlu Cym-reig). On that day, they were subject to no less than five waves of coun-terattacks from various German units as these arrived at the front; one by one, these were repelled with heavy losses: First, the Sturm-geschütz III (StuG III) assault guns from 3. Kompanie of schwere Heeres-Panzerjäger-Abteilung 559; next, a paratroop battalion under Oberstleutnant Rudolf Løytved-Hardegg, of Danish descent; then, a home guard battalion (Landesschützen-Bataillon) as well as an infan-try reconnaissance battalion and a company from Flieger-Regiment 22. These attacks had barely been fought back before the Welsh ran into a new home guard battalion; this one had no anti-tank guns and was completely annihilated by the tanks of 2il Fataliwn. "They were able to dispose of the Germans in their slit trenches, whereupon num-bers came forward waving white handkerchiefs and only too anxious to give themselves up", the Guards Armoured Division chronicle recounts.[47] Here, 150 Germans were taken captive.[48]

---

* Bataliwn 1af y Gwarchodlu Cymreig in Welsh.
** A field bridge system built from prefabricated framework.

But this was only the beginning. A battle raged for several days over Hechtel, 12 kilometres northeast of Beringen. As the Albert Canal had now been forced, Student desperately threw in all available resources in order to prevent the British from capturing this strategically important junction, where the road from Brussels crosses the highway north towards Eindhoven. The newly formed "Fallschirmjägerregiment Grassmel" was shifted to Hechtel itself. This unit consisted of one single battalion with four companies, mainly of the same motley crew as the rest of the paratrooper units in this sector. However, the unit commander, Major Franz Grassmel, was one of the most legendary German paratroopers. He had made combat jumps over Crete and fought on the Eastern Front in 1941–1943 and in Italy in 1943–1944. During the battle of Monte Cassino, he led Fallschirmjäger-Regiment 4, which fought back the Polish II Corps with bloody losses.*

Student himself went to the little village of Heppen, only four kilometres north of Beringen, in order to lead the battle personally. This is probably the most important explanation for the harsh resistance that developed in this sector. Student took parts of schwere Heeres-Panzerjäger-Abteilung 559 with him, with 11 StuG IIIs from 3. Kompanie and some Jagdpanthers from the staff.[49] Six StuG IIIs had been lost on 7 September, but on 8 September, the German battalion again clashed with the tanks of the Guards Armoured Division.

Just north of Beringen, eight StuG IIIs and three Jagdpanthers, together with the I. Bataillon of Fallschirmjäger-Regiment 2 (whose fitness for combat von der Heydte had dismissed in such strong language), tried to halt the Sherman tanks of the 2nd (Armoured) Battalion, The Irish Guards, as these came charging across the Bailey bridge to reinforce the Welshmen. The American-made Sherman was considerably inferior to the Jagdpanther in a tank battle – it had a weaker armour protection, and its 75 mm gun could not achieve much frontally against the German tank destroyers unless it came within quite

---

* In three days, the Poles were hit by a loss of almost 4,000 men. "Just eight hundred Germans had succeeded in driving off attacks by two divisions", Matthew Parker observes in his book *Monte Cassino: The Hardest-Fought Battle of World War II* (Doubleday, New York 2004), p. 308.

close range. Initially, the Germans managed to put five Shermans out of action, but soon found themselves compelled to yield to the superior force: after the Irish, the 5th Battalion, The Coldstream Guards, followed suit. While the Irish turned right and continued towards Helchteren and Hechtel to the east and northeast, the Coldstream Guards went north.

At Eindeken, just north of the little village of Beverlo, the British came across two Jagdpanthers and one StuG III that had been abandoned by their crews after getting bogged down in the marshy grounds.*

From there, the march towards Heppen, only a kilometre or so further north, continued.

In the neighbouring village to the east, Leopoldsburg, Major Erich Sattler had set up his command post for his schwere Heeres-Panzer-jäger-Abteilung 559 in the Carmelite monastery next to the Kamp Beverlo military training grounds. At about the same time as the Irish penetrated Beringen, Sattler and his adjutant Oberleutnant Erwin Seitz set off in Jagdpanther No. 01 – which is now on display at the Imperial War Museum in London** – and 02 respectively to reconnoiter towards Beverlo.

The experienced Sattler was supposed to stall the British on his own. The war diary of the 5th Battalion, The Coldstream Guards, noted, "The enemy had several S.P. guns, three of which were knocked out by the tanks, but one continued to give trouble firing down the road that runs into Beverloo from the North East."[50] This is consistent with Major Sattler's own account, according to which he sighted

---

* Today, the location is both sides of the street of Molenvijerstraat 45–47, a street that was lined with deep ditches in those days.

 ** QR5: VIDEO
Seitz's Jagdpanther at the
Imperial War Museum.

enemy tanks to the south after journeying a few kilometres from Leopoldsburg towards Heppen. At a distance of 1,200 metres, he opened fire. The war diary of the 5th Battalion, The Coldstream Guards, continues, "The squadron of tanks were unable to get up owing to a number of Anti-Tank guns firing from the right flank, which knocked out 7 of our tanks." [51]

Sattler now continued down the road ahead, with his adjutant at a distance behind him. When the firing had ceased, Major Lord Hartington (William John Robert Cavendish, commonly known to his men as "Billy") gave the orders to the infantry of his No. 3 Company of the Coldstream battalion to advance along the road to the railway station at the southern part of Heppen. But Sattler made it there before him, and opened up with his front machine gun. "No. 1 Company were unable to get into the station owing to a Panther Tank but they consolidated a position just short of it", the British war diary reads.

What Sattler had not expected, however, was an attack from behind. The Welsh and the 2nd (Armoured) Battalion, The Irish Guards, were at that moment engaged in fierce fighting with three German paratroop regiments that had just arrived at Hechtel and Helchteren. Nevertheless, a Cromwell tank was to intervene in the battle in a decisive way. The commander, the barely 21-year-old Lieutenant William "Hugh" Griffiths, recounted, "I was in charge of Headquarters Troop. I was with the command vehicles a little back from the battle when we got a report in that the village was being threatened from the west by a number of very large tanks. Our squadrons were fully committed. So I thought it might be a good idea if I would go and have a look and I asked the commanding officer and he said yes. So we drove off in the direction where the warning had come from."

Apparently, Griffiths followed the same road that Sattler had taken previously. A German lorry with mounted soldiers was unfortunate enough to get in the way of the British tank. Using a high-explosive shell, Griffiths' gunner, Sergeant Ivor Wilcox, shot the lorry to pieces. "The Germans got out and started running in all directions", Griffiths recounted, "I remember saying to my gunner: 'Come on! Shoot them! Shoot them!' But he said: 'No, I can't do it, sir. I just can't do it.' We then decided to go and investigate down the road. We drove towards the center of the village, where the main battle was taking place. Suddenly there was this huge Jagdpanther. He fired at us and mercifully missed us. We shot off the road to the left." Griffiths took for granted that it was one and the same Jagdpanther, but this was likely Jagdpanther No. 02 under Oberleutnant Seitz, positioned further back, which had discovered his Cromwell. Griffiths drove into a small forest road and suddenly came up behind Sattler's Jagdpanther, which had taken up position on the paved road at the railway crossing next to the little station at Heppes.[52]

Normally, the British Cromwell was not very suitable for tank battles; its short 75 mm Ordnance QF 75 mm L/365-type gun had the worst penetration ability among all Allied anti-tank guns – only 68 mm sloped at 30° at a range of 500 metres. That was not good enough against a Jagdpanther's frontal armour, which was 80 mm sloped at 35°. But now, Griffiths was less than 100 metres to the side of the Jagdpanther, whose side armour was only 45 mm sloped at 65° (that is, relatively speaking, only one fifth of the thickness of 68 mm armour sloped at 30°). The two tank commanders sat in their open top hatches and looked each other in the eyes. "Fire!" Griffiths cried. While the Jagdpanther reversed past the station building, it was hit by one, two, three, four shells, and caught fire.*

Finally, the Jagdpanther reversed across the railway tracks, and came to a standstill in the sand next to the station building (where there is a sandpit today). The crew made it out, but Sattler was wounded and was evacuated. His Jagdpanther became welcome booty when Heppen was captured by the British the following day; it was shipped over to England in 1945 and today is on display at the Imperial War Museum.**

Perhaps the most dramatic of all is that Generaloberst Kurt Student, the commander of German 1. Fallschirmarmee, was inside the station building while this battle was taking place in the street outside!

---

* The railway is now closed, but it used to run towards the west along the lower part of the present-day Kerkestraat. The old station building at Kerkestraat 69, however, still remains.
** It has been claimed that Sattler's Jagdpanther was knocked out near Hechtel, but photographs of the abandoned vehicle show that it was standing in the sand next to the railway station at Heppen.

A shell that struck nearby killed Oberleutnant Rudolf Beck, a company commander of Fallschirm-Regiment 6, who was also present there. Oberleutnant Franz Kopka, the commander of the 3. Kompanie of Sattler's battalion, was also at the location. But Griffiths, of course, had no idea about this, and withdrew quickly from the area.

Student ordered Kopka to assume command of schwere Heeres-Panzerjäger-Abteilung 559 and head off with his StuG III westwards, where the British had appeared. Kopka's position as battalion commander would not remain for long; west of Heppen, his StuG III was knocked out, probably by a Sherman Firefly,* and Kopka was also wounded and evacuated.

Oberleutnant Edmund Haile, who had been leading the 2. Kompanie until then, was appointed new commander of the battalion.[53]

At that stage, schwere Heeres-Panzerjäger-Abteilung 559 only had five left of the eleven StuG IIIs that had arrived with the 3. Kompanie the day before, and the only operative Jagdpanther was No. 02 under 24-year-old Oberleutant Seitz. This vehicle continued making quite successful raids against the British, but apart from that, the German troops were not particularly efficient. The British captured 150 prisoners from the I. Bataillon of Fallschirmjäger-Regiment 2 on 8 September alone. The following morning, a dejected battalion commander, Major Oswald Finzel, had to report that 40 men was all that was left of his unit.[54] Two of the German soldiers who took part in the fight on 8 September illustrate quite well what kind of soldiers the Germans had been scraping together to close the gap in the front: Unteroffizier Daniel Grams and Gefreiter Wilhelm Hartwig. Grams was born on 20 December 1909, and had thus begun the 35th year of his life. When the war broke out in 1939, he was, with his almost 30 years of age, already overage for frontline duty, and was at first placed in the home

---

* The Firefly was a Sherman that had been modified by the British, who had painstakingly squeezed a large 17-pound, 76.2 mm, anti-tank gun (at the expense of not having any room for the deputy driver, who would otherwise help the loader). The 17-pound gun could penetrate 131 mm armour sloped at 30° from a distance of 1,000 metres. Even if it could not be compared with the Germans 88 mm PaK 43 anti-tank gun (which could penetrate 165 mm armour sloped at 30° from the same distance), it was sufficient against a Jagdpanther's 80 mm frontal armour at a 35° angle. One tank in four in the Irish tank battalion was a Firefly.

guard, and, after that, from 1941, in Coastal Defence Division 719. When he was taken captive on 8 September, it was his first combat. Gefreiter Wilhelm Hartwig, born in 1926 and thus only 18 years old, had just been placed in Division 176, and arrived at the front at Beringen on 8 September, only to be badly wounded by shrapnel. Hartwig was then in a hospital until April 1945; on 25 April 1945, he collected a Polish-made rifle, which he however handed back three days later. The short combat on 8 September was most likely the only one he took part in.

An increasingly desperate Student issued a categorical order– "Stand your ground at the Albert Canal to the last man". But in Hechtel, at the crossroads on the northbound highway towards Eindhoven, the paratroopers of Fallschirmjägerregiment Grassmel, inexperienced in combat, started giving way under the pressure from British attacks. Student therefore ordered the II. Abteilung of the Fallschirm-Panzer-Ersatz- und Ausbildungs-Regiment "Hermann Göring", with almost 600 men and six training tanks and tank destroyers, into this sector, and sent in two SS batteries with powerful 10.5 cm guns that had previously been part of the German coastal defence in the Netherlands. By that, he won yet some more time.

Things were becoming increasingly frustrating for the British. The German resistance in Hechtel meant that the northbound highway remained blocked. In order to break the deadlock, Dempsey, the commander of British Second Army, ordered the 11th Armoured Division as well to regroup to the Hechtel sector. Parts of this division circumvented Hechtel from the south on 10 September, and clashed with a large group of paratroopers from Fallschirmjägerregiment Grassmel east of the town. These Germans turned out not to be particularly willing to fight – in fact, they were on their way of escaping from the harsh battle of Hechtel – but surrendered after a short fight which cost the British four killed and eleven wounded. The number of captured Germans was 400.[55] Among 30 killed Germans were the commander of the paratroop regiment's 1. Kompanie, Hauptmann Herzog.

Under increasing pressure, the remaining Germans in Hechtel had several civilians shot. One of the paratroopers, Jäger Wolfgang

Neff, testified after the war that 10–12 civilians had executed were Hechtel on 10 September. Even if Neff testified who the perpetrator was, this person escaped being brought to justice after the war. [56]

Meanwhile, the Guards Armoured Division circumvented Hechtel to the north from the west, with the Grenadier Guards to the left and the Irish Guards under "Colonel Joe" Vandeleur to the right. A reconnaissance force from the latter unit discovered a small, unguarded road, that was not marked on the British maps. This was Fabriekstraat (Factory Street), which connected Neerpelt and Overpelt, on the other side of the highway, with the large factories of Compagnie des Metaux d'Overpelt-Lommel, which at the end of the 19th century had been established on the south side of the canal, east of the bridge at Grote-Barreel.

The commander of the Irish reconnaissance force, Lieutenant Jack Creswell, hurried back to the command post in the small village of Ekel, northeast of Hechtel, to report. It was around nightfall, and "Colonel Joe" Vandeleur had intended to pause for the night, but when he received this message, he decided to attack immediately with a compound battle force. With the infantrymen of No. 2 Company of the 3rd (Infantry) Battalion mounted on the Sherman tanks of Major John Peel's No. 1 Squadron of the 2nd (Armoured) Battalion, as well as a group of engineers, the Irish set off. Vandeleur personally led the force.

With some difficulties, they made it across the terrain between Neerpelt to the east and the highway to the west. Today, the area is built over, but in those days, it consisted of large, open sand dunes, and was, hardly surprising, called "the Sahara" by the locals. To "Colonel Joe", who had been serving as a camel rider in Sudan in the 1920s, it almost felt as though he was back in the desert again. In the northern outskirts of this "desert", next to the canal, lay the ruins of the large factories where zinc and sulphuric acid had been produced. These had been completely bombed to smithereens by Allied aircraft, and therefore lay more or less abandoned.

Without having been detected by the Germans – with the exception of a lone German soldier who surrendered without further ado – the Irish made it to the factory area. "Colonel Joe" climbed up on top of one of the great slag heaps at the western edge of the factory area, and saw the river crossing from there, only little more than 200 metres away. The original steel bridge at Grote-Barreel had been demolished by the Belgians in May 1940, but the Germans had built a wooden bridge out of framework 150 metres east of it.

The British called it Bridge No. 9, and taking it was of course of utmost importance. While the Germans had blown up most of the bridges across the Maas-Scheldt Canal, they had kept this one and yet another one (farther to the east) for their troops south of the canal. The bridge itself was not defended by anything more than a couple of 88 mm anti-aircraft guns. The crews for these guns had been abandoned the day before by their commanding officer, who had left along the northbound road after urging them to "fight to the last cartridge".[57] The barrage that hit them from the factory area at nightfall on this 10 September came completely unexpected to them. The non-commissioned officer who had said that "the bridge must and will be blown up" immediately disappeared from the site.

The zinc works at Neerpelt and the so-called "Sahara". The Maas-Scheldt Canal runs just behind the factory area. The picture is taken from the southwest. Outside the picture, next to the building to the far left, were the slag heaps. Bridge No. 9 was another 200 metres to the left.

More out of fear than out of motivation to defend the bridge, the anti-aircraft gun crews returned the fire. In the midst of it all, a German Sd.Kfz. 7-type half-track with an 88 mm gun in tow appeared on the road from the north, rolling up onto the bridge. A shell from the other side tore the vehicle to pieces as soon as it had made it across to the other side. A German anti-aircraft gun crew opened fire against a tank that seemed to be crossing the highway 350 metres to the south, but missed it, and, at the next moment, the Sherman tank had disappeared behind the residential houses that lined the highway. This seemed to become the signal for terrible bombardment by artillery and machine guns of the area around the bridge. While their comrades fell to the right and to the left, the Germans hurriedly threw themselves into cover. The large house to the left of the bridge was hit in one of its roof trusses and caught fire.

In the next moment, the Irish attacked. Lieutenant Duncan Lampard commanded the troop of three Shermans that led the charge. It was Lampard's tank that had hit the German vehicle, which was now fully ablaze in the middle of the road. He had positioned Lance-Serjeant* Thomas Edward McGurren's Sherman on the left side of the road (it was this tank that the Germans had seen crossing the highway) and a Sherman with Serjeant Fred Steers as commander at the head to the right.

McGurren's tank stalled, but he still continued firing at the bridge, while Steers and Lampard continued down the road ahead, ceaselessly firing their frontal machine guns.[58] When they passed the bridge-master's house one hundred metres from the bridge, the infantrymen came flocking out from their hiding places; a platoon from the 3rd Battalion had sneaked forward into a position here before the attack. The platoon commander, Acting Captain John Stanley-Clarke, rushed across the bridge together with the leading tank and neutralised a German machine gun on the other side.[59] Eventually, only two surviving Germans remained, and they surrendered immediately. Captain Ronald Hutton, one of the engineers who had joined up, climbed down the pillars supporting the bridge from underneath and cut the wires for

* The British and New Zealand armies (but not the air forces) spelled this military rank with a "j" instead of with a "g" until 1953.

the explosives. The important bridge, that was to play a major role in the forthcoming offensive, had been captured undamaged![60] The War Diary of the 32nd Guards Brigade concluded, "The bridge was fully prepared for demolition with charges totalling a weight of 2,000 lbs, and the bridge was strongly defended. All the bridges to the east along the canal had been blown, and it is evident that this bridge and the one at 3097 were left for the evacuation of enemy forces, after which they also would have been destroyed".[61]

Major Peel, Lampard, McGurren, Steers, Stanley-Clarke, and Hutton were all awarded the Military Cross – the third highest award for valour for officers up to the rank of major in the United Kingdom – for their effort. Lieutenant-General Brian Horrocks, the commander of the XXX Corps, was so impressed by "Colonel Joe's" achievement that he gave the order to call Bridge No. 9 "Joe's Bridge" henceforth.[62] "They're a 'terrible' body of men, the Micks", one of the British soldiers wrote, referring to The Irish Guards, who were called The Micks. "They had rushed the bridge in the failing light and – 'Holy Mother of Jaizus' – they had got it in the bag, together with the four 88 mms and the startled Boche who had failed to defend it."[63]

The northbound road also lay open. The Grenadier Guards cleared the road to the bridge by wiping out the German force that held the smaller crossroads between the bridge and Hechtel to the south the same evening. Here, one StuG III, seven anti-tank guns, and three of the obsolete tanks from II. Abteilung of Fallschirm-Panzer-Ersatz- und Ausbildungs- Regiment "Hermann Göring" were destroyed. The commander of the "Hermann Göring" battalion, Hauptmann Willi Müller, was wounded as his Panzer III tank was knocked out, and was brought by his comrades back to Hechtel.

All that had to be done now was to break the German resistance at Hechtel. On 11 September, the British withdrew their forces from the town, which, during the following night, was subject to intense artillery fire. This eventually broke the German defence. When the Welsh Guards entered the town again the following morning, it fell into their hands quite quickly. The battle of Hechtel cost the Germans terrible losses. The II. Abteilung of Fallschirm-Panzer-Ersatz- und Ausbildungs- Regiment "Hermann Göring" was virtually annihilated. Only small groups of soldiers managed to escape. All tanks and artillery pieces, as well as all anti-tank and anti-aircraft guns were left behind in Hechtel.[64] Hauptmann Müller was taken captive as he lay wounded in the cellar of the ruins of the house where he had had his command post. Major Franz Grassmel, the commander of the paratroop regiment that bore his name, managed to escape, but his unit was dreadfully badly mauled. Leutnant Walter Schauf, who had taken over the 1. Kompanie after the fallen Hauptmann Herzog, was among those who were taken captive on 12 September, as were the commanders of the 2. and 3. Kompanies, Oberleutnants Karlheinz Schlizio and Günther Plaumann. The British took 575 prisoners, 200 of which were wounded, and rounded up the dead bodies of 150 German soldiers.[65] Only 89 Germans managed to escape the encirclement and withdraw to their own lines.[66]

The British had also suffered some serious losses; 1st Battalion, The Welsh Guards, counted almost 200 killed, wounded, and missing.[67] But Montgomery had many strong units left – quite contrary to the Germans, who would have to fight the battle during Operation "Market Garden" with the remains of units that had been so badly depleted between the Albert and Maas-Scheldt canals. In retrospect, it turned out to have been a huge mistake by Student to send his units across the Maas-Scheldt Canal at the same pace as they arrived. In that way, he deviated from the German military principle of power concentration, and ended up losing a large number of his new units as these were sent into combat piecemeal. Now, he did not have much left to hold back the British Second Army with.

Operation "Market Garden"

"LET US SAVE ENGLAND!"

On 8 September 1944, a terrible explosion occurred in the Maisons-Alfort quarters in the south-eastern part of Paris. Several buildings were blown out, six people were killed, and thirty-six wounded. An enormous crater testified to the impact of a bomb of some kind, but nobody in Paris knew what had caused the explosion.

Seven hours later, Chiswick in western London was shaken by a similar, sudden explosion. Immediately afterwards, a mysterious roaring sound was heard, and next, an enormous bang boomed high up in the air. The sound could be heard all over London. In Chiswick, eleven buildings were toppled and more than five hundred houses were damaged, fifteen of which so badly that they had to be evacuated. It was only sheer luck that the number of killed was limited to three.

The authorities hurriedly explained that the event had been caused by a "gas explosion". But they knew very well what it was all about. What had happened was that the Germans had begun their bombardment with A 4-type (Aggregat 4) ballistic missiles, which would later be renamed V 2 (Vergeltungswaffe 2, Vengeance Weapon 2). Just as the British Air Defence had started to overcome the V 1 flying bombs (which flew at a low altitude at about 600 km/h), the V 2s started emerging. This rocket was launched into the stratosphere and would dive at multiple-supersonic speed straight down into the ground. The sounds that the Londoners had heard were first the bang from the impact – which was powerful enough to fling 3,000 tons of matter up into the air – and only then the sound of the rocket engine, followed by the supersonic bang.

The military and political leadership on the Allied side knew of the A 4/V 2 after having been given the parts of two different V 2s from both the Polish resistance and the Swedish government (in both cases, test launches). Through air reconnaissance, it had been established that they were launched from the Hague region in the Netherlands, but from vehicle-drawn, mobile launch ramps, which made them almost impossible to fight with aircraft. It was, of course, also completely out of the question to shoot down the V 2s.

The beginning of the V 2 barrage caused panic in the Allied headquarters. British Prime Minister Winston Churchill feared that as many as 100,000 people could get killed when the V 2 offensive began for real.

After the Allies had crossed the river Seine, and begun their Blitz offensive in August 1944, Americans and Britons had been engaged in a tug-of-war over the insufficient supplies for the armies. U.S. General Patton was of the opinion that the bulk was to be assigned to his Third Army, which was advancing towards Metz and the Saarland on the southern flank. Montgomery, on the other hand, demanded that his army group, the 21st Army Group, and the northern American First Army be give top priority for a coordinated push to the north, through the Netherlands, and subsequently into Germany. The Supreme Commander, the American General Dwight D. Eisenhower, was wavering indecisively between these two positions.

Montgomery had been in command of the Allied ground forces during the Battle of Normandy, but on 1 September 1944, Eisenhower personally took over this position. The fact that Montgomery at the same time was promoted to Field Marshal was poor consolation for the British commander. The personal conflict between Montgomery and Patton did not exactly improve the situation, and Lieutenant General Omar Bradley, commander of the American 12th Army Group, begun leaning more and more in favour of Patton. When Montgomery on 17 August had presented his plan to Bradley for the first time, the latter seemed to agree to all intents and purposes. But three days later, Eisenhower advocated an advance on a wide front, with the same priority both for Americans and Britons, which received Bradley's support. But the logistics apparatus would not be able to manage this as long as the large port of Antwerp could not be used. Yet another problem was the large wastage during the long road transports – the Allies were confined to transports with the lorries of the American so-called "Red Ball Express" as all railways in northern France had previously been destroyed by Allied air attacks. This was problematic for several reasons. American historian Martin Blumeson wrote, "The Red Ball Express fostered the habit of poor road discipline, offered opportunity for malingering, sabotage, and black marketeering, and tempted combat units to hijack and otherwise divert supplies." [68]

During the following weeks, Eisenhower was put under heavy pressure from both Montgomery and Patton, and swung back and forth between their respective demands. Eventually, it was, ironically enough, Hitler's actions that settled the case. As the V 2 barrage begun, Eisenhower took the decision to give Montgomery's northbound push top priority: now, it was primarily a matter of entering the Netherlands and driving away the Germans from the launching areas of the V 2s; London was only just within range when these were launched from the Hague area.

On 9 September, Montgomery received a wire from the British War Office, asking how soon he would be able to occupy the Southern Netherlands. "In about a fortnight's time", was the self-confident reply. Montgomery understood that the hardening German resistance was only temporary, and was expecting that the Battle of the Albert Canal would break the Germans.

The next morning, he met in Brussels with Dempsey and Browning, the commanders of the Second Army and the I Airborne Corps respectively. These had expected to discuss Operation "Comet", which meant that the British 1st Airborne Division and the Polish Parachute Brigade would be landed at the bridges across the Rhine between Arnhem and Wesel in connection with the Second Army's northbound push. But now, Montgomery had changed his mind. In part that was because the stiffening German resistance had slowed down the pace of the advance, and in part it was because the Air Force had recommended Montgomery not to send in airborne forces against Wesel because of the very strong German anti-aircraft defences in the Ruhr area. But the thought of driving away the Germans from the Hague area, from where their V 2s were launched, was of at least as big importance. Montgomery recounted the telegram and said, "Let us save England!" [69]

"ONE OF THE MOST IMAGINATIVE PLANS OF THE WAR"

"The thrust line must be against Arnhem", Montgomery explained. By shifting the previously planned advance of Dempsey's army to the west, and having the eastern shore of the Zuiderzee as its first goal, the German units in Western Netherlands would be isolated, and no more V 2s would be able to be brought forward to the Hague area. The objective, Montgomery explained, was to "destroy all enemy west of the general line Zwolle-Deventer-Kleve-Venlo-Maastricht, with a view to advancing eastwards and occupying the Ruhr".[70]

Apart from that, the plan reminded of Operation "Comet". During the course of a few hours, Dempsey, Browning, and Montgomery drew up the main outlines of what would become one of the most famous undertakings in the history of warfare.

The attack would be carried out by Dempsey's army, which was to be concentrated to a 30 kilometre-wide sector between Turnhout to the west and Hasselt to the east. But the attack proper would be carried out on only 15 kilometres' width, with the XII Corps to the left and the VIII Corps to the right, and the XXX Corps advancing in the centre across the Maas-Scheldt Canal across Bridge No. 9 (which was given the name "Joe's Bridge" the same evening), and continue through Eindhoven and Nijmegen towards Arnhem – a 120-kilometre route by road. From there, the XXX Corps would continue north to Emmeloord, on the eastern side of the Zuiderzee (today's IJsselmeer), and establish bridgeheads on the eastern side of the river IJssel, the tributary river to the Rhine that flows northwards just east of Arnhem. By acting quickly and exploiting the fact that the Germans had moved most of their new units forward to the Albert line, where Montgomery expected them to be crushed, the plan predicted a Blitz advance in six days. Dempsey's attack would be combined with an attack by the U.S. First Army towards Cologne and Bonn at the Rhine to the south, while this army's northernmost army corps would cover Dempsey's eastern flank. As soon as the Americans had established themselves at the Rhine, it was time for the next phase, a pincer movement towards the German Ruhr area.

Due to the strained supply situation, Montgomery believed it necessary to give Dempsey's units top priority when allocating supplies, meaning that Patton's U.S. Third Army to the south had to be ordered to cancel their attacks. But it was only a matter of a short interruption. Montgomery's westernmost army, the Canadian First Army, would mainly be relieved from their efforts to capture the seaports that the Germans were still holding in the Pas de Calais area; as soon as Boulogne had been conquered, it would be sent in to drive the Germans away from the Scheldt Estuary in order to open the port of Antwerp for Allied supply traffic. This would in turn make it possible for all Allied units, including Patton's army, to resume the advance on a wide front that Eisenhower had been advocating. "Monty" argued that there was every reason to expect a victorious end to the war before the turn of the year through such an operation.

As with "Comet", the ground attack by Dempsey's army would be combined with an airborne operation with the objective of securing important watercourse crossings along the planned route of attack. The strength of the airborne units that were to be sent in was expanded from one division and one brigade to three divisions and one brigade. These would, in the words of Montgomery, lay "a carpet" for the British ground troops across eight bodies of water:

From south to north
- the Wilhelmina Canal north of Eindhoven
- the Dommel river at Sint-Oedenrode, seven kilometres further north
- the Zuid-Willemsvaart Canal, yet some five kilometres to the north
- the bridge across the Maas at Grave, 30 kilometres to the northeast
- at least one of the bridges across the Maas-Waal Canal, yet another ten kilometres away
- at least one of the bridges across the river Waal at Nijmegen, ten kilometres further north
- at least one of the Rhine bridges in the southern outskirts of Arnhem, yet another 17 kilometres to the north.

Thus, the foundations for the operations had been made clear. Montgomery now delegated to Dempsey to polish the details. The airborne units would be placed under his command, but only after they had been landed. It fell on the staff of the airborne army to work out the air landings. Therefore, the operation ended up consisting of two attack plans: Operation "Market", the airborne part, and Operation "Garden", the ground operation – taken together, "Market Garden".*

The historiography of Operation "Market Garden" bears much resemblance with the similarly failed German offensive through the Ardennes in December 1944/January 1945** in such a way that both military commanders and writers have been claiming after the war that the operation plan was "doomed on beforehand" and that many of the most important commanders opposed it – in spite of all available documents clearly refuting the latter.

Later the same day, on 10 September, Montgomery met with General Eisenhower aboard his twin-engined Douglas C-47 transport plane at Melsbroek Airport outside Brussels to brief the Supreme Commander of his plans. Much is often made of the fact that Eisenhower at one occasion during this meeting was annoyed with Montgomery's impudence (which was quite typical of the headstrong Englishman), but the most important outcome of the meeting was that Eisenhower received Montgomery's proposed plan with great enthusiasm. He was not the only one to do so, either. "I freely conceded", said the commander of the American 12th Army Group, Lieutenant-General Omar Bradley, "that it was one of the most imaginative [war plans] of the war".[71]

In the literature about "Market Garden", there are often references to what that the commander of the Polish Parachute Brigade, Major-General Stanislaw Sosabowski, muttered under his breath when the plan was presented, "But the Germans, General, the Germans". The problem with this is that Sosabowski expressed this implicit reservation not concerning "Market Garden", but concerning "Comet".[72]

---

* It has been claimed that the plan for the operation at first bore the name "Sixteen", but this is a misunderstanding based on the fact that it was the operational plan No. 16, while Operation "Comet", for example, was plan No. 15. A map of the battle area is available on page 27 and 400.

** See Bergström, *The Ardennes 1944–1945*.

Lieutenant-General "Boy" Browning is said to have put forward the opinion that it was "a bridge too far" – which has given the name for Cornelius Ryan's famous book on the subject, later the basis of the perhaps best-known Hollywood war movie ever. There are no memoranda supporting this, and it has been questioned whether Browning said these words at all. Geoffrey Picot, one of the veterans of Operation "Market Garden", said, "I doubt that he used the phrase because it would imply that he did not understand the strategy of the operation". This is, as Picot rightly points out, of course "inherently unlikely"; the importance assigned to the Arnhem bridge is evident not least by Montgomery himself calling the whole undertaking the "Arnhem Operation". [73]

Recently, however, evidence has emerged that Browning did in fact pass this remark – however, with a slightly different meaning than questioning the entire operation. A few years before his death in 1994, his chief of staff at the time, Brigadier Gordon Walch, lifted the veil by writing down the following, which was made accessible by the archive at the Imperial War Museum in London not long ago, "I have never previously broken my silence on this matter, but now, 45 years later, I think perhaps this statement may do more good than harm, if it gets any publicity. [...] On being asked by General [sic] Montgomery for his general opinion of the proposed operation, General Boy said he thought it was possible, but perhaps, they might be going a bridge too far with the airlift available. His opinion was understood and appreciated; the operation was planned in detail by General Boy and he would be in command until the ground forces joined up." [74]

As we shall see, events that could not possibly have been anticipated by Browning, would prove him right – but "Market Garden" would still, as such, and with the exception of one tactical setback, be brought to a mainly successful conclusion. This will be evident as a result of both of the volumes of the present work.

The Allies had more than 1,700 operational transport planes at their disposal – 1,274 American and 164 British Douglas C-47s and 321 four-engined British bombers that could be sent in to tow gliders. In addition, there were more than 3,000 gliders, almost 2,200 of which were of the Waco type, more than 900 Horsas, and 64 of the gigantic Hamilcars.

Douglas C-47, which was called Skytrain by the Americans and Dakota by the British, was a rebuilt version of the civilian DC-3 passenger aircraft. Therefore, it lacked both defensive armament as well as self-sealing fuel tanks, but could take on 28 paratroopers (10 more than the German equivalent, the Junkers 52). Each transport plane could take one glider. Among these, the American Waco CG-4 could house either 13 soldiers or four passengers and a jeep or three passengers and one 75 mm howitzer. The larger British Airspeed AS.51 Horsa could contain as many as 30 soldiers or one jeep or one 6-pound cannon. The biggest among them all was the British-made Gal. 49 Hamilcar, with a 33.5-metre wingspan, which during "Market Garden" was used for flying on great 17-pound anti-tank guns and 4-ton Bren Carriers to the Arnhem area.

Theoretically, this armada could fly in the 33,791 soldiers of the three airborne divisions and the brigade that was earmarked for the attack in one single flight. But with all the equipment these units brought along,, the numbers were limited to 16,500 men at any one time.[75] Browning immediately saw that this would become one of the operation's weakest points.

In theory, the transport aviation would be able to carry out two flights during the first day, and this was also something that Air Vice-Marshal Leslie Hollinghurst, the commander of the transport

Two C-47 transport aircraft with Waco gliders in tow.

aviation of the 38 Group of the Royal Air Force, proposed. But Lieutenant General Brereton, the American commander of the Allied airborne army, had given the task of planning for the flight to Major Paul L. Williams, the commander of U.S. IX Troop Carrier Command, and he decided that only one flight per day would be carried out. Williams argued, not without reason, that there would not be enough time during one single day to service the aircraft and get another airborne operation with the necessary concentration going, as the air units were based in England, more than 700 kilometres from the landing targets (taking into consideration that the route had been calculated so as to avoid German anti-aircraft fire to the greatest possible extent). With the cruising speed of the C-47 at 250 km/h, this meant that the aircraft would be airborne for more than six hours, including the time it took to gather the formations. According to Williams, it was complicated enough to organise such an enormous air operation in one day.

Neither did they want to fly by night, which was probably a sound decision. The previous Allied military airdrops – in North Africa, Italy and Normandy – had all taken place during moonlit nights. But when "Market Garden" was to commence, the moon was down, which made it very difficult to drop the paratroopers over the right spots. Moreover, the German night fighter aviation had been weak in these other areas, but over the Netherlands, very strong German night fighter units were operating. The German day fighter aviation was, on the other hand, strongly decimated, and did not pose as big a threat, which was why it seemed natural to carry out the airdrops by day.

Cancelling the operation because it was not possible to fly in the entire force during the same day was never an option – that would have been squandering a golden opportunity to finish the war in a short time. German Paratroop General Kurt Student, who without doubt was the commander with the largest experience of airborne operations, did not hesitate in his assessment after the war, "It was but logical in such a situation to proceed with airborne operations, by way of gliders and parachutists, in order to secure bridges intact." [76]

Moreover, Montgomery had assured Browning that the ground units would come to the aid of the airborne forces in Arnhem within two days. One infantry division, the 52nd (Lowland) Division, would also be flown in with transport aircraft that landed near Arnhem to reinforce the Allied units in this area: either, the division would be flown in to the Deelen airfield, a few kilometres north of Arnhem, but in case this did not work, an American engineer battalion would be landed in order to build a provisional airfield that could receive the division.

One thing that did drag on further, however, before the whole intended airborne force had been landed, was the need to fly in supplies for the forces that had been landed first. Therefore, the plan for Operation "Market" ended up comprising airdrops for three consecutive days.

In general, the beginning of Operation "Market Garden" was delayed by decisions that were taken by the U.S. commanders. At the meeting with Montgomery in Brussels on 10 September, Eisenhower, even though becoming enthusiastic about the new plan, had refused to give this operation the priority in allocating supplies that Montgomery deemed necessary. The following day, Montgomery returned to Eisenhower with a warning that under the circumstances, the units were not capable of carrying out their northern attack until 23 September at the earliest, perhaps not even until the 26th.[77] This was not made up; on 9 September, Dempsey had reported that "owing to our maintenance situation, we will not be in a position to fight a real battle for perhaps ten days or a fortnight".[78]

"This message produced results which were almost electric", Montgomery commented. On 12 September, Eisenhower's chief of staff, General Walter Beddell Smith, told Montgomery that Patton would be ordered to halt, so that Montgomery's offensive could get absolute priority in allocating supplies. This finally got things going. "As a result of these promises", Montgomery recounted after the war, "I reviewed my plans with Dempsey and fixed the D-Day for the Arnhem operation (Market Garden) for Sunday 17th September."[79]

Eisenhower would, however, turn out to be too weak to enforce his will against the charismatic George Patton. The message from

Eisenhower's staff that Montgomery received on 13 September showed that the "priority in maintenance" that he had been promised was not being honoured at all: Montgomery's army group would not receive more than an addition of 500 tons per day via highways and 500 tons per day that were to be flown in. This was not even half of the extra addition that Montgomery considered necessary, and moreover, the supplies that would arrive by air would cease as the armada of transport aircraft were sent in for the airborne attack operation.

After renewed correspondence between the two headquarters, Eisenhower issued a new directive on 15 September. Now, he promised again "priority in all forms of logistical support" for Montgomery's offensive until it had crossed the Rhine, and Patton would only be allocated resources sufficient for "security and reconnaissance".[80] "I must say that not only is [your plan] designed to carry out most effectively my basic conception with respect to this campaign but is in exact accordance with all understandings that we now have", Eisenhower wrote to Montgomery the following day. But the higher priority that Eisenhower had promised never materialised, because of Patton's manoeuvring in combination with Eisenhower's weakness. After the war, Patton revealed his tactics: "In order to attack, we had first pretend to reconnoiter, then reinforce the reconnaissance, and finally put on an attack."[81] By putting his army in risky situations in the Metz area – the very point on the entire Western front where the Germans were at their strongest – Patton made it impossible to cut down on supplies for his army.

This had serious consequences for the two corps in Dempsey's army that were responsible for protecting the flanks for the main assault force, the XXX Corps. As we have seen above, the insufficient supplies had forced Montgomery to prioritise, so that the VIII Corps and most of Dempsey's artillery had been left "stranded" at the Seine when the advance from this river was begun on 29 August; now, Dempsey was forced to wait to the last moment – the same day as "Market Garden" was to begin – with assigning fuel so that this corps could be moved forward. The XII Corps was also affected, albeit not as hard, but when the offensive began, the tank division of the corps, the

7th Armoured, had only been able to shift one of its three regiments to the combat area.[82]

This basically became the only result of Patton's manoeuvring – as the famous military historian Liddell Hart put it, "Patton's Third Army begun [...] crossing the Moselle already on 5 September, but had not made it much further two weeks later – or, in fact, two months later."[83]

MONTGOMERY vs. MODEL

Fifty-three-year-old Generalfeldmarschall Walter Model was the third great German commander that Montgomery had been opposing. He had defeated the other two – Rommel in North Africa and Gerd von Rundstedt in France. The man he was now facing was certainly very experienced, but the two others were undeniably more skilled. It was true that Hitler had called Model "my best field marshal", and he had gained a reputation as "the Führer's fireman" for the many occasions when he had saved the situation on the Eastern Front. Nor was there any doubt about Model's experience. He had been serving as a chief of staff in various units during the First World War and in the Reichswehr, and during the Second World War, he had made a quick military career and was now the commander of Heeresgruppe B – the German army group on the northern part of the Western front. Model was doubtlessly a good commander, but his shortcomings had become apparent during the battle of Kursk in July 1943, when his Ninth Army had failed completely.

The three years older Bernard Law Montgomery was at least as experienced. In fact, Model and Montgomery had much in common. Both of them served as battalion adjutants on the Western Front at the beginning of the First World War, and both of them had advanced from divisional commanders to corps commanders, commanders of an army, and, finally, commanders of an army group during the Second World War. They had both also been Supreme Commanders for the ground forces of their respective sides in the West for a short period: Montgomery from the invasion of Normandy and until 1 September 1944, when Eisenhower took over, and Model between August 1944 and 4 September, when Field Marshal Gerd von Rundstedt was reinstated in that position.*

Another similarity between the two was their obstinacy and sharp tongues when it came to contradicting superiors whom they believed they were right against. Here, however, the two armed forces' respective attitudes would decide the outcome: contrary to the prevailing clichéd image, the Nazi dictator Hitler could very well take being contradicted by his generals. At one occasion, a hot-tempered discussion played out between Model and Hitler over where a new army corps would best be sent in, whereby Model fixed his eyes on the Führer and hissed, "Who is really leading at the front, you or I, *mein Führer?*" – upon which Hitler yielded.

In Montgomery's case, his outspokenness constituted an obstacle for his military career for a long time, in spite of him being an admittedly skilled commander. In his memoirs, he describes how he served under General Claude Auchinleck as commander of the 5th Corps, adding sarcastically, "I cannot recall that we ever agreed on anything".[84] British writer Barrie Pitt describes Montgomery's criticism of Auchinleck as "a campaign of insubordination against his superior which bordered on mutiny".[85]

The question is, however, whether Montgomery must not be considered a cut above Model: he was, by early September 1944, one of the few generals in the Second World War who had never lost a battle. The negative reputation that Montgomery has been given in historiography can be explained almost entirely by American use of history; the American generals never got over him saving them out of the debacle in the Ardennes during the winter of 1944/1945.**

Three other very skilled British generals during Operation "Market Garden" were Major-Generals Sir Richard O'Connor and Brian Horrocks, and Brigadier "Pip" Roberts. As commander of the British

---

* Field Marshal von Rundstedt had been Supreme Commander in the West earlier as well, but was fired in July 1944 by Hitler, who, however, reinstated him again on 4 September 1944. Until then, Model had simultaneously been Supreme Commander in the West and commander of the army group Heeresgruppe B, which he found overwhelming.
** See Bergström, *The Ardennes 1944–1945.*

forces in Egypt, the moustached "Dick" O'Connor had won one of the most brilliant victories of the Second World War, as he in the winter of 1940/1941 defeated an Italian army many times larger than his own forces, taking 130,000 Italian soldiers captive without the British losing more than 500 killed and 1,300 wounded men. It was sheer bad luck that he happened to be taken prisoner by a German patrol shortly afterwards, but O'Connor escaped in 1943 and made it back to his own, who, in January 1944, put him in command of VIII Corps. Montgomery expressed on several occasions how impressed he was by O'Connor's skill as a commander – for instance, he proposed that O'Connor should succeed him as commander of the Eighth Army in Italy when he himself was sent to England in January 1944 to take command of the Allied ground forces that were to land in Normandy. Considering this, it is surprising that it was indeed O'Connor's corps that had to remain inactive at the Seine when the two other corps in Dempsey's army swept westwards in August and September 1944. The fact that O'Connor's VIII Corps was given a second-class position to cover the XXX Corps' flank during "Market Garden" becomes even more peculiar when considering that the VIII Corps also had the British Army's perhaps best armoured division, the 11th, called "the Black Bull". This was commanded by the renowned Major-General George Philip "Pip" Bradley Roberts, at age 37 the youngest general in the British Army and perhaps its most prominent armoured unit commander. He had been awarded the Military Cross for his success against the Italians in Libya when leading the 4th Armoured Brigade in 1940. Two years later, it was his brigade that halted Rommel at Alam Halfa, Egypt, and in December 1943, he assumed command of the 11th Armoured Division. This division had temporarily been lent to the XXX Corps for the sweep through northern France in August 1944, and it was this division that had taken Antwerp. Ahead of "Market Garden", however, it was returned to the VIII Corps.

The fact that Montgomery wanted the XXX Corps under Brian Horrocks at the head of Operation "Market Garden" is not particularly strange, however; Horrocks had been serving under Montgomery during two different occasions – first, as battalion commander of

Montgomery's division in France in 1940, and, after that, as a corps commander in Montgomery's Eighth Army in 1942–1943 – and "Monty" knew Horrocks's qualities very well: he considered him "one of my most able officers", which was rather an understatement. Horrocks was an aggressive and forceful commander who was only too happy to be at the frontline with his soldiers to give them courage. A disadvantage for him was, however, that he was suffering from the effects of the serious injuries he had suffered when being shot at by a German fighter plane in Italy in September 1943.

As for the rest, the Allied commanders of "Market Garden" were not of any calibre that could measure with the German generals, who usually were the most professional ones of the entire war. As we will see, this was a completely decisive factor for the way the battle went during "Market Garden".

The commander of British XII Corps on Dempsey's left flank was Lieutenant-General Neil Ritchie. He had, as had Montgomery, O'Connor, and Brian Horrocks, served in North Africa, but as opposed to them, he had not done so with any distinction: in June 1942, he was fired from his position as commander of the Eighth Army for his flagrant failures against the "Desert Fox" Rommel and his German-Italian Afrikakorps. It meant great humiliation to Ritchie to be demoted to a divisional commander (of the 52nd Infantry Division), but in December 1943, he was at least reinstalled by Montgomery as commander of the XII Corps.

Lieutenant-General Miles Dempsey himself, the commander of the Second Army, is described by military historian David Bennett as "more efficient than brilliant".[86] His infantry brigade had covered Montgomery's 3rd Division during the retreat to Dunkirk in May/June 1940, but lost 80% of its men in the process. Dempsey was the commander during the campaign in Italy in 1943 of an army corps that mainly distinguished itself for its very slow advance. Even if he did not concede it, it is possible that Montgomery, who after all had quite a sentimental disposition, chose Dempsey to lead the Second Army as a favour in return for him having saved Montgomery in 1940.

By contrast, Montgomery was not pleased with Major General Allan Adair, the C.O. of the Guards Armoured Division, and that was an opinion he seemed to share with Dempsey. Adair was considered to be too schematic in his leadership, and, according to Montgomery, he was lacking in drive, and was simply "not suitable for command of an armoured division".[87] The fact that Dempsey let Adair's division lead the main attack of "Market Garden" says perhaps something about Dempsey's own qualities as commander. This "lack of drive" that Adair had would soon be expressed in the impending offensive.

While Dempsey and Adair are quite anonymous in history writing, there are clear – albeit shifting – views of the commander of the British I Airborne Corps, Lieutenant-General Frederick "Boy" Browning, commissioned to plan and lead the airborne operation. As in the case of Montgomery's eccentricity, Browning's appearance has influenced many people's opinions about him: Browning was careful bordering on perfectionism with his appearance, always impeccably uniformed. It was also he who introduced the maroon beret* which gave the British paratroopers their name The Red Devils – in fact, an imitation of what the German paratroopers were called, *die grünen Teufel* ("the Green Devils"). It was also Browning who had commissioned an artist to draw the coat of arms he had chosen for the British paratroopers: Bellerophon of Greek mythology, riding the flying horse Pegasus, to fight the three-headed monster Chimaira.

But Browning was equally undiplomatically straight-forward as Montgomery, and constantly gained new enemies. He was appointed commander of the British Airborne Forces in the autumn of 1941, and formed the British 1st Airborne Division, but began by criticising the military command for "squandering" the airborne forces in commando raids. When he was sent to the United States in the summer of 1942 to visit American airborne units, he did not conceal the fact that he believed that the Americans had a lot left to learn, which caused much bad blood. This worsened when his British division and the U.S. 82nd Airborne Division would cooperate in North Africa in the winter of 1942/1943. Brigadier General Matthew Ridgway, the commander of the American division, became furious with what he perceived as Browning's condescending attitude towards the Ameri-

---

* It has been claimed that it was Browning's wife, the writer Daphne du Maurier, who introduced this beret, but it was probably done by Browning himself.

cans. James Gavin, who took over the 82nd Airborne Division when Ridgway was appointed commander of U.S. XVIII Airborne Corps, had a bad impression of Browning already at their first meeting. "He made a rather unkind remark to me about General Ridgway's not having parachuted into Sicily", Gavin recounted, continuing, "I stopped by the office of General Barker* and mentioned my brief meeting with General Browning. He remarked: 'Ah, yes, he is an empire builder'." [88]

It was probably Browning's bad relation with the Americans which meant that he was overlooked when a commander of the new First Allied Airborne Army was to be appointed in August 1944 – instead, this position went to the former commander of the American tactical Ninth Air Force, Lieutenant General Lewis H. Brereton, despite him having no experience whatsoever of airborne operations. Browning had to settle for being Brereton's deputy, while maintaining command of the I Airborne Corps, which he had been appointed to in April 1944.

As we have seen, Browning and Brereton clashed quite soon, when the former threatened to resign unless Brereton cancelled Operation "Linnet II" – which was the first operational plan that the new commander of the airborne army had developed. It turned into a violent conflict where Brereton was supported by Ridgway and the commanders of the two American airborne divisions, Taylor and Gavin. Browning was forced into a humiliating retreat.

It was thus a Browning that had been cut down to size who was appointed to plan and lead Operation "Market" only a few days later. Whether this circumstance is the explanation is difficult to determine, but the fact is that he was involved in a series of unfortunate decisions when planning the airborne operation.

As we have seen above, the Wilhelmina Canal north of Eindhoven was the first significant body of water that the airborne forces would need to secure for the XXX Corps. The task fell on the U.S. 101st Airborne Division under Major General Maxwell Taylor. The plan that Browning had devised for this division meant a series of airdrops along a 50-kilometre stretch from north to south, whereby the first five

---

* Ray Barker, Deputy Chief of Staff for Supreme Headquarters Allied Expeditionary Force.

bodies of water that XXX Corps met would be secured by this division. At each point, units from Taylor's division were to be landed on both sides of the watercourses, which, of course gave a greater chance of success.

But Taylor objected – he felt that his division would be too fragmented by that, and asked for the airdrop south of the Wilhelmina Canal at Eindhoven to be cancelled. Instead of sticking to his original plan – which was based on a basic doctrine for airborne operations – Browning quietly accepted the demand.

The 101st Airborne Division, "The Screaming Eagles", was an elite division by all criteria. Its traditions harked back to the American Civil War's 8th Voluntary Regiment in Wisconsin, which had a bald eagle named Old Abe as its mascot. That was where the unit's name originated from. The division's soldiers were hand-picked from volunteers, and their training was as tough as discipline was strict. They had been commanded by Major General William Carey Lee, the American military paratroop pioneer, who was commonly called "the Father of the U.S. Airborne". Under his leadership, they were trained for their effort during the invasion of Normandy – which Lee would not participate in himself; he suffered from a heart attack in February 1944, and was succeeded by Maxwell Taylor, who had joined the airborne forces from the artillery little over a year earlier.

Taylor's colleague, Brigadier General James Gavin, commander of the 82nd Airborne Division, was, with his 37 years of age, of the same age as "Pip" Roberts, the British Army's youngest general, but still much more experienced concerning airborne warfare than the six years older Taylor. During his time at the U.S. Military College West Point in 1940, he had been fascinated by and specially studied German paratroopers' conquest of the Belgian Fort Eben Emael in May the same year. This led him to write the field manual for the American airborne forces. In August 1941, he volunteered to the new American airborne forces and was appointed one year later as commander of the 505th Parachute Infantry Regiment (PIR). Another two years later, in August 1944, he took command of the 82nd Airborne Division.

The son of a coal miner, Gavin was a civil rights advocate. Although that gave him enemies among the more conservatively inclined, he took a clear stand against the race segregation in the U.S. Army. Gavin was also extremely popular among his soldiers for the care he showed them. The latter is possibly a contributing factor to his (and Browning's) decision to concentrate his division for defence once it had been landed; instead of prioritising the task that Montgomery and Dempsey wanted to see, securing one of the bridges across the river Waal, Gavin directed most of his division towards the Groesbeek Heights southeast of Nijmegen.

Gavin may have been the foremost among the commanders of the three Allied airborne divisions that were sent in during Operation "Market", but his decision to give the capturing of the Waal bridges less priority would have strongly negative consequences for the Allies. Neither was this decision opposed by Browning. "General Gavin and his staff", writes Karel Magry in the mammoth opus Operation Market-Garden Then and Now, "determined to put first things first and leave Nijmegen to be taken by ground attack after the other objectives were secured. This decision was later confirmed in very explicit terms by General Browning." [89]

Browning knew that he could not afford any further conflicts – Ridgway was clearly after his position as commander of the greatest airborne operation in history, and he needed to tread cautiously. It was possibly because of the lack of confidence he felt for the Americans' competence that he decided to take such a large part of the 82nd Airborne's first wave of transport aircraft for the landing of his own corps headquarters.

Lieutenant-Colonel John Frost, the British battalion commander, who was to hold the Arnhem bridge for three days, was strongly critical of landing any paratroopers on the Groesbeek Heights at all. "Nijmegen bridge was there for the walk-over on D-Day", Frost wrote afterwards, "The Groesbeek Heights, so called, are several miles from Nijmegen. They do not constitute a noticeable tactical feature and their occupation or otherwise has little or no bearing on what happens in Nijmegen or at Nijmegen Bridge." [90]

The 31-year-old Frost could perhaps be described as the best among the unit commanders of the Allied airborne units of "Market Garden"; being one of the first to volunteer for the newly-formed airborne forces in 1941, he was definitely one of the most experienced ones. The latter could hardly be said about his divisional commander, Major-General Robert Elliott "Roy" Urquhart.

Because of the film *A Bridge Too Far*, none of the commanders in the field have been associated as strongly with "Market Garden" as "Roy" Urquhart, played by Sean Connery in the film. As opposed to Browning and Gavin, Urquhart had no background in the airborne forces; neither had he led as a large unit as a division before he was appointed commander on 7 January 1944 of the British 1st Airborne Division. On top of all, Urquhart had a tendency for air-sickness!

The fact that this 42-year-old Scot was appointed commander of perhaps the most important airborne division during Operation "Market" is not entirely easy to explain – especially not as he succeeded one of the most experienced British airborne unit commanders, Major-General Ernest "Eric" Down, known as "Dracula" among his men. It was under Down's command that the 11 SAS* Battalion in September 1941 was reorganised into the 1st Airborne Division.

"Of all the British World War II Sky Generals, 'Eric' Down was probably the toughest – in every sense of that word", said Major Victor Dover, who served as company commander under Down. "There was nothing that the Battalion could do that he himself could not do better. March or run, ride or shoot, 'Eric' Down was superior", said another of Down's men.[91] When Major-General George Hopkinson, the first commander of the division, was killed in action in Italy in September 1943, it was considered natural for him to be succeeded by Down. In spite of his merits, however, he was still replaced with Urquhart in January 1944. The reason for this was said to be that Down was to set up a new airborne division in India, but it took a long time before he was even sent to India. As late as on 15 August 1944 – less than a month before Operation "Market" – he made a combat jump with the 2nd Parachute Brigade over southern France.

Many people have seen the replacement of Down with Urquhart as a symptom of Browning's lust for power. The fact that Urquhart

* Special Air Service.

was the one chosen is sometimes explained partly by him never being able to threaten Browning's position because of his lack of experience of airborne operations, and partly by Montgomery being well familiar with him. Urquhart had served under Montgomery both in North Africa and on Sicily, and Montgomery had even invited him to take a week's leave at his headquarters in September 1943.

However, "Roy" Urquhart had much combat experience and soon earned the full respect of the otherwise quite cocky paratroopers. In this, he was well helped by his "low-key manner, which sometimes bordered on diffidence", according to historian William F. Buckingham.[92] It is of course difficult for veterans from the battle of Arnhem to speak critically about such a popular unit commander who shared his men's tribulations and fought with them to the end. It is true that Lieutenant-Colonel John Frost (see above) did write, speaking about Urquhart succeeding Down, "The snag of bringing in a complete newcomer was that however good they might be, they were inclined to think that airborne was just another way of going into battle, whereas in fact [it was] very different."[93] But he chose to write this in general terms, adding soon afterwards concerning Urquhart that he very soon gained the full respect of the airborne men. The fact that Urquhart had never before led a larger unit than a brigade the size of a regiment was, however, without doubt a weakness.

As a newcomer, Urquhart also had no opportunity to drive through his wishes for the operation. First of all, he wanted to land his division as close to the large highway bridge across the Rhine in Arnhem as possible. The British transport aviation – which held the decision for air routes – is claimed to have been opposing this with a reference to the German air base Deelen, a few kilometres further north. In fact, following a series of Allied bomb raids, the Germans had evacuated this air base on 3 September 1944, whereby the anti-aircraft guns were also moved out. But there were other reasons why not to land the division near the bridge on the first day. Brigadier Gerald Lathbury, who led the 1st Parachute Brigade, whose main task it was to take this very bridge, wrote in a letter, which has until now remained unpublished, to the Australian war correspondent Chester Wilmot after the war:

"Urquhart wanted to drop one Brigade near the bridge. It would have had to be South of the river owing to Deelen on the North. It was carefully considered and turned down for the following reasons:

a)   The RAF did not want to do it because of flak at the bridge and in town. You say Hollinghurst denies this and we must assume that they would have agreed if he pressed. The general opinion, however, is that the RAF refused.

b)   It was considered that no gliders could have been landed with this brigade owing to dykes and bunds. Even if a few gliders could have landed, it was doubtful whether the jeeps and A Tk guns could have been got to a track without engineer work. This would have seriously weakened the brigade.

c)   The Division would have been split by the river. We must remember that at the time of planning we thought we might have a job to stop the Germans blowing the bridge. If they had, not only would the Division have been divided, but that brigade would have been on the wrong side of the river for a bridgehead." [94]

This undeniably sheds new light on the decision to drop the 1st Airborne Division in the open fields north of the Rhine, between 12 and 15 kilometres northwest of the road bridge in Arnhem – which actually were the closest places north of the Rhine where it was possible to carry out such large-scale air landings. Another thing that has puzzled many when Operation "Market Garden" has been discussed, is that the British neglected using the Driel ferry south of their own landing grounds to ferry units across the Rhine, so that the bridge could have been attacked from both sides of the river. Theories have been put forward that the British did not know of it, and in his classic *A Bridge Too Far*, Cornelius Ryan points out that the ferry was actually in service for civilian traffic at the beginning of the battle. In fact, Urquhart and the planners did know of this ferry, and chose not to use it. It was considered necessary to hold the 1st Airborne Division together north of the Rhine since it was landed with such relatively weak forces on the first day.

Urquhart had wanted to see two airdrop operations on the first day, but Major General Williams, commander of the U.S. IX Troop Carrier Command, disagreed, as we have seen previously. Furthermore, Urquhart's division was denied access to 38 transport aircraft that were being used for carrying the entire headquarters of Browning's corps to the 82nd Airborne Division's landing area.

While Urquhart had wanted to see a quick landing of the entire 1st Airborne Division with more than 12,000 men, plus the Polish brigade's almost 2,000 men, his division's effort on the first day became the numerically weakest, with 5,700 men out of a total of almost 20,000 airborne troops. In addition, on the first day, only about half of these 5,700 men (1st Parachute Brigade) could be sent in against the targets – the railway bridge, the pontoon bridge, and the road bridge in Arnhem – because the second half (1st Airlanding Brigade) was tied to hold the landing zones for the units that would arrive the next day. Due to the fact that so many aircraft were being used to ship Browning's headquarters, not even the entire 1st Airlanding Brigade could be sent in the first day; some of the companies had to remain in England and be flown in only on day two. Finally, on day three, the bulk of the Polish Parachute Brigade was to be air-dropped just south of Arnhem's road bridge, while its heavy equipment and the American engineer unit that would build a provisional landing ground for the landing of the 52nd (Lowland) Division would be landed by glider northwest of Arnhem.

On top of this came the fact that Arnhem was located so far from the British fighter and fighter-bomber units' airfields in Belgium that no regular air support could be expected for Urquhart's division.

The fact that the British paratroopers in spite of these obvious shortcomings of the plan still managed to both take at least the northern part of the road bridge at Arnhem and hold it for three days, is equally due to the quality of the paratroopers, "the Red Devils", and the weakness of the German units that they were facing.

GERMAN ARMOURED FORCES AT ARNHEM

hrough his information on German armoured forces in the Arnhem area, the British divisional commander's namesake, Major Brian Urquhart, the intelligence officer in Browning's Corps Headquarters, has been given a disproportionally large place in the historiography of Operation "Market".

After the war, Brian Urquhart told Cornelius Ryan how he had been able to identify German tanks and armoured vehicles underneath trees not far from the 1st Airborne Division's planned landing zones through photographs taken by a Spitfire reconnaissance aircraft on 13 September 1944.[95] The book and the movie *A Bridge Too Far* has immortalised the story of how Brian Urquhart – who, however, was rechristened "Major Fuller" in the movie – is trying in vain to warn the corps commander Browning about the consequences of what is on these photographs.*

There were six Panzer IIIs, two Panzer IVs, and seventeen French-made Renault Char B-1s in the area. On 12 September, some of these were captured on a photo by a Spitfire from No. 541 Squadron, RAF near Deelen.[96] But these were obsolete training tanks that posed no serious threat to the airborne force. Panzer III was taken out of production in 1943, the Panzer IVs were of an outdated early model, and the French tanks were from 1937. In fact, the Allied knew about the presence of German SS Panzer divisions in the Arnhem area when planning Operation "Market". Captain William Taylor, intelligence officer at the 1st Parachute Brigade, wrote in the brigade's intelligence report on 13 September about "a reported concentration of 10,000 troops SW of Zwolle on 1 Sep may represent a battle scarred Pz Div or two reforming".[97] Captain Hugh Maguire, intelligence officer of the

* QR6: VIDEO
See the scene with "Major Fuller" from
the film *A Bridge Too Far.*

1st Airborne Division, wrote in the division's intelligence report on 14 September that "tanks have previously been reported", adding, "German reactions to a successful Airborne landing in the Arnhem area will be immediate and to his maximum capacity. It is here that he is most favourably placed to produce troops from the East, North or West and any major reactions (which will include tanks) to the Airborne armies intrusion must be borne by 1 Airborne Division".[98]

Another reason why the 1st Airborne Division had the lowest number of air-landed troops among the three airborne divisions during the first day of the attack is that Urquhart gave such a priority for anti-tank guns. 392 PIAT-type close-range anti-tank weapons were also brought along.*

The idea that the British paratroopers would have landed straight on top of "two full-fledged SS-Panzer divisions" is, to say the least, a statement that needs to be corrected. Only fragments remained of 9. SS-Panzer-Division "Hohenstaufen" and 10. SS-Panzer-Division "Frundsberg", the ones in question, after the terrible losses that had been inflicted on them in the Falaise Pocket and during the retreat from France. Even if serious accounts of "Market Garden" are stressing this fact, a close investigation shows that the strength of these units still tends to be exaggerated. It is usually said that out of a nominal force of 18,979 men per division, each of these divisions had only about 3,000 men each at their disposal when Operation "Market Garden" was begun.[99] In fact, this corresponds to the total combat force of both of these divisions taken together. The reinforcements did indeed consist to a high degree of untrained recruits, but when "Market Garden" had begun, not many of them had made it there yet. A large part of the 9. and 10. SS-Panzer-Divisions' soldiers were highly motivated and skilfully led, but they were far too few.

One of the most common misunderstandings concerning Operation "Market Garden" is regarding the tank force of these units on 17 September 1944. It is doubtful that Cornelius Ryan's claim that the 10. SS-Panzer-Division had 20 Panther tanks on 17 September 1944 is based on any facts.[100] According to SS-Brigadeführer Heinz Harmel,

---

* PIAT was basically a one-man mortar which fired anti-tank grenades without leaving any smoke that could reveal the gunner's position. It was efficient against 100 mm thick armour at a range up to 100 metres.

the divisional commander, there was no information about how many tanks this division had at its disposal – if any at all![101] According to the unit chronicle for these two SS Panzer divisions, the 9. SS-Panzer-Division had no tanks at all on 17 September 1944.[102] This was confirmed by the then acting commander of 9. SS-Panzer-Division, SS-Obersturmbannführer Walter Harzer, who shortly after the war, polemicising against the notion of the presence of German tanks in the II. SS-Panzerkorps on 17 September 1944, wrote that "it is an established historical fact that, at the beginning of the battle, there was not one single tank available on the German side".[103] The three Panther tanks from the 9. SS-Panzer-Division that briefly entered the battlefield in western Arnhem on 18 September were not operational on 17 September, and had been given makeshift repairs.[104] The extremely few tanks that these two divisions had at their disposal on 17-20 September had, in any case, almost negligible influence on the battles for Arnhem and Nijmegen, and could not in any way motivate any change of the British operation plan.

The only armour that the Allied airborne troops in Arnhem and Nijmegen were originally facing consisted of a handful of obsolete training tanks from various training units in the vicinity – six Panzer IIIs, two Panzer IVs, and seventeen French-made Renault Char B-1s from the year 1937, captured by the Germans in 1940. All of them could be fought efficiently by the airborne troops.

On 10 September, 9. SS-Panzer-Division "Hohenstaufen" and 10. SS-Panzer-Division "Frundsberg" were ordered to disengage from the fighting in Belgium and move to the north, to the area north and northeast of Arnhem, to let the troops rest.[105] But they were also ordered by Field Marshal Model to form so-called "alarm companies" that were to be ready to be quickly sent into combat whenever a crisis occurred. The two divisions had hardly arrived in this area before they were ordered to second one battalion each back to the front in the south. 9. SS-Panzer-Division was ordered to commence the transfer to Germany in order to basically be reformed there as a Panzer division. The first units began their march to the east three days later. On 16 September, Harmel, the commander of 10. SS-Panzer-Division, went to the operative headquarters of the SS in Bad Saarow southeast of Berlin to discuss the rebuilding of his division.

Arthur Heinrich "Heinz" Harmel, born in 1906, was at this time one of the most experienced divisional commanders within the Waffen-SS, the military arm of the SS.*

Metz, his place of birth, is in the disputed Lothringen/Lorraine that Germany took from France in 1871, after which France retook the region after the First World War. The political convulsions after the First World War drove Harmel far to the right on the political scale. At age 20, he joined the Nazi Party, and in 1935, he entered the branch of the SS that would become the Waffen-SS. Harmel took part in the invasion of France in 1940, in the war in the Balkans in 1941, and in the battles on the Eastern Front between 1941 and 1944. Through this, he distinguished himself for his ability as a unit commander and was awarded the Knight's Cross with Oak Leaves.**

After the commander of the 10. SS-Panzer-Division had been seriously wounded on the Eastern Front, Harmel was appointed his successor in April 1944. Even if Harmel seems to have remained a Nazi, there were no war atrocities to charge him with after the war. Following two years in a British POW camp, he was released in 1947. His 10. SS-Panzer-Division "Frundsberg" – the name was taken from the German medieval knight Georg von Frundsberg (1473–1528) – was also an SS unit that was not accused of any war crimes whatsoever after the war.

* QR2: VIDEO
10:55: The German veteran Karl Heinz Herschel of the 9. SS-Pz-Div about the state of the SS-Pz-Div after the retreat.

** The Knight's Cross was Nazi Germany's equivalent to the highest German decoration for valor in the First World War, Pour le Mérite. The Second World War was not even one year old before Hitler instituted a higher rank of the Knight's Cross, the Knight's Cross with Oak Leaves. After that, new and higher ranks were instituted: With the Swords (1941), the Diamonds (1942), and the Golden Oak Leaf (1945).

II. SS-Panzerkorps ahead of Operation "Market Garden"
Commander: SS-Obergruppenführer Wilhelm Bittrich
Headquarters at Doetinchem

9. SS-PANZER-DIVISION "HOHENSTAUFEN"
Commander: SS-Obersturmbannführer Walter Harzer (acting)
Staff at Hoenderloo

- Division Headquarters, Begleitkompanie (guard company), Feldgendarmeriezug
  (field police platoon), Nachrichten-Kompanie (signal company)
  Total of 280 men[1]

SS-Panzergrenadier-Regiment 19 (anti-tank)
- I. Bataillon at Hamont
  300 men without heavy equipment[1]
- II. Bataillon at Zuthpen
  400 men*
  2 Jagdpanzer IV tank destroyers, 4 anti-tank vehicles (2 of which had one 75 mm
  gun each), 4 20 mm anti-tank guns, 1 75 mm light infantry gun, 1 120 mm mortar

SS-Panzergrenadier-Regiment 20 (anti-tank)
- I. Bataillon
  (Dissolved: II. Abteilung)
  About 400 men[1]

SS-Panzer-Regiment 19 (armoured) in Zuthpen
- I. Abteilung
  (Dissolved: II. Abteilung)
  450 men without tanks[1]

SS-Panzerjäger-Abteilung 9 (anti-tank) at Apeldoorn
  120 men[1]
  2 Jagdpanzer IV tank destroyers
  2 Marder III tank destroyers
  2 Pak40 auf 38H Selbstfahrlaffete tank destroyers

SS-Panzer-Aufklärungs-Abteilung 9 (armoured reconnaissance) at Hoenderlo
  400 men (95 of which were infantry)[1]
  About 20 armoured half-tracks[2]

SS-Panzer-Artillerie-Regiment 9 (artillery) at Dieren
- I. Abteilung
  120 men without heavy weapons[1]
  (Dissolved: II. Abteilung)

SS-Flak-Abteilung 9 (anti-aircraft) at Dieren
- 1. Kompanie
  87 men
  3 Ostwind self-propelled anti-aircraft guns, 4 20 mm anti-aircraft guns

SS-Panzer-Pionier-Abteilung 9 (engineer battalion) at Brummen
- 1. Kompanie
  60 men

SS-Sanitäts-Abteilung 9 (healthcare) at Velp
- 1. and 2. Kompanie

SS-Nachschub-Bataillon 9 (supplies) in Apeldoorn
- Two companies

SS-Wirtschafts-Bataillon 9 (rations) in Apeldoorn
- Bäckerei-Kompanie (bakers' company)
- Schlachterei-Kompanie (butchers' company)

First-line force: Less than 2,500 men[1]

10. SS-PANZER-DIVISION "FRUNDSBERG"
Commander: SS-Oberführer Heinz Harmel
Headquarters at Ruurlo

SS-Panzergrenadier-Regiment 21
- I. Bataillon in Deventer-Diepenven
  225 men
- II. Bataillon at Hamont
  200 men

(SS-Panzergrenadier-Regiment 22: Dissolved)

SS-Panzer-Regiment 10 (armoured) in Vorden
- (I. Abteilung dissolved)
- II. Abteilung in Vorden
  200 men, probably without tanks[3]

SS-Panzer-Aufklärungs-Abteilung 10 (armoured reconnaissance) in Borculo
  115 men
  9 armoured cars (Sdkfz 233 with a 75 mm gun and Sdkfz 234 Puma with
  a 50 mm gun) and 26 anti-tank vehicles

SS-Panzer-Artillerie-Regiment 10 (artillery) at Borkel en Schaft
- I. Abteilung
  12 Wespe self-propelled artillery vehicles, 6 Hummel self-propelled artillery vehicles
- II. Abteilung
  18 10,5 cm lFH 18 howitzers
- III. Abteilung
  18 10,5 cm lFH 18 howitzers
- IV. Abteilung
  6 10 cm guns

SS-Flak-Abteilung 10 (anti-aircraft) in Klaarenbeek
  3 st Ostwind self-propelled anti-aircraft guns

SS-Panzer-Pionier-Abteilung 10 (pioneer battalion)
  200 men
  3 half-tracks

In addition: guards, liaison, and various other rear zone units
In addition: SS-Panzerjäger-Abteilung 10 seconded to 7. Armee in Germany

First-line force against the Allied units in Operation "Market Garden":
About 1,200 men

1. Source: Walter Harzer, Combat Report. Gelders Archief. Dokument 2171. Collectie Boeree. 1. De Slag om Arnhem. 1.3. De Duitsers. Rapport van Harzer, p. 52.
2. On 1 September 1944 this unit had more than 28 armoured half-tracks, two of which were towing vehicles, and 26 of which were anti-tank vehicles, at its disposal. Source: Dugdale, Jeff. *Panzer Divisions, Panzergrenadier Divisions, Panzer Brigades of the Army and the Waffen SS in the West. Autumn 1944– February 1945. Their Detailed and Precise Strengths. Vol. I, Part 1. Refitting and Re-Equipment.* The Military Press, Milton Keynes 2000.
3. Some sources say that this battalion had 16–20 Panzer IV tanks at its disposal. There is, however, no information that any such tanks would have been deployed at Nijmegen or at Betuwe during the decisive days of 17–20 September, indicating that none of these at least were operational.

Harmel's colleague during the battle of Arnhem and Nijmegen in September 1944, the six year younger SS-Obersturmbannführer Walter Harzer of the 9. SS-Panzer-Division, was far from as experienced; he was not even a divisional commander, but only functioned as an acting C.O., since the regular unit commander, SS-Standartenführer Sylvester Stadler, had been wounded in July 1944. Harzer replaced the "regular acting" divisional commander, SS-Oberführer Friedrich-Wilhelm Bock, because of his very skilled leadership of the units that remained of the division during the retreat from France. Harzer was a member of the Nazi Party from 1930, and of the SS from 1931. Apart from a short stint at the front in Poland in 1939 (in the same unit as Harmel), and eleven months on the Eastern Front, he served in various SS training units until February 1943, when he was placed in the headquarters of the "Hohenstaufen" division, from April 1944 as chief of staff. On 10 October 1944, just after the end of the battle of Arnhem, Stadler returned to resume his position as divisional commander, and Harzer then became chief of staff in V. SS Mountain Corps.

Harzer was very close to SS-Obergruppenführer Wilhelm "Willi" Bittrich, the commander of II. SS-Panzerkorps, the corps that the two SS Panzer divisions were part of. He was a First World War veteran and had been serving in the German Reichswehr from the early 1920s. By the time of Hitler's seizure of power in 1933, he was already a member of the Nazi Party and of the SS. Bittrich participated as an SS officer during the campaigns in Poland in 1939, in France in 1940, and on the Eastern Front from 1941. He was awarded the Knight's Cross in 1941 and led the SS Cavalry Division "Florian Geyer" between August 1942 and February 1943. This division is infamous for its many war atrocities in combat with Soviet partisans, but during Bittrich's tenure as a commander, the unit took part in fighting at the front. In February 1943, he took over the command of 9. SS-Panzer-Division "Hohenstaufen" and led it with great success on the Eastern Front and during the Battle of Normandy – until the end of June 1944, when he was appointed commander of the II. SS-Panzerkorps. In August 1944, he received the Oak Leaves to the Knight's Cross.

Aged 50 by this time, Bittrich was something as unusual as a Nazi who was critical of Hitler. A few days before the attempted assassina-

93

tion of Hitler on 20 July 1944, Bittrich had promised Field Marshal Rommel to join his side against Hitler in case of a coup. Some time later, the Minister of Armament, Albert Speer, witnessed Bittrich's violent accusations against the Nazi Party. The SS leader Himmler tried several times to get the insubordinate SS General fired from his position, but he was defended by his commanders within the army, including Model. It was doubtlessly much thanks to Bittrich that the SS soldiers largely behaved as correctly as they did against their opponents during the battle at Arnhem and Nijmegen.

Equally doubtless is the fact that Bittrich, Harmel, and Harzer were among the most higher officers within the Waffen-SS. Together with Model, their experience and leadership talent would play a decisive role for the outcome of the battle.

The same could be said for Generaloberst Kurt Student, the German Paratroop Corps' founding father, and, during "Market Garden", commander of the 1. Fallschirmarmee. One of the most prominent British commanders during the battle of Arnhem, Sir John Hackett, has nothing but praise for Student in his biographical text about him, "His own personality and career exemplify some of the best characteristics of German professional soldiers ... his continuing determination and drive." [106] In fact, a handful of very experienced and skilled unit commanders on the German side could be said to have tipped the scale, preventing Operation "Market Garden" from immediately ending in total disaster for the German side in the war. Another one of these was Generalleutnant Kurt Chill, commander of Kampfgruppe Chill. He had in-depth experience of defensive combat from his tenure as commander of the 122. Infanterie-Division in the so-called "Demyansk Pocket", and at Staraya Russa on the Eastern Front – for which he was awarded the Knight's Cross. [107]

As for troop training and motivation among the soldiers on both sides, the situation ahead of "Market Garden" was more beneficial for the Western Allies than at perhaps any other occasion during the entire war. In general, the German soldiers were both more motivated and better trained than the British and the Americans. Ahead of "Market Garden", it was, for once, completely the other way around. The three Allied airborne divisions were an elite of selected volunteers, well-trained and highly motivated soldiers. The British Guards Armoured Division, which was to lead the XXX Corps, was, being a Guards division, an elite unit with strong unit pride and high morale; some of its battalions had a history going back to the 17th century.

The 7th Armoured Division, on British Second Army's left flank, was the famous "Desert Rats" that had been fighting against Rommel in North Africa. The 11th Armoured Division, called "the Black Bull", on the army's right flank, was generally considered one of the British army's best armoured divisions.

What this elite was facing was, in several cases, hardly worthy of being called regular military units. As we have seen, the German army in the West was, at this time, marked by low morale, and the scrapings that the soldiers who had hastily been thrown in to cover gaps in the front constituted usually neither had any troop training nor any combat experience worth mentioning.

"ALL IS FLOWING BACK"

"*Es strömt alles zurück* – All is flowing back, assault gun crews, pioneers, anti-aircraft crews, and the replacement battalion's officers are nowhere to be found. The English have crossed the canal on the bridge north of Helchteren (Broeseind) with 3 tanks and infantry. The bridge has not been blown up, the last assault gun is said to have shot it into flames. The English have also made it across the bridge 2 km north of Lommel." [108]

This disheartening message reached the HQ of German LXXX-VIII. Armeekorps in the morning of 11 September 1944, describing the situation at the front around the road north towards Eindhoven, Nijmegen, and Arnhem, after the British had taken "Joe's Bridge" across the Maas-Scheldt Canal at Lommel. The reinforcements that had been sent to Student's 1. Fallschirmarmee had been torn up and toppled. In addition, the British tactical air force, 2nd TAF, had been dispatched in powerful air attacks against German positions and troop concentrations, while the Luftwaffe, as so often during the last few months, was conspicuously absent. The road to the north lay virtually open. "There is no talk of any coherent frontline in this section", the staff of the LXXXVIII. Armeekorps concluded.[109] The disintegration of the German front is quite well illustrated by the fact that two British armoured Daimler Dingo reconnaissance cars were able that day to drive all the way north towards Valkenswaard, 15 kilometres north of "Joe's Bridge", in order to investigate whether the bridge across the watercourse south of the town was intact (which it was), and return to "Joe's Bridge" again.

"Normally, in such a situation, an infantry division would attack in order to try break open a hole through which the armour could pour", wrote military historian Alexander McKee.[110] But because of the approaching Operation "Market Garden", Montgomery decided to hold back his units so as not to risk that the Germans blew up the bridges, which must be considered a sound decision. The much-talked-about German "recovery" during the second week of September was, in any case, completely swept away by this time.

Generaloberst Student desperately gave the order of a counter-attack so as to drive the British away from the bridgehead at "Joe's Bridge"; all that could be mustered for this attack on 11 September was eight StuG IIIs and forty (40) paratroopers! The attack was, of course, beaten back, three StuG IIIs were destroyed, and several of the paratroopers were taken captive. This was followed by two relatively calm days, which British 32nd Guards Brigade spent clearing up the area south of the Maas-Scheldt Canal. "This did not prove to be a matter of much difficulty", its War Diary concludes.[111]

Meanwhile, the Germans were making frantic efforts to establish a new line of defence. Oberst Erich Walther, an airborne veteran who had been awarded the Knight's Cross and with combat experience from the beginning of the war, was detailed to lead a new battle group – Kampfgruppe Walther – in which what was left of the German units that were facing the XXX Corps was organised. But it was obvious to the Germans that this battle group was not able to offer any more than symbolic resistance. On 13 September, the LXXXVIII. Armeekorps reported, "Weakness in the area of the corps section, as before, on the left wing in the area north and northwest of Lommel.

If the enemy breaks through here, there is a danger that the entire position on the Maas-Scheldt Canal will be rolled up from the north and east." [112]

Student's last hope probably vanished when Oberst Walther's counterattack on 14 September – aimed at taking and blowing up "Joe's Bridge" – ended with another disastrous failure. Walther sent in the main part of his force – Kampfgruppe von der Heydte with an estimated 700 men remaining, four StuG IIIs in schwere Heeres-Panzerjäger-Abteilung 559, and Luftwaffen-Jäger-Bataillon z.b.V. 6. The latter was a penal battalion consisting of four rifle companies with about 400 Luftwaffe soldiers who had been sentenced for various crimes. These outcast men wore worn-out old tropical uniforms, had insufficient armament, and were as demoralised as all penal units.

The Germans were completely massacred by the tanks from the Irish Guards. 32nd Guards Brigades' War Diary gives an excellent account of the battle, "An enemy counter-attack against Joe's Bridge straight from the north, supported by four StuG III. Two of these were knocked out and a third was abandoned intact by its crew in panic after it had been hit by a 6 pounder. Meanwhile, another attack came in simultaneously from the north-west by infantry alone, the whole I. Bn of 6 Para Regt. The enemy infiltrated in several places into the woods and a considerable force equipped with several Bazookas got into some houses at the end of the track leading west from La Colonie. Two tanks of the armoured unit supporting us were knocked out, and it was some time before the enemy were liquidated. Skirmishing in the woods continued through the afternoon, but by 1400 it was evident that the attack had failed completely. Our casualties were not unduly severe, while the enemy lost no fewer than 170 PW, of which 40 were wounded. His dead must also have been considerable, as a great weight of artillery and mortar fire had been brought down on his concentrations. But the German shelling of the bridge and the crossroads continued and late in the evening an ammunitions lorry was destroyed and a small hole was made in the bridge. Traffic, however, was never interrupted and the damage was very soon made good." [113]

Serjeant Maurice Hollis, commander of a Cromwell tank, knocked out three StuG IIIs during this combat, after which the remaining one fled.[114] Kampfgruppe von der Heydte lost almost 200 men, 114 of whom were taken captive; nobody seems to have cared to count the penal battalion's losses. The British Guards units were now withdrawn behind the Maas-Scheldt Canal in order to prepare for the main attack, while other units arrived to take their place in the small bridgehead north of the canal at "Joe's Bridge". See map on page 27.

Ahead of "Market Garden", the British XXX Corps could muster around 40,000 men, 400 tanks, and 350 artillery guns against a German force of troops that was only one twentieth as large, without any tanks, and very weak in anti-tank guns and artillery – Kampfgruppe Walther:

At the Maas-Scheldt Canal west of the British bridgehead was the II. Bataillon of Fallschirmjäger-Regiment 18 with about 300 men. On its northern flank, Oberst Walther had placed the penal battalion Luftwaffen-Jäger-Bataillon z.b.V. 6, which was described by Hauptmann Gerhard Schacht, chief of staff of Kampfgruppe Walther, as being "without any value for combat".[115] On top of it all, the penal battalion's commander, Major Walter Veit, had been mortally wounded by shelling on 13 September, and no replacement had arrived before Operation "Market Garden" had commenced.*

Kampfgruppe von der Heydte was positioned right behind the penal battalion. But Heydte's unit was also very weakened, and had perhaps no more than 500 men left after the heavy losses in connection with the counterattack on 14 September. The weakest among its five battalions was I. Bataillon of Fallschirmjäger-Regiment 6, which had lost 80% of its force of 250 men in the counterattack on 14 September, and I. Bataillon of Fallschirmjäger-Regiment 2, which had no more than a few dozen men left. Schwere Heeres-Panzerjäger-Abteilung

---

* According to Kershaw's *It Never Snows in September,* Veit died on 16 September, but his headstone and the German Volksbund Deutsche Kriegsgräberfürsorge e.V. show that the correct date is the 13th. Walter Veit is buried in the German military cemetery in Ysselsteyn, Sector AA, Row 5, Grave 107.

559, which had been added to von der Heydte's regiment, had, in addition, only five operational StuG IIIs left. As the commander of this anti-tank battalion, Major Sattler, had been wounded on 8 September, the unit was led by the commander of the 2. Kompanie, Oberleutnant Edmund Haile (according to a conflicting source, Oberleutnant Franz Kopka, who had been assigned command on 8 September, but who was wounded on that same day, had recovered from his injuries and re-assumed his command).*

North of the bridgehead, Oberst Walther had positioned the two battalions that the SS-Panzer divisions had been ordered to relocate back to the front (see page 88): the so-called SS-Sperrverband Heinke under SS-Sturmbannführer Heinrich Heinke had two SS battalions at its disposal, plus one pioneer company and artillery. I. Bataillon/ SS-Panzergrenadier-Regiment 19 with 300 men and II. Bataillon/ SS-Panzergrenadier-Regiment 21 with 200 men were pitted against the British bridgehead's southeast corner. These regiments had been formed by scraping together the remnants of the now dissolved Panzergrenadier-Regiment 20 from 9. SS-Panzer-Division and Panzergrenadier-Regiment 22/ 10. SS-Panzer-Division respectively. SS-Hauptsturmführer Friedrich Richter, commander of the latter battalion, had only a week earlier been ordered by the divisional commander Harmel personally to report at Oberst Walther's staff. "When I arrived there", he recounted, "Oberst Walther asked me to take command of and try to bring some order into a shattered unit, whose battalion commander had had a nervous breakdown after the British tanks had broken through. The condition of the remains of this battalion was really miserable. The SS battalion really gave a mediocre impression. It consisted, apart from the remains of the HQ of the I. Bataillon/Panzergrenadier-Regiment 22 and a new regiment, of three grenadier companies with no more than 50 to 60 men each. Their armament consisted of a few light machine guns and carbines, and ammunition supplies were very scarce."[116]

---

* The recurring claim that SS-Panzerjäger-Abteilung 10 from 10. SS-Panzer-Division would have been present in this sector is erroneous; this battalion took part in the defence of Aachen against the Americans, 50 kilometres further southeast.

The artillery support, 2. Batterie, SS-Panzer-Artillerie-Regiment 10, only constituted 52 men with four 105 mm IFH 18 howitzers and an ammunition supply of about 80 shells.[117] It was supported by two platoons from the 10. SS-Panzer-Division's Panzer reconnaissance battalion.[118]

The Allies had an unchallenged air superiority. The British 2nd Tactical Air Force, tasked to provide the offensive with air support, had about 1,500 aircraft at its disposal. The Luftwaffe's force in the West only had about 300 aircraft left.

Student's only hope was with the possibility to get reinforcements, partly from Germany in the shape of newly-formed units, and partly from the west, where the 15. Armee was fully occupied with evacuating from the Pas de Calais area across the Scheldt Estuary in a sort of "German Dunkirk". In the morning of 17 September, it was reported that 70,000 men had been evacuated across the Scheldt Estuary.[119] In all, the Germans would be able to transfer 82,000 soldiers and 580 artillery guns from the Pas de Calais area, but these were also needed to hold the islands in the Scheldt Estuary. Indeed, parts of the 15. Armee were ordered to be rushed to the Tilburg area, 30 kilometres northwest of "Joe's Bridge", but they would, however, not make it in time to meet the XXX Corps' attack.

Both sides seem to have felt that the war was rapidly coming to an end. On 14 September, it was noted in the British 7th Armoured Division's War Diary, "GOC conference 1730 review past ops, importance of *good turnout and dress for when we go to Germany and after Armistice*" [italics by the author].[120] The same day, the German Supreme Commander in the West, Generalfeldmarschall von Rundstedt, issued an order to his soldiers that "the West Wall is to be held to the last cartridge and until complete annihilation". [121]

At 1000 hrs in the morning of 15 September, "Colonel Joe" Vandeleur summoned the officers of the 2nd (Armoured) Battalion, Irish Guards, informing them about the forthcoming attack, where the battalion would be the vanguard of the Guards Armoured Division. The battalion's war diary noted, "1000. The Brigadier gave orders for the break out from the bridge. We were to advance N up the main road ... Arnhem and then push on to the Zuiderzee at Nunspeet and consolidate and wait for the rest of the Second Army to arrive. The next advance would then be on Münster to cut off the Ruhr." [122]

The intelligence service described the situation on the German side quite accurately, "The supply of ammunition is very faulty, and that of food almost worse, very few PWs stating that they have had anything approaching their full rations during the last two weeks. Almost more serious is the difficulty of providing any supporting arms. So much heavy equipment has had to be abandoned and the lack of mobility makes it difficult to bring up such supplies as may be available in Germany." [123] On 16 September, the Allies intercepted a German order that all airfields west of the Rhine, with only a few exceptions, were to be prepared for being demolished. [124] Meanwhile, Horrocks was informed that the attack was to commence on 17 September.

At 1030 hRS on Saturday 16 September, Horrocks summoned his unit commanders at a small movie theatre in Leopoldsburg. "The inhabitants must have wondered", Horrocks wrote, "what on earth was happening as they found the British Military Police almost occupying their town early in the morning, and from about 0900 hrs onward a motley stream of officers in cars and jeeps of every description beginning to pour in. I have used the word 'motley' because no one was wearing standard uniform with steel helmets. I myself was dressed in a high-necked woolly with a battle-dress top and a camouflaged airborne smock, while nearly all the officers from the various armoured units wore berets of every colour. I have deliberately mentioned this because in the American Army the strictest rules as regards dress prevailed. If George Patton could have seen my audience that day, he would have gone through the roof. It is an interesting fact that two of Britain's best battle commanders, Wellington and Montgomery, never cared about how their troops were dressed, providing the clothing was serviceable and comfortable. The atmosphere of the conference was casual and cheerful. I knew most of the audience at Leopoldsburg personally. Some us fought side by side ever since Alamein."[125]

Captain John Gorman of the 2nd Irish Guards Battalion remembers, "Brian Horrocks was a natural actor. His stage presence was drama personified. On stage with an enormous covered map behind him he started to speak: 'Gentlemen, how would you like to have this all finished by Christmas?' The cheering from his audience gave him his answer."[126] After that, Horrocks started outlining the plan, "This is the biggest combined airborne and ground forces operation which has ever been attempted. The Corps will advance, and be supplied, along one road – the only major road available."[127] The northbound road that the British were to take north of the bridge was not wide, but it was paved and could carry heavy traffic. After the war, it was widened, asphalted, and given the designation N715.*

But the red porphyry paving that constituted the road in those days is still visible at certain places at the side of the road. Some distance into the Netherlands, it segued into the considerably better and wider concrete motorway Rijksweg 69, north towards Emmeloord, east of the Zuiderzee. (Today, it is designated the A 50.)

"Some 20,000 vehicles will be involved", Horrocks continued, "so traffic control posts will advance behind the leading troops and will be established at intervals along the road, linked by wireless to a central traffic control station. In order to avoid congestion no unit must put more than five vehicles on the road without a timing from traffic control." [128]

The Guards Armoured Division had been issued with supplies for seven days, including fuel sufficient for 190 miles (305 km), and 10,000 25-pound artillery shells.[129] This was necessary, because, as Horrocks warned, "supply may be difficult". After that, he turned to describing the obstacles that the units would meet: "Tough opposition must be expected and the country is very difficult – wooded and marshy – only possibility is to blast our way down the road. [......] There is a difficult country between here and Nijmegen, low-lying, intersected by canals and large rivers; bridges will almost certainly have been prepared for

---

* The considerably larger N74, which today crosses the canal 1,500 metres further east, did not exist in those days.

demolition. We have collected in one area 9,000 engineers and vast supplies of bridging material. Air photos of each bridge have been taken, and each handed over to a separate Royal Engineers unit which has made its own plan to repair or replace the bridge."

Then, he moved on to the beginning of the attack itself, and its support: "Guards Armoured Division will lead break-out and I have arranged for their leading Regiment, the Irish Guards Group (Infantry and Tanks), to be preceded by a barrage fired by 350 guns which are now in position and camouflaged. The Typhoons of the 83rd Group RAF will give close support to the leading formations and their control vehicle will be with H.Q. Irish Guards."[130]

The Allies had begun the Second World War without any doctrine for close air support for the ground forces, as opposed to the Germans, who by sending in air officers in the first line with direct radio liaison with aircraft perfected their Blitzkrieg tactics. However, during the fighting in North Africa, Montgomery and Air Marshal Sir Arthur Coningham had developed a similar doctrine for close air support, which contributed strongly to the victory over Rommel. The method was called "Cab-Rank", and also consisted of air officers at the first line being in direct radio contact with aircraft in the air. The supporting air units were divided into three circulating groups, where the first was attacking targets on the ground according to the liaison officer's directions, the second was on its way to the scene to replace the first, while the third was being refuelled and rearmed at the air base. The 2nd Tactical Air Force, the British air force on the continent, was led by Air Marshal Coningham.

The single-engined, single-seated fighter-bomber Hawker Typhoon, the main British aircraft for close air support at this time, was perfectly suited for this task. It was equipped with four 20 mm automatic cannons for fighting "soft targets", and eight 27-kilo RP-3 rocket projectiles. These had a range of 1,600 metres and were capable of blasting through the turret armour of the German Panther tanks. Even though firing precision was so poor that only 4% on average of the projectiles hit their targets during tests in England, the psychological effect of an attack with rocket projectiles often made the German tank crews abandon their vehicles, so that they could be fought with anti-tank guns. With a top speed at 663 km/h, the Typhoon could also outrun any German fighter, apart from the very few Messerschmitt Me 262 jet planes that had recently been put into service.

The 2nd Tactical Air Force consisted of four groups, two fighter-bomber and two bomb groups. No. 83 Group had main responsibility for air support for Operation "Garden", and had more than eight wings with a total of thirty squadrons of fighters and fighter-bombers as well as four squadrons of artillery spotters at its disposal. The three Typhoon wings, 121, 122, and 143 Wing, with a total of eleven squadrons and more than one hundred aircraft, would be in full activity over the bridgehead at "Joe's Bridge" on 17 September.

"Speed is absolutely vital", Horrocks continued during his run-through in the movie theatre in Leopoldsburg, "as we must reach the lightly equipped 1st British Airborne Division if possible in forty-eight hours." He repeated the last bit several times to impress the importance of trying to reach Arnhem in the afternoon on 19 September.

Horrocks had not yet been given the exact time for when the attack was to be launched, which was planned to be coordinated with the airdrop – it was dependant on the decision of Major General Paul L. Williams, commander of the American IX Troop Carrier Command, who took the decisions concerning transport aviation.

Captain John Gorman was breathless, "It was the most inspiring address I had ever heard and when it was ending he strode to the edge of the cinema platform. 'Now you must be wondering who is going to have the honour of leading this great dash which may end the war.' Pause ... 'THE IRISH GUARDS!'" [131]

On the German side, preparations were being made for what they understood would come, at least those at the bridgehead at "Joe's Bridge". SS-Untersturmführer Heinz Damaske, the adjutant of the II. Bataillon, SS-Panzergrenadier-Regiment 21, recounted, "Night-time shock troop raids showed that the English had been encouraged not only by the attention that we gave them by the bridge. Extensive columns of traffic on the Hechtel bridgehead road (partly vehicles with their headlights turned on), which also continued during the night of 16 September, indicated preparations to expand the bridgehead. Our shock troops reported a 'wide awake' and combat-ready enemy." [132] Oberst Fritz Fullriede, commander of Fallschirm-Panzer-Ersatz- und Ausbildungs-Regiment "Hermann Göring", wrote in his diary on 16 September 1944, "Every day, we are awaiting the enemy's main attack." [133]

Did the Germans know of the plan in advance?

After the war, it has been speculated whether the Germans knew of the Allied attack plan in advance. The notes from the German HQ conferences at the highest level indicate that this was not the case. However, it has been speculated that the Dutch double agent Christian Lindemanns, known as "King Kong", would have revealed the plans. Lindemann was a member of the resistance who had been pressed by the Germans to cooperate with them. He made it across to the Allied lines in the summer of 1944 and managed to induce them to recruit him to, among other things, the Dutch Prince Bernhard's military headquarters in France.

On 14 September, the British smuggled Lindemanns back across the frontlines in the Netherlands. Lindemanns himself claimed afterwards that he met Generaloberst Student in Vught, something that the latter however firmly denied. When the British liberated Valkenswaard on 17 September, they could also free Lindemanns – who had been captured by a member of the Dutch resistance who suspected him of being a double agent. Lindemanns was finally revealed to be a double agent and arrested, but the question is when he was unmasked. Officially, this took place in October 1944, but according to what Dutch resistance member of the resistance Maria de Meersman said after the war, she had unmasked Lindemanns already in the summer of 1944. This raises the question if Lindemanns's dual agent status was simply used by the Allies when they sent him to the Germans just before Operation "Market Garden", and in the very area where the operation would be carried out.

Oberstleutnant Hermann J. Giskes, the commander of the German counterespionage (Abwehr III f) in the Netherlands, the man who coordinated and ruled Lindemanns's activities as a double agent,

II. OPERATION "MARKET GARDEN"

must probably be considered credible when he denies that Lindemanns revealed the plans for Operation "Market Garden". After the
war, he wrote the following testimony, which is currently to be found
in the Liddell Hart Centre for Military Archives at King's College London, "I personally directed the activities of the English spy, Christian
Lindemanns, until the Arnhem battle. Lindemanns entered into my
service in March 1944. Lindemanns appeared two days before the
Arnhem air-landings coming from Brussels, and, on arriving in our
Dutch Abwehr HQ, he betrayed everything to us that he had learnt
through his connection with the Canadian-British Secret Service in
Brussels. But he did not mention Arnhem. It is quite obviously simply
because the objective of the planned air-land offensive was not known
to him. Lindemann's so-called betrayal of Arnhem is a legend."[1]

Lindemanns's further destiny has, which is quite typical of many
double agents, never been clarified. According to some sources, he
was detained in the Tower of London, where he was allegedly executed – mysteriously enough without any officially date of death, and
without any known grave. According to other information, he escaped
from the Dutch prison in Scheveningen in 1946. Yet other sources alle-
ged that he took his life by swallowing 80 aspirins at the psychiatric
clinic at the Scheveningen prison. In June 1986, however, an unregis-
tered coffin was found between Lindemanns's two parents' coffins in
the ground at the Crooswijk Cemetery in Rotterdam. An autopsy of the
dead body in this third coffin established that it probably was Christian Lindemanns. His brother Henk Lindemanns, however, claimed
with certainty that Christian Lindemanns at that time was still alive
but remained in hiding.

It is at least equally difficult to explain how the following note in
the German Navy's War Diary for 18 September 1944, as far as the
author can see, has avoided any attention whatsoever in all publications to date on Operation "Market Garden:

18 Sept. 1944.
Conference on the Situation with the Chief, Naval Staff at 1130.

I. In connection with the air situation:[2] 800 to 1,000 freight gliders
were landed in the area of Breda-Tiel-Arnhem-Nijmegen-Utrecht
and Hilversum; 500 parachute jumpers were reported in the Arnhem-
Nijmegen area; 650 of our fighters were on defensive missions.

The landing was already announced on 11/12 [sic][3] *by an agent
from London by way of the Air Force Attaché, Stockholm.* [Italics by

106

the author.] The corresponding report reads, "Two British armies will have reached the Maas, even the Waal, on a wide front by 24 Sept. Thereupon *strong airborne operations in the eastern and northern Netherlands* [italics original] and in the German border area are planned. Immediately after the airborne landing which aims at rolling up the German river positions in the rear, action by the Fusag in the eastern Netherlands and in the Heligoland Bight will take place. Strength of the Fusag is 29 to 30 divisions. Reports are intentionally spread in the circles of the Norwegian and Danish governments in Exile that an operation by the Fusag is planned in the north."[4]

Here, there is obviously a mix of authentic facts, disinformation, and a less serious mistake concerning dates. The FUSAG was the abbreviation of the fictitious "First United States Army Group", which was used in Operation "Quicksilver", which in May and June 1944 was intended to trick the Germans into believing that the Allies would land in the Pas de Calais area and not in Normandy. In any case, this note in the German Naval Command's War Diary is remarkable. There has been no explanation to be found for the background of this information.

1. King's College London. Liddell Hart Centre for Military Archives. 15/15: Papers of Reginald William Winchester ('Chester') Wilmot (1911–1954). 15/15/50/55. Arnhem: The German Side of the Story; in reply to Col. Pinto. Letter by Oberst-Letnant [sic] H.J. Giskens, former chief of Abwehr in the Netherlands, Belgium and Northern France.
2. Here, the first, preliminary German reports about Operation "Garden" on 17 September 1944 are invoked.
3. It remains unclear whether this refers to 11–12 September or if it should be "11/9".
4. Bundesarchiv/Militärarchiv, RM 7/64.

↑ "Arnhem in 1934. The contested road bridge is clearly seen in this photo, which is taken from the northwest. The large church building in the centre of the photo is the Sint-Walburgis Church. The Musis Park is located behind the smaller church with the twin towers on the left hand side. The distance from the Sint-Walburgis Church to the river bank is 250 meters as the crow flies.

↓ Dempsey (left) and Montgomery.

↑ "The Killing Fields" in the Falaise Pocket, a German tank crew.

↓ Lieutenant Sidney Beck (front left) and his comrades in the 341 Battery, 86th (East Anglian) (Herts Yeo) Field Regiment, Royal Artillery. Via Benjamin Beck.

↑   German paratroopers arriving at the front in September 1944.

↓   German paratroopers with a captured American M1919 Browning machine gun.

↑ American airborne troops from the 101st Airborne Division and Dutchmen at Drop Zone "C", in the fields three kilometres north of the Wilhelmina Canal.

↓ German propaganda image of how paratroopers armed with the Panzerschreck rocket launcher are destroying British tanks north of "Joe's Bridge" on 17 September 1944. The tank in the foreground is a Churchill, that was not present on that scene.

↑ British infantry mounted on a Sherman tank during the advance.

↓ Two soldiers from The Irish Guards in a battle position.

↑ American paratroopers from the 101st Airborne Division with German prisoners of war in Eindhoven.

↓ American paratroopers from the 101st Airborne Division and Dutchmen at an abandoned German 88 mm anti-aircraft gun in Eindhoven.

↑ Dutchmen dragging away a collaborator in Eindhoven while a British tank soldier is looking another way.

↓ Two German commanders during Operation "Market Garden": Bittrich, II. SS-Panzerkorps (left), and Harmel, 10. SS-Panzer-Division (right).

III.

Armoured attack
17 September 1944

Sunday 17 September 1944 dawned as a gloriously clear autumn day. "The morning was passed watching squadrons of bombers and fighters passing to and fro high overhead. Then came thrills. Lightning fighters and dive-bombers made daring low level attacks on enemy gun positions just across the canal."[134] This was how the British artilleryman Lieutenant Sidney Beck* described the wait for the attack to commence at Neerpelt in his diary.

The aircraft he and his men saw on that morning came from U.S. Eighth Air Force in England. 875 four-engined bombers and 703 fighters and fighter-bombers had been dispatched to fight the German anti-aircraft defence along the transport aircraft's flight routes. Two hundred P-47 Thunderbolt fighter-bombers flew at an altitude of between 600 and 750 metres as "bait" for the anti-aircraft defence. As soon as any anti-aircraft position opened fire, a group of fighter-bombers appeared, dropping fragmentation bombs and firing at the position with their heavy machine guns. In that way, one anti-aircraft position after another was knocked out. Meanwhile, the heavy bombers dropped more than 3,000 bombs against 117 different targets in the Netherlands, mainly anti-aircraft positions. The American air attacks lasted between 0930 and 1100 hrs.

This was the follow-up of the raids that 282 British bombers had carried out against the airfields at Leeuwarden, Steenwijk-Havelte, Hopsten, and Salzbergen, as well as against anti-aircraft positions at Moerdijk during the past night.[135] The third air operation in support of Operation "Market Garden" was carried out in the morning of 17 September by 85 British Lancaster heavy bombers and 15 Mos-

* 341 Battery, 86th (East Anglian) (Herts Yeo) Field Regiment, Royal Artillery.

quitoes, escorted by 53 Spitfire fighters, and was aimed at the German costal defence installations on the island of Walcheren in the Scheldt Estuary. The purpose here was to mislead the Germans into believing that an air landing was being prepared here. But no airdrop was taking place yet. By noon, the Irish, who were to lead, started marching up in a long row right before the bridge, and Horrocks went across to them in order to spend the day with them.[136] Major General Williams, the American commander of the transport aviation, believed that full daylight was needed for gathering the large air formations that the operation plan predicted, which was why the take-off from the air bases in England was set for the morning on 17 September – hence, Operation "Market Garden" would commence only in the afternoon. The first transport planes took off in England as late as at 1025 hrs. This was the first Allied mistake, since it limited the number of daylight hours when the units could operate during the first, important day.

Brigadier Gerald William Lathbury, commander of the 1st Parachute Brigade of British 1st Airborne Division, wrote in his diary, "Sunday, September 17th dawned a lovely day except for ground haze. Got to Barkston Heath Airfield at about 1015 a.m. Everyone in fine spirits. Emplaned 1115 a.m. and took off at 1147. Very good flight, but a bit chilly. Lovely and calm over the sea."[137] The 38-year-old Lathbury was predestined to play a key role during Operation "Market". He was a seasoned veteran who had formed the 3rd Parachute Battalion in 1941, after which he assumed command of the 1st Parachute Brigade, which he led in combat in Italy. For his effort in the airborne attack against the Primosole bridge in Sicily in July 1943 (Operation "Fustian"), Lathbury was awarded the Distinguished Service Order, one of the most prominent British war decorations. The award statement read, "This officer organised and led the attack by the 1st Parachute Brigade on a vital river crossing South of Catania in Sicily on the night 13th/14th July 1943. Although dropped by parachute 1.5 miles away, from a height of only 100 feet Brigadier Lathbury reached the objective, took part in its capture and directed the consolidation, during which he was wounded. Later, during a heavy counterattack by German parachutists, he remained at the bridge where he fought alongside his troops and provided an example and inspiration which contributed in no small degree to the success of the operation."

One of the non-commissioned officers in the 1st Airborne Division, Serjeant Bruce Cox, describes the approach on 17 September 1944, "I shall never forget that armada of aircraft: flight after flight of battalions in the air, wave upon wave, as far as the eye could see, and high above us Mustangs, Spitfires, Lightnings and Thunderbolts escorting us to our destination, with bombers in front for diversionary targets. This was going to be some battle. We sat looking at each other; some told rotten jokes, some even slept (cool bastards!)." [138]

Signalman Herbert Butcher, also of the 1st Airborne Division, recounts, "I was in the same plane as Colonel Frost, who sat next to the door reading from a heavy volume. I found myself speculating what it might be. 'Gone with the Wind' seemed appropriate. Across me was Sergeant Westall, his bagpipes across his lap in a black box. We were tied up tighter than Christmas parcels for overseas mailing, over our battledresses and airborne smocks was our equipment, ammunition pouches, waterbottles, entrenching tools, messtins, etc. etc. all held together with belts and braces, plus whatever other odds and end we needed for our own particular job, in my case a havesack of batteries. Then came the jumping jackets, a loose denim affair, zipped down the front, to stop everything else flopping about and getting tangled in the parachute. Then came the lifejacket, just in case we came down in the sea. Next came the parachute and finally the Sten gun and magazines tucked into the harness. We must have all at last resembled that favourite epithet of sergeant-majors, pregnant nuns." [139]

A less-known fact is that some of the British airborne soldiers were wearing body armour, which is described by Butcher: "Another item available to key personnel was body armour. It consisted of a padded steel plate that hung over the chest with another, about half its size hung from the webbing straps to protect the stomach and a tee-shaped back piece to shield the kidneys." [140]

All went like clockwork – or, at least, almost all: the glider that brought Lieutenant-Colonel Thomas Haddon, commander of the

117

British airborne division's 1st Battalion of the Border Regiment, was forced to make an emergency landing in England.

Meanwhile, the fourth bomber operation was launched: 122 twin-engined bombers from the 2nd TAF – 48 B-25 Mitchells, 24 Douglas Bostons, and 50 Mosquitoes – were sent in against German barracks and other targets in the Arnhem-Nijmegen area. There were especially tragic consequences by the attack against the psychiatric nursing home outside the small village of Wolfheze to the west of Arnhem, where the Allied reconnaissance aviation had discovered German artillery. This cost 93 civilians their lives, including 58 admitted patients, and the buildings were completely destroyed. During the following days, confused and agonised mental patients would wander around the woods in the area, in the middle of a raging military battle.

"EVERY MAN FOR HIMSELF!"

At 1100 hrs, the corps commander Horrocks went up on the roof of one of the buildings of the zinc works next to "Joe's Bridge" to observe. He felt confident of victory, but did not want to set the exact time for the attack until he could see the armada of transport aircraft in the air above with his own eyes. Beneath him to the left, the Guards Armoured Division's tanks and many other combat vehicles formed a column several kilometres long on the road up towards the bridge. (See map on page 27.)

"Suddenly", Horrocks wrote, "seemingly out of the blue, hundreds of aircraft were overhead, many transport planes, some towing gliders, with fighter cover swarming everywhere as the Armada flew steadily northwards."[141] Horrocks immediately gave the order to start the attack at 1435, with preparatory artillery shelling from 1400.

At 1400 sharp, 300 guns opened fire over an area 1.5 kilometres wide and 8 kilometres long in front of the bridgehead. Meanwhile, about 100 Typhoon aircraft dived down on all identified and all suspected German positions.

The Irish Guards Group under "Colonel Joe" Vandeleur was at the lead, with the tanks of the 2nd (Armoured) Battalion under "Colonel

Joe's" second cousin, Lieutenant-Colonel Giles Vandeleur, at the very front.*

Lieutenant Keith Heathcote was the commander of the first Sherman tank of No. 3 Squadron of the Irish battalion. At 1435, he gave a short order in his microphone, "Driver advance!" While the artillery barrage began crawling forward at a speed of 200 metres per minute, dozens of tank engines started. XXX Corps commenced its attack with No. 3 Squadron at the forefront. After them, the twenty Shermans of No. 1 Squadron and, after them, No. 2 Squadron, followed. The tanks rolled in perfect column across the 30-metre wide Maas-Scheldt Canal over "Joe's Bridge" and turned left onto the road that had been given the name "Club Route" in the Allied plan. At a speed of 12 kilometres per hour, they approached the first town, Valkenswaard, 15 kilometres north of "Joe's Bridge".[142] 2nd Irish Guards Battalion's War Diary reads, "The battalion advanced, keeping as close behind the barrage as possible. The clouds of dust raised made this difficult, but the leading tank managed to follow some 300 yards behind the shell bursts."[143]

All went well during the first ten minutes. Soon, the first tanks crossed the border between Belgium and the Netherlands, where the road surface changed from macadam to concrete. Up on a factory roof some distance from the road, civilians were standing, applauding. The leading column announced over the radio, "Advance going well – leading Squadron has got through!"

QR9: VIDEO
Listen to Australian radio reporter Chester Wilmot's radio broadcast from Joe's Bridge at 1435 hrs on 17 September 1944.

---

* In the film *A Bridge Too Far* from 1977, Michael Caine and Michal Byrne played the parts as the two second cousins. "Colonel Joe" himself served as an expert advisor during procution, and when he had seen the film, he is said to have expressed that Michael Caine's interpretation of himself was "first-class".

Four kilometres further northeast, outside the small "twin village" Borkel en Schaft, a battery of howitzers from SS-Panzer-Artillerie-Regiment 10 were positioned. They were lucky enough to be positioned beyond the British artillery's shelling. "Tank from the right! Eight hundred meters!" the warning call sounded. The artillery men lowered the elevation of the barrels and aimed their guns, but only two guns in the right platoon had a field of fire. The men were waiting breathlessly while the battery commander, SS-Hauptsturmführer Karl Godau, watched the tank column. When more tanks became visible, he decided to hold his fire. Now, nine tanks had passed, and more kept appearing behind the trees that obscured the road to the southwest. Godau counted 27 tanks and reported this to the HQ, which ordered him to regroup. Without firing a single shot, Godau's battery started preparing their departure.[144]

But the Irish would not escape unscathed much longer. Major Hellmut Kerutt, the C.O. of the I. Bataillon of Fallschirmjäger-Regiment 18, coolly watched the approaching tanks through his binoculars, while the 14. Panzerjäger-Kompanie vanished in a cauldron of exploding shells. Here, among several others, the company commander Hauptmann Paul-Gerhardt Brockes was killed (see image below). But the anti-tank platoon under Leutnant Günther Vinke had escaped annihilation and was now hiding in the ditches, masked under leafy branches, with all of their Panzerfausts and Panzerschreck anti-tank weapons ready.

"Let the first ones pass", Kerutt ordered. An account from the German side describes what happened next, "Breathlessly, his ten soldiers saw how the mighty, green colossuses rumbled past. *'Feuer!'* From all directions, there was fire. Panzerfaust grenades shot through the air with flames behind them towards the tanks. One British tank after another caught fire."[145]

Major Mick O'Cock, commander of the Irish No. 1 Squadron, watched with horror how a whole row of tanks erupted in flames in quick succession: first, the ninth tank in front of him, after that, the eighth, the seventh, and so on, until the tank right in front of his own was also hit and caught fire. The three rear tanks of No. 3 Squadron and the six tanks at the forefront of No. 1 Squadron had been hit and knocked out. It was a perfect ambush. "Burning men tumbled out of the tank trapdoors, seldom the full crew of five", Captain John Gorman of the 2nd Irish Guards Battalion recounts.

In Lance-Serjeant Dave Roper's Sherman from No. 1 Squadron, four of the crew members made it out, but the signalman, Guardsman William Moore, died inside the burning tank.

The Sherman that was at position No. 3 from the rear in No. 3 Squadron was hit by a Panzerfaust at close range, and burst into flames. William Parkes, the 33-year-old Serjeant-Major (warrant officer) of No. 3 Squadron, died where he was sitting in the turret hatch.

Moreover, a Cromwell tank of "C" Squadron, 15/19 The King's Royal Hussars,* with Captain Roy Norton Swanwick as commander, was knocked out by a Panzerfaust.[146]

Two Daimler Dingo vehicles from the armoured reconnaissance company "B" Squadron of the 2nd Battalion, Household Cavalry Regiment (2 HCR), that had turned off the road to avoid the fire, were blown up by mines.[147]

Brockes was mortally wounded by shrapnel in the head. He was buried in the cemetery of the German military hospital Hengstdal at Nijmegen. In 1947, his remains were moved to the German military cemetery at Ysselsteyn, where he currently rests in grave No. 14 in Sector V, Row 1 – one of 31,598 German soldier graves from the Second World War on this site.

* The unit designation stemmed from the merger of the two cavalry units 15th The King's Hussars and 19th Royal Hussars in 1922.

However, not knowing what had happened, the tanks at the front continued. O'Cock called them over the radio, "Hi! You've lost your tail!" From the German side, SS-Rottenführer Johannes Rüsing, who in the general commotion had been inserted into Fallschirmjäger-Regiment 18, recounted, "English tanks are on fire on the road. We fired with our machine guns and handguns at the unarmoured tracked vehicles and the soldiers that were jumping out of them. But after their assault, the anti-tank troopers withdrew to the heath, without informing us of this. I assembled my group and we ran off towards the northeast. We were twelve men who escaped."[148]

"Colonel Joe" Vandeleur immediately called in the Typhoon planes that were circling in the air above according to the Cab-Rank method. The RAF liaison officer was present at Vandeleur's command post with his radio car, and being in direct contact with the pilots, he could lead them towards the Germans. The tanks helped out by firing red smoke shells against the enemy's positions and marking their own positions with yellow smoke.[149]

The pilots attacked and hit their targets only a hundred metres in front of their own ground troops. Chester Wilmot, who was covering the attack for the BBC from a tall church tower only a kilometre or

Serjeant-Major William Parkes.

so further back, recounted, "There was no chance of mistake for the white road stood out against the dark forest and all the tanks carried on their backs large orange identification screens." [150]

At 1510 hrs, the intelligence officer of the 2nd (Armoured) Battalion, Irish Guards, Captain Denis FitzGerald, reported over the radio, "Air support very good – using it now!" [151] The War Diary of the 2nd Battalion, The Devonshire Regiment commented, "Air support was terrific. Typhoons were swooping down at all angles and there was a constant hail of rockets and machine gun fire from them on the enemy." The War Diary of Irish Guards' 2nd Battalion concludes, "In the next hour 230 sorties were flown and very low and accurate attacks were made on the enemy. Our tanks burnt yellow smoke abundantly and though the rockets landed within 100 yards of them, there was never any likelihood of a mistake, so sure was the pilot's aim. The effect of the rockets, combined with the aggressiveness of our tanks and infantry, was almost instantaneous. Enemy came running out of the trenches trembling with fright." [152]

Two infantry battalions from the 50th Division, 1st Dorset and 2nd Devonshire, and the Cromwell tanks of "C" Squadron, 15/19 The

Parkes and Moore are currently laid to rest in the Commonwealth War Cemetery south of Valkenswaard, Plot II, Row B: Parkes in Grave 8 and Moore in Grave 9.

King's Royal Hussars, had been detailed as immediate flank protection about a thousand metres on each side of the road. They, and the infantrymen of the Irish 3rd Battalion, assaulted the Germans in the ditches and among the trees on each side of the road. The Guards Armoured Division's chronicle describes the effect of the Typhoon planes' intense attacks, "Quite a few Germans were found crouching at the bottom of their slit trenches among the trees; most of them were frightened to death by the overpowering attack of the Typhoons and were heartily relieved at becoming prisoners, tears literally pouring down many of their miserable faces." One of the two platoons of the 10. SS-Panzer-Division's armoured reconnaissance battalion that had been detailed to the defence of the artillery was completely annihilated by the British tanks.[153] Gorman recounts, "The 3rd Battalion Infantry, sweeping the ground on each side of us, kept flushing out hundreds of Germans from their trenches and dugouts. Their faces were deadly pale, with little flecks of blood. I often noticed this effect of continuous heavy shelling."

The prisoners were rounded up at breakneck speed and were ordered to get going towards the British rear lines. One Unteroffizier stammered out that most of the men of the 14. Panzerjäger-Kompanie had been finished off. He was sent weeping down the road.[154] The prisoners were running for dear life, and continued running as they reached the divisional HQ a few kilometres further down the road, on the other side of "Joe's Bridge". But there, they were rounded up by military police, who in a short time were able to count in 250 prisoners of war in the division's prisoner cages. Interrogation with the prisoners showed that "most were new and ignorant recruits, others good fighters who had suffered Normandy

QR10: VIDEO
5:34: Authentic wartime footage from
this site immediately after the battle.

and the retreat".[155] Others, those who had escaped capture, simply fled for their lives. One of the German paratroopers, Obergefreiter Alfons Krüsch, recounts, "Suddenly, the commander said: 'Every man for himself!' The tanks had come within only ten metres. The MG 42 becomes useless, my machine gun gunner is already out of our common dugout. A few machine gun shots from a tank strikes him down. We were hunted by the tanks just as when you're hunting rabbits."[156]

In the general panic, Krüsch apparently did not notice that it was infantry and not any tanks that was pursuing them; the surrounding marshy terrain with deep ditches made it difficult for the tanks to leave the road. Out of the company that Krüsch belonged to, only 25 men remained in the evening of 17 September – of a nominal strength of 200.

1st Dorset, 2nd Devonshire, and "C" Squadron, 15/19 The King's Royal Hussars, cleared up the flanks, but the many anti-tank mines that had been laid out in the terrain effectively hindered a circumvention of the wrecks that blocked the road. Major Guy Courage of the latter unit recalled, "Near a hamlet called Petter, the infantry collected some scattered and dazed Germans who were still cowering in their foxholes. The Typhoons were still at work and we could see their rockets striking buildings and trenches alongside the road two hundred yards in front. Some Typhoons elected to return towards us firing their MGs at the enemy from his rear. The bullets came perilously close to us as well. There was a loud explosion close by, as SSM Sara's tank was blown up on a mine. On examination a few minutes later, it was clear that at least two Teller mines must have been under each track. The damage to the tank was very extensive and the driver, Lance Corporal [Walter] Batchelor* was killed. Serjeant Pearson and Trooper Dick were wounded and the others were badly dazed. The Commanding Officer [Lieutenant-Colonel Anthony Taylor] appeared in his tank alongside Squadron FHQ. Almost immediately his tank went up on a mine, to be followed a few minutes later by the 2nd Troop Challenger (Corporal Shirvill)."[157]

---

* Batchelor today rests at the Commonwealth War Cemetery south of Valkenswaard, Plot II, Row A, Grave 17.

An armoured bulldozer had to be brought forward to shovel away the destroyed tanks from the road. At 1630, the advance was recommenced, with Major Tyler's No. 2 Squadron at the head, under the same "artillery umbrella" as before, and with Typhoon planes circling in the air.

By then, the five StuG assault guns from schwere Heeres-Panzerjäger-Abteilung 559 had made it to the road from the village of Bergeijk, three kilometres to the west, where they had been when the attack began. But three of them were immediately knocked out. The commander of one of the remaining, Leutnant Hans Vögele, immediately ordered the driver to turn around and return to Bergeijk. The other remaining StuG III disappeared towards Valkenswaard.[158] One of the destroyed StuG IIIs had been knocked out by a Sherman Firefly from No. 2 Squadron with Lance-Serjeant Bertie Cowan as commander. The German crew bailed out, but Cowan stood up in the turret of his tank and ordered them harshly to come forward and climb up onto his tank. The shocked Germans did so without protests, and when they had got up, Cowan demanded that they point out the other German positions. The captured German did this as well, apparently in the belief that this was what they had to do unless they were to be executed.[159] In one hour, Tyler's No. 2 Squadron advanced six kilometres without encountering more than a little sporadic shelling from single mortars and handguns. At 1730, the little river Dommel was reached, where the road bridge was found not only to be intact but also capable of carrying tanks. On the other side, four intact 88 mm anti-aircraft guns were captured, when their crews surrendered as the Irish tanks appeared.

Major Tyler's tanks were only a few kilometres from the town of Valkenswaard, but by now, the large column of soldiers and combat vehicles had brought about a terrible traffic jam on the narrow road. This was not least because the Germans had laid out mines in the grassy edge along the road, which had cost several vehicles. Therefore, everyone stayed on the road. Further back in the column, the 1st Battalion of the Dorset Regiment tried to advance. The Battalion commander, Lieutenant Colonel Alexander Bredin, called "Speedy", recounted, "The main road was so congested along its entire length by double and triple banking of tanks and other vehicles that, not only did the battalion vehicles have great difficulty in moving up, but I, Commanding Officer, had to do a bit of pillion-riding on Corporal [Henry] Barnes' motor-cycle." [160]

It took time to take the column across the narrow stone bridge. While the troops prepared for attack on the north side of the river, the sun began to set. At half past eight, it was completely dark, and the only lights came from the fires in Valkenswaard, where British artillery shelling had set several buildings on fire. Tyler led his tanks in a careful advance towards the town. At 1955, they rolled in among the houses, their crews' eyes staying watchful. [161] The town was partly in ruins. In the streets, abandoned German equipment lay strewn. Every now and then, a shot rang out from individual German soldiers who had been hiding here and there behind corners of houses or hedges, but most Germans in the town had ran away. A number of them were completely taken by surprise by Major Tyler and his tanks, and surrendered straight away. The town's inhabitants were equally surprised. One of them recalled, "In the evening when the Tommies got near the village, we were sheltering in the cellar of the Town Hall. There was some firing outside and we could hear the tanks thundering on the streets. Then the door suddenly flew open. We saw two men who cried: 'Hands up!' We shouted: 'Hooray! Hooray! Tommies! Tommies! Come here! Come here!' We couldn't believe it. After all these years they had come at last." [162]

As at a given signal, the townspeople started flocking out of the houses and came to meet their liberators with cheers. Soon, the whole of Valkenswaard was draped in orange, the Dutch national colour. The BBC's Chester Wilmot reported from the town, "The town was gay with flags and orange colours - flowers, ribbons, paper caps and even freshly painted orange clogs. People danced in the streets and crowded round the BBC microphone to sing songs that had been banned for years." [163]

More and more units from the Irish Guards arrived in Valkenswaard and assembled in the square in the town centre. At around 2100 hrs, the town clerk came running to "Colonel Joe" Vandeleur, announcing that the German commandant in Eindhoven, Oberst

Hellmut von Hoffmann,* without knowing that the town had changed hands, had phoned to order that Valkenswaard should be held at any cost, and that reinforcements were on their way for a counterattack.

The Dutch official was beaming with joy as he announced what kind of strong language he had used against his former oppressor.[164]

The announcement that new German troops were on their way to carry out an attack in the dark was, of course, serious. Adding to this was that Vandeleur, by continued liaison with a friendly telephone operator in Eindhoven, had been given information that the Germans were still patrolling the streets of the major city and that no American troops were to be seen. But none of this could be considered having motivated the decision taken by the divisional commander, Major-General Allan Adair, to simply halt for the night. Patrols that were sent out could observe almost total disarray on the German side, and only weak and shattered German units along the road to Eindhoven, a little over five kilometres further north.

Horrocks, the commander of XXX Corps, is silent in his memoirs on this nocturnal halt. The fact that he did not intervene to get Adair going in this situation could possibly be explained by him constantly being afflicted by intermittent pain in his wounds (after having been badly injured by fire from a German aircraft in 1943) which rendered him unable to act.

* Previously the commander of Fallschirmjäger-Regiment 18.

IV.

"The Screaming Eagles"
17 September 1944

While the Irish tanks broke out of the bridgehead at "Joe's Bridge", the "airborne carpet", as Montgomery put it, was rolled out in front of them. Major General Maxwell Taylor's 101st Airborne Division, "The Screaming Eagles", was commissioned to secure the first bridges for the XXX Corps: At the Wilhelmina Canal north of Eindhoven; at River Dommel in Sint-Oedenrode, seven kilometres further north; at the Zuid-Willemsvaart Canal, another five kilometres north; and at the parallel river Aa, one kilometre further north. In addition, the city of Eindhoven was supposed to be captured by 2000 hrs on 17 September.

Four hundred and twenty-four Douglas C-47 Skytrain transport planes with 70 Waco gliders brought 6,695 paratroopers from 101st Airborne Division out across the English Channel. Private First Class Donald Burgett from the 506th Parachute Infantry Regiment looked for a long time at the white cliffs of Dover until they finally disappeared from sight. Taylor's division had been assigned four landing areas: Drop Zones "A", "B", and "C", as well as Landing Zone "W". Paratroopers were to be dropped over the first three, and the last was intended for the gliders.

Burgett and the rest of the 506th, as well as an engineer platoon, were to be dropped over Drop Zone "C", which was the southernmost, located in the fields three kilometres north of the Wilhelmina Canal. The regiment's primary task was to secure the crossings of this wide canal, which runs in an east-west direction just north of the city of Eindhoven.

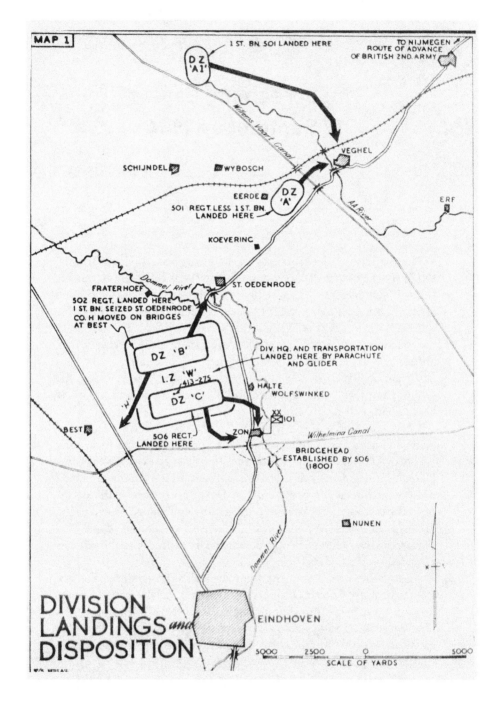

American military map from the war over the 101st Airborne Division's landings on 17 September 1944.

Next to the 506th, just a few hundred metres further north, the 502nd Parachute Infantry Regiment as well as the HQ of the 101st Airborne Division, including Major General Taylor, were to be dropped over Drop Zone "B". The 22-year-old son of Finnish immigrants T/4 (Technician 4th Grade) George E. Koskimaki* served as Taylor's signalman.

He recounted, "As we flew across the Channel, I watched the shadows of the planes in their formation on an almost placid sea. Air-sea rescue craft were everywhere, just in case planes ran into trouble. We picked up our fighter escort at mid-Channel and crossed into Belgium."[165]

Right between Drop Zones "B" and "C", Landing Zone "W" was placed, where the gliders were to land artillery, signal equipment, medical equipment, and jeeps.

Slightly to the side, little over five kilometres northeast of Drop Zone "B", the 501st Parachute Infantry Regiment was to be dropped by parachute at Drop Zone "A", just south of the Zuid-Willensvaart Canal.

The armada of aircraft with the 101st Airborne Division took the southern route in over the frontline. This went past the Thames Estuary to North Foreland, the pointed tongue of land at the very far end of the Estuary, and crossed the coastline six kilometres northeast of Ostend. At Beringen at the Albert Canal, the air armada turned north, and flew over the heads of the men of the XXX Corps on their way to Eindhoven. The approach was covered by six Fighter Groups of American Mustang fighters, which sufficed to keep the Luftwaffe at a distance. Another 142 aircraft from U.S. Ninth Air Force – Thunderbolt and Lightning fighter-bombers – were circling over the landing grounds from 1230 hrs, striking down on all identified anti-aircraft positions.

Meanwhile, General Hans Wolfgang Reinhard, the commander of German LXXXVIII. Armeekorps, was on his way back by car to his headquarters near Tilburg after an inspection tour of the front. "My route was through Winterle and Oirschot, and I noticed that the

* Koskimaki has contributed to the documentation of the 101st Airborne Division with several acclaimed books. He passed away in February 2016.

activity of the enemy fighter-bombers was increasing enormously", Reinhard recounted. "Very often I was forced to stop my car and take cover." When he arrived at the bridge across the Wilhelmina Canal at Oirschot, almost ten kilometres northwest of Eindhoven, he saw something that made him gasp for breath, "Directly above me and stretched far to east and west, huge fleets of enemy transport planes. Some of these were a scant several hundred meters above us and the cable attaching the gliders to the planes could easily be seen with the naked eye."[166] The terrified general estimated the number at two thousand transport planes and gliders – four times the actual number, which surely reflected the shock he must have felt.

When the formations flew in over the frontlines, they were met with furious fire from the ground. By then, they only had a few minutes left to their targets, but the rest of the flight virtually turned into running the gauntlet. "Our plane rocked and bounced with the nearby explosions", Burgett recounted. "Flak, machine-gun bullets struck our plane from time to time but no one was hit."[167] Lieutenant William Muir, Burgett's 30-year-old platoon commander, ordered the men to line up and hook up onto the static line. It felt like an eternity. Everybody's eyes were fixed at the red light that signalled to the paratroopers to get ready. Suddenly, the light turned to green. "Go! Let's go!" Muir cried. "Let's go! Let's go! Let's get out of this damned thing!" Burgett and his comrades cried, while they jumped out in quick successions into the freezing air, where the jet streams from the propellers grabbed hold of them and shook them up while the static lines opened their parachutes.

When Burgett had come out of the turbulence, he looked up, and saw in astonishment how the entire sky seemed to be full of parachutes. He looked down, and saw how large numbers of parachutes were touching down all over the fields. Then, the ground came rushing towards him, and he had touched down.

The American reporter Ed Murrows, who had joined in one of the 101st Airborne's C-47s, reported for CBS Radio. He was yelling excitedly into his microphone as the paratroopers on board his aircraft jumped out, "There he goes! Do you hear him shout? Three, four, five, six, seven, eight, nine, ten, eleven, twelve, thirteen, fourteen, fifteen, sixteen, seventeen, eighteen... There they go! Every man out – I can see their chutes going down now! Every man clear!"*

Out of the 424 transport planes that carried "The Screaming Eagles", 16 were shot down and 98 others were damaged by fire from the ground. But the main part of the 101st Airborne Division had been landed behind the German lines between 1301 and 1355 hrs, and the elite paratroopers now made themselves ready to secure their targets.

One decisive factor for the success was the Pathfinders – especially trained paratroopers whose task it was to guide the aircraft to and mark out the landing grounds – who had arrived on beforehand. The 101st Airborne's Pathfinders arrived between 1247 and 1255, and could, without encountering any resistance, switch on their small portable "Eureka" transmitters. These sent out a signal that was received by the "Rebecca", which the aircraft were equipped with, thus guiding the airmen to their targets.**

In addition, the landing zones were marked by large, coloured sheets of plastic and smoke signals.

* QR11: AUDIO
Listen to Murrow's broadcast.

** QR12: VIDEO
Documentary on "Rebecca".

501ST PARACHUTE INFANTRY REGIMENT – TOTAL SUCCESS

The aircraft that brought Colonel Howard R. Johnson's 501st Parachute Infantry Regiment met the fiercest flak out of all air units, resulting in the first paratroopers of the 101st Airborne Division's 1st Battalion being dropped five kilometres northwest of Drop Zone "A", on the wrong side of the Aa river, the north side. But this would turn out to be lucky.

The rest of the regiment was landed in the right place, south of the Zuid-Willemsvaart Canal (which runs south of and in parallel with the Aa, at between a few hundred metres' and one kilometre's distance). While the paratroopers assembled, scores of overjoyed Dutchmen started flocking to the site. One inhabitant of the town of Schijndel, just north of Drop Zone "A", described this unforgettable moment in his diary, "Many inhabitants are hurrying in the direction where it was littered with parachutes and where the liberators are greeted excitedly. They are returning with cigarettes, chocolate, coffee, etc., and parachutes, that they will later make children's dresses from. Everyone is overjoyed, as they believe that Schijndel is already liberated."[168]

Colonel Johnson managed to assemble 95 per cent of the 2nd and 3rd Battalions within 45 minutes. Already before 1400 hrs, the men were on their ways towards their respective objectives. Lieutenant Colonel Julian Ewell grouped part of his 3rd Battalion to the defence of the landing ground next to Rijksweg 69 – "Club Route", where the British XXX Corps was to advance on its way to Arnhem – and took Eerde, the little village by the landing ground. Lieutenant Colonel Bob Ballard's 2nd Battalion advanced to the northeast and secured the railway bridge and the road bridge across the canal. By then, shots were heard from within Veghel, just over a kilometre further east. It was the 1st Battalion that was fighting German troops in the town. This battalion was tasked with securing both of the bridges across the Zuid-Willemsvaart Canal and the river Aa at Veghel. Using commandeered lorries and bicycles, an advance guard had left the Heeswijk castle on the road to Veghel, followed by the main force. The only resistance they encountered was in the shape of a few German motor vehicles, which were quickly knocked out, and those aboard were killed or captured. Among other things, a German ambulance was captured, turning out to contain two wounded as well as Dr. Kampermann, the divisional physician of the 16. Flak-Division.

But what the Germans did not succeed with, the Dutch civilians accomplished. "Hollanders were coming to the road from all sides until their numbers became confusing", the American report says. "They crowded in trying to shake hands with Kinnard's men, offering them fruit and other gifts and asking if they could be of help." [169] This slowed the Americans to the point where they reached the outskirts of Veghel only after two hours – where they encountered some resistance, which, however, could be neutralised quite quickly. Some thirty Germans put their hands in the air. When the Americans entered the town, the population flocked out of their houses and gave their liberators an enthusiastic welcome. At 1630 hrs, the battalion could report Veghel and the important bridges secured and was able to establish liaison with the 2nd Battalion.

The fact that these bridges had fallen into the enemy's hands undamaged came as a shock to the German Paratroop General Student. "According to the plans for a further German withdrawal", he recounted, "all bridges had been prepared for demolition, and were guarded by strong detachments and special demolition commandoes. Each bridge had a responsible bridge commandant who had orders to blow up the bridge in the case of immediate danger." [170] But at the moment of truth, this failed in many places – the German soldiers and commanders responsible simply left the site in panic; "another proof of the paralysing effect of surprise by airborne forces",[171] Student commented.

QR13: VIDEO
00:00–14:24: Authentic wartime footage. The 101st Airborne before and during approach, and the landing. At 13:55, you can see a glimpse of the artillery commander McAuliffe in a jeep.

In the general state of disintegration and confusion on the German side, Student personally took command of the operations on the tactical level. "The airborne operation caused a shock among the troops in the front line of my army. I therefore stayed purposely with my general staff detachment at Vught in order to strengthen the morale of the fighting troops", he recounted.[172]

In a downed glider, the Germans came across at least the parts of the Allied operation plan that concerned the 101st Airborne Division, if not more. (See fact box on page 138.) These documents were handed over as early as during the afternoon of 17 September to Student. His problem was that he hardly had any forces available against the paratroopers. But in 's-Hertogenbosch, ten kilometres northwest of Veghel, Fallschirm-Ersatz- und Ausbildungs-Regiment 1 under Oberst Udo von Kummer was present. It consisted of 2,500 men of surplus personnel from air units that had gone through what was, in reality, infantry training – almost all of them had been deemed medically unfit for parachute jumps.[173] Together with guard soldiers and other forces in the town, this regiment had been put together as Kampfgruppe Dewald, under the town commandant, Oberst Eberhard von Dewald.

Student knew from his own experience that an airdrop is at its most vulnerable during the first few hours, and that it therefore had to be attacked immediately.[174] At 1355 hrs – that is, before the 101st Airborne Division even had been able to organise its men for the advance – von Dewald was given orders to organise his Kampfgruppe into six smaller battle groups, each designated after its commander.[175]

At 1420, Hauptmann Ewald's battle group, part of Kampfgruppe Dewald, was ordered to carry out armed reconnaissance towards Dinther, along the road to Veghel, and to Uden, northeast of Veghel.[176] Led by Oberleutnant Diedrichs, the 10. Kompanie came marching in two columns on the road next to Kasteel Heeswijk – the medieval castle with towers and pinnacles which even is surrounded by a moat. They immediately noted some activity, and on the ground around, there were clear traces of the American 1st Battalion's landing. While the Germans took up positions, they suddenly saw how a Red Cross flag was hung out of one of the castle windows. Oberleutnant Diedrichs gave the order to fire two grenades from a mortar against the castle yard. Twenty-one Americans came out with their hands above their heads. It was a small force under Captain William Burd that had been left behind to take care of twelve men that had been injured during the parachute jump.[177] The Germans rounded them up and confiscated their American cigarettes, which they smoked with much delight. Moreover, the German prisoners that the Americans had taken captive were liberated, including Doctor Kampermann and a Luftwaffe Leutnant with his driver.[178] Kampermann, however, did not show much gratitude, but gave Diedrichs quite a dressing down for having fired against a building flying the Red Cross.

Across the canal, a cruel surprise awaited the people of Schijndel, the little town with some 10,000 inhabitants. When the paratroopers had been raining down over the fields outside the town, the towns-people had been cheering, but it turned out to be too soon. One of the inhabitants recounted, "We thought that we were liberated, but the soldiers (Americans and Englishmen) had been assigned to hold the corridor from Eindhoven through Veghel and Nijmegen to Arnhem open. Schijndel sat in the line of fire. After the first shells had hit, causing fatalities, the eastern part of the Hoofdstraat (Main Street) towards Boxtel was evacuated. Every now and then, the Americans came to Schijndel again, and we thought that we were liberated at last, but the liberators then left again with lots of German prisoners of war." [179]

In the evening, two companies from Hauptmann Ewald's battalion fought their way into Schijndel, and attacked Lieutenant Colonel Ewell's 3rd Battalion east of the town.[180] The Americans, however, felt that these efforts were quite half-hearted, and could hold their positions without any major difficulties.

More serious, however, was the attack that was carried out against Veghel by the German paratroop training regiment's first through fourth companies commanded by Hauptmann Tuchstein.*

---

* Certain publications erroneously write the name Duchstein, but that can, however, be traced to a typo in a Dutch translation of Oberst Dewald's war diary.

Did the Germans come across the entire operational plan for "Market Garden"?

According to what General Student recounted after the war, a German soldier named Koch came across the complete plan for Operation "Market Garden" during the afternoon of 17 September, in the uniform of a dead officer in a Waco glider that had been shot down near Student's own headquarters in Vught. Student recounted:
"A few hours later the enemy orders for the complete airborne operation were on my desk; they had been captured in a glider which had been shot down near Vught. From these orders, the following was clear: The corridor Eindhoven-Veghel-Grave-Nijmegen-Arnhem was to be opened by a large air-landing operation and be held open; for this purpose, the bridges within this corridor were to be captured. Immediately after establishing this corridor, parts of the British 2nd Army were to thrust along this corridor at high speed and link up with airborne troops. Operationally employed were:

• The U.S. 101st Airborne Division in the area Eindhoven Veghel
• The U.S. 82nd Airborne Division in the area Grave-Nijmegen
• The British Airborne Division at Arnhem

The whole operation was under command of the British Airborne Corps. The Corps H.Q. accompanied the 82nd Division into the Nijmegen area." [1]

A few years after the war, Student clarified to Cornelius Ryan what the documents contained: "They showed us everything – the dropping zones, the corridor, the objectives, even the names of the divisions involved. Everything!" [2] This is, however, questioned in its entirety by the authors of *Operation Market-Garden Then and Now*, who point out that the glider in question was not a Waco, but a Horsa, which carried parts of Browning's Corps Headquarters, and that it did not crash at Vught, but at 't Broek near Dongen, 25 km further southwest. *Operation Market-Garden Then and Now* even claims to have identified the glider as Horsa No. 413, flown by Staff Sergeant Jock Campbell and Sergeant David Monk. Onboard were eight men, among whom the British intelligence officer Captain Peter Ashbury held the highest rank. According to this source, the documents that the Germans came across from this glider contained "not the full operational plan, as claimed by Student, but only the operational order of the 101st Airborne Division which opened with a general outline of Market Garden".[3] What we do know from the German documents that have been preserved is that the intelligence section of Heeresgruppe B at 1925 hrs on 17 September sent out the following message to all units in the area: "101 Americ. Airb-Div. has the task of capturing the crossings at Son – St. Oedenrode and Veghel and keep them open for the advancing Engl. army troops (Guards-Arm.-Div, 50. I.D. and 43. I.D.). The latter are advancing towards Eindhoven."[4]

Among the Orders of the Day, issued by Heeresgruppe B, there is a note that the captured documents contained "operational orders, forces, unit structure, and objectives for the landing operation".[5]
The question will probably never be answered, as the documents have probably not been preserved.

However, the acting commander of the 9. SS-Panzer-Division, SS-Obersturmbannführer Walter Harzer, plays down the significance of these captured documents. "Although we had the operational orders these were not all that useful", he said after the war. "The only precision they gave concerned the landing areas. So we did not really trust the captured plans. We did not know how the enemy would react. We did not even know for sure that the plans were genuine."[6]

1. King's College London. Liddell Hart Centre for Military Archives. 15/15: Papers of Reginald William Winchester ('Chester') Wilmot (1911–1954). 15/15/50/1. Notes from official sources and interrogation of Gen Kurt Student, Cdr 1 German Parachute Army on the German tactical response.
2. Ryan, *A Bridge too Far*, p. 254.
3. *Operation Market-Garden Then and Now*, p. 173.
4. Bundesarchiv/Militärarchiv, RH 24-88. Bestand LXXXVIII. Armeekorps: Ia-KTB mit Anlagen 1.7-31.12.1944.
5. Tagesbefehl Heeresgruppe B, Abschnitt 11, 16 September-10 Oktober 1944. 28.9.1944. File No. 259, Market Garden, Municipal Archives, Ede. ; Verhoef, The Battle for Ginkel Heath Near Ede, p. 109.
6. SS-Obersturmbannführer Walter Harzer. "Arnhem Interview." Gelders Archief. Archiefblok 2867. Collectie L.P.J. Vroemen. Doos nr. 30, p. 4.

General Student had personally issued the order to attack Veghel to "annihilate the enemy" and retake the bridge.[181]

Under cover of darkness and rainy haze, Tuchstein's force of 500 men managed to sneak up to positions at the same road from the castle that the American 1st Battalion had taken to Veghel. At 2010 hrs, they made a surprise attack towards the railway bridge, one and a half kilometres to the south. Here, the American positions were only held by "E" Company of the 2nd Battalion. Leaving seven killed behind, the American retreated to the bridge, and there, they managed to resist. Willi Schiffer, one of the Germans, remembers, "The light infantry companies walked straight into the machine gun fire of the Americans who were hiding in the station." Inexperienced in battle, the Germans withdrew to defence positions three kilometres further northwest. Here, they were exposed to intense shelling claiming further severe losses, including Hauptmann Tuchstein himself.

In total, the 501st Parachute Infantry Regiment managed to reach all of its objectives during the first day. Further south – the main direction for "The Screaming Eagles" – things were not, however, going as well.

502ND PARACHUTE INFANTRY REGIMENT – STUCK AT BEST

The 502nd Parachute Infantry Regiment under Colonel John H. Michaelis, along with the divisional commander Major General Maxwell Taylor, were dropped at Drop Zone "B", in the fields southwest of Sint-Oedenrode, some distance south of the 501st. Its main mission was to secure three of the bridges that Rijksweg 69 ("Club Route") crossed on its way north: two across the river Dommel at Sint-Oedenrode, five kilometres southwest of Veghel, and, seven kilometres further to the south, the bridge across the Wilhelmina Canal at Son just northeast of Eindhoven.

The main part of the regiment, however, was assigned to defend the landing area itself – a somewhat inflexible measure, as it turned out that there were no Germans to be seen in the area, while several civilians from nearby farms and villages, on the other hand, appeared in the field to welcome the liberators. The 1st Battalion under Lieutenant Colonel Patrick Cassidy advanced north to take Sint-Oedenrode, the little medieval town north of the landing fields. Here, the German Flieger-Regiment 93, a unit where Luftwaffe recruits received their basic infantry training, had set up its headquarters in the town hall. The German recruits showed little desire to sacrifice themselves, so, after dutifully having fired a few rounds, they put their hands in the air. 58 prisoners were counted in.

Captain James J. Hatch, Cassidy's operations officer (S-3), made it into the abandoned town hall, and just as he was there, the telephone rang. Hatch had been studying German, and picked up the receiver to try to get some information, but the voice at the other end sounded far too upset for him to be able to understand a word. Eventually, Hatch said *"Heil Hitler!"* and hung up.

Meanwhile, a small group of other German soldiers tried to blow up one of the bridges, but were detected by a few men from the American "B" Company – to the right of "C" Company – which wiped out the Germans with a Bazooka. Soon afterwards, the Americans were able to cross the undamaged bridges at Sint-Oedenrode, and at 1800 hrs, they established connection with units from the 3rd Battalion of 501st Parachute Infantry Regiment some distance to the north of the town.

However, in the direction of Eindhoven in the south, things were not going as well. While Student was organising his counterattacks, he made large efforts to prevent the Americans from seizing the crossings over the Wilhelmina Canal north of Eindhoven. Initially, he hardly had any forces at his disposal. In Eindhoven proper, the German garrison to all intents and purposes only consisted of anti-aircraft soldiers, guard soldiers, and headquarters personnel, and many of them had fled in various directions when the American landing took place. There were two large bridges across the canal at Eindhoven: on one of them, at Son to the northeast, Rijksweg 69 passed, and three kilometres to the west, at Best, both a railway bridge and the bridge on the road between Eindhoven and 's-Hertogenbosch passed. In neither of these places were there anything but small anti-aircraft units available to Student, but these were ordered to defend the bridge at all costs, and, as a last resort, to blow them up.

Meanwhile, Student's new chief of staff, Oberst Reinhard, rang around to scrape some reinforcements together. There was special emphasis on defending the large bridge at Best. The only available reserve consisted of one battalion, I. Bataillon of Grenadier-Regiment 723. This regiment was part of 719. Infanterie-Division, which was only just able to hold its positions northeast of Antwerp. Nevertheless, Student took the decision to regroup this battalion to Best. The replacement battalion Feld-Ersatz-Bataillon 347 was also ordered there, as well as what remained of the 59. Infanterie-Division of the 15. Armee after the evacuation across the Scheldt Estuary. This division arrived at Boxtel, almost ten kilometres northwest of Best, during the afternoon of the 17th and the following night.

Meanwhile, Oberst Reinhard's namesake, the commander of the LXXXVIII. Armeekorps, General Hans Wolfgang Reinhard, arrived at his headquarters outside Tilburg. In order not to offer too large a target for enemy fighter-bombers, he continued his journey from the bridge across the Wilhelmina Canal at Oirschot (see page 131) in the sidecar of one of the motorcycles of the escorting force.[182] General Reinhard received reports of Allied landings at Arnhem, Nijmegen, Eindhoven, and Udenhout, five kilometres north of the headquarters. With all other units already alerted, he contacted the chief of police at Tilburg, Oberst der Polizei Hans Otto Karl Böhmer. He had a battalion, I. Bataillon of SS-Polizei-Sicherheits-Regiment 3, in the town.

This was not a fighting regiment; it was the police regiment of the occupational force in the Netherlands, the so-called "Green Police" that the Dutch hated so deeply. Its task was to be sent in against strikes, carry out raids, and arrest and deport Jews to death camps.[183] Amongst other things, SS-Polizei-Sicherheits-Regiment 3 was responsible for the deportation train from Westerbork to Auschwitz on 3 September 1944 which carried Anne Frank.* The men were policemen aged between 35 and 45.[184]

---

* The regimental commander, Oberst der Polizei Böhmer, was sentenced in 1949 by a Dutch court in Amsterdam to two and a half years in prison. (Verfahren Lfd.Nr. NL110; BG/BS Amsterdam 490406. Marcus Wendel, *Third Reich Factbook-SS Police Regimenter*, skalman.nu/third-reich/polis-sspol-reg.htm.)

Reinhard ordered the police colonel to promptly send one of his three companies to Udenhout and two others to Best. (The company sent to to Udenhout was also redirected to Best when it turned out later that the reports of air landings at that place had been inaccurate.[185]) The mission was, "Defend the bridge to the last man!"[186]

But all of these units were given their orders only after the Americans had been landed, so the first hit would be taken by the small anti-aircraft units.

As far as the Allies were concerned, it was a prerequisite for the XXX Corps' advance that the major city of Eindhoven, five kilometres south of Drop Zone "B", was secured, as well as the bridges across the 25–30 metres wide Wilhelmina Canal – which runs in a westerly-easterly direction just before Eindhoven's northern outskirts. According to the plan, these objectives had to be reached no later than at 2000 hrs on this first day of attack. The main attack would be carried out by the 506th Parachute Infantry Regiment, which was landed just next to the 501st PIR, towards the bridge at Son in the east. Five kilometres to the west, the 501st would take the bridge at Best, a kilometre or so north of Eindhoven's western outskirts.

The mission was unnecessarily made more difficult by Taylor's far too strong emphasis on the defensive, and a complete absence of any tactical cooperation between the two regiments in the advance towards Best. All that could be spared from the 501st, when the 1st Battalion had taken Sint-Oedenrode and about 1,700 men had been positioned to defend the landing zone, was a reinforced company of about 260 men – the 3rd Battalion's "H" Company as well as an engineer platoon from the 326th Engineers and a machine gun squad from the battalion headquarters. Neither did this manage to fulfil its task in an optimal way.

Led by the company commander, Captain Robert Jones, the troop set off at 1440 hrs. Between the Americans and the bridge at Best lay five kilometres of forests and fields without a single German soldier, so they should have been able to get there within an hour. But because of the heavy losses during the fighting at Normandy, the unit consisted of many inexperienced recruits. They had apparently misunderstood an order to avoid damaging civilian property, so instead of cutting the many barbed wire fences running in all directions across the fields, they made the effort of climbing over them – which led to both screamingly hilarious and time-consuming situations. They were only lucky that there were no Germans nearby. When the battalion commander, the hot-tempered Lieutenant Colonel Robert Cole, was informed of this, he got furious. He had led the now-famous bayonet charge at Carentan in Normandy on 11 June – where half of the battalion was eradicated – and would not tolerate any "civilian conduct" in this situation. "Cut the God-damned wire and quit wasting time!" he hissed.[187] The fact that the high number of recruits in the battalion was due to Cole's very attack at Carentan was, of course, another story...

On top of all that, the Americans lost their way in the forest further ahead. The plan was to take advantage of the Sonsche forest, a belt of planted firs a kilometre wide on the north side of the Wilhelmina Canal, in order to make it unseen to the bridge. But when Jones and his men made it out of the forest, they discovered that they had ended up six hundred metres too far to the north. In front of them lay a field with farms, and beyond, a few hundred metres further away, the houses in the eastern outskirts of Best. It was then about a quarter to five in the afternoon. It had taken "H" Company three hours to cover five kilometres!

Penetration capacity for different German 88 mm guns hitting at a 30-degree angle at a 2,000-metre range

MODEL	GRENADE	PENETRATION ARMOUR
Flak 18/36/37	anti-tank shell 39	88 mm
KwK 36 L 56	anti-tank shell 39	99 mm
KwK 36 L 56	anti-tank shell 40	110 mm
Pak 43/KwK 43	anti-tank shell 39	139 mm
Pak 43/KwK 43	anti-tank shell 40/43	153 mm

The only German unit at Best was a reinforced anti-aircraft company, 3. Kompanie of schwere Flak-Abteilung 428 under Hauptmann Herbert Zeller, with eight 88 mm and two 20 mm anti-aircraft guns.[188] The latter was, with a rate of fire at 280 rounds per minute, a gruesomely lethal weapon against "soft targets", and the 88-millimetre anti-aircraft gun Flak 18/36/37 had proven very efficient against armour even at great distances already early in the war.

Right now, these guns were not immediately accessible to meet the Americans, who were obscured by houses and rows of trees lining the small roads that ran in all directions across the fields east of Best. But Seller had, of course, both seen and heard the massive airdrop just northeast of the little town, and every available soldier had been grouped to the east and the north in firing positions in houses and behind hedges and trees. When Jones's men advanced between the houses, they came under massive fire from handguns.

Fighting from house to house, the Americans still managed to press ahead towards the road that passes through Best on its way to the bridge. After about one hour, Jones's men had taken the crossroads between the main street in Best, Nieuwstraat/Hoofdstraat, and the highway towards Eindhoven. Oberleutnant Thomas Carstensen, one of the German anti-aircraft soldiers, noted at the same time that "the enemy is trying to circumvent us to the north".[189] It was Jones's 3rd Platoon doing a flanking movement northeast of the town.

Just as it appeared as though the anti-aircraft soldiers at Best would be outflanked, a motorcycle appeared on the road from the north, and 200 metres behind it came a column with twelve German lorries. It was the two German police companies that came with 300 men, and they were travelling in a column as if there were no enemies nearby. General Reinhard would later curse and lambast "the poor quality of its leadership".[190]

According to all rules of the art of war, they should have ended up in an American ambush and would have become neutralised – this was at least what Jones intended. He ordered his men, who were positioned on both sides of the road, to hold their fire until the column of vehicles had passed the crossroads. But one American soldier – at a guess, one of the recruits – seems to have lost his nerve, or Jones's orders might not have reached everyone. In any case, someone opened fire when the vehicles were about three hundred metres from the crossroads. The driver of the first German lorry saw how the motorcyclist was hit and fell, and immediately hit the brakes. The whole column stopped, and the policemen jumped into the road ditches for cover.

Soon, the battle was in full swing. The Americans now had Germans on two sides. Behind one of the lorries, a few policemen managed to disconnect a 20 mm gun that they had had in tow, and when it was put to use soon afterwards, the situation became very critical for the Americans. What had looked like a successful advance now turned into a hard battle.

Informed about what was going on, the regimental commander Michaelis gave the order to send the remainder of the 3rd Battalion marching towards Best, but, at that time, German reinforcements were also on their way from Eindhoven. One and a half kilometres east of Best, they set up firing positions, and when the American reinforcements from 3rd Battalion appeared a little further north, the Germans opened fire. The Americans hit the ground and started retreating towards the forest. There, they dug defences where they remained all night.[191] At Best, the Germans were able to reinforce their positions. Hauptmann Zeller's men soon managed to get one of the 88 mm anti-aircraft guns into firing position in Best against the remains of "H" Company and was able to force their enemy back. A quarter past eight in the evening, Leutnant Wöll from the anti-aircraft company could report, "Crossroads cleared from enemies!"[192]

Once again, Lieutenant Colonel Cole, the American battalion commander, flew into a rage over "H" Company's conduct. He could not understand how Captain Jones could let himself be drawn into a lengthy battle for Best when the task was to secure the bridge, two kilometres further south. Over the radio, he now ordered Jones to immediately send the 2nd Platoon as well as the engineer platoon and the machine gun squad straight to the bridge.

While the rest of the company was digging foxholes at the edge of the Sonsche forest east of Best, the 2nd Platoon under Lieutenant Edward Wierzbowski set off south through the forest, in parallel with the road towards Eindhoven. Instead of making a flanking movement a little further to the east, they moved in single file just a short distance into the forest, 500 metres from the road. But German combat groups that had made it into the forest were waiting in ambush. Wierzbowski and his platoon hardly got 30 metres into the woods before being fired upon. The sun had just reached the horizon and its rays filtered into the forest. The Americans found themselves in a planted forest where the fir trees stood in lines as straight as arrows with firebreaks every 30 to 35 metres. By rushing with one man at a time across these firebreaks, however, the American platoon was able to move ahead, albeit slowly. When the troopers finally arrived at the end of the little forest, Wierzbowski only had 21 men with him, plus 26 engineers.[193] At that moment, there was total darkness, and it had started raining. The Americans made it across the levee and down on the canal bank crawling.

A group of German soldiers on the other side of the canal detected the Americans when they were only 30 metres from the bridge. They threw two hand grenades straight across the canal, and then opened fire with automatic weapons, resulting in the Americans withdrawing across the levee and into the forest where they dug in.

Until three o'clock at night, the Germans bombarded the forest with mortars and artillery. "We were getting the hell shot out of us", reported one of the paratroopers, Sergeant Joe Ludwig.[194] Things were bad enough for Captain Jones to believe that the platoon had been completely wiped out, and he simply wrote it off. Thus, the advance towards Eindhoven was bogged down on this western flank.

THE 506TH PARACHUTE INFANTRY REGIMENT – TOWARDS EINDHOVEN!

The 506th Parachute Infantry Regiment under Colonel Robert F. Sink managed its mission only marginally better. It had been entrusted with the division's most important task, to take Eindhoven and establish contact with the British XXX Corps before nightfall.

Between 1312 and 1324 hrs, the 506th Parachute Infantry Regiment had made a perfect landing on the southernmost Drop Zone "C", three kilometres north of the Wilhelmina Canal. The primary target was to secure the crossings over this wide canal, which runs from west to east just north of Eindhoven's northern outskirts. The unit's command post had been set up already twenty minutes after the last drop. Within one hour, 80 percent of the force of 2,200 men had assembled. The 1st Battalion was the first one to depart. It constituted the vanguard towards Eindhoven and was in a hurry to secure the large bridge that leads Rijksweg 69 ("Club Route") across the Wilhelmina Canal at Son.*

About fifteen hundred metres west of the motorway, the 1st Battalion quickly set off southwards through the about one-kilometre wide Sonsche forest right between the Drop Zone and the Wilhelmina Canal. Latecomers were quickly organised into groups of 15 to 25 men who, led by an officer each, set off afterwards as quickly as possible. The plan was to advance to the canal one and a half kilometre west of Rijksweg 69 to carry out a flank attack against Son, while the regiment's main force attacked along the Rijksweg from the north. However, there were no plans to support "H" Company of the neighbouring regiment at Best, three and a half kilometres further to the west.

Son was one half of the "twin village" Son-Breugel, a hamlet with 3,500 inhabitants just off the northeast parts of Eindhoven. The village was divided in two by the Dommel river, which runs from south to north, and Son constituted the western part. The bridge was only defended by 4. Kompanie of the Luftwaffe's schwere Flak-Abteilung 428.[195] Two of its 88 mm anti-aircraft guns were positioned north of the canal fifteen hundred metres west of the main road.[196] When the men of the American 1st Battalion came out of the woods a few hundred metres north of the German position, it was probably exactly what these gun crews had expected; they must have observed the airdrops. With their barrels already aimed towards the edge of the forest, the Germans immediately opened fire. Hits in trees sprayed the Americans with deadly splinters. "A" company, which was at the head, immediately lost five dead and eight wounded. But the tough paratroopers would not be deterred, but stampeded right across the

---

* In certain accounts, the location is spelled "Zon", but the correct spelling is with an "s".

400-metre wide field and overpowered the gun crews, which imme-diately surrendered.

Meanwhile, the 2nd Battalion had certain difficulties with its assembly, as some of its men mistook the signals from the neighbour-ing regiment 502nd PIR for their own regiment's signals. The 502nd's Drop Zone was, after all, located just to the north of the 506th's Drop Zone "C". Moreover, the battalion commander was missing. This was unfortunate, as this battalion was to take the lead of the reg-iment's advance along Rijksweg 69, straight for Son and the great bridge. After some confusion, the battalion was assembled 30 min-utes after schedule, and could begin its advance along the road. Once the march got started, the Americans encountered no resistance on their way to Son.

During the approach in the transport plane, Colonel Sink had been observing some Panzer III and Panzer IV tanks just east of Drop Zone "C". These were the only remaining ones from the II. Abteilung of Fallschirm-Panzer-Ersatz- und Ausbildungs-Regiment "Hermann Göring", which had been withdrawn to the village of Wolfswinkel, just north of Son. Even though the tanks were outdated and being used for training, they would easily have been able to halt the lightly equipped American airborne battalion. But the demoralised Germans, who had experienced a terrible setback in Hechtel just a few days before, chose to flee rather than fight. While the infantry withdrew along the minor roads towards the east, tanks drove north towards Veghel.

The four tanks driving along the road had not even reached Sint-Oedenrode, three kilometres further up the road, before Amer-ican P-51 Mustang fighter-bombers dove down and knocked out three of them. The remaining managed to escape and made it to Veghel – only to run straight into celebrating Dutchmen and Americans in this recently liberated town! The German tank commander ordered full reverse and the tank disappeared as quickly as it had appeared.

Using commandeered bicycles and wheelbarrows for their equip-ment, the American 2nd Battalion hurried down the road to Son and entered the village. There, they were met by villagers coming out of the houses to welcome them, and an overjoyed priest handed out cigars left and right. In Nieuwstraat, which leads down towards the bridge, a German soldier on a bicycle rode in among the Americans at full speed. *"Kameraden!"* (comrades), he yelled in terror, and jumped off the bicycle with his hands above his head. At the same moment, a loud bang was heard, something whizzed past in the air, and a mighty explosion was heard, followed by a pressure wave and gravel and dust falling down over the Americans. Outside Sint-Aloysius's school for boys a little further down the road, more than 200 metres from the bridge, stood an 88 mm anti-aircraft gun from the 4. Kompanie of schwere Flak-Abteilung 428, and it was this that now opened fire on Americans and Dutchmen, who instantly took cover behind the houses on both sides of the street.

The German gun crew was either very courageous or inexperienced – it went into battle without any flank protection, so a group of Americans could quickly and unhindered dash around the corner of the street and into the parallel street of Klosterstraat. A well-aimed grenade from a Bazooka, fired by Private Thomas G. Lindsey, knocked out the '88. Leaving one of their bleeding comrades behind, the six remaining of the gun crew fled. Sergeant John F. Rice from the "D" Company arose and mowed down all of them at point blank range with his Tommy Gun.

But instead of making a quick advance through the small village, which occupies no more than a few kilometres from north to south, the Americans stopped, using their entire force to thoroughly comb through the entire town, taking two hours to do so. This, in the circumstances, exaggerated caution, would cost the Allies dearly. During this entire time, they left the bridge in the hands of the Germans, who thus had the opportunity to prepare blowing it up.

Suddenly, the entire village was rocked by a new violent explosion. The bridge had been blown up! The American battalion commander

QR14: VIDEO
Documentary about the 101st Airborne's approach, landing, and entry into Son.

Major James L. LaPrade, who was in the village together with the divisional commander Major General Taylor, realised that he had failed. He immediately set off rushing towards the canal. Two men followed suit.

The German resistance on the other side of the canal was not much better than it had been in Son. A handful of German soldiers remained passive, while American paratroopers peppered the two houses where they had taken cover. Captain Richard Winters, commander of "C" Company of LaPrade's battalion, remembers how comical it appeared as LaPrade was "tiptoeing from rock to rock, trying to make his way across the canal without getting wet. He had a forty-five-caliber pistol in one hand as he tried to maintain his balance".[197] In this place, the canal was not deeper than that you could wade across it.

But instead of immediately attacking, LaPrade and his men went into firing position just on the southern canal bank, in spite of a steady stream of American paratroopers joining them. In the meantime, engineers began to build a provisional footbridge, anchored to two smaller boats. When this bridge had been completed, the rest of the regiment started making it across, and LaPrade's "bridgehead force" – which had now grown considerably in number – started advancing along the Eindhovenscheweg towards Eindhoven.

"We moved between some houses south of the canal with very little trouble", Private Robert Wiatt recounted. "The enemy was still running",[198] Private First Class John Garrigan commented.

But on the north side of the canal, the regimental commander Colonel Sink heard from Dutch civilians that German reinforcements had arrived in Eindhoven. He conferred with Major General Taylor, and the two officers agreed to halt their advance and set up camp for

QR15: VIDEO
Authentic wartime footage showing American paratroopers making it across the Wilhelmina Canal at Son.

the night. So, the 506th Parachute Infantry Regiment halted in Bokt, the northernmost part of Eindhoven, one and a half kilometres from the demolished bridge at Son.

If the American paratroopers had continued into the city, they had probably been able to clear up the remaining ten kilometres towards Valkenswaard, and open up the road not only to the British tanks, but also to the engineers of the XXX Corps to the demolished bridge at Son. The German defence at Eindhoven was still very weak – mainly a few anti-aircraft and supply train soldiers. During the 506th PIR's march towards Bokt, it had become all too clear that the Dutch claims of German reinforcements were erroneous.

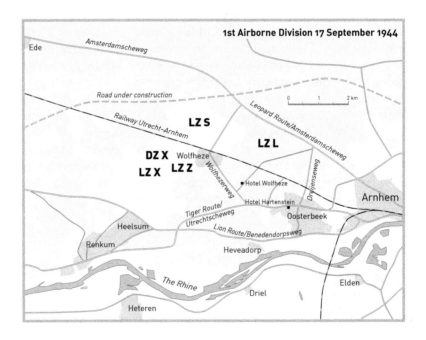

V.

"The Red Devils"
17 September 1944

"THE SKY WAS BLACK WITH AIRCRAFT"

However, Eindhoven and the 101st Airborne Division's other targets were stages on the northbound road that led to Arnhem and its large road bridge across the Rhine (which has become known as "a bridge too far"). Montgomery called the entire undertaking "the Arnhem Operation" not without reason. The task to secure this bridge had been assigned to the British 1st Airborne Division under Major-General "Roy" Urquhart. The British airborne troops, the so-called "Red Devils", were proud to have been allotted such an important mission, but many of them worried over obvious shortcomings in the plan. The largest threat to the success of the mission was that the division would be landed during the course of two days, between 12 and 15 kilometres northwest of Arnhem's road bridge, west and northwest of Oosterbeek, on the northern side of River Rhine. Only half (the 1st Parachute Brigade) of the 5,700 men who were to be landed on the first day could be used to secure the objective, while the other half (the 1st Airlanding Brigade) had to remain at the landing areas and hold them until the next day's second wave of air landings. Moreover, Arnhem was at too great a distance from the British fighter and fighter-bomber units' airfields in Belgium to allow any continuous air support.

The 426 transport planes that carried the 1st Airborne Division took the northern route. This crossed the British coast at Aldeburgh, about 100 kilometres north of London, passing the Scheldt Estuary's northern delta on its way in over the Netherlands. South of 's-Hertogenbosch, at Vught – where Generaloberst Student happened to have his command post – the route turned north and northeast, towards the Arnhem and the Nijmegen sectors respectively.

In Chapter 3, we have followed one of the non-commissioned officers in the 1st Airborne Division, Serjeant Bruce Cox, during the approach flight (see page 117), and shall now return to his depiction: "I looked out the window again, this was a sight I never wanted to forget. Down through the formation came four '109s, followed by about 20 Spitfires. Not a shot was fired at our planes. We could see the coastline now; not too much longer to go." [199]

As we have seen, Urquhart had wisely enough chosen to prioritize anti-tank weapons during the first day's air transport. Therefore, the gliders carried twenty-five 6-pound and eight 17-pound anti-tank guns. Staff Sergeant Ron P. Gibson from 16 Flight, 2 Wing, GPR, F Squadron, was the co-pilot of a Horsa glider loaded with a jeep and a 6-pound anti-aircraft gun. He recounts, "At 12.45 we passed over the dunes [on the Dutch coast] and we ran into some flak . . . black smudges of thudding smoke. Our tug pilot pulled us to starboard and into some cloud to avoid [it] . . . we could only see 12 feet of the tow rope in front of us. Sam dived the glider down and on emerging from the cloud the tug was 1000 feet below us; the rope tightened with a jerk and in twenty minutes we reached our first turning point at Hertogenbosch. Then we flew below cloud over flooded Lower Holland." [200]

The Paratroop General Kurt Student was astonished when the mighty armada suddenly came rumbling as in a parade for him. He recounted, "It was a beautiful late summer day. My H.Q. was, since a few days, at Vught (south of s'-Hertogenbosch), in a cottage. There was general quietness along the front line. Before noon, the enemy activity in the air suddenly became very great. I noticed from my house numerous formations of fighter-bombers and heard bombs falling, firing from aircraft guns and A A. artillery. About noon I was disturbed at my desk by a roaring in the air which more and more increased in intensity so that I left my study and went onto the balcony. Wherever I looked I saw aircraft: troop-transporting aeroplanes and large aeroplanes towing gliders. They flew in formation and they flew singly. It was an immense stream which passed at quite a low height near the house. I was greatly impressed by this mighty spectacle. I must confess that during these minutes I did not think of the danger of the situation, but reflected with regret the memory of my own airborne operations, and when my Chief of Staff* entered, I could not say more to him but: 'Oh, how I wish I had ever such powerful means at my disposal!' "[201]

The aircraft armada with the British paratroopers encountered nothing but very weak opposition from German Flak – a good grade for the preparatory air attacks and the fighter escort – and not one of the transport planes was shot down.

In Villa Walfriede at the Johannahoeve farm just north of Oosterbeek, west of Arnhem, SS-Sturmbannführer Josef "Sepp" Krafft, the commander of SS-Panzergrenadier-Ausbildungs- und Ersatz- Bataillon 16, had set up his command post.**

The 39-year-old Krafft was a highly experienced unit commander. He had served as company commander, and, after that, battalion commander with the SS division Das Reich during the invasions of Yugoslavia and Greece in April-May 1941, and on the Eastern Front in 1941–1942. In the summer of 1942, he was appointed security officer at SS leader Himmler's headquarters in East Prussia, Feldkommandostelle Hochwald. There, however, he was caught in the continuous intriguing around Himmler, and was transferred on 1 April 1943 to the Netherlands, where he was assigned to command the training battalion that would eventually be reorganized into SS-Panzergrenadier-Ausbildungs- und Ersatz-Bataillon 16.

This was originally a training battalion for the 12. SS-Panzer-Division "Hitler Jugend". But with the growing threat of an Allied landing on the Dutch coast, all SS training battalions in the Netherlands were also tasked to participate in the coastal defences in the spring of 1944. In June 1944, SS-Gruppenführer Karl Demelhuber, the commander of the Waffen-SS in the Netherlands, had between 8,000 and 10,000 men from such SS training battalions for the coastal defences in the Netherlands.[202]

---

* Oberst Walter Reinhard, who had assumed the position as chief of staff of the 1. Fallschirmarmee only two days earlier.

** This beautiful villa with its towers was razed during the fighting in September 1944. Today, a rest home for elderly missionaries from St. Joseph's Society for Foreign Missions instead occupies the site.

German soldiers at the railway station in 's-Hertogenbosch, waiting to be sent into combat.

On 3 September 1944, the same day as the Germans were driven out of the Belgian capital, the German Military Commander for the Netherlands, General Friedrich Christiansen, was ordered to hastily organise a rear defence line at the river Waal. Christiansen gave Generalleutnant Hans von Tettau, the Military Training Commander in the Netherlands (Führungs- und Ausbildungsstab Niederlande), the task of assembling the coastal defence, training, and guard units that were available into a new, improvised Division Tettau (also known as Stab von Tettau). Using units that were largely second-rate quality, von Tettau had to establish a 60-kilometre defence line no later than 5 September. Krafft's battalion was one of these units, but was held in reserve in the Oosterbeek area north of the Rhine. There, Krafft received an order to prepare to attack an Allied air landing.[203] The Germans at Arnhem were thus intent on meeting that very kind of landing – which, by the way, was also true for the 9. SS-Panzer-Division.

On this 17 September 1944, Krafft had just sat down at the table for lunch, when the calm was suddenly disturbed by the rumble from a large number of aircraft engines. Krafft went out into the yard and saw a formation of bombers that started to drop bombs over Arnhem. However, he did not let himself be disturbed by the bomb attacks over in the east, but went inside again and ate his meal, a large pork chop, and pudding for dessert. He had barely finished his meal before several fast-flying aircraft thundered by above the roof with such a roar that it rattled the china. It was Allied fighter-bombers. The German Flak now joined the fray.

From these fighter-bombers, the experienced Krafft drew the conclusion that it was probably a matter of such a landing that he had been given explicit orders to prepare for. His SS battalion had three companies at its disposal (2., 4., and 9.), plus a Stammkompanie in Arnhem (7. Kp), as well as a staff platoon, and one section each of anti-tank, flame-thrower, heavy mortar, and light mortar, plus two reconnaissance sections each, in total 13 officers, 73 non-commissioned officers, and 349 men.[204]

When the landing began, the 2. Kompanie was on training in the forests at Wolfheze, that is, just one and a half kilometres east of the

British landing zones. The 4. Kompanie and its staff was in Oosterbeek with the task to defend Field Marshal Model's headquarters.*

The 9. Kompanie was in Arnhem, a few kilometres east of Oosterbeek. Krafft immediately put his battalion on full alert and ordered the 9. Kompanie to prepare to move to Oosterbeek.

The 1st Airborne Division's Pathfinders – paratroopers whose task it was to mark the landing areas – opened the entire Operation "Market" as they touched down at 1240 hrs. They took fifteen German soldiers captive and immediately began marking the landing areas.

Just before 1300 hrs, the main formation of transport aircraft arrived over Landing Zone "S" (LZ "S") just northwest of Wolfheze – 134 machines with as many Horsa gliders. The first ones to touch ground belonged to No. 2 Wing. Staff Sergeant Ron Gibson, co-pilot of a Horsa, described the landing at LZ "S", "As we approached the landing zone at Arnhem we could see some big fires blazing in the town and along the railway line on one edge of the ploughed field where we had to land. We released from . . . 3000 ft and had to weave our way through a host of gliders that all seemed to aim for the same point. We touched down in a ploughed field on the side of a pine wood."

From Villa Walfriede, Krafft saw the gliders. One of his soldiers, SS-Sturmmann Karl-Hans Bangard, remembers, "The sky was black with aircraft. Some of us tried to count them, but it was impossible. Our commander, SS-Sturmbannführer Krafft, was standing in the yard. Calmly and soberly, he gave the command: 'Battalion! Get ready to march!'"[205]

Krafft ordered the commander of 2. Kompanie, SS-Hauptsturmführer Hans-Heinrich Köhnken, to attack the landing zone without delay. Krafft knew that the only possibility to hold your own against an airborne force that was superior in numbers was to attack without

QR16: VIDEO
0:00–0:40 shows footage shot secretly by Mrs. Clous in Oosterbeek of German vehicle columns passing through Oosterbeek, no later than 17 September 1944.

* This was situated at Hotel Tafelberg, a couple of hundred meters from Hotel Hartenstein, where the mess was located.

delay immediately after the landing.[206] "The last items were packed feverishly, steel helmets on, belts buckled up, rifle in hand, and out", Bangard recounted.[207]

After that, Krafft instructed his two other companies to set off by motor vehicles as quickly as they could to Hotel Wolfheze, a luxurious hotel 800 metres southeast of Wolfheze, where Köhnken had set up his temporary command post.* He went to this hotel himself, too, to lead the battle in person.

It has often been said that without this lightning-speed action by one single individual on the German side, Operation "Market Garden" could have taken a completely different course of events. But this is, to put it mildly, a statement that needs qualifying. SS-Sturmbannführer Krafft himself had a good portion of combat experience. But his men were mostly recruits that had not yet been fully trained, to whom were added officers and non-commissioned officers, who in many cases had spent many months in hospitals and in convalescence after being badly injured in combat, and who probably also were more or less seriously traumatised. Köhnken, the commander of 2. Kompanie, for instance, had been injured both in his left leg and left arm.[208] The commander of 9. Kompanie, Obersturmbannführer Günther Leiteritz, was a broken

Hotel Wolfheze before the war.

* Today, it is called Hotel Bilderberg, after the so-called "Bilderberg Group" held its inaugural meeting there in May 1954.

young man who had been kicked out of the 12. SS-Panzer-Division for corruption, theft, and black-marketeering, and who had recently been sentenced to five years in prison, to be served after the war.

In reality, not much became of the attack against the landing zone, in spite of 2. Kompanie with 132 men, equipped with heavy machine guns, training in the forest and in the fields east of Wolfheze, just next to the gliders' Landing Zone "S". A machine gun section at the railway crossing at Wolfheze, just a little over one hundred metres from Landing Zone "S", shot at the gliders when they came in to land. Lieutenant Alan Green remembers how a volley of bullets slammed into the Horsa that he was onboard. Private Ron Stripp was hit by a bullet in one arm, but no one else was injured. The German machine gunners withdrew after only a few minutes. The purported reason was that it was "heavily inferior in numbers" – which certainly was not uncommon for German units at this time. Normally, a German MG 42-type heavy machine gun – a so-called "bone saw" with a rate of fire at 1,200 rounds per minute and an efficient range at up to 2,000 metres – could pin down large enemy forces, however, providing that it was manned by experienced soldiers with a high combat morale.

It took fifty minutes to land all of the gliders in the field north of the Arnhem-Utrecht railway. During that time, the inevitable chaos that characterises even the most successful landing prevaled. Every twenty seconds, a new glider came thudding down onto the little field, which was no more than 900 x 1,000 metres. Several gliders slammed into others that had just landed, some overturned upon touching ground. Dazed and bewildered soldiers got out as good as they could and started unloading jeeps, guns, and all other equipment. If SS-Hauptsturmführer Köhnken's 130-strong company had attacked straight into this chaos, as Krafft had ordered, it would have cost the British very dearly. Instead, Köhnken led his men westwards, on the south side of the railway – as if he had known that the next landing would take place there.[209]

After the landing at LZ "S", 143 transport aircraft (out of 167 that took off) followed, releasing 143 gliders, including some of the great Hamilcars, over landing zone LZ "Z", the fields belonging to the Jonkershoeve far on the south side of the railway. Here, Gordon Walker, a photographer from AFPU, was onboard one of the first gliders. He quickly jumped out straight after the landing and started filming the incoming gliders. His film bears clear witness to the initial passivity of the SS troops.*

When the last glider had touched down, the 1st Airlanding Brigade under Brigadier Philip Hicks had been landed with a total of about 2,000 men and equipment including, amongst other things, six 17-pound guns, ten 4-ton Bren Carrier-type armoured personnel carriers, and several jeeps armed with Vickers "K" machine guns. The divisional commander Urquhart had arrived as well, with one of the last gliders.

Slowly but steadily, the Germans were losing momentum. At 1355 hrs, a new wave of Dakota planes rumbled in, dropping 2,280 paratroopers from the 1st Parachute Brigade under Brigadier Gerald Lathbury. Serjeant Bruce Cox recalled, "Then all of a sudden, 'Stand up. Hook up. Check lines and equipment.' My legs were wobbling, Must be all this bloody weight; full G.1098 fighting gear. Looking outside I could see green fields. The engine's revs died down. 'Stand to the door.' Red was on. 'Green on. GO.' Static line straps were banging. Move it, boys, move it! Suddenly I am gone, and automatically start checking my gear and looking for smoke – that's the place I have to head towards.

* QR 17: VIDEO
Gordon Walker's film.

QR18: VIDEO
00:00–5:33: Authentic wartime footage of the approach by the 1st Abn Div and the landing.

I can hear the crack of small arms. The ground is coming up, I assume landing position and remember to roll, keeping low. Another guy lands nearby; he looks scared, but gives the thumbs up and we both start moving. A cannister crashes to the ground – chute didn't deploy. Let's get out of this DZ, it could be dangerous!" [210]

Private Stephen George Morgan from 2nd Battalion of the 1st Parachute Brigade made his second jump ever here from a Dakota.*

He remembers, "Weighing me down were not only my Lee Enfield No. 4 rifle but my ration packs, 2 Hawkins anti-tank mines and three sealed boxes containing 250 rounds each for our Vickers machine gun. After landing I released my parachute and emptied my kitbag of three boxes of machine gun ammunition and two Hawkins anti-tank mines. A German reconnaissance vehicle appeared with a small armoured car and an open topped lorry full of soldiers. As I was about a hundred yards behind, I was not part of the fight but saw all the German soldiers either killed or captured."

RAPID GERMAN REACTION

At around one o'clock in the afternoon of 17 September 1944, Generalfeldmarschall Walter Model had sat down to dinner at the Hotel Hartenstein in central Oosterbeek – the little town that is about halfway between Arnhem and the British paratroopers' landing zones at Wolfheze. Perchance it occurred to him that it was one month to the day that he had been named by Hitler both as commander of the German Heeresgruppe B (after, until then, having commanded Heeresgruppe Mitte on the Eastern Front) and been awarded the Diamonds for the Knight's Cross with Oak Leaves and Swords – the highest

* QR19: VIDEO
The veteran Stephen George Morgan
recounts the landing.

award for valour of the Third Reich. It had been instituted solely for the great fighter pilot Werner Mölders when he, as the first pilot in aviation history, had reached 100 air victories in July 1941. When Model received the Diamonds, only fourteen men, apart from Mölders and himself, had received this coveted decoration. Not even the Supreme Commander in the West, the declared genius Generalfeldmarschall von Rundstedt, had it.

We do not know what Model was thinking of when he sat down to dinner, but in any case, soon other things would occupy his mind. By around two o'clock, a typist reported, announcing that Model's first general staff officer, Oberst Hans-Georg von Tempelhoff, had an urgent call from the headquarters.

General Friedrich Christiansen, the Wehrmachtbefehlshaber Niederlande, had been dining with his chief of staff, Generalleutnant Heinz-Hellmuth von Wühlisch, in Crailo, near Amsterdam, when they heard a mighty rumble of engines from the south. They immediately got in touch with the HQ, which reported that several hundreds of transport aircraft had flown in over the Scheldt Estuary on an eastbound course, probably towards Arnhem. Von Wühlisch advised against sending any troops there; he believed Arnhem to be "lost", but Christiansen objected that he was much too afraid of Hitler, who would hardly appreciate such a defeatist attitude.[211] The two terrified men asked themselves what should be done, and agreed to call Model. At Hotel Tafelberg, Model's headquarters, the response was that the Generalfeldmarschall was away for lunch at Hotel Hartenstein, where the mess was located, but they were put through to Generalleutnant Hans Krebs, Model's chief of staff.*

Krebs was very nervous – von Wühlich got the impression that he was hardly listening to what he had to say – and just said, "We're leaving immediately!"[212]

---

* Some confusion has occurred in the historiography since both Krebs and von Tempelhoff were called Ia, which actually means chief of staff. But von Tempelhoff was the First Chief of Staff (Erste Generalstabsoffizier), subordinate to the chief of staff, and had a more administrative function. Cornelius Ryan calls Krebs Chief of Staff and von Tempelhoff Operational Chief of Staff, which only adds to the confusion as the chief of staff is the operational chief of the staff. Krebs, Model's old chief of staff in Heeresgruppe Mitte, had succeeded Generalleutnant Hans Spiedel as Heeresgruppe B's chief of staff, as the latter was arrested on 7 September 1944 for participating in the 20 July assault on Hitler.

Someone called Hotel Hartenstein and asked to speak to von Tempelhoff urgently regarding a message from Christiansen. Von Tempelhoff had hardly hung up after receiving the ominous message before a series of large bomb explosions blew out the windows so that shattered glass flew around the room. Everyone dived for cover under the table, and then ran out into the yard, where they saw how the sky seemed to be absolutely filled with aircraft. Von Tempelhoff came running down the stone stairs, shouting to make himself heard over the aircraft engines, "What a mess! One or two divisions of paratroopers are over us!" Model quickly made his decision, "Everybody out! Rendezvous Terborg!" he ordered. With Model's passenger car, they drove past Hotel Tafelberg, where they came across a frightened Krebs outside, picking him up and then driving off at full speed. Terborg, 45 kilometres further to the east, was the site of the Army Group's logistics headquarters.

The rest of the staff stayed behind and packed all of their material as carefully as quickly – not a single document seems to have been lost – before following suit along the road that went through Arnhem and further eastwards.*

En route into Arnhem, Model met a discouraging sight – German soldiers who were fleeing in absolutely chaotic scenes to get out of town. A Dutch police report reads, "The German troops packed rapidly and moved in some panic (blew up houses before leaving). They did not move in battle order but in considerable confusion."[213] SS-Rottenführer Horst Jupe from the signals unit of 9. SS-Panzer-Division recounted, "Allied soldiers hovering by parachute in mid-air were being shot at. Our accommodation (the school or the gymnasium at the edge of the forest) was heavily bombed and it resulted in large losses of people. I left the town area with my two comrades shortly afterwards. During the following battles, I was no longer in town."[214]

---

* According to Cornelius Ryan's colourful, and, by now classic description – which seems to draw support from the Dutch historian Theo Boeree's notes – Model allegedly cried out in horror "They are coming for me" and dashed out into the yard in panic, where he dropped his suitcase, with the consequence that it flew open. In some propagated versions, even Model's underpants allegedly flew out into the yard by that. However, there is no evidence that this was the way it happened. Several details in Boeree's and Ryan's account of these minutes at Hotel Hartenstein differ from Walter Görlitz's Model biography (*Model*, pp. 207–208), which is based, amongst other things, on interviews with von Tempelhoff.

Model ordered the driver to take the route past the City Commandant's headquarters in the northern part of Arnhem. There, he stopped by, sending a message to General Friedrich Kussin, the field commander at Arnhem, that the enemy was carrying out a landing west of Oosterbeek, and ordered Kussin to inform Hitler's Führer Headquarters. After that, he set off for Terborg, in order to continue towards the HQ of the II. SS-Panzerkorps at Doetinchem, a few kilometres away. Kussin, on the other hand, followed Model's instructions, and ordered his driver, Gefreiter Josef Willeke, to drive him to the command post of the German unit at Oosterbeek, SS-Panzergrenadier-Ausbildungs- und Ersatz-Bataillon 16 under Sepp Krafft. By then, the paratroopers and the gliders had already touched down about five kilometres away to the west.

SS-Obergruppenführer Hanns Albin Rauter, the Senior SS and Police Commander in the Netherlands, reacted with quick resolve. He told von Wühlisch over the telephone, "Our front is now at Arnhem. I want every man who is still ready to fight to be there. My reserves have already been deployed!" [215]

"Mein Bataillon greift an!" – My battalion is attacking! – Sepp Krafft reported to his commander, Generalleutnant von Tettau. The latter had, only two weeks earlier, begun assembling the improvised "Division Tettau" out of hastily thrown-together units in the rear.[216] But the quality of most of these units left a lot to be desired, and Krafft's training battalion was no exception. Instead of striking against the landing zones when they were at their most vulnerable, during or just after the landing – which was what Krafft intended – the men of the 2. Kompanie remained standing by. The arrival of the 4. Kompanie, which increased Krafft's force at the "front" to about 300 men, did not improve the possibilities to act offensively. By that time, it was already three o'clock in the afternoon, and the 1st Airborne Division had landed 5,191 men.[217]

In that situation, Krafft had no other choice than to organise his force defensively, between one and two kilometres east of the landing zones. At a width of more than two kilometres in the forest between the Arnhem-Utrecht railway to the north and the main road between the two towns, the Utrechtscheweg, to the south – with Hotel Wolfheze in the middle – the SS men lay waiting for the British to arrive.*

BRITISH DELAY

On the British side, the situation was the exact opposite. The 1st Parachute Brigade, which was to carry out the advance towards the bridges in Arnhem, were the "the élite of a crack division", as military historian Geoffrey Powell put it.[218] The tough paratroopers, "The Red Devils", as they proudly called themselves, were eager to get going, and would doubtlessly have been able to sweep away all German resistance in short time if they had been allowed to attack at once. But in spite of it being more than an hour since the paratroopers had touched ground at Drop Zone "X" west of Wolfheze, and the assembling had been unexpectedly quick, there was no marching order.

Here, it was Urquhart, the newly appointed commander of the 1st Airborne Division, who delayed the attack. On the other side of the Arnhem-Utrecht railway, the gliders had landed most of the 1st Airlanding Brigade, assigned to hold the landing zones until the second wave of paratroopers would arrive the following day. With the jeeps that the gliders carried, the brigade's reconnaissance company, the 1st Airborne Reconnaissance Squadron under Major Freddie Gough, was to set off first of all towards the bridge in Arnhem to try to take it through a swift coup. However, it turned out that the radio liaison did not work.

The problem with the wireless radio equipment in Arnhem is quite well-known. The difficulties were due to a number of factors: the for-

QR2: VIDEO
12:20: The German Veterans Werner Krüger and Karl Heinz Henschel, both of the 9. SS-Pz-Div., recount 17 Sept in Arnhem (in German and Dutch).

ested and partly rolling ground, tall buildings in Arnhem, the sandy ground, and interference from German radio stations. In addition, the crystals in much of the landed radio equipment were damaged during the landing, and reserve crystals dropped by parachute on 18 and 19 September largely ended up with the enemy.[219] This was the first major setback, and it would worsen the situation considerably during the following days.

In order to establish a connection, Urquhart decided to personally go with one of the jeeps that the gliders had brought to Landing Zone "Z" next to Drop Zone "X" to find Brigadier Hicks, the commander of the 1st Airlanding Brigade. Perhaps Urquhart was also delayed by feeling ill – in spite of being the commander of an airborne division, he suffered from airsickness!

So, while Urquhart was bumping along in his jeep across the railway tracks, Brigadier Lathbury, the commander of the Parachute Brigade, had to wait for the divisional commander's return before giving marching orders. Lieutenant "Tsapy" Britneff, intelligence officer of the brigade's 1st Battalion, was furious that "we had to hang around for over an hour for Brigade's permission to move off".[220]

The first one to pay the price for this was WS/Lieutenant "Gerry" (Edgar Gerald) Wise, the 23-year-old intelligence officer in 9th Airborne Field Company Royal Engineers, which had been landed at LZ "Z". His company commander, Major Jack C. Winchester, had selected Hotel Wolfheze as his command post on beforehand, and sent a few men led by Wise as early as around two o'clock to reconnoitre towards the hotel. Wise was a veteran of North Africa and of the landings in Sicily and at Taranto in 1943. But now, he plunged straight into fire from a German machine gun hidden in a shrubbery at the crossroads 200 metres north of the hotel. Wise fell to the ground, wounded in both legs, his left arm, and his face.[221] He survived only by his men managing to take him to security, in spite of the German machine gun, and then carrying him back to the landing zone.*

---

* For Wise, participation in "Market Garden" ended as annoyingly as it had begun. He spent the rest of the operation among the growing number of wounded, and was captured by the Germans when they took over Oosterbeek on 26 September 1944. Having recovered from his injuries, he managed to escape from captivity, but was soon caught again. However, he did survive the war, and was promoted to Major.

Major Winchester ordered 30 men to take the hotel. They too were halted by German machine gun fire. WS/Lieutenant James Steel then set off on a motorcycle to try to find a way around the German position. Later, his motorcycle was found, perforated with bullet holes. Only after the war did Major Winchester learn that Steel had been wounded and taken prisoner.

Meanwhile, the first reconnaissance jeep with four men led by Lieutenant Peter Bucknall from the reconnaissance unit's "C" Troop set off. It was followed a few moments later by a second jeep with the 20-year-old Serjeant Thomas McGregor and another four men.

Bucknall turned, at full speed, to the right into the road to Wolfheze. Before the railway crossing, he made a short reconnaissance stop. There, he ordered Trooper Arthur Barlow to alight, and await the second jeep to show the way – which would eventually save Barlow's life. Then, Bucknall turned to the left into the Johannahoeveweg, a narrow mud road that runs in parallel with the railway on its northern side. A littler further on, at a culvert underneath the railway embankment, a reserve platoon under SS-Hauptscharführer Josef Wiegand that Krafft employed separately from the companies had taken up positions.

"*Feuer!*" The British could hardly have discerned the German command word, because at the next moment, the silence was torn apart by blasts of shots. At that moment, the second jeep came driving, ending up in the middle of the hail of bullets. While the driver, Trooper Reg Hasler, stepped on the brakes, Trooper Richard Minns was hit, falling off the vehicle, wounded.

All others bolted off the jeep. Minns, Hasler, and another man crawled in underneath it, McGregor dived head first into the shallow ditch, where he desperately tried to squeeze himself down, and Arthur Barlow and another man took cover behind some oak trees. Barlow produced his gun, and fired a few shots in the dark by aiming his weapon around the edge of the tree. Immediately, a whole series of German machine gun bullets clattered into the oak and tore off large chunks of the tree. When he looked to the side, Barlow saw how McGregor cautiously raised himself up on his hands from the ditch, probably to try to get to a position that offered better cover. "He fell flat on his face and died without making a sound", Barlow remembered.

During a pause in the firing, Barlow dared to peek out. Further ahead, he could see Germans moving quickly between the trees, but he did not dare to fire again, as those who were holding the Brits down with their fire were hidden behind bushes.

Reinforcements arrived in the shape of yet another reconnaissance group under Lieutenant Ralph C. Foulkes, but this too was forced to take cover from the German fire. After a while, Foulkes, the senior officer on site, realised the futility of the situation and ordered forward smoke grenades. Covered by the smoke, his group retreated. The next day, when a larger British forced arrived on the scene, which the Germans had been driven away from by then, they made a shocking discovery about what had happened to Peter Bucknall and the four men that he had had in his jeep when it had got into the ambush. Serjeant David Christie of the "C" Troop recounted, "They were laid in single file, about one yard between each man. None of them was wearing any equipment, nor had they any weapons. All had about ten bullet holes in the back or in the neck. We later found their equipment on the jeep. From this, it was obvious that the Germans had taken them prisoner and then shot everyone in cold blood. Lieutenant Bucknall had his face burned right off. I could recognize him by the blue polo-necked sweater he had been wearing and by his identity discs."[222] No-one could have been more shaken than Arthur Barlow, who had been ordered off of Bucknall's jeep only minutes before the ambush.*

THE ADVANCE COMMENCES

Urquhart, the divisional commander, was still in the glider brigade's area, when he was reached by the information about the German ambush against the reconnaissance patrol. Now, a farcical search began. Urquhart quickly wanted to get hold of the commander of the 1st Airborne Reconnaissance Squadron, Major Freddie Gough, so as to order him to redirect the rest of his reconnaissance unit, but did not know where he was. Gough himself had set off for the landing

---

* Today, Bucknall and the four men in his jeep, as well as McGregor, are resting next to each other in the Oosterbeek war cemetery, Plot 16, Row B, Graves 5 through 10.

zone of the parachute brigade in order to look for Urquhart. At the same moment that Urquhart set off for his command post in the parachute brigade's landing zone, Gough left it to continue his search for Urquhart. Unbeknownst to this, the two jeeps passed each other by a few hundred metres. Gough continued driving around, looking for Urquhart, and, at one moment, he was even close to driving straight into one of the Germans' positions – had he not been warned by a major at the last moment.

Back at his command post, Urquhart cursed the non-functional radio equipment. But now, at least the paratroopers' advance could get started. According to the plan, they split up across three roads. The 1st Para Battalion under Lieutenant-Colonel David Dobie went a bit to the north to circumvent the Germans at Johannahoeveweg, and then took the motorway that runs to Arnhem from the northwest. This was the so-called "Leopard Route".

The 2nd and 3rd Para Battalions marched towards the south across the fields and into the little village of Heelsum. There, they split up, so that the 2nd Battalion under Lieutenant-Colonel John Frost took the southern "Lion Route" to the east, while the 3rd Battalion under Lieutenant-Colonel John Fitch took the main route, the Utrechtscheweg, eastwards towards Oosterbeek and Arnhem, the "Tiger Route".

This plan has been called a tactical mistake; it has been proposed that it would have been better to concentrate the forces to one single road. But by moving forward two thirds of the paratrooper brigade on the only two roads that lead through Oosterbeek towards Arnhem, the largest concentration of forces was actually achieved; otherwise, nearly two thousand paratroopers would have had to march in a single, drawn-out column. Moreover, the southern "Lion Route" converged with the "Tiger Route" in western Arnhem, where the Utrechtscheweg turned in order to then continue eastwards just by the river Rhine. The 1st Para Battalion was to secure the area northwest of Arnhem, where the 52nd (Lowland) Division according to the plans would be flown in on 19 September.

On the German side, Krafft had detailed 2. Kompanie to hold the Utrechtscheweg just at the crossroads where it meets the Wolfhezer

Weg, which comes from the north. As far as can be judged, the soldiers of 2. Kompanie fled as soon as the first paratroopers from the 3rd Battalion appeared on the road, Lieutenant James Cleminson and the men of his No. 5 Platoon, "B" Company. Even if Krafft describes it as if 2. Kompanie was driven away after a hard skirmish that had cost the British dearly, the British report shows that no fighting at all took place in that situation – even though the Germans had ample opportunity to group for an ambush. Cleminson himself recounts what things looked like on the "Tiger Route"/Utrechtscheweg, "The first problem that I realised was that on both sides of this road was some fairly high wire fences. And I realised that if we ran into trouble we were going to have a very narrow front to organise ourselves on and we wouldn't be able to do anything about it." Because of this, the 3rd Battalion found itself extended along 1,000 metres of the road, which meant that even a small force of determined German soldiers would have been able to stop it and cause it heavy losses – especially if they had attacked the flank.

Cleminson's men had barely reached the crossroads before a Citroën 11CV Traction Avant-type private car, painted in a speckled yellow and green camouflage pattern, came driving at full speed from the Wolfhezer Weg. It was General Friedrich Kussin, the city commander at Arnhem, who was on his way from Krafft's command post at Hotel Wolfheze.

Kussin had visited Krafft at a quarter past five in the afternoon to inform himself of the situation. Krafft gave him a quick situation report to the extent of what he knew, and after that, Kussin ordered his driver to take him back to Arnhem. Krafft tried to dissuade him from this, since he did not know how far the enemy had made it, but Kussin persisted. "I must get back to Arnhem!" he said.[223]

As Kussin's car thundered ahead south on the narrow Wolfhezer Weg that meanders on towards the Utrechtscheweg, the men in Cleminson's platoon were marching along the Utrechtscheweg. Both sides were equally surprised as the Citroën rumbled straight in among the paratroopers at the crossroads. The paratroopers immediately opened fire with their Sten submachine guns. The car came to a halt, completely peppered to pieces with bullets. But the paratroopers were overcome with murderous instinct. Hooting and shouting, they continued shooting into the increasingly perforated wreck. Cleminson had to yell at them for quite some time before they came to their senses and stopped shooting.

Then, the advance continued. It was only after the war that Cleminson found out that he and his men had killed the city commander of Arnhem. A film team from the Army Film and Photograph Unit, which was following them, filmed and photographed the car wreck with the dead Germans.*

Kussin had met his ultimate fate with only a few minutes' margin. Shortly afterwards, at 1700 hrs, the 3rd Battalion encountered what, according to the unit's War Diary, was the first resistance in the shape of infantry and two armoured vehicles. It was the advance guard of Krafft's 9. Kompanie under SS-Obersturmbannführer Günther Leiteritz that had arrived from Arnhem, reinforced by one self-propelled anti-aircraft gun and one 3.7 cm tank destroyer.[224] But neither would this cause the thick-skinned paratroopers any major difficulties.

* Apart from General Kussin and the driver, Gefreiter Josef Willeke, it was Kussin's interpreter, the Arnhem-born Unteroffizier Max Koester, and Unteroffizier Willi Haupt. They were later buried by the Germans at the German "Heroes' Cemetery" Zypendaal at Arnhem, but today, they are resting in the German military graveyard in Ysselsteyn in the Netherlands. Kussin's grave is No. 143 in Row 6, Sector BL.

GERMAN MOBILISATION

The German countermeasures, however, materialised at a considerably higher speed than the operations on the British side. 9. SS-Panzer-Division's SS-Hauptsturmführer Klaus von Allwörden, commander of the anti-tank battalion SS-Panzerjäger-Abteilung 9, set off already before the paratroopers had started being dropped, with a motorcycle with a sidecar from Apeldoorn, about fifteen kilometres north of Arnhem, towards the area where the gliders had been observed.

40 kilometres east of Arnhem is the small village of Doetinchem. Outside the village, the Slangenburg castle is towering above a surrounding moat. There, SS-Obergruppenführer Wilhelm Bittrich, the commander of II. SS-Panzerkorps, had set up his headquarters. The 50-year-old Willi Bittrich, a well-known profile because of his bald head and friendly face, was perhaps the most prominent among all higher officers within the Waffen-SS. He had been oriented about the Allied landings as soon as they had begun, and immediately put the headquarters at both of the Panzer divisions of II SS-Panzerkorps, 9. SS-Panzer-Division "Hohenstaufen", and 10. SS-Panzer-Division "Frundsberg" on alert.

"Hohenstafuen's" acting divisional commander, SS-Obersturmbannführer Walter Harzer, was at the air base at Deelen (which had recently been evacuated by the Luftwaffe), about five kilometres north of Arnhem.[225] There, he had just awarded the commander of the reconnaissance battalion, SS-Hauptsturmführer Viktor Gräbner*, the Knight's Cross, and the commander of the artillery regiment, SS-Sturmbannführer Ludwig Spindler, the German Cross in Gold.

Harzer recounted, "As the troops approached the shelters and the officers went with me to the casino for a meal, we all saw the first British parachutes above Arnhem in the air. However, there was nothing there to indicate any major action". It must be assumed that it was the British Pathfinders that the German officers had seen. Harzer continues, "We sat down calmly to eat. During the meal, the first reports

---

* In certain literature erroneously called Paul Gräbner, but his full name was Viktor Eberhard Gräbner.

came by telephone from the division's staff headquarters in Beek-bergen."[226]

Spindler was ordered to immediately go to western Arnhem to organise a Kampfgruppe with the purpose of attacking the landed troops there, but he did not have much in terms of troops for this task. Since there was no radio connection between the staff of the 9. SS-Panzer-Division and Division Tettau, Harzer knew nothing about Kampfgruppe Krafft.[227] Moreover, he had been oriented that Gräbner's armoured vehicles had had their tracks removed and stood on a train that was about to take them to Germany. "Now what will you do with your vehicles?" he asked Gräbner. The short (170 cm) SS-Hauptsturmführer Gräbner quickly telephoned his engineer unit and then he was able to report, "*Kamerad**, they will be ready in three hours!"[228]

On 3 September, his battalion had had at its disposal 28 armoured half-tracks, two of which were towing vehicles and 26 of which were anti-tank guns (out of which five had one 20 mm anti-aircraft gun each, one had a 37 mm anti-tank gun, three had one 75 mm anti-tank gun each, and the rest had 7.92 mm machine guns) and two eight-wheel Sd.Kfz.234 Pumas (with one 5 cm gun in a revolving turret and one machine gun) as well as yet a number of transportation vehicles on wheels. Gräbner himself was leading with a captured British Humber reconnaissance car.[229] It remains unclear how many of these that remained on 17 September.

"After that, I immediately went back to the headquarters at Beek-bergen, in order to take further measures there to supervise the alerting of the division", Harzer recounted. "The warning orders for the alerting had already been given by the staff officers of the division."[230] Many of the soldiers of the 9. SS-Panzer-Division were at a small railway station close to Enschede on the German border, waiting for a train that would take them to Germany, when the order suddenly reached them, "The English are parachuting over Arnhem. Every man must immediately get to the landing area, how and with what doesn't mean shit!"[231] One of the SS soldiers recounts, "Guys from the neigh-

---

* Within the SS, it was forbidden to use the more conservative armed forces' rule of addressing superiors with "Herr"; instead, the use of "Kamerad" (comrade) was decreed.

The alarm companies of the 9. SS-Panzer-Division on 17 September 1944

The division's HQ company: about 120 men

SS-Feldgendarmerie-Kompanie: One platoon, 60 men

SS-Panzer-Regiment 9: One company with tank crews without tanks as infantry, one baggage train company

SS-Panzergrenadier-Regiment 19: Two companies without heavy weapons

SS-Panzergrenadier-Regiment 20: Two companies without heavy weapons

SS-Panzer-Artillerie-Regiment 9: Two companies of infantry without guns

SS-Panzer-Aufklärungs-Abteilung 9: Three companies, 400 men, some 20 armoured vehicles

SS-Panzerjäger-Abteilung 9: One company, 120 men without guns

SS-Flak-Abteilung 9: One company with 4 x 20 mm anti-aircraft guns, the rest, infantry

SS-Pionier-Abteilung 9: One company, 60 men

SS-Nachrichten-Abteilung 9: One company with 80 men for radio communications

Nachschubtruppen 9: One transport company (motorised)

SS-Wirtschafts-Bataillon 9: One company with 70 men as infantry, the rest, catering battalion

SS-Sanitäts-Abteilung 9: Two medical companies

Source: Walter Harzer, Combat Report. Gelders Archief. Document 2171. Collectie Boeree. 1. De Slag om Arnhem. 1.3. De Duitsers. Rapport van Harzer, p. 52.

bouring platoon are swishing past us in two commandeered cars. Their whole faces are grinning. We're running to the first best bicycles and setting off after them. My Unterscharführer from Cologne, who always has a joke at hand, is roaring past us on an antiquated motorcycle, calling out as he went past, *'Das neue Wunderwaff!'* – The new wonder weapon!"[232]

As we have seen previously (page 88), Model had ordered on 10 September the 9. and 10. SS-Panzer-Divisions to form so-called "alarm companies", that were to be sent quickly into battle in crisis situations. At four o'clock in the afternoon, an order came from Bittrich that Harzer's division was to go towards Nijmegen.[233] This split up the 9. SS-Panzer-Division, as Spindler had already marched off towards western Arnhem, but when Gräbner had had his vehicles unloaded off the railway cars, they set off towards Nijmegen.

10. SS-Panzer-Division "Frundsberg", with its headquarters located at Ruurlo, 35 kilometres northeast of Arnhem, was spread out along 30 kilometres between Dieren, ten kilometres northeast of Arnhem, and the area around Ruurlo. Not only did it have a major shortage of officers – some companies were led by non-commissioned officers – but the divisional commander, SS-Brigadeführer Heinz Harmel, had gone to Bad Saarow in Germany only the previous day to plan the reorganisation of the badly battered unit. In addition, his second in command, SS-Obersturmbannführer Otto Paetsch, the commander of the Panzer regiment, was temporarily absent when the British landing took place. Meanwhile, one of the platoons from 10. SS-Panzer-Division's armoured reconnaissance battalions, which had been seconded for the defence of the artillery at the front near "Joe's Bridge", was completely wiped out by the British tanks.[234] At around half past one in the afternoon on this 17 September, the division's chief of staff, SS-Haupsturmbannführer Wilhelm Büthe, received an order by telephone from the corps commander Bittrich to put the division on high alert.

At four o'clock in the afternoon, Bittrich returned and ordered 10. SS-Panzer-Division to secure the bridges across the Rhine at Arnhem and Oosterbeek. Büthe urgently called SS-Sturmbannführer Hans-Georg Sonnenstuhl, who led the division's SS-Panzer-Artillerie-Regiment 10. Sonnenstuhl had recently crossed the road bridge at Arnhem from the south on his way to his new command post at Zutphen, 40 kilometres northeast of the town. "Enemy parachutists have landed in Arnhem, the commander is still in Berlin at the SS headquarters, and Obersturmbannführer Paetsch cannot be reached anywhere!" Blüthe yelled into the receiver, "Therefore, as the highest-ranking officer, you must take command of our Arnhem defence area! Centres of attention are especially the Rhine bridges. Alarm units are already on the way and I shall be sending you still more reinforcements." [235]

There was not much at Sonnenstuhl's disposal, as he recounted himself, "As far as manpower was concerned I had just two alarm companies at my disposal. One of these was the crew of a light battery that had already been sent as infantry to 'Sperrverband Heinke'.* All I could assemble were 65 NCOs and three officers, with only light weaponry – no machine guns!" [236]

But reinforcements were soon underway. When Hitler was informed of the Allied attack, he immediately ordered that combatting the landings should be given top priority. He demanded that the entire German fighter aviation command in the West – about 300 aircraft – would be sent in against the landing zones, and that all accessible ground units should regroup towards Arnhem, Nijmegen, and Eindhoven. In western Germany and as far away as in Denmark, frantic efforts began to scrape together all available units, almost regardless of whether they were fit for fight. Panzergrenadier-Ausbildungs- und Ersatz-Regiment 57, a training unit at Wehrkreis VI (Military Area 6, Westphalia, the Northern Rhineland, and Eastern Belgium) was ordered to send two battle groups – Kampfgruppen Knaust and Bruhn – to Elst east of Arnhem. These had been formed in connection with the German reserve army being mobilised on 1 August 1944. [237] The commander of the former unit, Major Hans-Peter Knaust, recounts, "I was in the area east of Bocholt organizing a Panzer battlegroup which had a long way to go before it was ready for service. On the Sunday of the landing all was quiet with us, no special preparations had been made. Between four and five o'clock I received a message by telephone about the air-landing and an order to move into the Arnhem battle-area. Proof of the complete surprise was, for instance, the fact that we had no petrol, no Panzer-Faust and that my Panzers were at that very moment being loaded [presumably on trains] at Bielefeld and Herford." [238]

At the tank drivers' school in Bielefeld, Oberleutnant Wilhelm Mielke, company commander in Panzer-Ersatz- und Ausbildungs-Abteilung 11, was ordered to have all available tanks loaded onto railway cars and go to Arnhem. From the SS officers' school

---

* At "Joe's Bridge to the south. See Chapter 3.

SS-Junkerschule in Bad Tölz way down in southern Bavaria – 750 kilometres from Arnhem – came SS-Sturmmann Alfred Ringsdorf along with a few other cadets with a freight train.[239]

At about three in the afternoon on 17 September, Generalfeldmarschall Model arrived at Slangenburg, where he met Bittrich, the commander of II. SS-Panzerkorps.[240] He had now been given more information about both Allied landings and the British tank attacks in the south. The two commanders agreed that the top priority for the SS Panzer corps had to be to hold the Waal bridge at Nijmegen to prevent the Allied main force from uniting with the British airborne forces at Arnhem. At half past five in the evening, Model's and Bittrich's operation plan was completed, and was sent out to the units. The operation area was divided into three parts in accordance with the Allied units:

- General Student takes charge of the defensive battle against the British XXX Corps and the American 101st Airborne Division at the Eindhoven sector in the south. For this purpose, Student was supplied with Panzer-Brigade 107 from Germany, as well as 59. and parts of 719. Infanterie-Division from 15. Armee, which had just been evacuated across the Scheldt Estuary.
- "Korps Feldt" under General Kurt Feldt with Division z.b.V. 406 as its main fighting unit is to be sent in against the American 82nd Airborne Division south of Nijmegen.*
- Bittrich's II. SS-Panzerkorps fights the Allied bridgeheads at the Rhine (Arnhem/Oosterbeek) and the Waal (Nijmegen) with 9. SS-Panzer-Division "Hohenstaufen" in the former and 10. SS-Panzer-Division "Frundsberg" in the latter sector. Division Tettau is subordinated to the II. SS-Panzerkorps and attacks from the west, and will annihilate the British units that have landed north of the Rhine.[241]

* Korps Feldt had only recently organised his staff from Wehrkreis VI (military area 6). Division z.b.V. 406 was actually not a fighting unit, but it was the name of a staff that led the home guard battalions of Wehrkreis VI. These were now hastily reorganised into fighting units.

As for the alarm companies, a strict order was issued that "only active and energetic officers with strength of mind are to be assigned command of own forces in the combat against the landed enemy. Rank and position will be of no importance. In case of units under a weak command, commanders with front experience are to be assigned the leadership or the units concerned are to be broken up." [242]

However, as of yet, the German units were in disarray and the headquarters did not have a clear picture of the entire situation. After the meeting with Model, Bittrich set off by car to western Arnhem to meet the commander of the 9. SS-Panzer-Division's artillery regiment, Sturmbannführer Spindler, who had been tasked with organising the counterattack against the landed forces from the east. [243]

What is significant for this first day of confusion is that Model changed Bittrich's original orders that the 10. SS-Panzer-Division was to secure the Arnhem Bridge and that the 9. SS-Panzer-Division was to secure the Nijmegen bridge, so that things instead turned out the other way round. This had the very unfortunate consequence for the Germans that the important Arnhem bridge ended up "between two stools", so that virtually no German forces were available at the road bridge at Arnhem when the British arrived at it in the evening of 17 September – more on this later.

Remarkably enough, Model has escaped the judgement of history for this, while, on the other hand, Generalleutnant Hans von Tettau, commander of Division Tettau, especially in German accounts after the war has been made the scapegoat for the failure to quickly strike against and occupy the British landing zones. It has even been put forward that Tettau lacked the necessary military experience for this operation.

This criticism against von Tettau does not stand up to closer scrutiny. First of all, von Tettau had genuine experience of having led an infantry regiment during the invasions of Poland and France in 1939–1940, as well as the 24. Infanterie-Division on the Eastern Front between June 1941 and February 1943. His qualities as a division commander were confirmed when he was awarded the Knight's Cross in September 1942 for his excellent leadership during, amongst other things, the conquest of Sevastopol on the Crimean Peninsula.

Later, he would also be awarded the Oak Leaves to the Knight's Cross.

However, von Tettau's units were spread out all the way over to the Waal estuary south of Rotterdam, and his staff at Grebbeberg in the northern Rhine bank some 20 kilometres west of Oosterbeek received a stream of contradictory and confusing information. While Sepp Krafft reported that the enemy had been landed north and northwest of Wolfheze – which was also consistent with the multitudes of transport aircraft that the headquarters personnel had been able to see with their own eyes – reports were coming in (erroneous, as it would later turn out) of landings at Utrecht (25 km northwest of the command post), at Tiel (on the other side of the Rhine, ten kilometres southwest), at Dordrecht (at the estuary of the river Waal, 50 kilometres further to the west), and at Veenendaal, just a few kilometres northwest of the headquarters. Moreover, those of von Tettau's units that had drawn up in array at the Waal west of Nijmegen had reported the massive American landing only a few kilometres south of the river (the 82nd Airborne Division). For a while, it looked as though von Tettau's command post at Grebbeberg was about to be surrounded, and, as far as the Germans knew, this could be the beginning of the seaborne landing on the Dutch west coast that they had feared for so long.

The small town of Ede, only three kilometres west of the British landing zones, had been subject to repeated bomb attacks just before the landing. It began just before midnight during the night of 16/17 September, when bombs fell both over the military camp of the Simon Stevin barracks on the eastern outskirts of town, and over residential areas. Twelve hours later, the town was attacked by 30 Mitchell bombers and 13 Boston bombers from the British 2nd Tactical Air Force. When a formation of 71 RAF bombers then carried out a third attack at 1515 hrs, just after the landing that was clearly visible from Ede, the Germans feared that the British were planning an attack towards the west to take Ede.*

---

* These bomb attacks cost the town's inhabitants 69 dead, while 25 Germans were killed and 60 were wounded.

The German town commandant, SS-Obersturmführer Karl Labahn,* barricaded himself at the Simon Stevin barracks, and ordered the town garrison – his own 7. Kompanie from the SS-Panzer-grenadier- Ausbildungs- und Ersatz-Bataillon 4, a small detachment of Luftwaffe staff and the marines of the Schiffstamm-Abteilung 20** – to group for defence eastwards.[244]

Later during the afternoon, SS-Standartenführer Paul Helle, the commander of SS-Wachbataillon 3, arrived at Ede. Earlier that day, he had been spending some supposedly nice moments together with a lady friend, and his adjutant, the SS-Untersturmführer Albert Naumann, had been given strict orders not to disturb him. Therefore, Naumann did not dare to inform his commander when a phone call from the town's German mayor announced that British gliders had been landed. It was only when SS-Obergruppenführer Hanns Albin Rauter, the highest-ranking SS and Police Commander in Holland, called the headquarters, that Naumann dared to alert Helle.[245] During the following hours, his battalion, which had previously been guarding the concentration camp at Amersfoort some 15 kilometres northwest of Ede, arrived, but by then it was too late to attack the British landing zones.

Von Tettau could thus hardly be blamed for failing to immediately regroup all of his forces against the landing zones at Wolfheze, where Krafft's battalion was already fighting. Moreover, as we have previously seen, most of the units of the hastily assembled Division Tettau were of second-rate quality. In fact, it was only the SS non-commissioned officers' school SS Unterführerschule Arnheim that could be counted as experienced in battle, but it was so far being held in defensive positions at River Waal south of Grebbeberg, ready to strike should the reports of landings at Tiel turn out to be correct (which they were not).

---

* In certain publications, he is erroneously called "Lebahn", but his own combat report, which has been preserved at the city archives of Ede, shows that Labahn is the correct name.
** This was, however, far from such elite soldiers as, for instance, the American Marine Corps was made up of. The German Navy's so-called Schiffstamm battalions consisted of able seamen who were currently not at sea.

At half past five in the afternoon, when Model's instructions went out to the units, von Tettau was unaware that Krafft's training battalion was already more or less shattered. In fact, Krafft himself had not been reached either by this information at his command post at Hotel Wolfheze; at 1740 hrs he wrote that the 9. Kompanie was offering the British successful resistance, keeping them from advancing any further.[246] In reality, the 9. Kompanie failed as well, having attacked the British parachute brigade's 3rd Battalion right after it had killed General Kussin at the Utrechtscheweg west of Oosterbeek. The 30-year-old Irishman Major Mervyn Dennison, commander of the 3rd Battalion's "A" Company, knew exactly what to do. He was a hardened veteran who had taken part in the fighting both in Sicily and the Italian mainland. Now, he brought two platoons along, made an outflanking movement through the forest next to the road, and attacked the Germans in the rear. Howling wildly, Dennison's men assaulted the Germans, who fled in all directions. Eighteen of them were captured by the paratroopers, who also seized several heavy machine guns. Twenty fallen SS soldiers lay on the ground. The British losses were restricted to five wounded. The 3rd Parachute Battalion could continue down the road.

While Krafft thought that his 9. Kompanie was holding back the British, his beaten battalion was fleeing in small groups back through the forest towards Oosterbeek to escape getting surrounded. The 2. Kompanie had been annihilated, and the battalion's two other companies, which had not been seeing as much action, did not seem too eager to sacrifice themselves.

But confusion was not less on the British side. In the midst of the fighting, yet another British general had appeared at the contested crossroads, between the Wolfhezer Weg and the Utrechtscheweg, the British divisional commander Urquhart. He had not given up his still fruitless search for the reconnaissance unit's commander Gough. With his jeep, Urquhart had first been following Frost's 2nd Battalion on the southern road, but having been able to establish that Gough was not there, he ordered his driver to turn around and drive back in order to search at the 3rd Parachute Battalion instead. They arrived there just as the fighting began east of the crossroads where the dead

General Kussin was sitting in his bullet-riddled car. Urquhart had his jeep parked at the crossroads and stepped out. He did not find Gough, but he found Brigadier Lathbury, the Parachute Brigade's commander. Since radio connections were not working, Lathbury had no idea about the situation for the 1st Battalion on the "Leopard Route" way up north. When Urquhart later returned to his jeep, he saw that his driver and a signalman had been wounded by shrapnel and were being carried away on stretchers.

Further down the Utrechtscheweg, the 3rd Parachute Battalion now arrived at the first houses in Oosterbeek. There, the battalion commander, Lieutenant-Colonel John A. C. Fitch, detailed "C" Company to the left, that is, to the north, in order to advance in parallel with the railway towards Arnhem, while the rest of the battalion continued down the Utrechtscheweg.

A few kilometres away in the east, in the western outskirts of Arnhem, SS-Sturmbannführer Ludwig Spindler, the commander of 9. SS-Panzer-Division's artillery regiment, and his adjutant, SS-Obersturmführer Eitel-Fritz Steinbach, were desperately struggling to bring some order into and establish a connection within the new battle group, Kampfgruppe Spindler. There was complete chaos. Obersturmbannführer Leiteritz's company from Krafft's replacement battalion, had just set off towards Oosterbeek, and what was left behind in western Arnhem was only a few anti-aircraft soldiers with two Möbelwagen,* one 88 mm gun, and one 20 mm automatic cannon, as well as a smaller unit of sappers.

Spindler and Steinbach were lucky to be unaware of the real situation – that all German resistance between them and the opponent's airborne division had been swept away.

A group of thirteen stragglers from 10. SS-Panzer-Division's anti-aircraft battalion and SS-Panzergrenadier-Regiment 21, which during the previous night had reached Arnhem after the retreat from Belgium, reported for service, and was quickly sent off towards Oosterbeek.[247] SS-Hauptsturmführer von Allwörden arrived exemplarily quickly on motorcycle from Apeldoorn. After him followed

---

* An anti-aircraft assault gun built on the chassis of a Panzer IV tank with a 37 mm anti-aircraft gun fitted in an open turret.

the battered remains of his SS-Panzerjäger-Abteilung 9, which was now named Kampfgruppe Allwörden – two Jagdpanzer IV tank destroyers and 120 men. After that, Kampfgruppe Möller arrived, which was the new name for the pioneer battalion SS-Panzer-Pionier-Bataillon 9. On paper, it consisted of three companies, but the total force, no more than 100 men and two armoured reconnaissance vehicles, was less than at a company. The battalion commander, SS-Hauptsturmführer Hans Möller, describes the situation as it appeared when he arrived at western Arnhem at around half past four in the afternoon of 17 September: "Everybody was running around each other screaming. No-one knew anything. The enemy was everywhere where there was shooting".[248] Spindler seconded the two anti-aircraft assault guns to von Allwörden, one tank destroyer with a 20 mm automatic cannon (Sd.Kfz. 10/5) and a few anti-tank vehicles for troop transportation, and ordered him to immediately set off to attack the landing areas. Von Allwörden's units set off down the Amsterdamscheweg towards the northwest, while the pioneers were sent down the Utrechtscheweg towards Oosterbeek on the heels of the small group of thirteen SS soldiers.

Since no more units appeared, and the radio liaison did not work the way it should either on the German side, Spindler ordered his adjutant to send in his SS-Panzer-Aufklärungs-Abteilung 9 as well against the enemy west of Arnhem. The fact that this unit had left for Nijmegen was nothing they were aware of. By then, both Oosterbeek and Arnhem with their bridges lay almost completely defenceless to the British, whose 3rd Parachute Battalion made it through Oosterbeek along the Utrechtscheweg without encountering any serious resistance.

QR 20: VIDEO
Private film by the Monné family in Oosterbeek showing British paratroopers in town on 17–18 September 1944.

Hotel Hartenstein was occupied by Lieutenant Cleminson's men. Inside the building, they discovered a ready laid table with food that had gone cold, which they immediately threw themselves over – ignorant of the fact that it was Field Marshal Model's own unfinished meal.

Slowly, it started to dawn on SS-Sturmbannführer Spindler how critical the situation was. But when things were looking its darkest, an unexpected report suddenly came: The British have paused at Hotel Hartenstein in central Oosterbeek! It seemed incredible – there was hardly any reason for the British to stop their advance, now that the road lay virtually open. As unexplainable as it may seem, it is a fact that the men of the 3rd Parachute Battalion were ordered to halt for the night and dig in as soon as they had captured Hotel Hartenstein at around nine o'clock on the evening of the 17th. The divisional commander Urquhart and the brigade commander Lathbury were quartered in a house at Utrechtscheweg 269, only a few hundred metres east of the place where General Kussin still lay dead in his Citroën. As they were sitting and eating porridge for supper on the ground floor of the house, they could verify for themselves that "there was very little firing outside".[249] That was the other fateful mistake that the

Utrectscheweg in Oosterbeek, 250 meters to the east of Hotel Hartenstein.

British commanders were guilty of that day. The Parachute Brigade had already been unnecessarily delayed by Urquhart insisting to get in touch with Lathbury before giving marching orders from the landing grounds, and now, in the evening of the 17th, the soldiers were cursing the fact that they were forced to dig in in spite of "twopenny-ha'penny opposition" from the Germans, as one of them put it.[250]

Meanwhile, von Allwörden managed to halt the British on the northern flank. The Amsterdamscheweg which he was advancing down – that was the "Leopard Route", down which the 1st Parachute Battalion under Lieutenant-Colonel David Dobie was advancing with the task to secure the heights north of Arnhem. During the march, von Allwörden's column was spotted by a British reconnaissance patrol, which returned to the 1st Battalion reporting "tanks on the road".[251] Of course, it was Kampfgruppe Allwörden's two Jagdpanzer IVs that the British mistook for tanks – the Germans had no tanks at this time. But the Jagdpanzer IV was enough of a deterrent for these Britons. This 24 ton heavy, 1.85 metre high tank destroyer on tracks had no turret and was built on the chassis of a Panzer IV tank. The armament consisted of one 75 mm gun and one 7.92 mm machine

Jagdpanzer IV.

gun. A British PIAT anti-tank weapon could not penetrate its 60 mm frontal armour sloped at 45°; for that, a 17-pound antitank gun was needed, and Dobie had none of those immediately available. Therefore, he decided to let his main force turn southwards, in order then to advance eastwards through the terrain. Company "R" continued down the highway, reaching contact at around five o'clock with von Allwörden's frontline unit, which withdrew.

"R" Company was led by Major John "Tim" Timothy, a very experienced officer who had been taking part in the fighting in Tunisia and Italy in 1943, and had been awarded the Military Cross with one Bar. Nevertheless, his company let itself walk straight into an ambush that von Allwörden has organised a bit further up the road. SS-Rottenführer Alfred Ziegler recounted: "We were lying in ambush in the woods. They came marching straight down the road in company file! What a nonsense! We were so few! They should have taken a route through the trees. We were told first to let the British through, and then we opened up from all directions and cut the first lot down." [252] Perhaps the previously weak German resistance had led the British to become so incautious; according to Ziegler, between 30 and 40 Britons were captured, who were "so beaten and submissive that it only needed one man to march them off to the rear". The SS soldiers that Timothy's men met here were cast in a completely different mould that the first German soldiers that they had met. The British report, however, gives a different version: "Major Timothy commanding R Company was ordered to attack infantry positions covered by four tanks. Despite the heavy fire he put in a most skilful attack, covered by two inch mortar smoke, and drove a superior force of enemy back thus securing an important cross-road. There, although attacked by tanks and infantry of a battalion strength, he held his ground until ordered to withdraw. He did this bringing out his casualties which amounted to 50% of his company." [253] With the advance down the highway repelled, von Allwörden's men were entangled into confused fighting with Dobie's paratroopers in the pitch black of the woods between the Amsterdamscheweg to the north and Oosterbeek to the south throughout the following night.

But all could be lost for the Germans because of the advance by British 2nd Parachute Battalion on Benedendorpsweg, the road leading along the southern outskirts of Oosterbeek. It was also there that this battalion was closing in on the bridges across the Rhine. Neither the railway bridge at the eastern outskirts of Oosterbeek nor the road bridge in Arnhem, three kilometres further east, had been blown up. Neither did Spindler have any idea that the British had also taken the southern route – he had dispatched Möller's pioneer soldiers along the Utrechtscheweg, about one and a half kilometres north of the railway bridge. But there was yet another force, and that was the thirteen SS soldiers from 10. SS-Panzer-Division's anti-aircraft battalion and SS-Panzergrenadier-Regiment 21 who had reported first of all. They decided to ignore Spindler's orders to follow the Utrechtscheweg.

THIRTEEN MEN DECIDE THE BATTLE

"Daar zijn ze! Daar zijn de Tommies!" – "There they are! There are the Tommies" – the shouts were sounding in the streets as the 2nd Parachute Battalion late in the afternoon of 17 September entered Oosterbeek from the west along the Benedendorpsweg, which runs in parallel with the river Rhine and separates Oosterbeek from the fields to the south, down towards the river.[254] This was the "Lion Route" in the British operational plan. The "Lion Route" segued about one and a half kilometres further east, on the other side of Oosterbeek, into the Klingebeekscheweg, and continued in Arnhem on the Utrechtscheweg in parallel with the Rhine straight towards the large highway bridge, the main target for the 1st Airborne Division. On the road there, the "Lion Route" passed the two other bridges, the railway bridge and the pontoon bridge. It was no coincidence that the 2nd Battalion under Lieutenant-Colonel John Frost, the most experienced one of the three battalion commanders in the parachute brigade, had been awarded the main task.

The Dutch watched the tough "Red Devils" in admiration as they came trudging in columns, their weapons ready to fire. At Heveadorp, the little village at the Rhine just before Oosterbeek, Frost's men had recently met the first resistance. Soldiers from SS-Obersturmbann-führer Leiteritz's 9. Kompanie in Krafft's battalion had opened fire at them from the heights in the north that slope down towards the river. To the paratroopers, it was an easy task to quickly chase the Germans away, and fifty men who did not make the escape were captured.[255]

But just as with many of the Americans further to the south, the paratroopers in Frost's battalion were soon stopped in their advance by crowds of elated Dutchmen coming from all directions in order to – often in quite a hands-on way – welcome their liberators. Jeanne Meeter Endt, a woman who at the time was 63 years old and living at Bildersweg 6 in Oosterbeek, wrote in her diary: "Indeed there was a whole bunch of Tommies that unhindered came marching along the Benedendorpseweg! We ran to meet them, leaving everything behind, even the potato cake that was left to burn, half mad with joy like all the other villagers who flocked together. They shouted hurray, they danced, they shouted, they 'shook hands' with the Tommies and we welcomed them with apples, pears, tomatoes and gin. That gin bottle from the barman went from mouth to mouth and that crazy moment saw even Ditha drink. Everyone suddenly was wearing orange; Rie Chits provided us with little flags and flowers, Ditha pulled out a large orange brush; Friso put the Chitsen's flag on a pole, and there even was

The road into Oosterbeek from the west on the Benedendorpsweg. Image from the early 1940s.

189

a flag flying from the church tower!" [256] An elderly gentleman offered to lend Frost his car, so that he would be able to move ahead faster and more comfortably, but being well aware of what would happen to the vehicle in that case, Frost declined kindly but firmly.

There were no German troops whatsoever between the railway bridge on the eastern outskirts of Oosterbeek and Frost's men, and they did not meet any further resistance either until they reached the little railway station Oosterbeek Laag just north of the railway bridge. [257] Now, one of The Second World War's most fateful and, at the same time, least known clashes was to follow.

From the railway station in Arnhem, two lines ran in parallel westbound. One towards Utrecht to the west, and this was the one that separated the British landing zones from each other. The other turned left between Arnhem and Oosterbeek towards the south, passing the railway station Oosterbeek Laag, and going via a large steel bridge across the Rhine, after which it went via another one across the Waal to Nijmegen. Both of these bridges were important targets for Operation "Market Garden".

While the paratroopers of the 2nd Battalion made their way as best as they could through the clusters of hundreds of cheering Dutchmen on the Benedendorpsweg, SS-Sturmmann Helmut Buttlar and three other SS soldiers climbed the railway bank at Oosterbeek Laag. Buttlar belonged to the anti-aircraft battalion of 10. SS-Panzer-Division "Frundsberg" and had been retreating all the way from Falaise.

Especially in one respect, German soldiers during the Second World War were considerably more efficient than their opponents, and that was about taking initiatives of their own. While other armies, to a great extent, inhibited the soldiers' own initiatives through a far too strict hierarchy of issuing orders, personal initiatives were encouraged in the German Armed Forces through the so-called mission tactics (*Auftragstaktik*). This comprised carefully initiating the troops – including the unit commanders at lower levels and even private soldiers – into the purpose and objectives of the mission, after which the smallest unit at the front was relatively free to solve the task in the way that the situation allowed. In that way, the soldiers were trained to think for themselves and act with powers of initiative even when officers were absent.*

During their training, the German field manual impressed upon the soldiers that "the conduct of war is an art, depending upon free, creative activity, scientifically based".[258]

Nineteen-year-old Helmut Buttlar, however, stretched these own initiatives a little too far from time to time. He had made himself infamous among the officers for his wilfulness, and especially his commander at the 3. Batterie, SS-Obersturmführer Hans Fröhlich, had grown tired of him. Three times had Buttlar been punished for breaches of discipline, and he had a one-year prison sentence hanging over him, "to be served after the final victory in the war". However, through his independence, he had also been awarded the Iron Cross (2nd Class) – after having managed to save an anti-aircraft gun using a horse and carriage in the evening of 8 September from Liège in Belgium, in spite of the city meanwhile being taken by the Americans. This was, however, after the conflict with Fröhlich had led to Buttlar being transferred to the 4. Batterie. His new commander, SS-Obersturmführer Gottlob Ellwanger, also had him promoted to SS-Sturmmann (Corporal) – "probably without the knowledge of the division's judge", Buttlar commented with a wink.

During the continued retreat on foot from Belgium, Buttlar had fallen behind after having stopped to rest his aching feet. In the evening of 16 September, he arrived at Arnhem, where he spent the night together with twelve other stragglers from the anti-aircraft battalion and the "Frundsberg Division's" SS-Panzer-Grenadier-Regiment 21 in the SS Police Barracks in the southern part of town. It was these thirteen men who were the first ones to report to Spindler in western Arnhem in the afternoon of 17 September. They had "commandeered" a city bus and, by their own initiative, set off in the direction where they had seen the gliders land, and were stopped on the western outskirts

---

* Those among the soldiers on the Western Allied side who had the closest resemblance to the German Auftragstaktik in terms of taking own initiatives actually were the British paratroopers. The most unflexible army among Germany's opponents was most likely the American army. However, one needs to bear in mind that many of the scantily trained German soldiers who were sent into battle during Operation "Market Garden" had not had this training and were still only recruits who had learned merely to obey orders.

of Arnhem by SS-Sturmbannführer Spindler, who gave them orders to continue along the road to report to Krafft.

While on their way, Buttlar and his comrades met a group of fleeing German baggage train soldiers who told them that Oosterbeek was already occupied by "the evil enemy". In that situation, the thirteen SS soldiers decided to hold, as Buttlar put it, "a Frundsberg council of war". They elected Sturmmann Buttlar as their leader, and he decided that they would turn to the left onto the smaller road, in order to avoid what could be the British main force on the Utrechtscheweg. By that, they came onto the "Lion Route", which would take them straight into the arms of Frost's 2nd Battalion. The Germans continued carefully forward in three small groups. Buttlar describes the sight that met him when he had made it up the railway bank just north of the railway station, "On an elevation near the railroad station Oosterbeek-Laag there were hundreds of curious Dutch people of both sexes and of all age groups moving about. Among them, almost in their midst, were several British paratroopers, who were being greeted by the Dutch at the top of their voices and refreshed with tea or whatever from thermos bottles. We were standing about 50 meters away from this drama as

The viaduct under the railway at Oosterbeek-Laag, seen from the west. The railway station Oosterbeek-Laag is just to the left, out of picture. Image from 1910.

the crow flies, more perplexed than paralysed up on the embankment which led to the railroad bridge over the Rhine and upon which we had climbed to watch out for the enemy." [259]

Two Britons emerged from the crowd and approached along the road that led to the viaduct under the railway. Buttlar and his comrades opened fire and forced the British to take cover. But soon, three more paratroopers emerged, and they undauntedly attacked and forced Buttlar's group to retreat with one of their comrades lightly injured. However, as had been impressed upon him during his training, Buttlar immediately organised a counterattack with his twelve men. Now, the Britons were the ones who were at a disadvantage, and the Germans had soon recaptured their positions. They now had a tactical advantage where they took up fighting positions on top of the three-metre-high railway bank. Buttlar hurried to group his men down to the left, towards the railway bridge eight hundred metres further down. From there, the thirteen Germans were able to hold back Frost's entire battalion.

It was in that situation that the divisional commander Urquhart arrived at the 2nd Battalion's rear – this was before he went to the 3rd Battalion. He recounted: "On the southern road east of Oosterbeek, I caught up with the rear elements of Frost's battalion. They were moving in single file staggered along each side of the road, and moving very slowly. Farther on, others were halted. Frost was not at his HQ; he had gone ahead because some of his leading elements had run into trouble. I tried to impart a sense of urgency, which I hoped would be conveyed to Frost." [260]

The latter was highly superfluous. Frost himself had organised an attack on the railway bank. Mortars were set up in firing positions and began shooting their projectiles with little bangs. But the Germans were well-protected. After a while, the "Red Devils" broke through across a width of four hundred metres. They were met with intense firing which felled several of them before the remaining ones decided to withdraw.

Frost left the "C" Company behind with the task to capture the railway bridge, and ordered the "A" and "B" Companies to turn to the left to circumvent the railway station. They made it up onto the

Twin brothers

By cross-referencing British and German accounts, it has been possible to identify the two Britons who clashed with SS-Sturmmann Buttlar at the first contact with the enemy at the railway station Oosterbeek-Laag. Twenty-two-year-old Private Thomas Gronert and Private Jack Edwards – two old childhood friends from Cornwall – constituted the reconnaissance group in the British battalion's "B" Company's No. 6 Platoon under Lieutenant Peter Cane. Edwards has given the following detailed account of the event:

"Tommy Gronert and I were the forward scouts and we were shot at almost immediately. We took cover behind a rise. The order came through to push on, which we did. Virtually straight away a bullet hit the track exactly between Tommy and myself. It looked as if there was a sniper in the vicinity. We again took cover. Tommy carried on and reached the end of a sort of railway barrier made of upright railway sleepers. I heard Tommy shouting that there were Germans approaching from the other side of the railway track."

More paratroopers from Cane's platoon joined in, including Serjeant Larry Ansell's group, and the British attacked. "Tommy left his cover", Edwards recounted, "and moved onto the railway track along with others from the first section. They were Lieutenant Peter Cane, Sergeant Henry Hacker and Corporal Edgar Rogers." Buttlar and his comrades received them with raging fire. A few bullets hit the smoke grenades that Corporal Rogers carried in his belt, and the phosphor caught fire in an explosive way. Screaming and engulfed in flames, Rogers was hit by a bullet and dropped dead. Lieutenant Cane kneeled down to open fire at the Germans, but was hit by a bullet in the chest. Serjeant Ansell, who had thrown himself to the ground for cover next to him, asked: "Now what do we do?" Cane responded through clenched teeth: "Charge the bastards!" Soon afterwards, he was hit again.

"Tommy" Gronert managed to make it up the railway bank. "Then I heard Tommy call out that he had been hit", Edwards recalled. "Apparently he had been shot in the mouth, the bullet passing through the back of his neck. It all happened in a few seconds." "Tommy" Gronert's twin brother, Private Claude Gronert, served in the same platoon and heard him scream that he was wounded. Their little brother Bernard recounted after the war, "Tommy and Claude, like many young men, had left their protected jobs underground at South Crofty mine to fight fascism. They didn't tell my parents what they were planning to do, and when they came home and said they'd joined up it broke my mother's heart. I can still see her crying and asking them why they'd done it."

Without a thought of his own safety, Claude rushed forward to help Thomas, and was hit by a bullet in the head. Edwards' account continues, "When we returned after the shooting had died down it was a terribly sad sight that met our eyes. Serjeant Wallbank went on ahead to assess the situation. Serjeant Hacker was badly wounded but was still alive. Lieutenant Cane said a few words and then died. Corporal Rogers' body was burning.

Tommy and Claude Gronert, the twins, lay close to one another. Both dead. Claude had received three bullets through the top of his helmet. For me it was a shattering blow because we had been friends for a long time. All three of us came from Cornwall and had joined the Paras in 1943 from the same unit. Their army numbers were 5511523 and 5511524, while mine was 5511508."

As the British Army regulations dictated that a soldier could only be registered as killed in action when an officer could confirm his death, and since all officers who could confirm the Gronert twins' death were killed or captured during the Battle of Arnhem, it took until June 1945 before their parents were informed. Their mother, Lyn Gronert, never got over the shock.

Claude (left) and Thomas Gronert.

A few years later, she also lost her husband, Robert. When her youngest son Bernard received his conscription documents, Mrs Gronert went straight to her local MP demanding that he get an exemption warrant. Today, the Gronert twins are buried next to each other at Oosterbeek's military cemetery, Plot 18, Row A, Graves 17 and 18. Lieutenant Peter Cane is buried together with the remains of an unidentified British paratrooper three graves away, in Graves 13-14. Lyn Gronert passed away in 1969, but Bernard Gronert is still alive.

Sources:
David G. van Buggenum, *B Company Arrived*, pp. 28–33.
Cornwall Live, 13 September, 2014: "Carn Brea's Bernard Gronert remembers twin brothers 70 years after they died in the Battle of Arnhem".
baroque4.rssing.com/browser.php?indx=3543695&item=7424.

QR21:
Larry Ansell appears in one of the most published images of the Battle of Arnhem.

Utrechtscheweg and continued under the railway viaduct 700 metres north of Oosterbeek-Laag. On the other side, the road ran across the southern spur of a hill called Den Brink (also known as the KEMA area). "A" Company under Major Allison Digby Tatham-Warter climbed up the woody hill, which in fact was a park with trees, bushes and hedges between a couple of houses. "B" Company continued down the road, and it did not take long until one of Kampfgruppe Möller's Sd.Kfz. 222-type armoured reconnaissance cars appeared from behind the trees on the north side of the road. In terror, the Germans opened fire straight into the lead, consisting of three men from "B" Company with a 20 mm automatic gun and handguns. Two Britons fell, hit by the German fire, while the others threw themselves into cover on the side of the road and the armoured vehicle disappeared back at full speed. Apparently, the vehicle crew was unable to warn the rest of the Germans. Soon afterwards, Digby's men clashed with another group of SS pioneers. SS-Hauptsturmführer Möller, the German battalion commander, recounts, "About 100 metres after the church, at the approach into Oosterbeek, such a fierce armed attack

Oosterbeek-Laag, railway station seen from the south. The heights at Den Brink/the KEMA area can be seen in the background. The viaduct under the railway runs just below the spot where the photographer is standing.

suddenly occurred against the two companies at the front that the attacking lead had to take cover. [SS-Untersturmführer Erhard] Voss with his 2. Kompanie on the right flank sustained the first casualties – where did that come from? The enemy was attacking from an ambush. Had we walked into a trap? Steinert, with 1. Kompanie on the left side of the road, slowly and carefully sneaked forward through the front gardens, but after a while, 1. Kompanie was also fired upon, and forced to take cover – the enemy was invisible".[261] Ten Germans were captured. In one of their pockets, the British found a map showing the German positions.[262] It appeared as though the road towards the two other bridges lay open. Now this was not entirely correct, since Kampfgruppe Möller's advance was not marked on the map. But the pioneer soldiers did not stand much of a chance against the men of Digby's "A" Company. An attempted counterattack by the Germans in the Den Brink Park/KEMA area brought about the conclusion, described by Möller:

"As quiet as cats and covered by the late dusk, Voss and Pötschke penetrated the large park with their pioneers. From here it was only about

The railway viaduct at Den Brink/the KEMA area. The image is taken from the eastern side of the railway and the villa in the park is outside the picture to the right.

50 metres to the villa – quiet and soundless – no resistance – no enemy – eerie – but leaning very closely to the well-groomed hedges and groups of bushes, they went forward carefully and at full cock.

Right next to the gravel patch, which stood out brightlwy from the dusk, any noise was unavoidable. And then it lay before them, this white villa, only 15 metres from the stairway with the magnificent portal above it, cased in fine wood and brass and furnished with heavy bolts. A large rhododendron provided good cover. Still quietly and soundlessly – oddly enough – Pötschke turned to the right with his pioneers, to reach the back of the house, and all was quiet here as well – a trap? Behind the rhododendron, Voss armed his explosive device and fitted it with a hook. Suspense was at its highest, and then another glance of approval, from comrade to comrade – pressing each others' hands yet again. All uncocked their submachine guns, ready to fire. It was dark now – Rottenführer Mass leapt forward, dashed up the stairway, hurried to the top, reached the portal, hung the explosives onto the doorknob and leaped back – taking cover

The large white villa in the Den Brink park which the SS-Untersturmführer Erhard Voss and his pioneer soldiers attacked in the evening of 17 September 1944. The image from 1925 is taken from the south, from the Utrechtscheweg, about 150 metres east of the viaduct under the railway.

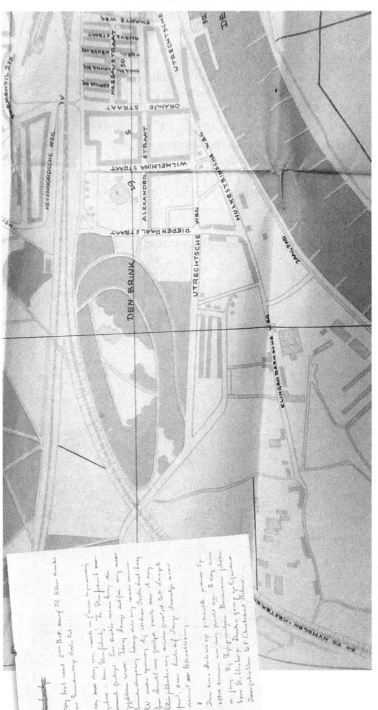

Far left in the map, forming an arc down to the left, is the railway Arnhem – Nijmegen, leading to the south and outside the image to the railway bridge across the Rhine. The viaduct under the railway at the Oosterbeek-Laag station at the Benedendorpsweg is bottom left. Den Brink/the KEMA area is in the middle of the image, with the viaduct leading the Utrechtscheweg under the railway. The rail yard, where Möller's men dug in after having been defeated at Den Brink, is top right. (British city map from the war. National Archives, WO 171 393 HW 1st AbnDiv.)

The inserted photo shows a report from two Dutch locals who accompanied Frost's battalion as guides. This source confirms that elements of this battalion took the detour around Den Brink/KEMA area as it writes: "In the KEMA area B Company is still involved in fighting". (Boeree Collection, Gelders Archief.)

behind the stone candelabrum – then a terrible explosion. Voss leapt out with his 5 pioneers, dashed up the stairway, where Maas was already waiting for him. The house door was gaping into the house – the great hall – the wide marble staircase – the precious carpets – then four large chaps on the middle landing. All raised their submachine guns and fired – a terrible hail of bullets – hand grenades ringing in the hall – two Canadians sank down and rolled down the stairs, Voss tumbled and collapsed, they must have fired simultaneously – hand-to-hand fighting – from the rooms on the upper floors came other paratroopers and from the cellar they came pouring out as from a hornets' nest. Pötschke and his pioneers came running around the house – flares after flares now lit up the snow-white façade of the villa and their pale light fell on the bushes and trees in the great park, and flares rose from further right as well, the entire front seemingly having come into movement. The superior strength of the opponents, but above all, their determination, forced us to retreat. We had completely misjudged them. Voss and two other wounded pioneers were dragged away by Pötschke and his men. It was a heavy and difficult loss and a bitter discovery at that! Obersturmführer Steiner had been bombarding the villa with a hail of bullets from the other side of the road. In the same way, the furious and well-aimed fire from our armoured personnel carrier had also enabled the brave pioneers' retreat and prevented the enemy from going into pursuit".[263]

The 23-year-old Voss was a close friend and former schoolmate of Möller's . He was buried at first in the cemetery at Brummen, but the body was moved after the battle to the German Heldenfriedhof at Grebbeberg.*

While Frost's "Red Devils" marched on along the Utrechtscheweg and into Arnhem without meeting any resistance, Möller's soldiers sought refuge among the residential houses next to the shunting yard in western Arnhem, only a few hundred metres north of them. "It was now getting dark", Frost recalled, "and though at times bursts of fire swept across the road, we could afford to ignore them. Up to this

---

* After the war, Voss's remains were moved to the German military cemetery Ysselsteyn and are resting today in Sector AC, grave 6:133.

time we had very few casualties and our progress had been highly satisfactory." [264]

From the German side, Möller claimed that "I had absolutely not been able to stop [the British advance] with my weak forces".[265] But as the events the next day would show, this was not as much due to the strength in numbers of Kampfgruppe Möller as the disorganisation it had found itself in after having been beaten by Digby's company. One of those hiding in the dark together with Möller and his men was no one less than the commander of the II. SS-Panzerkorps, SS-Obergruppenführer Bittrich, who had just arrived at Spindler's command post in western Arnhem. In Bittrich's own words, "[I] was caught in the turbulence of a fight, which bore all the characteristics of confusion. The enemy had advanced into the town from the west and made it to the road bridge. Enemy and German combat vehicles were swirling around each other. I stayed at a makeshift advanced command post on the northern outskirts of town during the night of 17 September." [266]

Had the British Paratroop Brigade's 3rd Battalion not set up camp for the night in central Oosterbeek, one and a half kilometres further to the west, but continued its advance along the Utrechtscheweg, it would have been able with its 300 men from the "A" and "B" companies to join the 2nd Battalion without further ado. ("C" Company was advancing meanwhile in parallel with the railway further to the north and would later join the 2nd Battalion further ahead.) There is even the possibility that they could have killed or captured both Spindler and Bittrich.

The men of Frost's 2nd Battalion hurried forward to the pontoon bridge,* 1,500 metres from Den Brink, and with the large road bridge another 700 metres away. They had been seriously delayed and now they were in a hurry! When they arrived among the houses in Arnhem along the road on the northern side of the riverbank, Dutchmen started pouring out from the houses. Private James Sims recounted, "One young Dutchman was charging about on a bike completely drunk and offering swigs of gin to one and all. Our officer lost his tem-

---

* Today, the modern Nelson Mandela bridge is built on the site of the old pontoon bridge.

per and threatened to shoot him and any of us who touched a drop. We were losing time and he realized that this semi-triumphal entry into Arnhem was not going to last." [267]

The situation on the German side in Arnhem by then was certainly reminiscent of this drunk Dutchman reeling around on his bicycle. Bittrich was stuck in north-western Arnhem, and due to the contradictory orders first from Bittrich at four o'clock and then from Model at half past five in the evening, the German units had been sent in all directions – away from the important road bridge at the eastern part of Arnhem. At around six o'clock, the column of vehicles of SS-Hauptsturmführer Gräbner's Panzer Reconnaissance Battalion of the 9. SS-Panzer-Division came rumbling along the Velperweg inside Arnhem from the northeast, turned to the left along the Nijmeegscheweg and roared across the road bridge, disappearing towards the south. Their task was to reconnoiter at Elst on the other side of the Rhine.

This air photo is taken from due south, in the air above Betuwe. At the row of trees just above the northern riverbank top left, the road Onderlangs runs. Along it, obscured by the next row of trees, the Utrechtscheweg runs. To the right of the pontoon bridge, the Rijnkade runs along the riverbank. It was this route that the paratroopers of the 2nd Battalion took during their march towards the large road bridge, which is situated about 450 metres beyond the right edge of the image. Top right is the railway station (at the near side of the railway) beyond the Willemsplein.

At 1900 hrs, they were able to report this place free from enemies, and then continued southbound towards the Waal bridge at Nijmegen. While Gräbner's units disappeared to the south, SS-Sturmbannführer Ludwig Spindler's desperation grew, as he had not only failed to halt the British, but was now cut off himself. And the road bridge remained undefended – while Lieutenant-Colonel Frost's men, without the Germans' knowledge, came careering towards it along the northern side of the river Rhine.

Spindler's adjutant, SS-Obersturmführer Steinbach, had – with SS-Unterscharführer Mayer as his driver – set off with a Volkswagen Schwimmwagen towards Arnhem to search for Gräbner, without knowing either where he or the British paratroopers were. They stopped in front of a large building with carousel doors. Steinbach saw how Mayer entered through the carousel doors, only to immediately follow them around and rush back into the car, his face ghastly pale. "The ground floor is full of English!" he yelled, leaping up into the vehicle. Mayer stepped on the accelerator and the car sped away for all its worth.[268]

While "A" Company continued towards the road bridge, "B" Company stopped by the pontoon bridge as soon as Möller's pioneer soldiers had been swept away from Den Brink. Already before the British had boarded the aircraft over in England, Frost had been informed that the air reconnaissance had established that the Germans had dismantled the middle section of the pontoon bridge so that it was currently out of use. But "B" Company's task was to try to find boats and other vessels with whose help it would perhaps be possible to repair the bridge provisionally. However, it eventually turned out that this was not possible. But two large, intact bridges remained – for a few more minutes.

Time was approaching half past seven in the evening when "C" Company's No. 8 Platoon fired smoke grenades and, after that, opened up a violent barrage against the riverbank north of the railway bridge further back, where Buttlar's SS soldiers were still standing their ground. Covered by a smokescreen and all the firing, the rest of the company charged ahead across the marshland towards the bridge. But the smoke was soon dispersed. The company commander Major

Victor Dover remembered, "The Polderweg along which we made our way was little more than a track. There was no cover and we were exposed to fire from the far side of the river. Number 9 Platoon was in the lead, followed by Company HQ and 8 and 7 Platoons. The German positions in a brick kiln on the north side of the buildings had been demolished. The opposition to our approach was light and was quickly overrun. 9 Platoon continued its advance of the escarpment of the railway bridge without trouble until they reached the foot of the escarpment of the railway track itself. Here it came under heavy fire from a machine-gun and from snipers on the far side of the river. The remainder of the Company took up covering fire positions in the area of the wrecked buildings." [269] Lieutenant Peter Barry, the commander of No. 9 Platoon, felt how he was hit by a bullet in his right arm. "[The bullet] made a small hole in front and a large gash coming out. Of course I know today it fractured the humerus. I had no idea what it had done then, but my arm suddenly began going round and round in a circle. I wondered what the devil was causing it to do that. At any rate, we couldn't afford to remain where we were much longer. I stood up and shouted that we were going back and we retreated…" [270]

But through this, the thirteen Germans in Helmut Buttlar's group had finished up their ammunition and were forced to retreat themselves. All of them had survived, with nothing but a few small wounds, but this was nothing they felt any joy about. "Howling with rage" they watched how a group of British paratroopers – from Barry's platoon – made their way up onto the railway bridge and started running towards the southern riverbank. [271] If they would make it, Operation "Market Garden" would practically be completed! Right then – as though directed in a movie – there was a yellow flash of light and with a mighty rumble, followed by a shockwave, the bridge blew up in front of them. Without Buttlar knowing it, a group of German pioneers had made it to the bridge from the south in the middle of the battle, and primed explosives that demolished the bridge at the very last moment.

Major Dover arrived at the northern abutment while debris was raining down around him. One of the men who had been on the bridge, 20-year-old Private Leslie Sadler, came down the railway bank towards Major Dover. The next moment, he fell straight to the ground, lifeless.

But the road bridge remained! Joannes van Kuijk, a Dutch telex and telephone answerer at the police station just north of the bridge, recounted, "Before the landings there were no troops at the bridge except the usual guards, 20 to 25 men with some light flak. There were garrison troops - men of 45 to 50 years of age, who had only just been called up. During the afternoon, these men fled, and I walked across the bridge at 7.30 p.m. there was not a single man in the defences. The first British parachutists reached the bridge half an hour later, but before they arrived some SS troops came up from the direction of Nijmegen and occupied defences at the southern end." [272]

Both sides were closing in on the bridge that so far was unoccupied. From the north came soldiers from the 9. and 10. SS-Panzer-Division careering in small groups. "The front is where the shooting is!" was the directive. On foot, on bicycles, or on motorcycles, in cars or with horses and carriages, a small exodus of SS men was moving towards Arnhem. Twenty lorries were shuttling back and forth, driving soldiers.

In Rheden, northeast of Arnhem, SS-Hauptsturmführer Karl-Heinz Euling was ordered to regroup his II. Bataillon/SS-Panzergren-adier-Regiment 19 of 9. SS-Panzer-Division to Nijmegen. He did not dispose of any more than two companies with a total of 400 men, but set off down the road that runs in parallel with River IJssel.

Horst Weber, an SS-Rottenführer of 10. SS-Panzer-Division's SS-Panzergrenadier-Regiment 21, arrived at Arnhem late in the afternoon. Weber had never seen any combat action when he was posted to the regiment a few days earlier. SS-Panzergrenadier-Regiment 21 was in a terrible state. The nominal strength of a German Panzergrenadier Battalion was 860 men, but when Weber was placed at the regiment's I. Bataillon, only 80 men remained after the disaster in France. In reality, this was more or less the entire regiment, after the II. Bataillon had been seconded to the LXXXVI. Armeekorps at the bridgehead at "Joe's Bridge" (see Chapter 3). The unit was soon filled up with recruits. Most of them were 17-18-year-olds with no more than three months' training as soldiers. SS-Unterscharführer Adolf Lochbrunner recalled,

"With the exception of a handful of comrades from my company, who made it reasonably unhurt from Normandy (Franz Schulze-Bernd, Rudolf Trapp, Wagner, Waigel and a few others), there was a plethora of unknown faces. Many of the replacements came from the so-called 'Hermann Göring account', that is, ground staff from the Luftwaffe who were not needed in their units anymore because of the shortage of aircraft".[273] One of the recruits was 18-year-old Horst Weber, who was made chief of staff to the battalion commander SS-Obersturm-führer Ernst Vogel. Weber was placed in the 3. Kompanie, which had 150 men out of 225 in the I. Bataillon, and was rushed to Arnhem. Weber recounted, "Who should be in charge we would find out on our way. On the 17th we had no officers at all at the scene!" [274]

The Germans did not even have vehicles enough to transport this SS company to Arnhem. Weber used a car that had been comman-deered from the Dutch civilians, but Adolf Lochbrunner, his comrade SS-Rottenführer Rudolf Trapp, and many others, had to ride the fifty kilometres from Deventer on bicycle.[275] Even though the common image of Holland is of a completely flat country, the road went uphill and downhill, but ended – presumably to the great relief of the SS sol-diers – in a four-kilometre descent. When Trapp and his comrades were approaching Arnhem, they were met by many other Germans on their way to flee north. With panic beaming out of their eyes, they were shouting, "Run away! The Tommies have landed!" [276]

From the west, "A" Company in Frost's battalion was approach-ing. The company commander, the tall and lanky Major Allison Digby Tatham-Warter, looked like a cross between a paratrooper in a parade and a tourist guide as he, wearing the paratroopers' maroon beret instead of a helmet, was urging his men forward by wielding a large black umbrella.*

They passed the SS police barracks where Helmut Buttlar and his comrades had spent the night twenty-four hours earlier. The barracks were still on fire after the bomb attack that had preceded the landings.

---

* Digby of course is the model to the likewise umbrella-equipped fictive charac-ter "Major Harry Carlyle" in the film *A Bridge Too Far*. However, there are two important differences between him and the real Digby: The real person sur-vived the war (he became 75 years old), and actually was even more colourful than the film character, as shall be seen in Volume 2.

Several dead Germans lay outside, SS men and a young woman in a Luftwaffe uniform.

But the Germans were the first ones to the bridge. A handful of soldiers took position in an anti-aircraft turret up on the northern part of the bridge. Then, the British were upon them. Many of them were veterans from the fighting in North Africa, and there they had learned new battle cries. Howling "*Woah Muhammed!*" – the British paratroopers' battle cry – the British charged up the abutment. Using PIAT anti-tank weapons and flamethrowers, they put the anti-aircraft turret out of action. Gruesome screams from men being scorched to death inside the narrow concrete building reached the paratroopers, and then, a few shocked Germans came out on trembling legs, their hands in the air. Some of them were weeping uncontrollably.

"A" Company reached the bridge at the last moment in order to take the northern abutment. Soon afterwards, a column of German armoured cars came rolling down the road which runs from the east towards the northern abutment. They belonged to 10. SS-Panzer-Division's Panzer Reconnaissance Battalion,* which was now designated Kampfgruppe Brinkmann after its commander, SS-Sturmbann-führer Heinz Brinkmann.

He was in Borculo, sixty kilometres northeast of Arnhem, when the order came to regroup to the Waal bridge in Nijmegen. Brink-mann immediately sent the 1. Kompanie under SS-Obersturmführer Karl Ziebrecht with nine armoured cars armed with 20 mm automatic guns, and these were the ones that were now approaching the bridge. Quite unexpectedly, they came under fierce fire from the northern abutment, and were forced to retreat. Lieutenant-Colonel Frost's men, who were well-equipped with PIAT anti-tank weapons and also four anti-tank guns, were in command of the bridge – or at least its northern abutment!

For a short while, the British were kept from making it across to the southern abutment by exploding ammunition flying in all directions from an ammunition depot that had been hit. When things cleared, Gräbner's Panzer Reconnaissance Battalion of 9. SS-Panzer- Division,

---

* SS-Panzer-Aufklärungs-Abteilung 10.

which had hurried to the site from the nearby Elst to the south, had started taking up positions on both sides of the southern abutment. Meanwhile, a few marines from Schiffstamm-Abteilung 14 arrived. The latter were, on 17 September, at Betuwe – the marshy land between the Rhine and Waal rivers that the Allies would call "the Island" – and were ordered to send in the 2. and 3. companies to the Arnhem bridge, the 6. company towards Oosterbeek, and the 4. and 5. companies to Nijmegen.

Frost decided to establish defensive positions around the northern abutment to await the rest of the 1st Airborne Division.

Had it not been for the 13 men led by a teenage SS-Sturmmann named Helmut Buttlar, the 2nd Para Battalion would not only have been able to take the railway bridge before the Germans could demolish it, but would also have been able to occupy the road bridge across the Rhine in its entirety. Thus, the 1st Airborne Division would have been able to not only establish a bridgehead on both sides of the Rhine, but would also have been able to attack towards the south to take the Waal bridges across Nijmegen in cooperation with the American 82nd Airborne Division – something that would have crowned Operation "Market Garden" with a 100% success.*

However, it would be to say too much that Buttlar and his comrades alone had a prolonging impact on the war. the Allies still had the possibility to bring the whole operation to a victorious end. Frost's blocking of the Arnhem bridge efficiently thwarted Model's and Bittrich's efforts to place focus of the defensive battle to the crucial Waal bridges in Nijmegen, and 36 hours after Frost had consolidated

* As we will see later, after a decisive battle in the morning of 18 September, the Germans had no more than a few hundred leaderless men remaining of the by then fallen Gräbner's battalion, as well as the motley crew of 750 soldiers of mixed quality – to put it mildly – in Nijmegen and at Betuwe, the patch of land between Nijmegen and Arnhem. If the 1st Airborne Division had managed to set up a bridgehead south of the Rhine, these Germans could have ended up in a vice on 18 September between two Allied airborne divisions. Even though large parts of them were seconded for defensive tasks to the north and to the south, the Allies could have had multiple superiority in numbers in the area between Arnhem and Nijmegen.

his positions at the road bridge, British XXX Corps reached Nijmegen. Several external factors also made the Buttlar group's defensive fight at Oosterbeek so important, including the 3rd Battalion's halt at Hotel Hartenstein – which Harzer, 9. SS-Panzer-Division's acting commander, in astonishment called "a great tactical mistake".[277] But the fact remains: Under the given circumstances, Buttlar's and his group's intervention in the battle had an absolutely decisive impact – which has been overlooked both by Buttlar's commanders and post-war historians. It is worth noting that this event, or at least its importance, was overlooked by Cornelius Ryan in his classic *A Bridge Too Far*, while the divisional commander Urquhart himself experienced and described how Frost's battalion was halted in the eastern outskirts of Oosterbeek. In hindsight, one can see that several circumstances made Buttlar's and his men's efforts tip the scale, prolonging the Second World War by six months. The most important contributing factor to this was the disastrous mistake in terms of priorities made by the 82nd Airborne Division, which was landed south of Nijmegen.

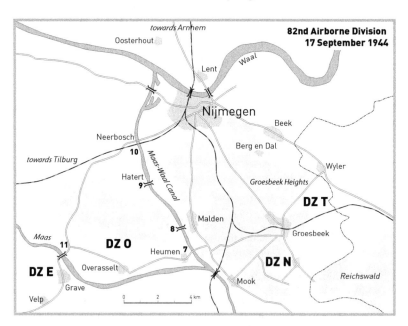

VI.

Wrong Priorities
Nijmegen 17 September 1944

SECURE THE BRIDGES!

Standing in the doorway to the C-47 transport aircraft at an altitude of 200 metres at a quarter past one in the afternoon of 17 September, the American paratrooper John Thompson was able to see the bridge on the river Maas north of Grave only a kilometre or so away. With its nine arched spans, it almost looked unnaturally large against the surrounding plains and the small town. In those days, it was Europe's longest bridge. It was Thompson's main target.

The green jump light signalling that it was time to jump was on, but Thompson ordered his men to wait until they had come closer to the bridge. Sporadic fire came from some anti-aircraft positions by the bridge, and from the crowd of houses in the small town of Grave which the transport aircraft just flew over, south of the bridge, but it was not as powerful as could be expected – the low-flying Mustang aircraft from the 78th Fighter Group had done a good job. While the air behind them was filled with parachutes in various colours, Thompson and his men threw themselves out over the fields 600 metres southwest of the bridge. Once down on the ground, he assembled his platoon of fifteen men, and, protected by the deep draining ditches criss-crossing the fields, the rushed with all their might towards the abutment. There was no time to lose here! Thompson was not going to wait for the "latecomers" in the other platoons of the company that had jumped farther back.

The twenty-seven-year-old John "Jocko" Thompson was a First Lieutenant and Platoon Commander of "E" Company in U.S. 504th Parachute Infantry Regiment. Two thousand men from this regiment of Brigadier General James Gavin's 82nd Airborne Division were raining down over the so-called Drop Zone "Oscar" (DZ "O"), in the triangle between the river Maas to the south, the Maas-Waal canal to the east, and the railway line Nijmegen-Tilburg to the north. Gavin had declined using any Pathfinders for most of his landing zones – he wanted to accomplish a maximum surprise effect – but he considered Drop Zone "Oscar" important enough to make an exception and had Pathfinders landed there. Their smoke signals gave clear guidance for the transport aircraft as they came in just after one o'clock in the afternoon of 17 September.

The 504th Parachute Infantry Regiment under Colonel Reuben H. Tucker had been inflicted with severe losses in Italy in 1943/1944 – where it had been participating in the invasions of both Sicily and at Salerno and at Anzio. Therefore, the unit had not taken part in any fighting since March 1944 and was thus both rested and well-equipped. The replacements for the losses consisted of well-trained and highly motivated paratroopers. The regiment's first task during "Market Garden" consisted of securing the passage for the British XXX Corps from the 101st Airborne's sector in the south and to the major city of Nijmegen, eight kilometres northeast of Grave. That meant that they had to take not only the Maas bridge at Grave, but also at least any of the four bridges across the Maas-Waal canal that run towards the north from the Maas to the parallel river Waal, seven kilometres further to the north, west of Nijmegen. Drop Zone "Oscar" had been placed on the great, open fields north of the Maas, more than three kilometres west of the southernmost of the bridges across the Maas-Waal canal, called Bridge No. 7 – the great sluice bridge at Heumen, only a thousand metres north of the point where the canal separates from the Maas.

QR22: VIDEO
Authentic wartime movie footage and from 1:18 a re-enactment at the Bridge at Grave.

The top priority for the 504th Parachute Infantry Regiment was taking the 400-metre bridge across the river Maas at Grave. Not only was this necessary for the advancement of the British XXX Corps; the division commander Gavin considered the task "essential to the division's survival", since it ensured 82nd Airborne Division's contact with the Allies' rear area. Hence the sending in of Pathfinders at Drop Zone "Oscar" north of Grave. Moreover, Tucker's regiment was dropped on both sides of the Maas; the "E" Company in the fields on the left side of the river, and the rest of the regiment at Drop Zone "Oscar" on the other side of the Maas. The 504th Parachute Infantry Regiment made a perfect landing on both sides of the Maas and the bridge at Grave.

The 925-kilometre river Maas (Meuse) begins at the Langres plateau in northern France, and runs to the north, past the city of Sedan, straight across Belgium, and into Holland, where it continues towards the north close to the German border. Quite some distance southeast of Grave, the river bends to the northwest, only to finally, some ten kilometres northwest of Grave, bend to the west and discharge itself into the North Sea south of Rotterdam. At Grave, the river runs in a north by north-westerly direction.

Grave, a small town with a few thousand inhabitants, is situated on a 400-metre-wide strip of land that is delimited by the lowland stream Graafse Raam to the west and the Maas to the east. The great bridge is located about half a kilometre north of the town itself. About two hundred metres northwest of the (south-)western abutment, the Graafse Raam discharges itself into the river. From the fields where Thompson's men had landed, it was possible to proceed to the Maas bridge on a small bridge across the stream, at the power plant 250 metres from the mouth. Here was the powerhouse, which some of Thompson's men

QR23: VIDEO
Film from the air of the Grave bridge today.

subjected to fierce fire, while others rushed ahead across the field on both sides of the small bridge. They threw themselves into the stream, which was no more than a little over a metre deep, wading across it with their firearms raised above their heads. On the other side, the soaking wet paratroopers charged the sluice house without meeting any resistance. When they penetrated the building, they came across a terrified, wounded German soldier next to four dead comrades.

Suddenly, in the middle of the firefight, a couple of motorcycles came rumbling along the road from Grave to the south. The terrified riders gave full throttle, swept past the bunker, took the curve as narrowly as they could, and disappeared across the bridge. Everyone was probably equally surprised. But when two lorries followed immediately afterwards, the Americans were ready. Sergeant Roy Tidd aimed for the driver's cabin of the first lorry and hit the driver with a well-aimed shot from his M1 Garand. The lorry skid and came to a stop, which forced the driver in the following one to

Air photo of the Maas bridge at Grave. The image is taken from northwest. The lowland stream Graafse Raam and the little bridge with the powerhouse are visible in the foreground. A glimpse of Grave is visible top right. The fields on the other side are the Drop Zone "Oscar". This picture was taken before the war, before the bunker at the bridge had been built.

hit the brakes. Clusters of German soldiers – between forty and fifty, according to Thompson's estimate – jumped off the flatbeds and disappeared behind the road bank on the eastern side.

But even though they were three times as many as the Americans, these Germans turned out to have little interest in fighting. A few volleys from the BAR light machine gun that the Americans had taken along were enough for the Germans to leave their position and flee back towards Grave.

The last obstacle now was a square, grey concrete bunker one hundred metres south of the sluice bridge, just west of the Maas river. On top of it, the Germans had built a new section out of wood and sandbags, and there, a 20 mm anti-aircraft gun had been erected. The Germans tried to open fire on the Americans with it, but must have felt very frustrated when they discovered that the enemy was on lower terrain, so low that the automatic gun could not be aimed at them.

The bunker from 1936 had concrete walls that were 1.5 metres thick, and two underground floors. Electric ventilation equipment made sure that the gunpowder gases were pumped outside. But it was no match for the American paratroopers of Thompson's platoon, who had brought along two Bazookas. Private Robert McGaw dragged his Bazooka into firing position twenty metres from the bunker, and fired three rockets in quick succession. One missed, but two went straight in through a loophole and exploded. After that, the fire fell silent. Other paratroopers stormed the building, where they came across two dead and one wounded German soldiers.

By that time, paratroopers from the other platoons of the "E" Company had arrived at the southern abutment, which was now in the Americans' hands. Meanwhile, the main part of the 504th Parachute Infantry Regiment had been landed well at Drop Zone "Oscar", more than a kilometre further east, on the other side of the Maas. The 2nd Battalion set off at full speed towards the bridge at Grave, with the "F" Company at the lead. Just like Thompson's men, the paratroopers made their way through draining ditches. Just in front of the abutment, they knocked out two German anti-aircraft positions. "They took no prisoners", "F" Company's combat report stated dryly.[278] Then, a squad carefully made it out onto the bridge and started advancing towards the other side, where Thompson's men had just suppressed the last German resistance. "The most important bridge of all", as Gavin put it, was in American hands. Without First Lieutenant Thompson's initiative to jump as close to the bridge as possible, and storm it immediately afterwards without waiting for the rest of the "E" Company, the Germans had probably been able to blow it up.*

Now, the Americans cut the cables to the explosives, which had been primed in advance, with their field spades. The next step was to storm Grave. It did not take long to make the town's 400-strong German garrison to either give up or flee. At 2000 hrs, Grave was reported as secure.

Meanwhile, the 1st Battalion of the 504th Parachute Infantry Regiment had been advancing eastwards from Drop Zone "Oscar" to secure the bridges across the Maas-Waal Canal, which runs out from the Maas six kilometres west of Grave and ends in the Waal west of Nijmegen seven kilometres further north. "B" Company under Captain Thomas Helgeson assembled quickly after the landing and took the shortest route to the southernmost bridge, the sluice bridge at Heumen – the paved country road that runs along the northern riverbank of the Maas. As they approached the bridge, they were met with fire. The paratroopers threw themselves for cover into the ditches, and quickly got their BAR light machine guns going.** The Germans fled back towards the sluice house on the little island in the middle of the 70 metre wide canal, just where the bridge is. This made it possible for American engineers to crawl ahead, protected by the elevated terrain, and cut all the cables to the explosives on the bridge.

At the same moment, a new force of Ameerican paratroopers came rushing from the eastern side of the canal. Caught between two

---

* John Samuel Thompson was a professional baseball player both before and after the war. He passed away on 3 February 1988, aged 71. In 2004, the bridge at Grave was given the name "the John Thompson Bridge".

** BAR, abbreviation of M1918 Browning Automatic Rifle, was a light American infantry machine gun with a firing rate at 500 rounds per minute. With cartridge magazines and a front stand, it could easily be operated by a single man.

fires, the Germans on the little island surrendered almost immedi-ately, and the Americans seized the captured 75 mm Soviet anti-air-craft gun that their opponents had been using. The Americans on the eastern side belonged to the 2nd Battalion of the 505th Parachute Infantry Regiment. It had been flown in wiht forty-five Skytrain planes, which had been met with fierce anti-aircraft fire during their approach. Since this forced the aircraft up to an altitude of between 800 and 900 feet – instead of the ordered 600 feet – most of the sol-diers of the 2nd Battalion were dropped north instead of south of the town of Groesbeek. This was unfortunate, as the unit had been tasked with establishing contact with the 504th Parachute Infan-try Regiment at the Maas-Waal Canal, and the distance there now became longer. The battalion commander, the legendary Lieutenant Colonel Benjamin "Vandy" Vandervoort, divided his unit so that two strong patrols went westwards, towards the Maas-Waal-Canal, while the rest of the force was tasked with establishing connections with the rest of the regiment at Drop Zone "N" south of Groesbeek. It was one of the former patrols that arrived at the sluice bridge at Heumen from the eastern side.

But fifteen hundred metres further up the canal, the next bridge across the Maas-Waal Canal, the Blankenberg bridge at Malden (Bridge No. 8), was blown to pieces just as the "C" Company and a platoon from the "A" Company of the 504th Parachute Infantry Regiment's 1st Battalion were preparing to storm it. A patrol from Vandervoort's battalion arrived on the eastern side of the canal only a few minutes too late. But they "cleared the house" from German defenders, the 5. Kompanie of the home guard battalion Landesschützen-Bataillon II/6. Thirty-two of them were taken prisoners.[279]

QR24: VIDEO
American instruction film about the BAR.

Yet another two kilometres to the north, at Hatert, was the next bridge, designated as No. 9. There, the German home guard captain Hauptmann Ernst Sieger received a report on the evening of 17 September from Feldwebel Ingendahl, whose platoon was holding the left flank of Sieger's 4. Kompanie in Landesschützen-Bataillon II/6, that contact with the 5. Kompanie to the south had been lost. Ingendahl's home guard men had also happened to get into battle with a group of American paratroopers that had turned up. Sieger sent forward two machine gun sections to support them, and a machine gun section from Pionier-Kompanie 434 also joined them. They formed a semi-circle-shaped defence south of Hatert, and were able to count their blessings as the Americans for the rest of the afternoon and evening did not make any serious attempts to attack – in spite of them having one battalion each from the 504th and 505th PIR on either side of the canal at Malden, only three kilometres further south.

Just after seven o'clock in the evening, a man arrived from Pionier-Kompanie 434 on motorcycle from Malden, reporting that the village was devoid of troops – both German and American! A little over half an hour later, an Oberleutnant turned up with a message

The sluice bridge at Heumen.

from Hauptmann Max Runge, commander of a company from the Fallschirm-Panzer-Ersatz- und Ausbildungs-Regiment "Hermann Göring", that Sieger's company was to fall back to Neerbosch, a few kilometres north. This company had been retreating back towards Germany when the American landings had commenced. When Runge saw how weakly defended the two bridges – one railway bridge and one road bridge – at Neerbosch (No. 10) were, he decided to order a halt and position his unit for defence. The road bridge in this place was doubtlessly the most important bridge across the Maas-Waal Canal, as it led the main road from Grave to Nijmegen across the canal. This bridge had not been subject to any attacks either. To the Allies, it was of course enough that they had taken the sluice bridge at Heumen. Sieger gave orders that the bridge at Hatert was to be blown up – this was carried out at 2015 hrs – and then set off on the northbound road.

It may seem curious that the Germans at these important bridges did not come under any harder pressure during 17 September, but the 504th Parachute Infantry Regiment had only sent in its 1st Battalion with more than six hundred men to secure these objectives across a width of more than five kilometres. The 2nd Battalion was positioned at the Grave bridge to defend it and the 3rd Battalion remained passive in order to hold the landing area and the approaches from Grave to the Maas-Waal Canal.

In fact, most of Gavin's 82nd Airborne Division – about four thousand men from the 505th Parachute Infantry Regiment and the 508th Parachute Infantry Regiment – were not sent in primarily to open the road for the British tanks, but simply to defend themselves. This was observable already in Gavin's orders for taking the bridge at Grave, but mainly by him seconding two thirds of the force that had been landed first to defend the landing zones against an imagined German force in the Reichswald forest on the Dutch-German border.

The two other parachute regiments that the 82nd Airborne Division landed (apart from the 504th), the 505th and the 508th Para-

---

* Today, this bridge is in the middle of Nijmegen, but in 1944, it was surrounded by the countryside around the little village of Hatert, more than three kilometres southwest of the built-up areas in Nijmegen.

chute Infantry Regiments, were landed quite some distance to the east of the Maas-Waal Canal, in the low-lying fields north and south of the Groesbeek Ridge. This forested massif rises mightily between 50 to 70 metres above the landscape just southeast of Nijmegen. Here, the terrain is completely different to the otherwise flat Dutch landscape.

The commanders of the 505th and the 508th both had Swedish ancestry, Colonels William Ekman and Roy Lindquist. The largest force of the division was landed at Drop Zone "N", south of Groes-beek: the 505th PIR with 2,100 men, the 376th Field Artillery Battalion, Brigadier General Gavin and the division staff, as well as Lieutenant-General Browning, commander of the I Airborne Corps, and his extensive staff. Out of the 480 transport sent in for the 82nd Airborne Division, 213 and all of the 50 Waco gliders were seconded to Drop Zone "N". Quite characteristically, Gavin forwent his fourth regiment – the 325th Glider Infantry Regiment – in the first wave of landings, in favour of the landing of an artillery battalion, the 376th Field Artillery Battalion with 42 tons of equipment, including twelve 75 mm howitzers, which was quite a defensive measure.

In Mook, a few kilometres west of the landing zone, was the 21-year-old Unteroffizier Jakob Moll of the German Grenadier-Ersatz-Regiment 520. When the American aircraft came in in large numbers, he and his comrades expected a bomb attack. "Instead", he recounted, "the plane hatches suddenly opened and paratroopers began jumping out. In second it seemed the sky was filled with red, blue, green and yellow bobbles". Moll admits that he was completely demoralised at the sight of this superior force.[280]

The main task for the 505th PIR was to establish defence positions towards the southeast. Unteroffizier Moll's German company was ordered into the forest on its way north to attack the American landing zone. Among the trees, Moll suddenly came across two American soldiers. He took off his German steel helmet and waved at them, and the two Americans waved back – they probably took him for one of their own. When Moll and his comrades soon afterwards arrived at the edge of the forest, they were met by a dreadful sight: "The field was covered with gliders and paratroopers were dashing about, getting

equipment together, unloading the cargo gliders. Jeeps, guns, ammunition, all sorts of equipment". The German company commander
asked if they would attack, but Moll advised him against this. It would
be lunacy to storm this mass of elite soldiers with nothing else than
a poorly equipped company of wounded convalescents. Instead, the
Germans retreated back to Mook to set up defence positions where
the Maas-Waal Canal meets the river Maas. When they reached the
country road to the south, they found it filled with fleeing German
labour soldiers. "They were panic-stricken and asked what they should
do", Moll recounts. Then, he and his comrade set up battle positions in
trenches on both sides of the road.[281] Soon afterwards, the Americans
emerged from out of the woods.

The 505th PIR's 1st Battalion managed, without meeting any
resistance, to assemble 90 per cent of its forces within 20 minutes of
the landing. "B" Company under Lieutenant Harold E. Miller went
into the woods on their way southwards and eastwards. "We saw
Germans dug in on a line northwest to southeast about two hundred
fifty yards", Miller recounts, adding laconically: "These enemy troops
offered little resistance and thirty-three prisoners were taken".[282] Moll
was one of the first on the German side to be wounded, and managed
to get away. He spent the remains of the war in a German hospital. He
recounts that he felt relief when being wounded and getting out from
the war.

Somewhat further down the road, a squad of American soldiers
under Lieutenant Stanley Weinberg carried out an ambush against a
private German Opel car. They took three Germans captive, one of
them, with a severe head injury, Oberstleutnant Siegfried Hanisch,
commander of the pioneer units at Wehrkreis VI (Military Area 6).
Hanisch was so badly injured that his life could not be saved.

Gavin may have been cautious, but he was not a coward. Leading
of a group of soldiers, he set off on foot along the way into the woods
west of Groesbeek, in order to make it to the place at a crossroads
inside the forest that he had designated his command post. Suddenly, a
clattering sound was heard, and a series of machine gun bullets whist-
led past the paratrooper general, who immediately dived straight into
the ditch. The next moment, Captain Arie Bestebreurtje had the white

patch of skin between the rim of the German's helmet and his machine gun in his sight. He softly squeezed the trigger of his gun – and the upper part of the top of the German's head flew backwards, together with the helmet, in a single bloody mess.

Gavin turned to Bestebreurtje: "Whatever your role in this division, you're a mighty hand to have around!" he said. Bestebreurtje served as Gavin's Dutch liaison officer. In 1941, he had made it over to Great Britain illegally, where he eventually was enrolled by the OSS.* In the 82nd Airborne he went under the moniker "Captain Harry", since the Americans found it so difficult to pronounce his surname.

In the forest that Gavin's group had entered, there turned out to be a German ammunition cache and a force of 200 German soldiers. The machine-gunner who had been firing at Gavin was part of this unit, but most of his comrades fled without putting up any resistance. The 3rd Battalion of 505 PIR entered the little town of Groesbeek without much difficulty. At three o'clock in the afternoon, the town was reported to be under complete control by the Americans. Most of the Germans had fled or surrendered. This battalion reported the Reichswald to be weakly held by Germans, and definitely too dense to allow any tanks to operate there.

AMERICANS AT THE NIJMEGEN BRIDGE

One often neglected fact in historiography is that the Americans took control of at least the southern abutment of the large road bridge in Nijmegen already during the night between the 17 and 18 September. The fact that they gave up this crucial bridge after that – and then repeated the entire process less than a few hours later! – is not so much due to the almost non-existent German resistance at that point. The result was that they eventually had to fight a bloody battle to make it across the river Waal at Nijmegen.

* Office of Strategic Services, the predecessor of the present-day American intelligence agency, the CIA.

At twenty-five past one in the afternoon of 17 September, about 120 Skytrains arrived with almost two thousand paratroopers from Colonel Roy E. Lindquist's 508th Parachute Infantry Regiment, 82nd Airborne Division, at an altitude of 200 metres above the Groesbeek Ridge. As the paratroopers were standing in the open doors of their aircraft, hooked up onto the aircraft's static lines, they could see the crowd of houses in Nijmegen only a few kilometres away clearly. "*Let's go!*" In quick succession, the men rushed forward, throwing themselves out over Drop Zone "Tango" ("T") northeast of Groesbeek, just inside the border to Germany. The 21-year-old Private First Class James Wickline fell to his death as his parachute failed to deploy.*

But in general, it was a perfect landing with only minor casualties. Major Louis Mendez, commander of the 3rd Battalion, wrote afterwards: "We could not have landed better under any circumstances". Within 90 minutes, 90 percent of the regiment was gathered and ready for battle. But there would not be much of a battle. The few Germans who were in the area quickly scuttled away or surrendered. Private First Class Ralph "Zig" Boroughs recounts:

" We could see rifle fire coming from a building across the track. A trooper fired a rifle grenade into the building. After the smoke cleared, a white flag was hung out of a window. We held our fire. Then twenty to thirty men, with hands raised, filed out. The fight was over. None of our men had been injured in the skirmish.

As we moved down the embankment, bodies of dead and wounded enemy soldiers lay in our path. One of our paratroopers pulled out his pistol to finish off a wounded German. The German reached up and caught the barrel of the pistol with one hand and pleaded, '*Nein! Nein!*' The words fell on deaf ears. The wounded man was blasted into eternity. This was my first view of dead people other than carefully

---

* Wickline currently rests in Grave 21, Plot I, Row 17 in the American war cemetery in Margraten, Holland. A 13-year-old Dutch boy named Maarten Vossen decided in 2002 to "adopt", that is, maintain, Wickline's grave, and he has done so ever since.

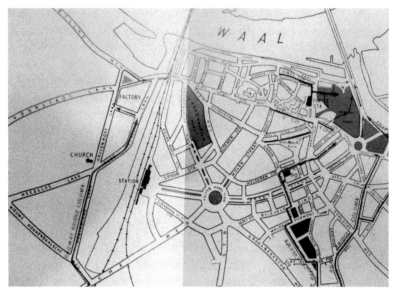

The bridges in Nijmegen. The road bridge to the east (right) and the railway bridge to the west.

James Wickline. (Images via Maarten Vossen.)

prepared bodies laid out in neat caskets at funerals. I can still envision those ashen faces and eyes fixed in a frightful stare, but we had no time for morbid emotions that day. Survival demanded that we push on and shove those kinds of thoughts into the subconscious.

We followed a dirt road leading east from the railroad through open farmland. It was hot, and our equipment was heavy. We soon loaded all the demolition equipment on the backs of the prisoners. That made the march easier for us and harder for the prisoners to escape. Brooks, who could speak some Pennsylvanian German, found out that most of the prisoners were Czechs and Poles who had been drafted into the German army.

Soon we approached a Dutch farmhouse on the side of the dusty road. A curious couple came from the house to look at the strange creatures marching by. The woman was very attractive, and one of our lusty troops hollered to his buddies, 'I sure would like to take that broad to bed!'

The woman heard the remark and responded with a broad smile. As we passed close by, another trooper asked the woman, 'Do you speak English?'

'Yes,' she replied. 'I understand English very well.' " [283]

In Drop Zone "Tango", there were two German anti-aircraft guns: One group of paratroopers landed right on top of one of them, which was immediately rendered harmless, and the other was soon also put out of action. The Groesbeek Ridge, the little villages of Berg en Dal and Beek as well as the Nijmegen suburb De Ploeg were quickly occupied almost without meeting any resistance at all. Then, the Americans dug themselves into trenches just on the outskirts of Nijmegen – while the Germans in the town itself fled in panic. The main German force of troops in Nijmegen was made up of a battalion from Landesschützen-Regiment 6 with three companies of home guard soldiers and one anti-aircraft company, in all perhaps 400 men, largely old men or boys aged 16 to 17 years.[284]

The sight of the thousands of paratroopers descending right out-side town was enough for the Germans in Nijmegen to lose heart completely. Harmel described these soldiers as "grandpas, musicians, and base wallahs" who were not satisfactorily armed either: "They had very old carbines from the First War, and also from 1870".[285] Most of them hardly felt like fighting against well-equipped American elite soldiers. The town *Kommandant*, Hauptmann Hagemeister, set off by car across the bridge northbound, as did the head of police, General-major Hellmuth Mascus.[286] The three home guard companies simply disintegrated into thin air; Major Rasch, the adjutant of the German Division z.b.V. 406 (see below) concluded that " the three companies in Nijmegen must be regarded as write-offs; no more reports were ever received".[287] In the evening of 17 September, even a train packed with fleeing Germans rattled straight through the American-held Groes-beek, on its way towards Germany. Major «Doc» Daniel McIlvoy, the regiment physician at the 508th PIR, recounted: "Within a matter of short time, less than an hour after moving into a girl's school the gates came down and a train passed. In the cars' open doors there were Ger-man troops. We waved, they waved back. As it later turned out, this was a train full of German soldiers that had escaped from Nijmegen by simply starting up and driving through our whole troop concentra-tions, no one stopping to think that this might very well be an enemy train getting out of the area"[288]

An immediate and resolutely carried out attack by the 508th Parachute Infantry Regiment from Drop Zone "T" would doubt-lessly have led to the last few Germans being thrown out of Nijme-gen and the road bridge across the Waal, which by then was still unmined, passing undamaged into American hands. But the regi-mental commander Lindquist only gave orders at around six o'clock in the evening of 17 September, four and a half hours after the land-ing, to his 508th Parachute Infantry Regiment to begin its advance towards the bridges in Nijmegen. Pater Hermanus van Driel at the Neboklooster monastery on the southeast outskirts of Nijmegen wrote in his diary: "The Germans left everything behind and fled for their lives. The residents in our neighbourhood were let out and from all directions we could hear [the patriotic song] 'Oranje boven'. Convinced that they had continued to Nijmegen, we called them in the evening, but there were no soldiers to be seen and you could not believe that." [289]

The men and women of the Dutch resistance, wearing orange armbands and with a variety of armaments, appeared and were able to disarm demoralised Germans in many parts of the town. At the PGEM's* large power plant in north-western Nijmegen, on the eastern side of the Maas-Waal canal's discharge in the Waal, a small resistance group called "De Pandoeren Club" under the 22-year-old student Jacobus G. Brouwer managed to persuade the ten German guards to surrender.

After that, the Dutch took control of the plant themselves, having a good view all over the area on the other side of the river from its elevated roof. This would eventually be of great importance to the Americans.

Lindquist gave the task of advancing towards the bridge to the 1st Battalion, which sent forward a reconnaissance patrol. It advanced through streets that were completely abandoned by the German soldiers, but, on the other hand, packed with Dutchmen celebrating that the hates occupants had left, and reached the bridge without incident before the sunset, which takes place just before eight o'clock in the evening. The 19-year-old Private First Class Joseph "Chuck" Atkins** tells the previously quite unknown story about this mission: "I was called on to take the point going into Nijmegen. As we entered the city, a crown of people gathered around us, and we had to push our way through. Three of us in the lead became separated from the other troopers behind us by the crowds of Dutch people. We three continued to make our way into the city until we came to the bridge. At the bridge, only a few German soldiers were standing around a small artillery weapon. I had a Thompson sub and a .45 pistol. The other two were armed with M1 rifles. They covered me as I jumped up and yelled, 'Hände hock!' [sic] ('Hands up!')

The Germans were so surprised; the six or seven defenders of the bridge gave up without resisting." [290]

The fact that three paratroopers sufficed to occupy one of Operation "Market Garden's" most important objective really says

* Provinciale Geldersche Electriciteits Maatschappij.
** Joseph Atkins lived in Heritage Lake, Indiana, after the war. He passed away in May 1997, only 69 years old. Atkins has had a crossroads named after him in Normandy.

everything about how weak the German resistance was. Atkins and his comrades remained at the site, more or less being the sole masters of the bridge. Meanwhile, Gavin's more than seven thousand landed elite soldiers – with artillery guns, anti-tank guns, and jeeps – were fully occupied with reinforcing defensive positions in the countryside south and west of Nijmegen against an enemy that hardly existed. The reconnaissance patrol was followed by a platoon, Lieutenant Robert Weaver's 3rd Platoon of "C" Company, 508th PIR's 1st Battalion.

Weaver's men lost their way in the throng of streets in the city and decided to pause to ask a Nijmegen resident to show them the way. Meanwhile, frustration was growing among many townspeople that no Allied soldiers arrived in spite of the Germans having left. One of them, a young member of the resistance named Gert van Hees, made it out of town and found Lindquist's command post, where he arrived just after Weaver's platoon had decamped. He told them excitedly that the Americans had to hurry up, since there neither were any Germans in the town nor at the road bridge. Lindquist immediately contacted Lieutenant-Colonel Sheilds Warren, commander of the 1st Battalion, ordering him to send his "A" and "B" companies as well as the battalion's mortar and machine gun squads marching towards the bridges. Van Hees would lead the way on bicycle.

But Joe Atkins and his comrades at the road bridge knew nothing about this. They now started to despair. It had now been an hour since they took the bridge. "It began to get dark", Atkins recounted. "None of our other troops had showed up. We decided to pull back away from the bridge, knowing we could not hold off a German attack. The German prisoners asked to come with us, but we refused, having no way to guard them. As we were leaving, we could hear heavy equipment approaching the bridge."[291] This was the vehicles of SS-Hauptsturmführer Gräbner's Panzer reconnaissance battalion of the 9. SS-Panzer-Division arriving from the north – after having crossed the still free Rhine bridge at Arnhem – to find out about the situation in Nijmegen. They arrived just as Atkins and his men had left the site, but were quickly summoned north again as there were reports that British paratroopers had taken the northern road bridge abutment in Arnhem, keeping the 10. SS-Panzer-Division from quickly crossing the Rhine and occupying the Waal bridges in Nijmegen. Gräbner only left two armoured personnel carriers behind in Nijmegen.[292]

Gavin has justified the failure to quickly strike against Nijmegen by pointing at air reconnaissance having localised large German Panzer forces in the Reichswald forest, and that it was therefore absolutely necessary to set up a defence line against them before moving on. After the war, there have been attempts to find these air reconnaissance reports that Gavin claims to refer to, without any success.[293] This still does not explain Gavin's continuedly defensive stance, as the 505th PIR already in the afternoon of 17 September reported that the Reichswald was not only considerably weaker held by Germans than had been expected, but also was too dense for any tanks to be able to operate there.

Gavin had been tasked with securing the large bridge in Nijmegen, but he himself did not issue any written order about this, but stressed the defence at Groesbeek instead. According to himself, he gave the commander of the 508th PIR, Colonel Lindquist, an oral order on 15 September to send his 1st Battalion towards the bridge in Nijmegen "without delay after landing". But according to Lindquist, Gavin's oral orders on the contrary meant that "no battalion was to go for the bridge until the regiment had secured its other objectives, that is to say, not until he had established defensive positions covering his assigned portion of the high ground and the northern part of the division glider landing zone".[294] This is consistent with what was told by the commander of this 1st Battalion, Lieutenant Colonel Shields Warren, who attested that he had been ordered by Lindquist to first take an "assigned initial objective" close to the Nijmegen suburb of De Ploeg at the road between Nijmegen and Groesbeek. According to Warren, he was to first set up defence positions there, and after that only "be prepared to go into Nijmegen later".[295] As we have seen previously, the corps commander Browning believed that taking the Nijmegen bridge should wait until all other tasks had been solved in a satisfactory way and the Groesbeek-Berg en Dal heights were secured.[296]

17 SEPTEMBER 1944 – A SUMMARY

On this 17 September 1944, 1,044 American and 335 British transport aircraft landed 431 gliders and more than 19,000 paratroopers. Out of the latter, 7,440 men were included in nine battalions and support forces in the 82nd Airborne Division, which also landed 12 artillery guns, eight anti-tank guns, 24 jeeps, and more than 250 tons of equipment. The resistance they had encountered was mainly weak and half-hearted, and therefore, all of this enormous landing operation had been crowned with success everywhere. And still, until the evening of 17 September, they could not spare any forces to take any of the absolutely most important targets, the bridges across the river Waal in Nijmegen. It certainly seems as though the decisive bridge in Nijmegen was "a bridge too far" for the 82nd Airborne Division.

Further south, at Eindhoven, U.S. 101st Airborne Division had been more successful by securing all of its river crossings except for one, the one at Best. But the other bridge across the Wilhelmina Canal, at Son, had been demolished by the Germans right before the very eyes of the Americans, who thereafter halted for the night on the northern outskirts of Eindhoven. The British Guards Armoured Division had done the same in Valkenswaard, a little over five kilometres south of Eindhoven, after it had swept away the German defence to the south without any major difficulty. As we have seen, Field Marshal Montgomery was already unhappy with the commander of the tank division, Major-General Allan Adair, who was accused of "a lack of enterprise". The situation was similar at the British 1st Airborne Division, where one of the two brigades remained defensive to protect the next day's landings, while most of the other brigade, the parachute brigade, had either been stopped by the Germans or – where resistance was almost non-existent – been ordered to halt for the night. Without any doubt, all of these Allied divisions had squandered good opportunities for even bigger success during this first day of "Market Garden". But one battalion, the British 2nd Parachute Battalion under Lieutenant-Colonel John Frost, had, by taking of the northern part of the road bridge across the Rhine in Arnhem, created the basic prerequisite for the entire enterprise to succeed, causing the Germans serious problems.

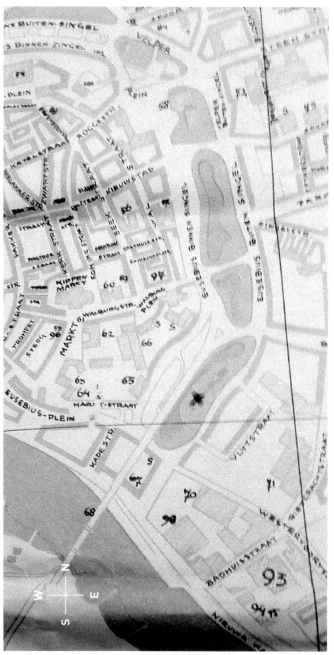

British deployments around the bridge on 18 September 1944: BETWEEN KADESTRAAT AND THE BRIDGE: No. 1 and 2 Platoon/"A" Company of the 2nd Bn.; HQ/"A" Company of the 2nd Bn.; Machine-Gun Platoon/"A" Company of the 2nd Bn.; Anti-tank Battery HQ. **WEST OF KADESTRAAT:** HQ/"B" Company of the 2nd Bn.; No. 5 and 6 Platoon/"B" Company of the 2nd Bn. **AT NO. 62, 63 AND 64:** Parts of the HQ and Support Companies, glider pilots; No. 2 Platoon/9th Field Company, Royal Engineers. **AT NO. 65:** HQ/2nd Bn.; mortar platoon/2nd Bn. **AT NO. 66:** 1st Para Brigade HQ; 1st Para Brigade Defence Platoon. **AT THE CROSS:** The Van Limburg school: HQ and No. 9 Platoon/"C" Company of the 3rd Bn.; 1st Para Squadron. **ON THE OTHER SIDE OF THE STREET, TO THE RIGHT OF THE CROSS:** Artillery observers and parts of the signals group. **AT NO. 70 (ALL OF THAT QUARTER):** Part of the 1st Para Bn.'s Defence Platoon. **AT NO. 71:** Part of the 1st Para Brigade HQ's Defence Platoon. No. 8 Platoon/"C" Company of the 3rd Bn. (National Archives, WO 171 393 HW 1st AbnDiv.)

232

VII.

Frost's bridge
18 September 1944

"WE FELT PRETTY COCKY"

Even though the German Paratroop General Student may have captured the complete Allied operational plan in a downed glider, the full situation had not cleared on the German side by the evening of 17 September. A situation map dated 1630 hours on 17 September at the German Armed Forces' Supreme Command shows that the Germans thought that Allied landings had been carried out – apart from at the real sites – at Veenendaal, twenty kilometres west of Arnhem; at Betuwe (the "Island") just north of Nijmegen; at Tiel north of the Waal, 25 km further west; at Zaltbommel, another 15 km to the southwest, south of the Waal; and even at Deelen, 10 kilometres north of Arnhem as well.[297] Above all, it seems as though all units believed that "someone else" would secure the important road bridge across the Rhine in Arnhem. This was something that the advance force of the 2nd Battalion of British 1st Airborne Division could exploit. At around eight o'clock in the evening of 17 September, the northern abutment was in their hands, whereby the Germans were kept from quickly dispatching their 10. SS-Panzer-Division to the Waal bridges at Nijmegen.

SS-Unterscharführer Adolf Lochbrunner and many other soldiers from 3. Kompanie of SS-Panzergrenadier-Regiment 21 had made it to Arnhem on bicycle the fifty kilometres from Deventer to the north. When they arrived during the night of 17 September, nobody seemed to know anything. "The situation wasn't only completely confused", Lochbrunner recounts, "but it was completely impossible to get an overview of it. Everywhere around us, in houses and gardens, there could be English paratroopers."[298]

As we have seen (Chapter 5), nine armoured cars leading Kampfgruppe Brinkmann (the remains of the 10. SS-Panzer-Division's Panzer reconnaissance battalion) had been halted by the British east of
the Arnhem bridge's northern abutment in the evening of the 17 September. This vanguard, led by SS-Obersturmführer Karl Ziebrecht,
was followed successively by the rest of SS-Kampfgruppe Brinkmann,
twenty-six armoured personnel carriers with a few hundred men, and
Kampfgruppe Euling. The latter, actually the 9. SS-Panzer-Division's
II. Bataillon/SS-Panzergrenadier-Regiment 19 under SS-Hauptsturmführer (Captain) Karl-Heinz Euling, was also on its way towards
Nijmegen. Euling had not been able to establish any radio contact with
the divisional headquarters, and was surprised when he was stopped
by soldiers from the 10. SS-Panzer-Division reporting that the road
was blocked by the enemy and that the commander of the combat
group, SS-Sturmbannführer (Major) Heinz Brinkmann, was yet to
be seen. Euling's 400 soldiers, however, with two Jagdpanzer IV tank
destroyers, four armoured personnel carriers (two of which with one
75 mm gun each), four 20 mm anti-tank guns, one 75 mm light infantry gun and one 120 mm mortar, constituted a reinforcement that was
more than welcome to Ziebrecht's weak units.

The British also received reinforcements at the road bridge. The
vanguard was joined by the battalion headquarters under Lieutenant-Colonel Frost and the headquarters company with another hundred men. At around a quarter to nine, the headquarters of the 1st
Parachute Brigade also arrived – commanded by Major Anthony Hibbert – and three reconnaissance jeeps under Major Freddie Gough.
Missing, however, was the brigade commander Lathbury, who had
been left behind together with the divisional commander Urquhart in
Oosterbeek.

Lieutenant-Colonel Frost quickly positioned his men into a circular defence in the surrounding buildings 200 metres upwards
from the bridge and 150 metres to each side from the bridge ramp.
The 1st Parachute Brigade's command post was set up in a two-storey house in the Eusebiusbinnensingel, the street running in parallel with the road towards the bridge on its western side, and two
houses further down, Frost set up his own command post in another

two-storey building. Here, SS-Kampfgruppe Sonnenstuhl led by SS-Sturmbannführer Hans-Georg Sonnenstuhl, the commander of SS-Panzer-Artillerie-Regiment 10, came storming. Arriving in northern Arnhem, he came across a platoon of labourers from the Reichsarbeitsdienst (RAD), whom he immediately sent in as combatant units. Sonnenstuhl recounted, "Then, having advanced so far without enemy resistance, I thought it was now just a simple sprint to the bridge, still approximately 300 metres ahead of us. But we were hardly half way when we were fired at from both sides. The bridge ramp was occupied!" [299]

Trooper Ronald Brooker from the 1st Airborne Reconnaissance Squadron was one of those who had been detailed to keep watch at the British brigade headquarters. He was sitting in his jeep with a Vickers machine gun when suddenly a German lorry came driving along the road down from central Arnhem. Brooker opened fire and peppered the German vehicle which stopped. When he rushed up to the lorry, he found a single bloody mess of shattered glass and dead Germans; none had survived. The fallen Germans were dressed in black SS Panzer uniforms. "As we learnt later from the prisoners we interrogated, the enemy had been greatly surprised: Waffen-SS", Sonnenstuhl recounted.[300]

The traces from the first fighting saved other German units from being subject to similar ambushes. As the soldiers of the 3. Kompanie, SS-Panzergrenadier-Regiment 21 approached the bridge, they discovered a tram with wounded people that had been shot to pieces, and realised that the British were in the vicinity, so they abandoned their bicycles and sneaked up to the bridge – where they however were greeted with fire from the British and had to take cover.

According to German reports, the 9. and 10. SS-Panzer divisions fought bitterly for the abutment throughout the night of 17 September – with the 3. Kompanie of SS-Panzergrenadier-Regiment 21 west of the abutment, Brinkmann's SS-Panzer reconnaissance battalion to the north, and Euling's unit to the east. However, there is not much to support this version. On the British side, there is talk of a relatively calm night. Frost describes the situation after the taking of the northern abutment: "The rest of the night was fairly quiet. Every now and then the comparative stillness was disturbed by the flames near the bridge discovering fresh boxes of ammunition to destroy. There was a great flash as each petrol tank flared up and we were warmed and very comfortable. I visited various people, among them 'A' Company, who were in great heart, as they indeed had every reason to be." [301] This calm seems to be confirmed by SS-Unterscharführer Lochbrunner, who recalled that "during the night [of 17 September] we withdrew, with strong sentries, to the cellar of a house in a cross-street with the bridge ramp in sight".[302] Another of the SS soldiers in Arnhem, SS-Sturmmann Wilhelm Balbach, spent the night together with some comrades in a Panzer reconnaissance vehicle. He remembered: "In the middle of the night, one of my comrades said: 'You can kiss my ass, I'm not completely mad. Am I supposed to try to sleep in such an uncomfortable tin can as this when the houses around us are full of soft beds? I'm going out to find a better place to sleep!' I said: 'Cut it out, don't be foolish!' But without heeding my warning, he climbed down from the vehicle and tried to make it into the next house. Immediately, several hand grenades exploded, having been thrown from the top floor of the house. We all jumped out and took cover under the vehicle. From there, we opened fire with all weapons, so that the façade of the house was completely illuminated by all tracers. Then, all fell quiet again".[303]

"We felt quite cocky", the British chief of staff Major Anthony Hibbert recounted.

On the other hand, the Germans engaged small groups of straggling paratroopers who had made it into Arnhem, but, for various reasons, had fallen behind, and now, during the course of the night, were trying to make it to the bridge. A force of 35 engineers – the "A" Troop of 1st Parachute Squadron, the Royal Engineers – led by Captain Eric Mackay were bravely struggling ahead with carts loaded with ammunition along Arnhem's dark streets to provide the men at the bridge with necessary ammunition.[304] They fell into repeated skirmishes with German soldiers, but made it through to the bridge without any personnel losses whatsoever – on the other hand, one of the ammunition carts had been blown to pieces. At one occasion, a group of German soldiers tried to sneak up on the men, but when Mackay and six other para engineers rushed towards the Germans with lowered bayonets, they fled. "They had no stomach for cold steel", Mackay said. "We pursued them to their building with grenades and gave them a taste of their own medicine."

The supreme German command on site, SS-Sturmbannführer Sonnenstuhl, did not even know that there were other German units than his own positioned against the bridge until the next day.[305] Sonnenstuhl had the same problems as his British opponents with malfunctioning radios (see page 166).[306] "The first day, we hardly had any contact with each other, and we were clashing as well as we could with the English, who were fighting quite outstandingly", one of the German soldiers told war correspondent Wilhelm Droste.[307] In addition, due to the lack of transportation, many of the German units arrived in more or less of a state of disarray, in small groups, and drawn out throughout the night and the following day, which made coordination of the operations even more difficult. Only by around ten in the morning of 18 September did the commander of the 10. SS-Panzer-Division's Panzer reconnaissance battalion, 30-year-old SS-Sturmbannführer Heinz Brinkmann, make it to the combat area at Arnhem. He was shown to Sonnenstuhl's command post, about a thousand metres north of the bridge. Brinkmann explained that he had been surprised by fighting in Arnhem and had been forced to take a detour across garden walls and in small footpaths. After that, he set off again, believing that he would be able to make it across the Rhine to Nijmegen. In reality, he was soon issued a counter-order – he was to take command of all German forces at the Arnhem bridge.* Neither did the German maintenance function properly. The then 19-year-old SS-Rottenführer Rudolf Trapp recounted how he and his comrades in the 3. Kompanie, SS-Panzergrenadier-Regiment 21, had to plunder food cellars in nearby residential houses during the first night to get anything to eat, as no rations arrived.[308]

As we have seen, the British parachute brigade's 3rd Battalion had been ordered to halt for the night on 17 September at Hotel Hartenstein

---

* Some accounts claim that SS-Kampfgruppe Sonnenstuhl was incorporated into SS-Kampfgruppe Knaust, or vice versa, but the fact is that these were two separate battle groups, both included in SS-Kampfgruppe Brinkmann.

in central Oosterbeek, four kilometres further to the west. However, this order did not reach the "C" Company, which, led by Major Peter "Pongo" Lewis, was advancing in parallel with the Utrecht-Arnhem railway on the northern flank. On the road to Arnhem, the British did not come across any more than a few single German vehicles, which were quickly disposed of. When the paratroopers penetrated the city, they found empty streets.

At around midnight in the night of 17 September, the men of the 3rd Battalion reached the city's railway station, 800 metres northwest of the road bridge. They found the station completely deserted, and continued. At Willemsplein, just in front of the railway station, they discovered a vehicle with German soldiers in the dark night. "Pongo" Lewis ordered his men not to attack but to behave "normally" so that the Germans would believe them to be their own soldiers. This succeeded; the British were able to sneak past and continued forward. At Velperplein, 400 metres to the east, they met a small group of Dutch

Air photo from 1925 of Arnhem's railway station. The image is taken from the south. In front of the railway station lies the Willemsplein square. On this side of the Willemsplein, central Arnhem begins. From the railway station and in a straight line cutting through the bottom right corner of the image is the road bridge, 800 metres away.

policemen commanded by Inspector Hendrik Stuvel, who willingly showed them the way to the bridge: Just continue down the road, 600 metres further ahead.

The British had not come far before they spotted some German armoured vehicles. One of them turned on its headlights and lit up the British, but "Pongo" Lewis quickly gathered his wits. *"Licht aus!"* ("Lights out!") he commanded sternly in German, and the headlights were quickly turned off. But in the myriad of side streets that constitute central Arnhem, No. 7 Platoon lost their way and were taken by surprise by soldiers from 3. Kompanie of SS-Panzergrenadier-Regiment 21. SS-Rottenführer Horst Weber describes this from the German side: "We advanced along the houses on the Beekstraat, Koningstraat and the Eusebiusbinnensingel [northwest of the bridge] towards the bridge. The British in the centre were completely surprised and we took some prisoners fairly easily."[309] Half the British platoon was lost, and the remaining men made it to the bridge only much later. But most of "C" Company of the 3rd Battalion joined Lieutenant-Colonel Frost's unit in the small hours, bringing its strength to about 700 men with support from four 6-pound anti-tank guns by dawn on 18 September. Soon, the airborne artillery in Oosterbeek would also provide them with support.

The commander of British 3rd Airlanding Light Battery, Major Dennis Munford, had made it to the road bridge together with the brigade headquarters in the evening of the 17th. His objective was to lead the artillery fire from Oosterbeek against the Germans at the road bridge. When they failed to establish radio contact with Oosterbeek, Munford did not hesitate to simply head off back to Oosterbeek together with the driver, Lance-Bombardier William Crook, in a jeep. They drove at full speed down the road along the Rhine bank, past the very sparse positions held by 3. Kompanie of SS-Panzergrenadier-Regiment 21. In western Arnhem, SS-Sturmbannführer Möller's German pioneers still remained hidden in the houses some distance up the hill from the Rhine, together with SS-Sturmbannführer Spindler and the German corps commander Bittrich. Arriving in Oosterbeek, Munford briefed the divisional headquarters about the situation at the bridge, and calibrated his radio equipment so that it could communicate with the fire control radio at the artillery regiment's headquarters. Then, he and Crook set off again, and made it back to the bridge unhurt.[310] All of this shows the possibilities that had been available if most of the 3rd Battalion had continued the advance instead of pausing for the night in Oosterbeek in the evening of 17 September.

The radio set (Wireless Set No. 22), weighing almost 17 kilos, was hauled up the stairs to the attic in the two-storey house where the brigade had set up its headquarters. To Munford's incredible frustration, it refused to work! It seemed as though some vital part had been damaged during the wild journey through enemy lines. But it did not take long before Bombardier J. Leo Hall, with the help of another radio set that had been carried up to the same position, made contact with Lieutenant-Colonel "Sheriff" Thompson, the commander of the artillery regiment, using a radio that had been placed at the top of the church tower over in Oosterbeek. Munford immediately wanted the artillerymen in his battery – with eight guns at their disposal – to fire a couple of shells against the southern abutment to get something to aim for.

The Germans of SS-Kampfgruppe Gräbner, who had set up positions south of the bridge, screamed with fear as the six shells came tossing down in quick succession, exploding in their midst. Munford contacted Thompson, who gave this spot the designation "Mike One".

However, no artillery was needed to beat back what turned out to be a half-hearted German attempt to attack in the dawn of 18 September. SS-Rottenführer Rudolf Trapp remembers how 19-year-old Grenadier Franz Schulze-Bernd started weeping with fear as he was detailed as driver of an armoured personnel carrier that was to try to make it from the western to the eastern part of the bridge with wounded; he realised that it would never work. And sure enough – the vehicle only just made it in under the bridge ramp before taking a direct hit from the British anti-tank guns, killing Schulze-Bernd.*

The other men on board jumped out and were scattered in all directions. In panic, Trapp threw some hand grenades against a cou-

* Franz Schulze-Bernd is buried today in the German military cemetery of Ysselsteyn, Sector U, Row 12, Grave 280.

ple of British "Red Devils" that appeared, and then ran towards the riverbank and jumped into the water and swam across to the other side.[311]

ENTER HARMEL

When "Pongo" Lewis and his men of the "C" Company from the parachute brigade's 3rd Battalion reached the Velperplein square in Arnhem, 600 metres north of the road bridge, they were actually only a hair's breadth from bumping into the commander of the 10. SS-Panzer-Division, SS-Brigadeführer Heinz Harmel.[312] He had been at the SS headquarters in Bad Saarow in Germany to organise the rearmament of the division when the message reached him about the British air landings. Harmel immediately jumped into a car and set off back to Holland. He went non-stop all of the more than 600 kilometres to Ruurlo, about thirty-five kilometres northeast of Arnhem, where he had had the division's command post set up. When he arrived, he was exhausted; the night before, he had barely had any sleep either. "I was totally unaware of the situation and its seriousness", he recounted.[313] But his second in command, SS-Obersturmbannführer Paetsch, had moved the command post to Velp just outside the north-eastern outskirts of Arnhem. During his journey there, Harmel heard the ominous sound of gunfire from within Arnhem.

SS-Obersturmbannführer Otto Paetsch sighed with relief when Harmel stepped into the new command post. He immediately briefed the divisional commander about the situation, to the extent of what he knew himself, and about corps commander Bittrich's orders. The experienced Harmel felt that "everything was confused and uncertain". He recounted, "After speaking to Paetsch I spoke to Bittrich by 'phone. He repeated the orders more or less as I had already been given. I then decided to take a look for myself and left for the centre of Arnhem. On the way to Arnhem along Velperweg [from the northeast in towards the city], I stopped off at Sonnenstuhl's command post where I requested and was given two tanks. I continued on with the two tanks until I reached Velperplein [600 metres northwest of the bridge] and left one behind there. I went with the other tank along Eusebiusbinnensingel towards the bridge. It had already been blocked with British anti-tank mines and the fighting was intense." [314]

In Eusebiusbinnensingel, just below the medieval Sint-Walburgis church, was the two-storey house where Frost had set up the 1st Airborne Brigade's command post. Harmel was now stopped in the same place as Sonnenstuhl had been the evening before.

Meanwhile, new German units had arrived at the flank position east of the bridge. Some time during the small hours of 18 September, Major Hans-Peter Knaust reported to II. SS-Panzerkorps's command post. 38-year-old Knaust was a veteran from the first days of the war, and had, amongst other things, led a rifle battalion during the invasion of France in 1940. As a battalion commander in the 16. Panzer-Division, he was badly wounded in December 1941 on the Eastern front, and his right leg had to be amputated. He now commanded Panzer-Grenadier-Ausbildungs- und Ersatz-Battalion 6, which had arrived from Bocholt with 200 men in the shape of Kampfgruppe Knaust (see page 177). A German account describes the state of this battalion: "Almost all of the officers of this battalion were unfit for the front. Several of them had had legs and arms amputated, their commander, Major Knaust, wore a prosthetic leg himself and led his battalion in battle leaning on a walking stick.

The battalion itself only consisted in small part of recovered, experienced frontline soldiers. Most of the soldiers were recruits of all ages with four to eight weeks' training". [315] Knaust recounted that he himself was tormented by constant pain in the stump of his leg. [316] The fact that Panzer-Grenadier-Ausbildungs- und Ersatz-Battalion 64 was employed at Arnhem shows just how far down the barrel the German military had had to scrape for resources. This was actually the replacement unit for the 16. Panzer-Division, which had been terribly mauled during the Soviet Lvov-Sandomierz offensive in July–August 1944.

Bittrich ordered Knaust to position his unit in eastern Arnhem, where he was to be put under SS-Sturmbannführer Brinkmann's command. Knaust was also supplied with "Panzerkompanie Mielke" from the replacement battalion Panzer-Ersatz- und Ausbildungs-Abteilung 11. Commanded by Oberleutnant Wilhelm Mielke, this company had quickly been put together from six old Panzer III and two Panzer IV tanks from the tank driver school in Bielefeld. Most of the crews lacked combat experience, and many of them had not even turned 18. For example, Hans-Otto Wittenberg, born in 1927 and thus 17 years old, had no other previous military service than three months at the anti-aircraft unit Heimat-Flak-Batterie 87/ XI in Hannover and four months in Germany at the Panzer-Ersatz- und Ausbildungs-Abteilung 11. Mielke's company was merged with Kampfgruppe Knaust, which was ordered to relieve Kampfgruppe Euling when it set off eastwards to try to make it to Nijmegen by taking a ferry across the Rhine.

When Harmel arrived in the combat area – this would have been about some time after six o'clock in the morning – the Germans had already made their first serious attack to retake the abutment. This was before Knaust's unit could be sent in. But the attack, which came from the north and northeast, was met with heavy fire from "Pongo" Lewis's company. The British had spent the night turning the stone houses surrounding the bridge into virtual fortresses. They had knocked out all window panes to avoid being injured by flying glass, furniture had been stacked in large piles to reinforce protection against enemy fire, and bathtubs and all kinds of buckets, tubs, and pots that they came across had been filled with water to have at hand when and if the Germans cut off the water supply. Wilhelm Droste gives a colourful description from the German perspective of the battle that he himself took part in:

"Part of our groups succeeded in entering the houses, and more than once there were Tommies on the ground floor of a house, on the first floor, Germans, and on the second floor, Tommies again. Everybody is shooting at everybody. Of course, the English were confused by this kind of fighting and soon even knew as little as we did where friend and foe were standing.

Five of us are lying by the fence of a large flower bed. A house opposite us makes any advance impossible. We stumble through the smoke towards the corner of the house. Ricochets are whirring from somewhere or other. My Unterscharführer, who had just reached the door, turns around immediately and slides slowly along the wall of the house. The hand grenades are soon hanging on the veranda door. We are jumping aside and going behind the stone terrace for cover. The door is blown open. 'In you go!' I shout and empty the magazine of my sub-machine gun into the dark hallway.

'Watch out for the doors!' A burst of fire – the first door swings open. In the corner, there are two wounded Tommies lying on mattresses stacked on top of each other, staring at me with eyes wide with fear. At the same moment, there is a crash, mortar crumbling off the walls. I am already out of there, watching through an open door. The Sturmmann is standing with his sub-machine gun cocked in front of for Brits, who have their hands raised. From above, I can hear Fritz bellowing: *'Go on!'* They have caught five men and one severely wounded there.

'Come on, Wenzel, barricade the door, or we'll be done for!' We lock up the Tommies in the cellar. The wounded one goes with the other two. The healthy ones have to give up their first aid kits in the infirmary. Fritz rushes over to the machine gun in the loft. Meanwhile, the Unterscharführer has been shot in the shoulder.

Then, the Tommies have already discovered us, covering us with fire from the other houses. Two of us are dragging the wounded, one after another, into the cellar, or otherwise they will eventually be killed by their own comrades. Thirst is driving us crazy. We are drinking the juice from preserving jars, throwing the rest away.

Wenzel is now securing the street, the Sturmmann goes to the side of the garden. I am panting to Fritz. This house is a trap! The front façade is under a machine gun sniper's fire. There are whistles and banks all over the stairs and corridors. I have not quite reached the top, when there is a dreadful crash. Smoke is coming out of the hatch in the floor. Then Fritz is also already there: 'We have to get out, they've just got us stuck in here. The Tommies are advancing in the streets. They've got the big building on the corner again and they're pulling out an anti-tank gun!' We are leaping behind the sandbags by the bay window. Wenzel is pulling the trigger of the machine gun. Beneath us, the Tommies are leaping from door to door. We fire our magazines right in the middle of the leaping figures. Thick clouds of smoke billows through the staircase, making our stay a misery. There is crackling and sizzling from the roof trusses. Red flames are coming through the dark clouds...

'Junka, we gotta get out, or they'll fry us', Wenzel pants, pointing towards the balcony, lying on level ground.

'The Tommies!' the Sturmmann shouts, shooting wildly into the garden. Then they are here as well. Two are leaping straight across the garden wall, a third one is covering them from behind in the shrubs. Then one MG 42 is being engaged over there, and then another one. The Tommies have taken cover behind fences, mounds of earth, and flowerbeds. I can still see how one of them is pulling himself up onto a stone plinth, and I withdraw. Then there is loud fire against us. A shockwave throws me back. Next to me, everyone is screaming – then I feel a blow against my shoulder and in my side and I hear myself screaming. Dirt and stones comes rattling down over me. I stumble to my feet. A hand pulls me up again. I notice that the window frames have been torn out. Next to me, Franz is kneeling on the stairs, shooting through the window.

Out there, the 'Devils' are coming roaring this way. Then, Wenzel yanks up a door, and immediately, the Sturmmann is on the balcony. Suddenly, there are figures appearing in the doorframe. Muzzle flashes flare through the smoke. I automatically pull the trigger. An enormous crash pierces my ears. The figures at the entrance collapse as though hit by a whip, falling on top of each other. One of them has fallen in the corridor.

My neighbour shouts something at me, but I can hardly understand him. My head is pounding as if from being hit by a hammer. I am looking into a pale, dirty face, with a thin stream of blood in it, from the nose to the mouth. 'There, now they are also on the other side in there. Come on, get out!' I can hardly see anymore. The thick smoke is forcing tears across my face. In a few bounds, we are on the balcony.

Then, Wenzel beckons me from the corner of the house, I press myself against the wall next to him. Inside right, by the opposite house, three figures are sneaking along, throwing themselves this way, firing – camouflage jackets! Those are our lot! 'Let's go', I yell, 'come on, Wenzel!' He understands immediately, gets on the railing, throws his steel helmet over it and sets off after it. We are shouting and waving. Then, we dash back into the burning and smoking house. In there, we lose our breath. The cellar door is open, it is completely empty. The Unterscharführer has thus taken them with him as well. – As we, half-suffocated, are back in the open, we bump into Wenzel. Next to him, six men are standing together with an Oberscharführer from another company, with a bloody wound across his face."[317]

Harmel arived at the combat zone when the attack had already been repulsed, largely owing to fire support from the artillery of the 1st Airlanding Light Regiment, Royal Artillery in Oosterbeek. He remembered how he saw the body of a fallen German soldier lying in the middle of the bridge ramp without any of the other soldiers daring to come forward to retrieve it, since it was in the middle of the British line of fire.

On the British side, Lieutenant-Colonel Frost felt inner satisfaction. "I felt everything was going according to plan", he later said. Moreover, the radio equipment that Bombardier Hall had assembled had reached a short but important connection with the XXX Corps to the south. "It meant", Frost wrote, "that they were well on their way towards us and though we didn't actually know how far they were, the signals were so strong that we felt we should see them arriving before very long."[318]

His opponent, Harmel, was less satisfied. He recounted: "There were many enemy snipers in the cellars and on the roofs of the surrounding houses. I decided that the only way to deal with them was to use heavy artillery on the houses."[319] With the help of tractors, two large 10 cm artillery pieces from Sonnenstuhl's SS-Panzer-Artillerie-Regiment 10 had been brought into position in the Musis park, 500 metres north of the bridge.

Harmel had them positioned in the middle of the Nijmegscheweg, which leads up to the bridge, and ordered fire: "We began directly under the eaves and fired metre for metre until the houses collapsed. I lay on the ground between two guns and directed the fire."[320]

One of the buildings that was subject to this heavy artillery fire was the one where Frost had set up his headquarters. "The arrival of a 150 mm gun, firing a shell weighing nearly 100 lb. from point-blank range at our building", Frost wrote with a slight exaggeration of the German guns, "was a rude shock. Each hit seemed to pulverize the masonry and the appalling crash of these missiles against our walls scared the daylight out of Headquarters. Just as I made up my mind that something drastic would have to be done, our mortars got the range, one direct hit killing the entire crew."[321] Harmel only barely avoided being hit himself. He, too, overestimated his adversary's equipment: "We couldn't go on for too long because the British had set up a heavy gun in a bunker [a small house on the west side of the northern bridge ramp] and concentrated their fire on our artillery. We had to pull back."[322]

Soon afterwards, the corps commander Bittrich appeared at Brinkmann's command post, where Harmel had gone from the Musis park. "The 10. SS-Panzer-Division is to break all resistance at the Rhine bridge and advance to Nijmegen by the quickest means possible and create a blocking line south of the river Waal!", Bittrich said sharply. Having had to hide from British paratroopers in western Arnhem during the night, Bittrich knew how critical the situation was. Harmel could only ask himself: With what was this supposed to be done? He went to the 9. SS-Panzer-Division's command post in northern Arnhem, where he met the deputy divisional commander Walter Harzer.

"You have a nerve being away in Berlin and not with your troops at a time like this", Harzer said jokingly as his colleague entered the villa that had previously been the now dead General Kussin's command post.

"I had bad luck", Harmel responded peevishly, continuing: "I am ordered to go down to Nijmegen with my division. We don't have the bridge open yet. Get rid of these Tommies, Harzer!"

Harzer stared at the commander of the 10. SS-Panzer-Division. "Me?" he exclaimed: "I'm seeing that the paratroopers don't get into Arnhem. I don't have time to take care of the bridge at the same time. The bridge is your look-out. You figure out how to free it." Then he said that he had already sent Gräbner's Panzer reconnaissance battalion south towards Nijmegen before the British blocked off the bridge.[323]

However, soon afterwards, there was a new order from Bittrich, who by now had had time to get better informed about the situation: "Kampfgruppe 9. SS will speedily break the enemy resistance on the Arnhem road bridge; it is crucial that the bridge be usable again as quickly as possible. A barrier line west of the bridge will stop the enemy's reinforcements from Oosterbeek."[324] Harzer asked his adjutant, SS-Hauptsturmführer Wilfried Schwarz, to contact Gräbner by radio and order him to attack across the bridge, annihilate the British force, and establish a defensive position towards the west.[325]

MASSACRE ON THE BRIDGE

Thirty-year-old SS-Hauptsturmführer Viktor Gräbner was a very experienced soldier. He had joined the SS in June 1934, and became a member of the Nazi Party in October, 1937, but served at the beginning of the war as a company commander in a Wehrmacht unit. He distinguished himself especially well during the battle of Rzhev on the Eastern Front in 1941–1942, for which he was awarded the German Cross in Gold. As the commander of the 9. SS-Panzer-Division's Panzer reconnaissance battalion, he had retaken Noyers-Bocage southwest of Caen on 16 July 1944 from British XXX Corps. It was for this accomplishment that he had received the Knight's Cross on 17 September (see page 17). We do not know what this experienced officer thought about the order to charge straight across the bridge – which meant that his vehicles had to run the gauntlet between British positions on both sides of the northern abutment – but the fact that he has been blamed for this in post-war literature is unfair. As SS-Hauptsturmführer Schwarz has attested, the attack took place under orders from above, and not on Gräbner's initiative, as it is sometimes claimed.

The survivors of Gräbner's battalion recounted that at 0930 hrs in the morning of 18 September, after a short briefing, the column of vehicles set off at full speed up onto the bridge. What followed is among the most well-known scenes during the Second World War,

German units at the Arnhem bridge on 18 September 1944

EAST OF THE BRIDGE
• Kampfgruppe Brinkmann (SS-Sturmbannführer Heinz Brinkmann)
   SS-Panzer-Aufklärungs-Abteilung 10 (SS-Sturmbannführer Heinz Brinkmann)
   Kampfgruppe Knaust (Major Hans-Peter Knaust)
   Panzer-Grenadier-Ausbildungs- und Ersatz-Battalion 64
   Panzerkompanie Mielke (Oberleutnant Wilhelm Mielke)

NORTH OF THE BRIDGE
• Kampfgruppe Sonnenstuhl (SS-Sturmbannführer Hans-Georg Sonnenstuhl)
   Two companies from SS-Panzer-Artillerie-Regiment 10
   (SS-Sturmbannführer Hans-Georg Sonnenstuhl)
   RAD platoon
   1. Kompanie, SS-Panzergrenadier-Regiment 21

WEST OF THE BRIDGE
• Staff/I. Bataillon, SS-Panzergrenadier-Regiment 21
   (SS-Obersturmführer Ernst Vogel)
• 3. Kompanie, SS-Panzergrenadier-Regiment 21

SOUTH OF THE BRIDGE
• Kampfgruppe Gräbner (SS-Hauptsturmführer Viktor Gräbner)
   SS-Panzer-Aufklärungs-Abteilung 9 (SS-Hauptsturmführer Viktor Gräbner)
   2. and 3. Kompanie/Schiffstamm-Abteilung 14

and has been staged quite well by the immortal screen adaptation of Cornelius Ryan's *A Bridge Too Far*.

"Armoured car coming across the bridge!" cried the signaller at the radio equipment in the attic of the airborne brigade's command post. "For one moment", Frost recounted, "I and many others wondered if this was the vanguard of XXX Corps". Perhaps this is not particularly strange, considering that Gräbner's conquered British armoured Humber reconnaissance car was at the lead. But when the vehicles opened fire, the British realised what was going on.

The paratroopers indeed gave their enemies a warm reception. The Germans had not even made it up onto the bridge itself before artillery shells exploded among the vehicles. All the British artillery major Munford needed to do was to signal "Target – Mike One!" to the artillery over in Oosterbeek. A couple of German motorcyclists were torn to pieces by the shells, which, however, were unable to do any damage to the armoured vehicles. When these drove up onto the bridge, the British artillery fire ceased.

The distance is about 200 metres from the southern riverbed to the ramp between the houses, where the British held their positions. The German vehicles were able to cover this distance before hell seemed to open its gates. PIAT anti-tank weapons and anti-tank guns knocked out some of the foremost vehicles. Serjcant Cyril Robson, the gunner at a 57 millimetre 6-pound anti-tank gun in position some fifty metres west of the bridge, fired a hole in the wall of the western edge of the bridge. In a window on the first floor of a house next to the gun, Lieutenant Tony Cox was shouting out directions to Robson, who thus was able to take precision shots at the German vehicles. SS Panzer grenadiers who leapt out of the immobile vehicles were mowed down with machine guns and firearms. A completely open Leichter Zugkraftwagen 10-type half-track with room for eight men turned away from the bridge ramp and steered into the narrow sliproad that went past the three-storey Van Limburg school, where

The road bridge at Arnhem, seen from the south bank of the river. The image was taken six years before the battle. To the left, the Sint-Walburgis church is visible.

the "C" Company under Major "Pongo" Lewis and Captain Eric
Mackay's engineers were holding the fort. Mackay recounted:

"I heard a clanking just below the window. On looking out, I saw
a half-track just below me. It was about 5 feet away and I looked
straight into its commander's face. I don't know who was the more
surprised. His reaction was quicker than mine; for with a dirty big
grin he loosened off three shots with his Luger. The only shot that
hit me smashed my binoculars, which were hanging round my neck.
The boys immediately rallied round, and he and his men were dead
meat within seconds. The halftrack crashed into the northern wing
of the school".[326]

One of few survivors on the German side, SS-Unterscharführer
Mauga, recounts: "Suddenly all hell broke loose. There were explosions
all around my vehicle, and all at once I was in the middle of confusion.
A few wanted to carry on, while others wanted to go back. Gräbner was
in a captured British armoured car. We have no idea where he got it
from. Later we took the car into central Arnhem, but the commander
was nowhere to be found. We were unable to recover his body." [327] SS
soldiers jumped down into the water from the bridge, 13 metres high.
Others rushed without weapons towards the German positions in the
north, where many of them collapsed in a state of panic. On one of the
stopped vehicles, the signal horn had jammed, and was screaming for
quite some time before the battery ran out. From his attic floor, Major
Munford counted 27 destroyed German vehicles* on the bridge ramp
– both from Gräbner's annihilated battalion and such that had been
knocked out earlier – and at least 70 dead SS soldiers.

It was over as quickly as it had started. The sight of Gräbner's
armoured column, turned into burning, twisted scrap in a tangled
mess of destroyed vehicles, strewn wreckage, and dozens of bodies
of SS soldiers, met the Germans who lay in position on the northern

---

* Out of these, it has been possible to establish by air photographs that nine
were armoured half-tracks (eight Sd.Kfz. 250s and one Sd.Kfz. 10) and the rest
were lorries – including those who were transporting petrol barrels filled with
sand, which were intended to serve as protection for the SS soldiers as they
were to set up their defensive position towards the west.

riverbank as a severe shock. There was no trace of Gräbner himself. Survivors have recounted how they saw him standing on the bridge, urging his soldiers forward. But air photographs taken just afterwards do not show any destroyed Humber on the bridge. It is possible that Gräbner was one of the German soldiers who jumped into the river to avoid the fire – his body has never been found.*

PANZER ATTACK

The German attacks against Frost's men at Arnhem on 18 September undoubtedly bear the characteristics of desperation. The Germans knew that the Americans could occupy the bridge at Nijmegen at any time, and they had to get reinforcements across the Rhine in time to meet them. That was why they, quite contrary to their military doctrine, set in their attack piecemeal. Kampfgruppe Knaust with Mielke's Panzer company had not been ready for combat when Gräbner attacked. It took a while until Knaust's units had been positioned for attack, but it was next in line. In the afternoon of this 18 September, the new order to attack was given, but all that could be mustered in terms of operational tanks were Panzer IVs. Together with a number of armoured personnel carriers, they rolled out onto the Westervoortsedijk, which ran just next to the riverbank from the east, straight towards the bridge, continuing underneath the ramp.

Cyril Robson had, by then, repositioned his 6-pound anti-tank gun to the western outskirts of the area that was controlled by the British. A terrible duel broke out between him and the foremost German Panzer IV. Robson's first shot, fired at a range of 250 metres, had no effect on the German tank's 80-millimetre frontal armour. The tank crew

* QR25: VIDEO
12:55: British veteran Stephen George Morgan, at the time a Private with Headquarters Company in the 2nd Bn., tells about the fighting at the bridge on 18 September 1944.

had now discovered Robson, and with a tremendous bang, they fired a shell that indeed missed its target, but hit the house façade behind Robson. With brick and mortar coming down around him, Robson hit the fire lever on the left side of the bolt. Still no discernible effect. The tank had arrived on the same side of the bridge ramp as Robson, at the CAMIX Dairy, when Robson had the next shell in his bore. This time, it hit from a distance of only 50 metres and went straight through the frontal armour, causing the tank to stop abruptly.

This made the German advance grind to a halt, and gave Serjeant William Kill, the gunner at another 6-pounder, an excellent opportunity. Earlier in the day, he had moved his anti-tank gun to a firing position among the trees in the little park that was located in the corner of Westervoortsedijk and Ooststraat on the eastern side of the bridge ramp, and from there, he got a direct hit that penetrated the thinner armoured side of the rear of the two Panzer IVs. Private James Sims describes the destruction of the German attack force:

"As the tanks slowed down the paratroops poured a withering fire into them. The German AFVs were knocked out one after another as they tried to disengage and negotiate the flaming metal coffins." [328] Now, the British artillery over in Oosterbeek also joined the fray. One of the German soldiers, Martin Busch, remembered: "We encountered artillery, mortar and rifle fire. The bullets seemed to come from all sides although there was no enemy in sight, it was really scary. I was hiding behind a lamppost for a while. It occurred to me much later that the tiny lamppost hid only a small part of my body." [329]

While the surviving Germans pulled back, the foremost Panzer IV, the one that had been knocked out by Robson's anti-tank gun, was standing helplessly still in the middle of the British area, while the flames spread inside the doomed Panzer vehicle. Sims recounted: "Black smoke belched from the leading tank, now well ablaze, but any movement from our position still brought a stream of well-aimed machine-gun fire from the turret guns. The paratroopers shouted to the SS man to come out, promising to spare his life, for they were impressed by his fanatical courage. The only reply was further burst of fire. As the flames got to him we could hear his screams of agony, muffled by the steel turret..." [330]

The battle cost Major Knaust two of his company commanders, Oberleutnant Karl-Heinz Heeren and Leutnant Karl Gansmann. Martin Busch remembers the shock he had when he saw himself in a mirror after this terrible clash with the "Red Devils": "We entered a deserted ground floor apartment and there I saw my own reflection in a wall mirror. I was shocked at what I saw. I seemed to have aged by years and years. My face was ashen, drawn and full of wrinkles that never had been there before..." [331]

The badly battered Germans to all intents and purposes kept their heads down during the rest of 18 September. Instead, they subjected the British bridgehead to artillery and mortar fire that continuously kept gaining strength as more artillery guns arrived. "To send in soldiers would be suicidal, we used the word '*Himmelfahrtkommando*' for such an attack", said SS-Rottenführer Horst Weber. "We were cautious the first two days. We never expected to be able to recapture the bridge. It was our artillery that beat the Paras in the end." [332]

All the time, a motley crew of German soldiers continued arriving in Arnhem. One of them was the then 21-year-old SS-Sturmmann Alfred Ringsdorf. His account is quite illuminating for the condition on the German side: "I belonged to a Reserve Battalion in the 16th SS-Panzer Division.* Two friends of mine, Robert Klapdor and Paul Rosenbach, and myself were on our way to Arnhem from Bad Tölz in Germany. We were supposed to be outfitted there. We were on a freight train and when we arrived outside Arnhem on September 18 we could not go into the city. It was about eight o'clock in the morning. Then we heard bombers and we sprang from the train and took cover under a viaduct nearby.

While we were under this viaduct two officers came along in a Volkswagen and told us to report to the Gefechtstand Sonnenstuhl [Sonnenstuhl Command Post]. My friends and I reported to this Command Post. The major there attached me to the 1st Company of the 1st Battalion of the 21st SS-Panzergrenadier Regiment. I took over command of the 1st Squad in the 1st Platoon.

---

* There was no such division. The 16. Panzer-Division, which Kampfgruppe Knaust had been the replacement unit for, is probably the one referred to. It did happen that SS soldiers served in Wehrmacht units, and vice versa.

When we arrived we had no arms. It was late Monday afternoon when we were given arms in a villa which had an anti-tank gun near it. We were handed out machine guns, carabines, hand grenades and a few bazookas. There was only a limited amount of ammunition. I think that I received only three magazines which was not very much. But we were supposed to be getting more supplies later."[333]

When the sun set behind the horizon in the evening of 18 September, Frost's paratroopers at the bridge felt full of confidence. They had shown their superiority against their opponents both in close combat as well as in combat tactics and morale. One event during the following night illustrates the insufficient level of training of many of the Germans that were employed against the bridge. All of a sudden, some paratroopers from the 3rd Battalion's "C" Company, who had been grouped in the three-storey Van Limburg school* where the Musis Park begins north of the bridge, discovered a platoon of German soldiers just by one of the house façades.

One of the Britons, Lieutenant Len Wright, describes what happened: "We all stood by with grenades. We had plenty of those. Then Major Lewis shouted 'Fire!' and the men in all the rooms [on] that side threw grenades and opened fire down on the Germans. My clearest memory is of Pongo Lewis running from one room to another, dropping grenades and saying to me that he hadn't enjoyed himself so much since the last time he'd gone hunting. It lasted about a quarter of an hour. There was nothing the Germans could do except die or disappear." [334]

Martin Busch, who had been lucky enough to survive Knaust's failed afternoon attack, was in this one as well. Through him, we know

QR26: VIDEO
34.48 Ringsdorf tells the story himself, many years after the war.

that this was not a question of any German attempt to attack, but that the Germans simply did not know the exact British positions, so that they in their inexperience were standing talking without any preparedness whatsoever when the attack took place. Busch recounts: "Our commander asked for support from some tanks and they arrived sometime later. They started to shoot at everything which moved in the area of the school house. Unfortunately what moved were mostly German soldiers trying to get away from that area. I was very upset and climbed upon one of the tanks and with my rifle banged at the turret hatch but the men inside probably did not hear it".[335] Len Wright recounted: "When it got light, there were a lot of bodies down there — 18 or 20, perhaps more. Some were still moving, one was severely wounded, a bad stomach wound with his guts visible.... Some of our men tried to get him in, showing a Red Cross symbol, but they were shot at and came back in, without being hit but unable to help the German." [336]

During their first day at the bridge, the "Red Devils" under John Frost had not only succeeded with their objective to hold the bridge, but they had also inflicted terrible losses on their opponents. Exactly how high these losses were during the fighting this day is not known, but approximately 150 Germans had been killed and probably twice as many had been injured. That means that the German units at the bridge at Arnhem had lost about half of their personnel during the first day alone. For example, three of the four company commanders of Kampfgruppe Knaust were killed during this 18 September alone. The commander of the I. Bataillon, SS-Panzergrenadier-Regiment 21, SS-Obersturmführer Ernst Vogel, had also been killed. In addition, most the German combat vehicles, including three of the eight tanks, had been knocked out. The losses on the British side were limited to ten killed and about thirty wounded.[337]

Apart from this, Frost and his men virtually served the important Waal bridge at Nijmegen, 15 kilometres further south, to the Americans on a silver platter: Since they blocked the Arnhem bridge against the German reinforcements that were supposed to move to Nijmegen, the Waal bridge was still being held by utterly weak units.

---

* This school building was destroyed during the fighting and has never been rebuilt.

Nijmegen and Oosterbeek
18 September 1944 – Failed Attacks

THE AMERICANS REACH THE NIJMEGEN BRIDGE
A SECOND TIME

While the American 82nd Airborne Division gave Nijmegen the lowest priority among their targets for attack, this town became the centre for the German defence measures. Bittrich, commander of the II. SS-Panzerkorps, had made the correct assessment early to give top priority to holding the Waal bridges at Nijmegen. As we have seen (Chapter 5), Generalfeldmarschall Model had sent out the operational plan for the defensive battle at around half past five in the evening of 17 September. General Kurt Feldt, commander of the newly-formed "Korps Feldt" (the Feldt Corps), thereby assumed command for the defence in the Nijmegen sector. The units that sent into combat in this sector were organised into Division z.b.V. 406, which had previously led the home guard battalions in Wehrkreis VI (Military Area 6). In addition, the 10. SS-Panzer-Division "Frundsberg" was ordered to regroup to Nijmegen.

On 17 September – before the commander of the 10. SS-Panzer-Division "Frundsberg", SS-Brigadeführer Harmel, had returned from Berlin – the deputy divisional commander, SS-Obersturmbann-führer Otto Paetsch, had assigned SS-Sturmbannführer Leo Reinhold, commander of the II. Abteilung of SS-Panzer-Regiment 10, with the task of taking command of the division's battle force, from now on Kampfgruppe Reinhold, and regroup from the area north of the Rhine and to Nijmegen. However, this was not all that easy, due to Frost's British paratroopers by the Arnhem bridge. Therefore, General Feldt handed over direct command in Nijmegen to Oberst Fritz Hencke, who was the commander of the paratroop training staff Fallschirm-Lehrstab 1, ordering all available units to the new Kampfgruppe Hencke.*

Arriving during the night of 17/18 September were, apart from two armoured personnel carriers from Gräbner's Panzer reconnaissance battalion of the 9. SS-Panzer-Division, also a company of stranded seamen from Schiffstamm-Abteilung 14 and a company from Hencke's paratroop school, as well as eight old Panzer III and Panzer IV training tanks from III. Abteilung/ Fallschirm-Panzer-Ersatz- und Ausbildungs-Regiment "Hermann Göring". Hencke ordered his units into defence positions on the southern bank of the river, by the railway bridge in the west, in the Hunner Park just left of the large road bridge, and strategically at the Keizer Karelplein, the large roundabout that connects the main roads from the south with the railway and road bridges – a thousand metres further away to the northwest and the northeast respectively.

It has been claimed that Kampfgruppe Hencke reached a strength of about a thousand men during the night of 17 September, but that is a considerable exaggeration. The real number was probably not half as large, and with the only possible exception of the handful SS soldiers that had arrived, the men were of quite low fighting qualities, most of them being overage.[338] It was their sheer luck that the Americans were not particularly strong in Nijmegen either.

As we have seen (Chapter 6), it was not until at around six o'clock in the evening that Colonel Lindquist, commander of the 508th Parachute Infantry Regiment, gave his 1st Battalion orders to advance towards the bridges in Nijmegen. This advance was carried out in a remarkably indecisive manner, piecemeal, and was, moreover, disturbed by large crowds of celebrating Dutchmen in Nijmegen, which had largely been abandoned by the Germans. First of all, a reconnaissance patrol set off. It got stuck among the Dutch, who were intoxicated with joy, and only three men made it through to the southern part of the road bridge, which they were able to occupy without any difficulties.

* Sometimes erroneously spelled Henke.

Soon afterwards, the same evening, Lieutenant-Colonel Sheilds Warren, commander of the 1st Battalion, received orders to send forward his "A" and "B" Companies together with the battalion's mortar and machine gun squads towards the bridges. But "A" Company deployed before "B" Company had arrived, so it was thus three separate American battle forces, without either coordination or contact with each other, that went into Nijmegen

The Dutch resistance member Gert van Hees showed the way on bicycle. Each time "A" Company arrived at a crossroads, van Hees cycled ahead to the next crossroads to ensure that the coast was clear. Thus, the advance went in intervals. The increasingly dark streets were still full of celebrating, singing Dutch. They tried offering the paratroopers all possible kinds of alcohol, they fattened them with sandwiches, pastries, and fruit, and women of all ages clung around their necks. But Captain Jonathan Adams Jr. managed to keep his "A" Company together. It was pitch black outside when they arrived at the crossroads just south of the Keizer Karelplein. Gert van Hees signalled to the paratroopers to wait and disappeared into the darkness on his bicycle. A reconnaissance patrol consisting of two men, that was sent forth, was met with fire that killed one and wounded the other.

But the Germans apparently had no idea that there were more Americans right behind these. Hidden by the darkness, the 2nd Platoon under Lieutenant George Lamm sneaked forward towards the roundabout. Lamm recounted: "Rifleman LeBoeuf slipped into a Kraut foxhole, still occupied, and used his trench knife on the unlucky German. Sergeant Henderson's men checked out the foxholes we passed over and collected a couple of AA gun crews, who were rather on the elderly side. Rifleman Stork took the POWs to the rear and returned promptly."[339]

As "B" Company finally joined up at the roundabout, Lamm and his men, together with the company commander Adams, continued forward through the dark town, towards the Belvédère Tower in the middle of the Hunner Park just next to the road bridge. Van Hees had said that the detonator for the explosives on the road bridge was to be found there.[340] Apparently, the Germans by then – as it was approaching midnight on 17 September – still only had weak forces in Nijmegen. Led by a townsman, Lamm's unit advanced across gardens and through back streets. Here and there, they took a German position by surprise, silencing its crew each time with trench knives. In Lamm's platoon, there were two sergeants who had made a name for themselves as specialists of trench knives, Alvin Henderson and Charles Gushue. Henderson had been captured by the Germans during the fighting in Normandy, but he managed to overpower his guards and escape, stole a boat, and sailed across the English Channel, reporting for service at his unit one week before Operation "Market Garden"![341]

The small Hunner Park was Kampfgruppe Hencke's most important position by far in Nijmegen: from its tree-lined hill, you could control the road bridge below it, and at the very top, in the middle of the park, was the tall watchtower from the 16th century that was called Belvédère. There, the Germans were ready, and met the Americans with intense fire from five machine guns. But the fighting quality of these soldiers was not better than that the two Americans Alvin

Nijmegen's bombed-out central parts. The image is taken from southwest and shows the road bridge in the background. There is a glimpse of the trees in the Valkhof Park top right, and beyond it (outside the picture) is the Hunner Park and the Belvédère tower.

Henderson and Charles Gushue could overpower them. Gushue threw hand grenades while rushing forward with a bayonet mounted on his rifle. One machine gun nest was destroyed by his hand grenades, and then, Gushue was over the Germans, slashing four of them with his bayonet. While the blood-curdling screams from the dying Germans cut through the night, Henderson attacked another German machine gun nest, killing two men with his bare hands. He managed to kill four more with his bayonet before the remaining Germans put their hands in the air. But Henderson had also been hit himself, and fell flat across one of the captured machine guns, dead.

The Americans now quickly advanced up the steep hill to the Belvédère Tower. They blasted the door open with a Gammon grenade and stormed inside with rattling submachine guns. It was as if taken from a classic Hollywood war movie! Terrified Germans jumped out of the windows. Inside the now partly burning building, Adams found what he thought was the detonator, and smashed it to

The Belvédère tower in the Hunner Park in Nijmegen. The image from the early 20th century is taken from the northwest, from the river bank below the Valkhof Park, which is located just west of the Hunner Park. The bridge is outside the image, down to the left below the hill where the tower is. The road from the south up to the bridge goes below the hill, on the other side of the tower. The river Waal runs just below the hill, to the left outside the picture.

"For extraordinary heroism"

Staff Sergeant Alvin Henderson was posthumously awarded the Distinguished Service Cross, the second highest decoration for valour in the USA, for his feat at the Nijmegen bridge on 17 September. The citation reads: "For extraordinary heroism in connection with military operations against an armed enemy on 17 September 1944 in Nijmegen, Holland. Staff Sergeant Henderson was platoon sergeant of the 2nd Platoon, Company A, 508th Parachute Infantry, and while on patrol in the city of Nijmegen killed two Germans in hand-to-hand fighting and bayoneted four others. He led his patrol in the accomplishment of three separate missions during the attack by his battalion, during which time he personally destroyed four enemy machine gun positions and assisted in the capture of six prisoners. When the point of the battalion advance became pinned down by enemy machine gun fire in the city of Nijmegen, Staff Sergeant Henderson led a squad from the advance guard and pushed forward, destroying the enemy position. He attacked a circular plaza to his front and cleared it of enemy. Later, at the bridge, he personally destroyed two machine gun positions and caused the crew of the third to withdraw. During this attack he was killed by enemy fire. The gallant and courageous actions of Staff Sergeant Henderson contributed greatly to the destruction of enemy resistance within the city and rendered a most vital and distinguished service in the accomplishment of the division mission. The conduct of Staff Sergeant Henderson reflects the finest traditions of the United States Army."

Quoted from en.ww2awards.com/person/38215.

pieces. In fact, it was not a detonator – by then, the bridge had not yet been mined.

A hundred metres further ahead, and below, was the southern abutment of the road bridge. For the second time that night, the Americans were essentially masters of this absolutely crucial bridge – and withdrew from there. With the Dutch guide gone, the Americans tried as best as they could to find their way back to the Keizer Karelplein roundabout through the myriad of small streets and alleys in the pitch-black night. It did not succeed very well. Obviously lacking a compass, they went west instead of south. The hours passed, and more and more German soldiers arrived in Nijmegen. Eventually, when the day started breaking, they entered completely bombed-out quarters where the skeletons of the houses were gaping empty and silent – the result of an American bomb raid in February 1944. They found refuge in a warehouse in Lange Helzestraat, and there, they remained hidden, while the Dutch supplied them with food and beverages until the area was liberated by the British on 20 September.

The 82nd Airborne Division's operation against Nijmegen was not only half-hearted, but also completely uncoordinated. The German soldiers who had been retreating from Keizer Karelplein when the American 1st Battalion took it over were stopped by officers who forced them to go back, and organised a counterattack. But the weathered paratroopers met them in close combat in the middle of the roundabout, and soon, the Germans were fleeing again. The Americans seized the opportunity and pursued them. The hunt went along the main road leading up to the road bridge, and before the Americans knew what had happened, they found themselves below the Hunner Park! Only there did they come across stronger resistance in the shape of especially the two armoured vehicles that Gräbner had detailed for the defence of Nijmegen – and fell back to the Keizer Karelplein!

At 0655 hrs in the morning of 18 September, at 82nd Airborne Division's command post, Gavin received a report that Lindquist's 508th PIR had "a patrol on the bridge".[342] The airborne general immediately set off in his jeep to Lindquist's headquarters, where he was briefed that that report was, unfortunately, not correct. Lindquist had in no way any clear image of the situation for the 1st Battalion, but at the battalion's command post in the Marienboom School not far from there, Gavin met the battalion commander Warren, who gave a disheartening report: "His battalion was broken up into small groups in the city, there were far too few troopers for the task at hand."[343]

Gavin returned to Lindquist's command post to try to get the attack against the bridges going. 508th PIR's 3rd Battalion was also in a favourable position for an attack. It had, in the afternoon of 17 September, taken the little village Berg en Dal quite easily, and from there, the soldiers were able to get an overview of the city of Nijmegen, 50 metres lower and a few kilometres away to the northwest. Since they had not come across any serious resistance, the battalion commander, Major Louis Mendez, ordered Lieutenant Russell C. Wilde's "G" Company to march towards Nijmegen. The men set off down the hill and, without having seen any enemies, entered the south-eastern suburbs of Nijmegen. "But since Wilde had not received the word to advance on the bridge, he set his company down for the night", Guy LoFaro laconically concluded in the 82nd Airborne Division's chronicle.[344]

Only at a quarter to eight in the morning of 18 September did Lindquist, on direct orders from Gavin, contact the 3rd Battalion, ordering "G" Company to resume its advance. The company advanced in full daylight down the sloping Berg en Dalseweg, which began to fill up with Dutchmen. "The crowds lined the streets and cheered as if the troops were on parade", Private Angel Romero recounted.[345] But as the Americans were approaching the bridge, the lines started thinning out, until no more civilians could be seen at all. At around ten o'clock, the Americans were standing in front of the Keizer Lodewijkplein roundabout*, and on the other side of it, the Hunner Park, and only three hundred metres further ahead the coveted Waal bridge. But they could not make it any further.

On the other side of the river, at Oosterhout, three kilometres northwest of Nijmegen, V. Abteilung/ SS-Artillerie-Ausbildungs-und-Ersatz-Regiment had set up battle positions with two batteries of howitzers. Now, they opened fire on Keizer Lodewijkplein with devastating effect. The artillery battalion's commander, SS-Hauptsturmführer Oskar Schwappacher, noted: "Our soldiers were already streaming back to the rear, when the attack was brought to a halt with precise salvoes dropped among the leading waves."[346]

Meanwhile, it had taken until about four o'clock in the morning of 18 September before Kampfgruppe Reinhold from 10. SS-Panzer-Division could be detached from the Arnhem bridge, where it was relieved by Kampfgruppe Knaust. Instead of circumventing Arnhem to the

---

* Today, this roundabout is gone, and has been replaced by the Keizer Traianus-plein.

north to take the road bridge at Renen – a distance of 25 kilometres – the Germans intended to cross the Rhine using the ferries at Huisen and Pannerden, twenty kilometres east of Arnhem. But the Huisen ferry turned out to have been sunk by the Dutch resistance, and the transfer on the only small civilian ferry at Pannerden took painfully long. In addition, it was unable to carry the heaviest vehicles of the 10. SS-Panzer-Division. The first ones to get across to the south side of the river were the pioneers of 1. Kompanie/SS-Panzer-Pionier-Abteilung 10 under SS-Untersturmführer Werner Baumgärtel. They headed off – many of them on bicycles – along twenty kilometres of narrow roads down to Lent, north of the road bridge at Nijmegen, where they arrived in the morning of 18 September.[347] There, they were briefed about the situation, and were ordered to start priming explosives on the bridges.

Over at Pannerden, Kampfgruppe Reinhold became even more delayed as the overloaded ferry capsized the same morning. This forced the SS pioneers to return to the site of the ferry to start constructing improvised rafts, so that the transfer could continue. Among the first things the divisional commander Harmel had to do after returning

The ferry at Pannerden.

to Velp during the night of 17 September was to call different Wehr-macht staffs to try to find more pioneers. Eventually, he got access to Pionier-Abteilung 6 in Minden, which put together a larger ferry in record time. Thus it was possible to carry the heaviest vehicles across the Rhine. Kampfgruppe Reinhold could not compare with the 82nd Airborne Division. The German battle group consisted of barely 1,000 men (many of whom were tank crews without vehicles), one artillery battalion, two Jagdpanzer IV tank destroyers, four armoured vehicles (two of which with one 75 mm gun each), four 20 mm anti tank guns, one 75 mm light infantry gun and one 120 mm mortar. The river cross-ing was protected from air attacks by the SS-Flak-Abteilung 10, whose three Ostwinds (self-propelled anti-aircraft weapons with 37 mm guns) were reinforced with a number of 20 mm automatic guns and a few 88s from the air force. Moreover, out of this force, only Kampf-gruppe Euling (I. Bataillon from the SS-Panzergrenadier-Regiment 22, previously II./19) under SS-Hauptsturmführer Karl-Heinz Euling with 400 men that was transferred to the southern river bank of the Waal at the road bridge in Nijmegen.

"The Panzer reconnaissance car company of Euling's battalion and the battalion staff rolled at full speed across the road bridge, which lay under hostile artillery fire", Harmel wrote. "Only part of the elements of the battalion that arrived during the afternoon [of 18 September], partly on lorries, partly on bicycles, could pass the bridge, because of the increasing artillery fire, other parts had to make it across the Waal in inflatable boats upstream." [348]

But their adversaries were still busy with defending the area south and east of Nijmegen, so the Kampfgruppe Euling only met the American "G" Company. "Our own infantry, now reinforced from the rear and supported by further artillery fire, was able to force the enemy well back to the south", Schwappacher reported. "The northern roundabouts came back into our possession. During the afternoon the initiative changed from the enemy back to our own forces." [349]

After that, there was not much fighting during the rest of the day, at least not according to SS-Hauptsturmführer Euling, who told about a peculiar event: "There was a warehouse near Nijmegen where there was brandy and food stocked up. Some of our soldiers got in there and started bringing things out. When they got to the middle there were some Americans doing the same thing on the other side of the ware-house. They did not shoot but agreed that the Germans could work on one side and the Americans on the other."[350]

Driving off "G" Company was not particularly hard for the Germans – especially not since the 1st Battalion had abandoned its positions at the Keizer Karelplein, eight hundred metres to the southwest. This was because of counterattacks that the Germans had set in during the morning of 18 September.

GERMAN COUNTERATTACK

To the east and southeast of Nijmegen was Division z.b.V. 406 under Generalleutnant Walter Scherbenning. It consisted mainly of home guard battalions with an average age of 59 years among the men, as well as the NCO schools in Jülich and Düren, one company from Grenadier-Ersatz-Regiment 520, a few battalions of discarded Luft-waffe personnel, and a number of so-called *Magen*- and *Ohren*-bat-talions (units that had recently been formed by men with stomach or hearing problems that were so severe that they during ordinary circumstances would have been discharged). General Franz Matten-klott, the commander of Wehrkreis VI, described most of the units in the division as "without any fighting qualities".[351] Oberleutnant Hans Wierichs was the commander of the 1. Kompanie of the home guard battalion Landesschützen-Bataillon I/6, which was part of this divi-sion. He describes his soldiers as "all low-quality men, ranging from 18-60. The troops were not fit for combat duty". Moreover, they were lacking both artillery and anti-tank guns.[352]

The Lufwaffe battalions of the division had no training in ground combat, apart from what the soldiers had received during their basic training, and in the "ear" and "stomach" battalions, a large part of the men was constantly on the sick-list because of the damp and cold weather. "The individual formations had very few vehicles", the corps commander General Feldt concluded, "and, as a result, were not suffi-ciently mobile. There were practically no field kitchens and no means of signal communications at all, even for the artillery, which was very limited in strength."[353] Scherbenning's division staff was, according to a German report, "not at all prepared or equipped for its task".[354]

But Feldt was an experienced commander who had led the 1. Kavallerie-Division in Poland in 1939, during the campaign in the West in 1940, and on the Eastern Front, where he had been awarded the Knight's Cross in August 1941. As early as during the afternoon of 17 September, he ordered Scherbenning to regroup his divisional headquarters to the Kruegers Manor at the German-Dutch border, a few kilometres northeast of Groesbeek, and sent the men of the NCO school at Kempen (of about the size of a battalion) and one pioneer battalion in Roermond at breakneck speed by lorries to the eastern side of the Maas river at Mook, just south of the point where the Maas-Waal Canal breaks out from the Maas. He gave the command to Oberst Goebel, with the objective of not allowing the Allies to break through to the south or to the southeast.[355]

During the following night, the Germans scraped together all soldiers they could muster in the area and sent them towards the area east and southeast of Nijmegen, where they were positioned in different Kampfgruppen in Division z.b.V. 406. General Feldt ordered a coordinated attack from the north and the south to be initiated at 0630 hrs in the morning of 18 September.

In total, 3,200 men were assembled – *Magen-* and *Ohr*-battalions, cadets, old home guard men, guard soldiers, and others of mainly inferior fighting qualities. "I had no confidence in this attack, since it was an almost impossible task for the 406th Division to attack picked troops with its motley crowd", Feldt wrote. "But it was necessary to risk the attack to forestall an advance of the enemy to the east and deceive him in regard to our strength."[356]

The main force, positioned to the north at a width of about five kilometres between Beek and Kranenburg, attacked with 1,300 men towards Groesbeek and the northern Drop Zone "Tango".[357] Supported by a low-level attack by fifteen Messerschmitt 109s, the Germans could here initially make some territorial gains, and even captured the 508th PIR's ammunition cache in the open fields below the Groesbeek Ridge. But there, the Germans also were caught in the crossfire from 2nd Battalion, 508th PIR on the ridge and in the forest to their right, and from 3rd Battalion, 505th PIR south of Groesbeek. From these positions, the Americans could also direct their fire against the Germans from the guns of the 376th Parachute Field Artillery Battalion.

When Scherbenning, the commander of Division z.b.V. 406, was informed that Panzerjäger-Ersatz- und Ausbildungs-Abteilung 6 with 450 men was lying under cover without moving forward, he became furious and ordered his adjutant, Major Rasch, to personally relieve the battalion commander, Hauptmann Grünenklee. Together with a machine gun section from the headquarters, Rasch made his way forward to the men – or, rather, the geriatrics – who were lying under cover at the edge of a forest grove. They were all grey-haired veterans from the First World War. "We charged this hill already in 1914", they shouted at him. "Now it seems as though we dotards will have to do it all over again", said one of the veterans, adding sarcastically: "All we have to do is to put Tommy to flight!" [358]

Up on the hill, from the top floor of a house on the outskirts of Groesbeek, the Germans were being observed by Gavin. He saw their infantry assemble for an attack, and then starting its advance in the open fields below the heights where the Americans sat. The 376th Field Artillery Battalion opened fire and large, black fountains of earth burst up among the Germans dressed in grey down there. Next, the men of the 505th PIR opened fire with machine guns and mortars. "I felt confident that it [the artillery] could hold them", Gavin recounted.[359]

But it was important that the landing zones were cleared of Germans, since a new airborne wave with reinforcements was on its way, so Gavin decided to launch a counterattack with two engineer companies, followed by the 1st and 3rd Battalions of 508th PIR.

Thus, the 1st Battalion was detached from its positions at Keizer Karelplein in Nijmegen, and after a seven-kilometre march, they immediately charged. These men had by then been in combat all night, and had not had any sleep for 24 hours, but carried out their mission with flying colours. The battalion commander, Lieutenant Colonel Shields Warren, recounted, not without pride: "The line of departure was on the right flank of the German attack, and rolled them up like a piece of tape, capturing 149 prisoners and killing approximately 50, and knocking out 16 dual 20mm guns."[360] With that, Drop Zone "Tango" was cleared.

It went just as quickly and efficiently when "C" Company of 505th PIR's 1st Battalion attacked the Germans at Drop Zone "N" south of the Groesbeek Ridge. Lieutenant Jack Tallerday recounts: "The C Company troopers were firing and the Germans were running away from us. It looked like a line of hunters in a rabbit drive and the Germans looked like rabbits running in no particular pattern."[361]

When then the armada of transport planes – 439 Skytrains with one Waco glider each – appeared just after two o'clock in the afternoon on 18 September, the Germans, inexperienced in battle, broke down completely. "The renewed air landing in the attack zone caused panic among the attackers", General Feldt wrote. "It was with the greatest difficulty that General Scherbenning and I succeeded in halting the troops in the jump-off positions. On this occasion I just managed to avoid being taken prisoner myself in the area of the Papen Hill."[362] Mattenklott, Wehrkreis VI's commander, stated resignedly: "Considering the low fighting quality of the motley troops, we did not gain any decisive success."[363] This was, if anything, an euphemism. Model was more straightforward when he stated that "our own forces sent in to attack at Kranenburg made an about turn as soon as the enemy attacked".[364] Major Rasch added: "A new attack with these troops would not be possible."

It was decided to withdraw the remains of Division 406 from the battle area as soon as the II. Fallschirmkorps had arrived.

Nothing could illustrate the German failure better than the sight of the great swarms of gliders descending into the fields that Scherbenning's units were supposed to have taken. Generalleutnant Feldt fumed over what he considered "a failure by the battle group". Instead, he complained, "a defence line was laboriously constructed west of Kranenburg".[365]

When Feldt shortly afterwards arrived at the command post at the Kruegers Manor, he found that both Generalfeldmarschall Model and General Eugen Meindl, the commander of the II. Fallschirmkorps, were there. Model demanded that Meindl's paratroopers immediately be dispatched in a renewed counterattack, but this was impossible as the units had not yet arrived.

With this new landing, Gavin was supplied with another 1,600 men with 31 howitzers, 13 anti-tank guns, 177 jeeps, 106 trailers and 211 tons of supplies. 320 of the 452 Waco gliders were used to fly in three new artillery battalions, the 319th and the 320th Glider Field Artillery Battalions, and the 456th Parachute Field Artillery Battalion. The fourth regiment in Gavin's division, the 325th Glider Infantry Regiment, had however still not been given any room in the air transports (according to the plans, that regiment was supposed to be flown in only on the third day, 19 September).

Twenty minutes later, about 130 four-engined B-24 Liberator bombers from the 20th Bomber Wing of the Eighth Air Force came rumbling in over the area, dropping twenty canisters each with a total of 258 tons of supplies. The air above them was almost completely covered by hundreds of escort fighters. The Americans were met by murderous anti-aircraft fire that took a terrible toll, especially from the escort fighters: 20 of them were shot down, while eight Skytrains and four Liberators were lost, and in addition, more than a hundred transport planes and 38 Liberators were damaged.

To sum up, both Americans and Germans had failed at Nijmegen on 18 September. The same can be said about Arnhem, where the Germans the same day failed to drive away Lieutenant-Colonel Frost's paratroopers from the road bridge while the main part of the British 1st Airborne Division over in Oosterbeek had not yet succeeded with its mission to relieve Frost.

WESTERN ARNHEM: BLOCKING GROUP SPINDLER HOLDS ITS GROUND

At around six o'clock in the morning of 18 September, darkness slowly started to give way in Arnhem. To the nineteen-year-old SS soldier Helmut Buttlar and his comrades, the night must have felt as a painful eternity. The previous day, the thirteen Germans had completed their self-assumed task to stall the British paratroopers at the railway bridge

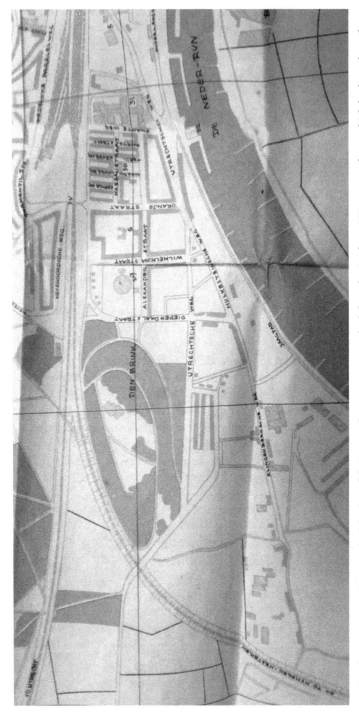

Arnhem's western outskirts. At the left edge of the image, forming an arc to the left, is the Arnhem–Nijmegen railway, which leads to the railway bridge across the Rhine to the south outside of the picture. There, the viaduct underneath the railway at the Oosterbeek-Laag station leads the Beneden-dorpsweg to the Klingelbeekscheweg, which segues into the Hulkesteinscheweg. The Hulkesteinscheweg reaches the Utrechtscheweg, which continues eastbound into Arnhem. The first side street to the north from the Utrechtscheweg after Hulkesteinscheweg is the Oranjestraat. The next side street from the Utrechtscheweg is the Zwarteweg. At No. 32 is the Rijnpaviljoen hotel. No. 31 is the Sint-Elisabeth hospital. (British city map from the war. National Archives, WO 171 393 HW 1st AbnDiv.)

272

at Oosterbeek until it could be blown up, and had also made it without any major injuries (see page 205). They had also managed to pull back and take refuge in an abandoned house just down by the Rhine on the western outskirts of Arnhem. Throughout the night, they had been lying low there, completely silent and still in the dark abandoned house, on tenterhooks, listening to the sound of marching nailed boots and every now and then voices speaking English in the street outside. Since they had used up all of their ammunition during the battle at the railway bank, there was nothing else to do than to stay hidden, and hope that they would not be discovered. And they were lucky – no British paratroopers showed any interest in the dark, lonely house.

As time went by, Buttlar and his men were tormented by what eventually became almost unbearable thirst, and hunger tore at their intestines. They had used up all of their provisions and emptied their field bottles, and the house turned out to be devoid of food and lacking water. Their only thought was to find something edible. But in order not to run across a British patrol in the dark of the night, they had decided to wait until light before going out to, primarily, search for food, and secondarily, to find their way back to their own lines.

Slowly, slowly it became brighter. Eventually, the SS men decided not want to wait anymore, but carefully sneaked out in the yard. No English could be seen or heard. In the cellars of the surrounding houses that they entered, the Germans found juice and dried and tinned fruit that they greedily consumed. It must have seemed as a goldmine to the tormented young men. With their hunger and thirst quenched, they were overwhelmed by terrible fatigue, so they returned to the house where they had spent the night to get some sleep before trying to make it back to their own lines, wherever those were.

When they awoke, the garden was bathed in sunshine, and they could clearly hear intense gunfire from the quarters somewhat further north. Buttlar selected four men, and armed with a few hand grenades, they sneaked out to try to make it up to the battle area. But they did not get far before a group of Dutch civilians spotted them and started yelling *"Moffen!"**

---

* An old Dutch pejorative term for Germans, derived from a word for "grumpy".

The SS men threateningly raised their handguns and were thus able to silence the Dutchmen – who could not be expected to know that the Germans had used up all of their ammunition – but realised that they could not get any further. So they fell back to their hiding place where they decided to change tactics: They would now wait for the darkness to try to make it through. All day they heard the noise of intense fighting from outside.[366]

Another German who had been forced to hide from the enemy in the same area, just a few hundred metres further north, was the commander of the II. SS-Panzerkorps, the SS-Obergruppenführer Bittrich. As we have seen (page 202), he had been in western Arnhem in the evening of 17 September, when Kampfgruppe Möller fled in among the houses at the shunting yard after having been beaten by Lieutenant-Colonel Frost's 2nd Battalion of 1st Parachute Brigade. There, the Germans remained hidden, while the "Red Devils" marched past the them on the road a little further down the hill.

The situation was saved for the Germans by the uncertainty about the situation on the British side. There, two major mistakes had been made on 17 September – the late start of the advance from the landing zones and the order to the Parachute Brigade's 3rd Battalion to pause the advance in central Oosterbeek for the night. A more daring officer would have let this battalion go on towards the road bridge in Arnhem, which by then was held by Frost's 2nd Battalion. But the British divisional commander Urquhart had spent most of the time since the landing driving back and forth in his jeep searching for the commander of the brigade's reconnaissance company, Major Freddie Gough (who in fact had continued straight ahead until he reached the road bridge). Therefore, and because radio liaison did not work, he had an utterly unclear picture of the situation as he joined the 3rd Battalion in the evening of 17 September, where he came across the brigade commander Lathbury. This is the backdrop for the decision to halt the 3rd Battalion during the night of 17 September.

This, which came unexpectedly for the Germans, gave SS-Obergruppenführer Bittrich an opportunity to make it back to his headquarters. On his way there, he stopped by at General Kussin's command post north of Arnhem to be briefed about the situation by the field commander. To his surprise, Bittrich discovered that this was now the command post of the 9. SS-Panzer-Division. When he stepped inside, he met Harzer, the acting divisional commander, who told him that Kussin was missing. But Bittrich quickly collected his wits. "Well, Harzer, how are things going?" he greeted him, asking: "How have you divided the different units? Where are you going to use them?" [367] Harzer told him what he knew, and Bittrich realised just how unclear and serious the situation was. He called the command post of the 10. SS-Panzer-Division and got to speak to the divisional commander Harmel, who had just arrived from Germany. After that, he set off towards the front at the road bridge in Arnhem (see page 247).

To SS-Sturmbannführer Ludwig Spindler, who was responsible for the defence of Arnhem further to the west, the British pause in Oosterbeek meant that he had the opportunity to reorganise his units. Spindler, who had been awarded the German Cross in Gold by Harzer on 17 September, was very experienced in battle. He was one of the first Waffen-SS soldiers, and had been fighting since May 1940. Through SS-Hauptsturmführer von Allwörden, whose battle group held the British at bay in the northwest, Spindler was informed about the situation on the right flank. He realised that the possibility of annihilating the landed forces had passed him by – at least for the moment – and therefore, he focused on forming a "blocking line" to stop the rest of the British forced from entering the city. Thereby, he exploited the terrain and the surroundings skilfully.

Between the road bridge in Arnhem and Oosterbeek, the Rhine bends to the north, passing only 200 metres from the large shunting yard on the Arnhem-Utrecht line. The British would have to cross this narrow sector during their advance in towards the central parts of Arnhem. The defence of this sector was facilitated by the steep descent down towards the river. At the top, in the north, at the shunting yard, Spindler positioned the 2. Batterie of the SS-Flak-Abteilung 9 under SS-Hauptsturmführer Heinz Grop. He only had 85 men with one 88 mm and one 20 mm cannon at his disposal, but they were aimed along the Parallelweg/Zwartenweg that runs straight down towards the Utrechtscheweg (which runs from west to east just above the river, connecting Oosterbeek and Arnhem), eight metres below.

West of the Parallelweg/Zwartenweg, there was a myriad of side streets and residential houses between the shunting yard and the Utrechtscheweg, and on the other side of the street to the east, Sint-Elisabeth's great hospital complex was spread out. Here, Spindler positioned the main part of Kampfgruppe Möller, the not even one hundred men remaining of the SS-Panzer-Pionier-Bataillon 9 under SS-Hauptsturmführer Hans Möller. The pioneer battalion's 2. Kompanie was the most badly battered one, having lost its commander, SS-Untersturmführer Voss, the previous day. He was succeeded by SS-Hauptsturmführer Josef Schmatz.[368] His company and the 3. Kompanie under SS-Untersturmführer Gerhard Engel kept ground between the shunting yard and the Utrechtscheweg. Down by the southern side of the road – in and around the Rijnpaviljoen* hotel building in Onderlangs 10, a small parallel street on the southern side of the Utrechtscheweg, just down by the river – was the 1. Kompanie/SS-Panzer-Pionier-Bataillon 9 under SS-Obersturmführer Karl Georg Steinert.

Behind Kampfgruppe Möller stood 120 artillerymen from the I. Abteilung in Spindler's own SS-Panzer-Artillerie-Regiment 9. Since this unit had been forced to abandon all of its artillery guns in France, the artillerymen were now sent in as infantry. Even further back was SS-Kampfgruppe Harder – 450 men from SS-Panzer-Regiment 9 with three Panther tanks under SS-Obersturmführer Adolf Harder, commander of the Panzer regiment's 7. Kompanie. But at dawn on 18 September, these were engaged in battle with "C" Company from the British parachute brigade's 2nd Battalion inside Arnhem, and could therefore not be sent in to the west.

The equipment that these weak units had at their disposal left much to be desired, according to SS-Obersturmbannführer Harzer: "Not one of the units in the battle had a sufficient amount of vehicles at their disposal. There were no field kitchens whatsoever at these units.

* The hotel still remains in place, and is now called Rijnhotel.

They had only captured rifles from all European armies with only little ammunition that fitted them. Immediate additions could only be made by capturing weapons from the 1st British Airborne [Division] on the battlefield." [369]

Urquhart and Lathbury were awakened at three o'clock in the morning on 18 September in the house on the western outskirts of Oosterbeek where they had spent the night. One hour later, Urquhart ordered that the British parachute brigade resume its advance by taking the road into Arnhem running along the river Rhine. To Lieutenant-Colonel David Dobie and his 1st Parachute Battalion, it came as a great relief. They had been tied down throughout the night in heavy night fighting with Kampfgruppe Allwörden and its Panzer vehicles in the forests north of Oosterbeek.

But it was the 3rd Parachute Battalion that took the lead, breaking up from its positions in the park at Hotel Hartenstein. Urquhart and Lathbury joined the men as these marched down the hill in the streets leading to the river. They passed beautiful villas with lush gardens and came down to the Benedendorpsweg, which marks the southern edge of Oosterbeek. The paratroopers followed this road to the left (east), arriving after a few kilometres at the viaduct under the railway at Oosterbeek-Laag Station, where Buttlar's thirteen SS men had halted the 2nd Battalion the day before. Until then, they had not met any resistance. On the other side of the viaduct, the road segues into the Klingelbeekscheweg. This road passes by a considerably less densely built-up area with several small forest groves. Here, they were suddenly shot at. But it was only a few German snipers who could quickly be neutralised or chased away. Here and there, a few Germans had secured themselves with ropes up among the tree branches. When they were discovered and shot by the paratroopers, they came crashing down until they were left dangling in the ropes a bit below the foliage. It was a bizarre sight for the men following suit further back in the column.

The march continued eastbound, all the time in parallel with the Rhine, a couple of hundred metres to the right of the soldiers. However, the river was obscured from the road by trees and bushes. Eight hundred metres from the railway viaduct, the Klingelbeekscheweg segued into the Hulkesteinscheweg. Here, the paratroopers entered the western outskirts of Arnhem, and here, the houses were closer together and were bigger. After yet a few hundred more metres, the Hulkesteinscheweg turned to the left in a small uphill slope, reaching the major thoroughfare Utrechtscheweg at a T junction. Lieutenant Cleminson's No. 5 Platoon, "B" Company – the ones who had shot General Kussin dead and taken Hotel Hartenstein the day before – were the first ones to get up on this wide road. It was paved and had dual tram tracks. The Utrechtscheweg led to central Arnhem, but Cleminson and the other paratroopers would not make it that far.

One hundred and fifty metres ahead of them to the right, down by the Rhine, lay the Rijnpaviljoen hotel, and there, SS-Obersturmführer Steinert's German pioneers were positioned, without the British knowing anything about this. Diagonally up to the left in front of the British, a large block of several two-storey houses was visible. Here,

This is where the British paratroopers came up onto the Utrechtscheweg (from where the picture is taken) from the Hulkesteinscheweg (at the back of the picture). Image from 1925.

between the Oranjestraat to the west and the Zwarteweg to the east, SS-Hauptsturmführer Möller had his foremost position.

The Germans were prepared. "During the night", Möller recounted, "I had had my two flamethrowers set up forward, and anti-tank weapons as well as smoke grenades, all of them indispensable weapons for house-to-house and street fighting, which we had practiced so often earlier during our training." [370]

It was about seven o'clock in the morning of 18 September, and it was still quite dark as the first British paratroopers appeared on the road below Möller's main force. The British ran crouching in small groups up onto the Utrechtscheweg, and turned to the right. (See map page 272) So far, everything was quiet.

Cleminson and his men continued down the road at the head of the "B" Company, suspiciously spying both sides of the road. Now they arrived at the street corner, where a side road to the left climbed up the hill. This was the Oranjestraat. On the other side of this street, a quarter of two- and three-storey tenement houses towered. Behind the windows in the darkened apartments, watchful eyes were following the continued advance by the British along the road.

A smaller street swung to the right, but the British continued along the Utrechtscheweg, which now entered an uphill slope. Further up the hill, on the other side of the next cross-street (Zwarteweg), the large hospital was visible. To the right, below it, was the Rijnpaviljoen, and behind the hotel, the British could catch a glimpse of the Rhine, only some fifty metres away. On tenterhooks, the first men passed the Zwarteweg. Where were the Germans?

"*Feuer!*" The night turned into day as the 88 mm gun opened fire at the top of the Zwarteweg. The British disappeared from the road. After a few minutes' confused firefight, all fell silent again.

The first sunrays made their way in among the houses, but the giant hospital complex threw long, black shadows over the Zwarteweg, and the houses on the other side were still obscured by darkness. Suddenly, some of SS-Untersturmführer Engels's men saw how the British tried to sneak around the Sint-Elisabeth hospital. Intense fire from the German side, supported by the SS flak soldiers on the other side of the railway, drove the British back.

They withdrew to the six tenement houses west of the hospital. The paratroopers rushed inside with their weapons ready to fire and with hand grenades in their hands. Terrified tenants came rushing out of their flats, pointing out to the British where the Germans were. Doors were knocked down, the staircases were lit up by exploding hand grenades and rattling submachine guns. Screams and noise, and the air was filled with gunpowder smoke. Then, the British were the masters of the houses. But soon, there were new bangs, as German volleys of bullets from the other side of the road slammed into the façade of the house, smashing window panes, making dust fly as they hit the walls. The paratroopers crawled up to the windows and returned the fire.

"Woah Muhammed!" The British paratrooper's battle cry echoed between the houses. After a while, there was yet another pause in the

The Sint-Elisabeth hospital with the Utrechtscheweg in the foreground, the Zwarteweg to the left, and, in the background, the shunting yard where the German anti-aircraft battery was positioned. To the left of the image, the tenement houses where the British "B" Company barricaded themselves are visible. Just outside the image to the left is the house in Zwarteweg where the divisional commander Urquhart was forced to hide in the evening of 18 September. The first (lower) cross-street to the left from the Zwarteweg is the Alexanderstraat, where Lathbury was wounded. The air picture from 1930 is taken from a position in mid-air above the Rhine to the south.

fighting, as always in this kind of battle. Cleminson and the other British officers were handing out orders. Soldiers were running up the stairs and down the stairs to find better firing positions. Wounded soldiers were being dressed, furniture was being dragged to the outside walls to reinforce them. The tenants dug out food and beverages that they offered to their liberators. In one of the houses, a little girl was shot in her leg as she passed a doorway. She collapsed, and a British medic tried to dress her wound, while her mother, who had gone absolutely hysterical by seeing her daughter being shot, was screaming and trying to tear away the medic from the little girl.

The British soon discovered that they were isolated. There was no sight of "A" Company, which was supposed to have followed suit – together with all of the battalion's mortar and machine gun sections as well as three of its four anti-aircraft guns. Having been further back in the column, they had encountered another group of Germans who had been infiltrating the back of the vanguard of the "B" Company, which thereby found itself cut off.

Meanwhile, the fighting in western Arnhem was focused on the "C" Company of 2nd Parachute Battalion, which, under Major Victor Dover, had attempted to capture the railway bridge between Oosterbeek and Arnhem when the Germans blew it up. After that, Major Dover had led his men against the German military command post in Nieuwe Plein 37–39 in Arnhem, about one kilometre east of the Sint-Elisabeth hospital. But here, they were encircled by SS-Kampfgruppe Harder. Eventually, as the Germans had set fire to all the surrounding houses and taken the building where the British had taken shelter under direct fire with the cannons from their Panther tanks, the one hundred remaining paratroopers led by Major Dover were forced to surrender. Only a small group managed to make it out of the German encirclement and join the rest of the battalion at the road bridge.

In that way, Kampfgruppe Harder could be freed to support Möller's unit. In the morning of 18 September, the battle group was ordered to attack in order to annihilate the British "B" Company in the residential homes west of the hospital, but were met with embittered resistance. It was probably here that Harder lost one of his three

Panther tanks to a PIAT. Yet another one was destroyed by a Gammon grenade launched by Major Peter Waddy, commander of the "B" Company. After that, the Germans turned to firing at the buildings that the British were holding, using mortars, however without causing them much losses.

Then, in the afternoon, the rear British column broke through – after the 1st Battalion had joined them from the north – and made it to the company that had been cut off. The first reinforcement to arrive was between 20 and 40 men with a Bren Carrier loaded with much-needed ammunition. Peter Waddy seems to have become so enthusiastic from seeing that relief force that he forgot all caution and rushed out into the street – where he was immediately killed by an exploding grenade.*

Since the commander of "A" Company, Major Mervyn Dennison, had been wounded by a stab from a bayonet in close combat just before that, the 3rd Battalion had thus lost two company commanders.

The sight that met the men who had made it through to the battlefield was not encouraging: Everywhere in the street lay dead paratroopers and Germans. Private James Shelbourne recounted, "I was startled to find an upturned German helmet filled to the brim with bright red arterial blood".[371]

But the British did not succeed with more than relieving the "B" Company. Late in the afternoon on 18 September, the positions were completely locked, with both sides on each side of the Sint-Elisabeth hospital complex, which became a sort of no man's land where the hospital staff continued caring for their patients in the midst of the raging battle. The giant Red Cross flag that they had hung on the front was actually respected by both sides.

QR2: VIDEO
18:30: The German veteran Karl Heinz Henschel, machine gun gunner at the 9. SS-Pz-Div., about the battle at the Sint-Elisabeth hospital complex (in German and Dutch).

---

* Waddy was first buried in the garden of Utrechtscheweg 148. Today, he rests in the military cemetery in Oosterbeek, Plot 27, Row C, Grave 4.

Urquhart and Lathbury realised by now that they could not be of any more use in western Arnhem, but that they needed to make it back to the headquarters in Oosterbeek (where they, by the way, had already been written off) to get an idea of the battle as a whole. Together with Lathbury's intelligence officer, Captain William Taylor, they intended to make it across the backyards and through the houses on the north side of the Alexanderstraat, which runs eastwards straight towards the Sint-Elisabeth hospital. In that way, they intended to try to avoid the German fire coming from the east. Lieutenant James Cleminson, commander of No. 5 Platoon of the 3rd Para Battalion – who had taken the lead in the advance the previous day and shot General Kussin dead – discovered how they were about to turn the wrong way – straight towards the Germans – and joined in as a guide.

But when they crossed the Alexanderstraat, Lathbury was hit by German fire. The three others pulled him into a residential house in Alexanderstraat 135 (on the north side of the road). Then, the three men set off to try to find a medic for him, stumbling in through the garden door of Anton Derksen's home in Zwarteweg 14, which runs past the hospital on its western side. The despairing Derksen explained as best as he could in Dutch that German soldiers were at the front of the house. Having established, to their horror, that this was the case, the three British made their way up into the small attic of the house. According to Urquhart, they could see a German armoured vehicle through the window from there, parked in the street below. The Derksen family left the house through the back door.

From about half past four in the afternoon of 18 September and throughout the following night, the British divisional commander, Captain William Taylor (the 1st Parachute Brigade's intelligence officer) and Lieutenant James Cleminson remained hiding in the dark house in extremely arduous conditions. At any time, the attic could be hit by a shell, or German soldiers could come storming in. Urquhart recounted, "There was neither food nor water in the house – the Germans had cut off supplies of water at the main", adding the perhaps most outright unpleasant thing of all: "The lack of indoor sanitation was a nuisance, we hated having to soil this family's living quarters". [372] Ironically enough, it was in a house just nearby that SS-Obergruppenführer Bittrich had been forced to stay hidden the previous night!

Reinforcements for "The Red Devils" 18 September 1944

CONCENTRATION OF FORCES

While these battles continued in western Arnhem, the 1st Airborne Division was waiting for the second landing with reinforcements. This kept up the British courage, and the Germans probably also were waiting for this second landing. Even though it has not been possible to establish what kind of documents it was that the paratroop general Student came across in a downed glider on 17 September – if it was the entire plan for "Market Garden" or just the operational plan for the American 101st Airborne Division – the events point to the former.

The second landing at the Arnhem sector was, according to plan, be carried out in three waves, starting at 1100 hrs on 18 September. It was to land Brigadier John Winthrop Hackett's 4th Parachute Battalion as well as supplies of various kinds. First of all, the main part of the 4th Parachute Battalion was to be dropped by parachute over Drop Zone "Y", the Ginkel Heath three kilometres northwest of Wolfheze, and only a kilometre or so east of the town of Ede. After that, gliders were to land a few more troops, including some from the 4th Parachute Battalion, in Landing Zone "S", a few kilometres further east, and in Landing Zone "Z". The latter was the four-square-kilometre Renkum Heath, south of the Utrecht-Arnhem railway, just west of Wolfheze. Finally, supplies were to be dropped by parachute over Drop Zone "L" northwest of Oosterbeek, a few kilometres east of Landing Zone "S". (Map page 292.)

Landing Zones "S" and "Z" had been used on 17 September – the latter had then been called Drop Zone "X" and was the landing site for the 1st Parachute Brigade. The Ginkel Heath, Drop Zone "Y", the most important landing zone on this 18 September, had not been used on the first day – it was way too far away to the west. In fact, it still was, eight kilometres from the new objectives – the heights northwest of Arnhem, but the problem for the British was that they needed to use the closer-lying landing zones for their gliders with invaluable equipment that could not end up in enemy hands.

The 4th Parachute Battalion's task to occupy the heights northwest of Arnhem was because there it was planned to land a battalion of engineers on 19 September who would build a provisional airfield to the British 52nd (Lowland) Division could be flown in.

The three battalions of Brigadier Philip Hicks's 1st Airlanding Brigade, which had been flown in on 17 September, were tasked with holding the landing zones on 18 September: The 7th Battalion, The King's Own Scottish Borderers (7th KOSB) at Drop Zone "Y" (the Ginkel Heath) to the northwest; the 2nd Battalion, The South Staffordshire Regiment at Landing Zone "S"; and the 1st Airlanding Brigade at Landing Zone "Z" to the south.

Meanwhile, German Division Tettau under Generalleutnant Hans von Tettau, the commander of military training in the Netherlands, was busy marching up across twenty kilometres west of the British units. Von Tettau has been blamed after the war for a belated reaction to the British landings, but he actually acted both quickly and efficiently on the incoming information about the landings. His unit had only just taken up battle positions along the river Waal to the south when the first landings took place on 17 September, and during the following hours, there was a torrent of incoming reports indicating landings in all directions, creating much confusion. But when Model's operational orders went out at half past five in the afternoon on 17 September, von Tettau quickly got his units going. With the exception of a few minor forces that were left behind by the Waal, the entire division regrouped – often with nothing else than bicycles for transportation – in a flanking movement and set up battle positions in a semi-circle against the British landing zones.

In the far north, at Ede and north of the Ginkel Heath, SS-Wachbataillon 3 and about 500 recruits that SS-Obersturmführer Karl Labahn had had under his command, stood under SS-Standartenführer Paul Helle. To the right (south) of these units, the SS Unterführerschule Arnheim (the SS NCO school in Arnhem) lined up two battalions. The II. Bataillon (SS-Alarm-Bataillon Eberwein) with 600 men under SS-Sturmbannführer Eugen Eberwein was positioned at Bennekom, one kilometre south of Ede. To the right of it stood the I. Bataillon under SS-Hauptsturmführer Günther Schulz. As he had left his 1. Kompanie behind at the Waal, Schulz only disposed of three companies, but received reinforcements in the shape of Fliegerhorst- Bataillon 3, which was to hold the sector between the two SS NCO school battalions. Down by the river Rhine, the Navy battalion Schiffstamm-Abteilung 10, Panzer-Kompanie 224 (with seventeen old French tanks in German service) and one reserve force, Artillerie-Regiment 184 (450 artillerymen without artillery guns), were positioned.

Interestingly enough, von Tettau's plan consisted of a pincer operation aimed at the Ginkel Heath (Drop Zone "Y") and the Renkum Heath (Landing Zone "Z"). Did he have advance information about the British plan?

SS-Standartenführer Paul Helle was to attack from the north and advance through the forest between the Ginkel Heath and Landing Zone "S" to the east, so as to reach the railway that formed the southern border for these landing zones. There, Helle's units were to link up with SS-Alarm-Bataillon Eberwein, whose four companies were ordered to fight their way forward in a north-eastern direction from Bennekom. If this were to succeed, Drop Zone "Y" would be cut off, and Eberwein's unit would then advance further to the east along the railway.

Further to the south, the SS NCO school's I. Battalion, Fliegerhorst-Bataillon 3, Schiffstamm-Abteilung 10, and Panzer-Kompanie 224 were tasked with attacking due east along a few kilometres, to drive away the British from the Rhine bank southwest and south of Oosterbeek.

The plan looked good on paper, and with around 3,000 men against the about 2,000 men of the British 1st Airlanding Brigade, von Tettau was superior in numbers – and in addition, the British had no equivalent of his Panzer and armoured personnel carriers.

The problem was that von Tettau's men were mainly of second-class quality, and they were put against some of the toughest and most well-trained soldiers on the Allied side.

Fliegerhorst-Bataillon 3 (Airfield Battalion 3) consisted of discharged ground crews from the Luftwaffe, who, according to one description, "had never been trained in anything else than rolling barrels of petrol".[373] Schiffstamm-Abteilung 10 consisted of 600 seamen, most of whom were in their 40s and 50s, and who had never before seen a land battle. The battalion commander, Korvettenkapitän Theodor Zaubzer, had previously been First Officer of the training ship *Schleswig Holstein*, adjutant in the motor torpedo boat inspection, and the liaison officer for the Navy at Luftflotte 2, but he too lacked experience of infantry fighting. Zaubzer was worrying about the upcoming encounter with the British elite soldiers, and, ahead of the attack mission, he had in vain been trying to get more experienced officers and non-commissioned officers for his unit. He was supplied with the 6. Kompanie from Schiffstamm-Abteilung 14, but this was no better prepared for infantry fighting. Harzer considered this unit "not really suitable for use as infantry".

The only unit in Division Tettau with a majority of soldiers experienced in battle was the SS Unterführerschule Arnheim, which consisted of SS soldiers who had been selected for NCO training after at least twelve months of service at the front. The two battalion commanders Schulz and Eberwein were veterans from the German Polizei-Division* on the Eastern Front.[374] The commander of the SS NCO school, SS-Standartenführer Michael Lippert, had been badly wounded on the Eastern Front in the summer of 1942, after which he had been transferred to a position as a troop trainer. He also had a background as a police officer, but above all, he was a veteran of the SS, which he had joined already in 1933. During "the Night of the Long Knives" in 1934, it was Lippert and the infamous Theodor Eicke who had murdered the SA leader Ernst Röhm. Lippert also played a key role in the formation of the concentration camps, and became a Waffen SS soldier early on. This contributed to the chasm of con-

---

* The Polizei-Division was a military frontline unit of German policemen formed in 1939. Later, it was transferred to the SS.

fidence that had arisen between von Tettau and his subordinate SS units. One of the cadets at the SS Unterführerschule told the British military historian Robert Kershaw many years later that von Tettau was a real "SS hater". [375]

But the SS NCO school was, according to Lippert, not equipped for any attack missions. This was even more the case with the rest of the units in Division Tettau. There was a dearth of more or less everything – weapons, ammunition, signal equipment, medical staff, and even rations. "Rations had to be purloined from the Dutch population", Lippert said laconically.

Now, taken by itself, the latter did not constitute any problem for SS-Standartenführer Helle's SS-Wachbataillon 3, which was positioned against the Ginkel Heath with its five companies of Dutch "volunteers" and a company of Ukrainians. The Dutch military historian Lou de Jong describes SS-Wachbataillon 3 as "an undisciplined, lawless gang". [376] The Dutch troop included a large number of sheer criminals who had been promised amnesty if they let themselves be enrolled, Dutchmen who had been faced with the choice of either letting themselves be enlisted or be sent to Germany for slave labour, and even former patients from mental institutions. The unit's task had been to undertake "dirty" work during the occupation, which the Germans themselves did not want to handle. In one of the trials against Dutch war criminals after the war, it was established that "criminality in this battalion had been particularly high, even when disregarding purely military offences (desertion, absence without leave, escaping one's guard, insubordination etc.) in this verdict. With these military offences included, they become as large in the Wachbataillon as in all German units of the Waffen-SS and the police taken together... Among the men of the Wachbataillon, just about all kinds of elements from civil criminal law occurred, such as theft, fraud, embezzlement, looting, unlawful raiding of houses and appropriation of other people's property, extortion etc." [377] The officers of the Wachbataillon mainly consisted of veterans from the Waffen-SS, in many cases with a background in the German police, who had been so badly wounded that they, in spite of often long-term hospital care were considered "unfit for frontline service". For example, the battalion's adjutant, the 36-year-old SS-Untersturmführer Albert Naumann, had had one arm paralysed through an injury on the Eastern Front; he could not even use a pistol without someone first having loaded and cocked it for him. Moreover, many of the German officers of SS-Wachbataillon 3 were highly traumatised by their experiences on the Eastern Front.

The more than 700 Highland soldiers of the 7th KOSB were positioned in the afternoon of 17 September for the defence of the Ginkel Heath. The battalion commander, the 47-year-old Lieutenant-Colonel Robert Payton-Reid, was described as a real "old-fashioned tough guy". Not many battalion commanders had his vast experience as a soldier: Payton-Reid's military career had started as early as in 1915, when he had joined The King's Own Scottish Borderers, a unit where he would remain. The divisional commander Urquhart spoke about him as "a tough, ruddy complexioned lieutenant-colonel who had no respect whatsoever for the Germans".

Payton-Reid was "extremely surprised", as he put it, by not having met any resistance, in spite of his battalion marching out to their positions right in front of the eyes of "600 German soldiers in Ede". The latter was based on information that the Scots had retrieved from prisoners of war that had been taken.[378]

The German passivity has a very simple explanation. The city commandant of Ede, SS-Obersturmführer Karl Labahn, had about 500 men at his disposal on 17 September, mainly newly called-up recruits, in the 7. Kompanie of SS-Panzergrenadier-Ausbildungs- und Ersatz-Bataillon 4, Fliegerhorst-Bataillon 3, and Schiffstamm-Abteilung 20. "The reservists have mainly been extracted from the cultural sector and state business, and with very few exceptions, you can only characterise them as sissies", Labahn wrote in a report two weeks later.[379] The vast majority of these recruits had arrived only two days earlier, without any previous military training whatsoever. Many of them had even been unable to collect a uniform, but arrived in their civilian clothes. "The newly arrived reservists had to dispose of their civilian clothes when taking up their positions and put on uniforms",

Labahn wrote: "Non-commissioned officers had to teach the men in the trenches how to load and uncock [a rifle] and in the use of hand grenades." In fact, these units were ordered to attack from Ede in the evening of 17 September, but the recruits deserted *en masse* rather than going into battle![380] Labahn was beside himself with rage. He demanded that "all these wretched cowards" be summarily executed; however, he was forced to withdraw this order as he realised that it would mean demoralising mass executions.

DIVISION TETTAU ATTACKS

The fighting at the Ginkel Heath begun as skirmishes that intensified during the night of 17/18 September. The four companies of the 7th KOSB were positioned on both sides of the two-by-two-kilometre heath, Drop Zone "Y". It was delimited to the north by the Amsterdamscheweg, the motorway between Ede and Arnhem (N 224), and to the south by the yet to be completed new Arnhem road (today's A 12/E 35).*

The surrounding terrain was dominated by deciduous forests. Apart from the Scots having superiority in numbers against them, the forests that surrounded the moor made liaison more difficult, and no radio contact could be established. Therefore, Payton-Reid did not know more than that the enemy, judging from the sound of gunfire, was present in the dark forest.

The first clash took place when two German vehicles, one of them being an ambulance, drove into a roadblock that had been set up by the "A" Company of 7th KOSB where the Amsterdamscheweg met the new Arnhem road.**

The Germans stopped and immediately surrendered. It turned out that the ambulance was full of heavily armed soldiers! [381]

---

* The Germans had started building this motorway in the summer of 1940 for transports to the coast in the run-up to the intended invasion of the British Isles. However, when the invasion did not happen, construction slowed and eventually ceased. In 1944, it was made up of a wide sandy track on top of a high viaduct.

** Where the A 12/E 35 today passes underneath the N 224.

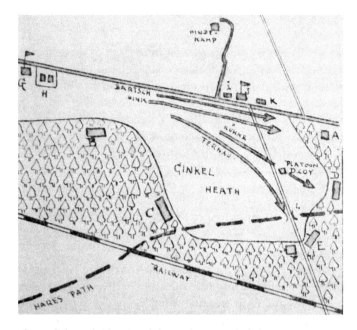

The Ginkel Heath (above) and the Renkum Heath (below).

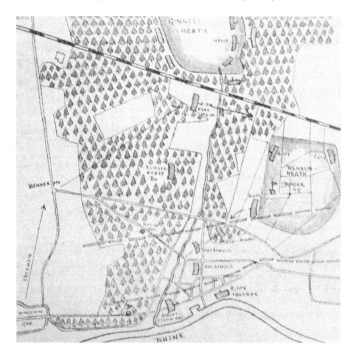

One kilometre further to the west, thirty men from the so-called "hunting commando" of Helle's SS-Wachbataillon 3, specialised in hunting down inmates that had escaped from the concentration camp at Amersfoort, came bicycling along the road when they ran into an ambush by "A" Company's 4th Platoon under Lieutenant James Strang. Most of the "hunting commando" was mowed down mercilessly. The soldiers that had not been hit fled into the woods, where many of them simply chose to desert. Only four men returned to Ede. One of them was the unit commander, SS-Unterscharführer Sackel, who was badly wounded. (He later died from his injuries at the hospital in Apeldoorn.) [382]

From SS-Flak-Artillerie-Abteilung 10 in Ede, too, a reconnaissance force was sent out into the dark. The patrol returned without the SS-Unterscharführer van Duellen and Walter Bunzel, and with SS-Scharführer Behm having a head wound.[383] Helle's mistake was to order his units to attack piecemeal, as they arrived in Ede, which was especially unwise given the lack of morale among the men. At a quarter to nine in the evening, Lieutenant Strang's men observed a new German vehicle column on the half-finished road. This was 4. Kompanie of SS-Wachbataillon 3, which, under SS-Hauptsturmführer Ernst Bartsch, was advancing with all of the battalion's motor vehicles – only to be stopped by raging gunfire.

The fact that Bartsch received some reinforcement by the 3. Kompanie of SS-Wachbataillon 3 did not change the situation; every time they tried to attack, Strang's men fired flares, and then covered the German lines with machine gun fire. In spite of their inferiority in numbers, and in spite of Bartsch having an armoured personnel carrier at his disposal, Strang's platoon managed to repel three attacks. The commander of the 3. Kompanie, SS-Obersturmführer Karl Hink, was badly wounded himself, and was evacuated. For each time, the attackers' firing lines grew thinner – which was not only due to losses in combat; many of the Dutch SS soldiers deserted under cover of darkness.[384]

Briefed about the difficult situation, Helle asked for advice from his adjutant, the one-armed war veteran SS-Untersturmführer Naumann. He was then able to explain to Helle what a mistake it was to carry out these frontal attacks – instead, the units ought to do flanking movements through the forest.[385] At 0450 hrs, when Helle had been able to get five of the six companies in SS-Wachbataillon 3 to the beech forests at the north-eastern corner of the Ginkel Heath, he launched a concentrated attack against the flank of Strang's platoon. Mortars and three 37 mm anti-tank guns as well as armoured personnel carriers with 20 mm guns subjected the Scots to a fierce gunfire. When the Germans then attacked, Strang saw his way clear to order a retreat towards the east, where the staff of the "A" Company was located. In that way, the Dutch SS soldiers managed to take No. 16 Platoon of 7th KOSB's "D" Company by surprise, as it had been positioned in a small labour camp for relocated Dutch civilians 600 metres further into the forest, on the eastern side of the heath. The battle raged in the midst of panic-stricken Dutch civilians – which the SS men took advantage of. Seven of the Scots were killed and fifty were taken captive.

Scenting victory, Helle headed off to the Café Pension J. Kramer*, a two-storey red-brick guest house, located on the northern side of the Amsterdamscheweg at the north-eastern corner of the Ginkel Heath, where he set up his new command post.

By then, his Dutch SS soldiers controlled the north-eastern part of the heath where the 4th Parachute Brigade according to plan was supposed to be dropped only a few hours later. But the report he sent to Generalleutnant von Tettau, that "all enemy advances westward have been halted", was nevertheless totally misleading.[386]

On the other side of the woods, Landing Zone "S", the field north of Wolfheze (where the 1st Airborne Brigade had been landed the previous day) was secured, by 2nd Battalion, The South Staffordshire Regiment. It had been landed with three companies on 17 September; the remainder was to follow suit on the 18th. Not much of the embittered fighting was noticeable here, and above all, nobody knew what was going on – neither to the west nor to the east. Here, the glider pilot Staff Sergeant Victor Miller woke up on a cold morning on 18 September. "Our own area remained strangely quiet, except for a small

* Called Zuid Ginkel Café in some accounts. Today, it is called Juffrouw Tok.

engagement being fought out on the edge of the woods we had left the previous night", he wrote in his diary.[387]

In fact, no one on the Allied side had any overview of the situation in its entirety in the morning of 18 September. In the residential house at Duitsekampweg 10 north of the railway in Wolfheze, where the 1st Airlanding Brigade had set up its command post, the brigade commander Brigadier Philip "Pip" Hicks had great difficulties establishing connections with his various subordinate units.*

The problems with the radio connections had still not been solved. A photograph taken by Serjeant Dennis M. Smith from the AFPU (Army Film & Photographic Unit) inside Duitsekampweg 10 in the morning of 18 September shows Hicks seriously absorbed by a map over the combat area; in his facial expression, one can almost sense his irresoluteness about the situation.

The 1st Airborne Division's headquarters, billeted in a few gliders on the Renkum Heath, were in a state of even larger uncertainty about the situation. Colonel Charles Mackenzie, the chief of staff, was worrying because he had not heard or seen anything from his commander Urquhart since last afternoon. Neither was it possible to reach Browning's Corps Headquarters in Nijmegen nor Montgomery's headquarters with the radio transmitters. On the other hand, there was regular contact with Frost over by the road bridge in Arnhem, who could get artillery support from the 1st Airlanding Light Regiment, Royal Artillery, thanks to correcting signals to radio equipment that had been placed in the tower of the church in Oosterbeek. They were thus well informed that Frost's battalion was isolated and in urgent need of reinforcements. The fact that the division at that point was without a commander of course did not do, so Hicks assumed command of the division, as was decided in the event of Urquhart passing on. In the divisional Headquarters' War Diary for 18 September, it was noted: "0900 – No information as to movements of General Officer Commanding. 0915 – Brig. Hicks, Comd, 1 Air Ldg

---

* According to Cornelius Ryan, Hicks's command post was located to a house by the road between Heelsum and Arnhem, but the brigade's war diary shows that it was the Duitsekampweg 10 in Wolfheze. (National Archives, WO 171/589. H.Q. 1st Airlanding Brigade, January–December 1944.)

Bde arrived Div H.Q. and assumed temporary command in absence of the General Officer Commanding." [388]

Hicks was best informed by the situation of the 2nd Battalion, The South Staffordshire Regiment, which, from its positions at Landing Zone "S" next to the Brigade's command post made the following note in its war diary: "The 18th September also started fairly quietly while the Bn prepared to wait for the arrival of the 2nd lift." [389] Under the impression of this, Hicks immediately issued an order for this battalion to leave its positions and march off towards Frost's men at the bridge. The unit decamped at half past nine in the morning of 18 September. [390] Moreover, Hicks decided that as soon as the 4th Parachute Brigade had been landed, its 11th Parachute Battalion was to be subordinate to his 1st Airlanding Brigade and march towards Arnhem to relieve Frost as well. Mrs. Clous at Lebretweg 1 in Oosterbeek, 650 metres east of Hotel Hartenstein, captured a few of The South Staffords on film during the afternoon as they marched by.

By then, Hicks knew very little about what was going on in the north, where the Dutch SS soldiers were pressing on; in the east, where two thirds of the 1st Parachute Brigade had got stuck at the outskirts of Arhem; or in the south. Through Colonel Mackenzie, he was of course informed about the situation on the Renkum Heath south of the railway (Landing Zone "Z"/Drop Zone "X"). There, too, the situation seemed calm in the morning of 18 September. Here, 1st Battalion, The Border Regiment – the third battalion of the 1st Airlanding Brigade – was responsible for the defence. Two of its three companies had been positioned around the heath itself: the "A" Company up by the railway, south of Landing Zone "S", the "C" Company east of the heath and south of Wolfheze, and the "D" Company just south of the heath. The battalion headquarters, which had set up its command post at the Jonkershoeve Farm in the middle of the heath, had good liaison with these three companies. However, the battalion commander, Lieutenant-Colonel Thomas Haddon, was not present. He, too, had disappeared without a trace; as we have seen previously (page 117), his glider had made an emergency landing in England during its approach. In his stead, the battalion was commanded by Major Stuart Cousens,"D" Company's commander.

To the "B" Company, the situation was completely different: it had the hardly enviable task of blocking the road that runs just north of the Rhine from Grebbeberg – where von Tettau had his command post – and to Oosterbeek. That meant that this unit was quite isolated, some two or three kilometres south of the rest of the battalion. The company commander, Major Thomas "Tommy" Armstrong, decided to concentrate the defence around the Juffeswaard brickworks right down by the river. Here, one could entrench oneself well, and control the road. "We dug in and the Germans left us quiet during the remainder of the night", one of Haddon's men, Second Lieutenant Arthur Royall, remembered.

But the calm was not to last. When the seamen of Korvettenkapitän Zaubzer's Schiffstamm-Abteilung 10 advanced along the southern road into Renkum at a quarter past six in the morning of 18 September, they went to sheer slaughter – at least, that was how the British soldiers at the brickworks saw it. One of them, Private Jim Longson, clearly noticed that the German unit commander seemed very insecure. He – it could have been Zaubzer – was pointing towards the brickworks, leading his men against it, straight across the open, treeless terrain. "The target was too good to be true", Longson commented.[391] Armstrong's men had two 7.7 mm Vickers machine guns and two 81.5 mm mortars ready. They breathlessly held their fire until the Germans had closed in at 200 metres' range. "Fire!" A hellish storm of bullets and grenades hit against the seamen, who were killed in droves.

Soon afterwards, the Germans sent in Panzer-Kompanie 224. Six big tanks came clanking down the road. These were Char B-1 type, made by Renault in France, and captured by the Germans in 1940. With a flamethrower fitted to the front, apart from the 47 mm

QR16: VIDEO
0.40-2.22 shows Mrs. Clous's footage of British paratroopers in town on the 18 September 1944.

gun in the turret, and two 7.5 mm machine guns, the 2.79-metre tall armoured giant was a terrifying sight. But the British did not let themselves be impressed. They aimed both of their 6-pound anti-tank guns, and soon, the first tank was in flames on the road. One after one, these so-called *Flammwagen auf Panzerkampfwagen B-2(f)* were knocked out. It was a classic example of how better training and motivation among soldiers often outweigh superiority in numbers among the opponents – Zaubzer had a more than five times as large a force at his disposal as did "Tommy" Armstrong, and in addition, he also had tanks.

The conditions were the same in the north, at the Ginkel Heath. As we have seen, the 5. Kompanie of SS-Wachbataillon 3 had managed to take No. 16 Platoon of 7th KOSB's "D" Company by surprise in the labour camp in the forest south of the heath, halfway between the old and the new Arnhem roads, taking most of the Scots prisoners. This 5. Kompanie was led by the heavily built 30-year-old SS-Obersturm-bannführer Hermann Kühne. His frontline experience was limited to four months in SS-Gebirgs-Division "Nord" on the Finnish front.

The brickworks at Renkum (right). The picture is taken from the east, on the northern side of the Rhine. The brickworks is gone today, but the tall factory chimney still remains in the sandy field east of the Parenco paper mill.

298

Before that, he had, amongst other things, served as a guard at the Lichtenburg* and Sachsenhausen concentration camps for several years in the 1930s.

Judging by his personal report, his posting as adjutant for Helle in SS-Wachbataillon 3 had been less than successful, which was why he had been transferred to the position as commander of the 5. Kompanie in the spring of 1944.[392] Even though the report described him as "quite hard", he seems to have been having difficulties to get his company to fight with any major efficiency. After the relatively simple takeover of the labour camp, the SS soldiers turned out to be unwilling to defy the fire from Lieutenant-Colonel Robert Payton-Reid's Headquarters Company of the 7th KOSB a little further south. Of course, this was the main plan – that the SS-Wachbataillon would push southwards in order to join the SS-Unterführerschule in a pincer operation aimed at the Ginkel Heath.

Only when the 6. Kompanie and what remained of the 3. and 4. Kompanies joined in – through the flanking movement in the forest that Naumann had recommended – was it possible to carry out an attack. But on the other side of the new road, one kilometre further ahead, the men in Payton-Reid's Headquarters Company lay in position among the trees. They received the SS soldiers not only with gunfire, but with sharp-edged bayonets. In the starry and chilly night, Helle's attack was completely upended. When 6. Kompanie's commander, SS-Obersturmführer Wilhelm Fernau, later was to explain to Helle what had gone wrong, he claimed that many of the Czech-made Vz rifles that his unit was equipped with had turned out to be out of order.[393]

When the SS soldiers had been driven off, Payton-Reid ordered No. 13 Platoon of the "D" Company to push ahead north so as to secure the northern edge of the heath. The company commander, the 27-year-old Major Gordon Sherriff, from Edinburgh, personally took command

---

* Lichtenburg in Saxony is one of the less-known Nazi concentration camps. It was intended for male prisoners, and initially housed about 70% Communist and 20% Social Democrat prisoners. During the time when Kühne was serving as a guard there (in 1934–1937), a growing number of male homosexuals were placed there. Lichtenburg was the first concentration camp to introduce the so-called "flogging table", a particularly merciless instrument of torture which was regularly used to punish the prisoners.

of this battle group. The 7th KOSB's War Diary states dryly: "That was the last seen or heard of [No. 13 Platoon] for the rest of the day and the CO was left, owing to failure of R/T, without further knowledge of [their] movements, though sounds of heavy firing came from the woods." [394] This platoon would find itself entangled in fierce fighting with the SS Dutchmen in the forest east of the Ginkel Heath almost throughout the day of 18 September – until the evening, when contact with the headquarters was re-established.

But initially, they did not see anything of the enemy. The Wach-bataillon's badly battered 3. and 4. Kompanies had withdrawn to Café Pension J. Kramer to protect Helle's new command post, Fernau's 6. Kompanie turned towards the eastern edge of the Ginkel Heath, and Kühne returned to the labour camp with his 5. Kompanie. There, the SS soldiers gluttonously helped themselves to the workers' breakfast, when someone suddenly shouted that there were Englishmen outside the window! What the Scots of the 13th Platoon were met by when they approached, intending to establish contact with the 16th Platoon, was hardly what they had expected – window panes were smashed, from inside the barracks there was screaming and shouting, and immediately afterwards, handguns started rattling against the Scots, who threw themselves into cover. Under cover of a smoke grenade, they pulled back. Major Sherriff instead decided to circumvent the camp. In that way, he and his men ended up in a drawn-out battle with Fernau's 6. Kompanie. To Kühne's less-motivated men, the sight of the British platoon, however, was enough for them to abandon the camp.

The Scotsmen's defence mission became easier as the day broke. "B" Company, 7th KOSB discovered a column of combat vehicles – probably from 1. Kompanie of the SS-Wachbataillon – on the half-finished road from Ede. Serjeant George Barton, gunner at the Scottish company's anti-tank gun, fired a shell that hit a half-track. The SS soldiers quickly abandoned the vehicle – only to find themselves in a murdering hail of fire from a Vickers machine gun.

By then, there were probably not many among the soldiers of the 7th KOSB who did not glance at their watches every now and then. The second landing – with all of the 4th Parachute Battalion as a reinforcement that was more than welcome – would, according to plan, arrive at 1000 hrs. Mortars and machine guns were being prepared, bayonets were being attached, and everybody was getting ready to attack and chase away the SS soldiers from the north-eastern corner of the Ginkel Heath that they held the moment the transport aircraft arrived.

But there were others who prepared for attack as well. At 0940, Leutnant Karlheinz Sundermeier and 70 other German fighter pilots in the Luftwaffe's fighter group JG 11 took off from the air base at Gütersloh and set their course for Arnhem, 150 kilometres to the west.[395] The single-engined Messerschmitt 109 and Focke-Wulf 190 fighters were commanded by Major Günther Specht, a tough guy who had been in first-line service since the war broke out in 1939. Specht had been shot down and badly wounded several times, having, amongst other things, lost one eye, but he continued to fly combat sorties in spite of his bodily injuries causing him severe pain during air combat. He wore the coveted Knight's Cross around his neck since April 1944; he had received it for shooting down 31 British and American aircraft, 17 of which were heavy bombers. 193 German fighters – that was all that could be mustered from the Luftwaffe units in the west – were sent in against the landing zones at Eindhoven, Nijmegen, and Arnhem.

Over at the Ginkel Heath, the Scots were feeling sure that it would be quite easy to drive off the obviously untrained SS soldiers.

At 1000, when it was supposed to be time for the air landing, an optimistic note was made in 7th KOSB's War Diary: "Situation reasonably well in hand." [396]

However, no transport planes arrived. Instead, it was single-engined fighters that appeared in the clear blue, almost cloudless sky. "Hurricanes* – our planes!" one of the British glider pilots at Wolfheze cried, waving his arms enthusiastically at the aircraft. But Staff

* Hawker Hurricane was a British single-engined, single-seater fighter aircraft.

Sergeant Victor Miller did not think it sounded like British Merlin engines. He looked up. A quick glance through the foliage was enough – he had not been teaching airplane recognition for one year for nothing. That was no British Hurricane! The "evil snub-nosed aircraft" that he saw was a German Focke-Wulf 190 fighter! "Enemy aircraft overhead!" Miller cried, throwing himself down for cover.

A second '190 with a roaring BMW engine appeared behind the treetops, followed by another one, and yet another one. Soon, Miller could count ten German fighters flying in wide circles, like vultures waiting for their prey. The air was filled with the roar from their engines, and they seemed to get lower and lower for each circle. Suddenly, their machine guns and automatic guns started pounding. Hundreds of leaves came floating down over the men who were cowering together in an attempt to hide underneath the branches. A black figure flashed past above Miller. He tried to get his machine gun up into firing position, but the German aircraft was already gone.[397]

This was Specht's '190s and '109s, with black crosses under their wings that seemed to grin scornfully against the 1st Airborne Brigade's men down on the ground. The German aircraft remained circling in mid-air – "to intercept the second wave of landing forces", according to the Polish military historian Janusz Piekałkiewicz.[398] This undoubtedly constitutes strong evidence that it actually was the entire operational plan that had fallen into German hands on 17 September.

But the expected transport planes did not appear. Eventually, drying fuel in the airplanes' tanks forced the German fighter pilots to turn back. But before that, they threw themselves over Landing Zone "S" and the Renkum Heath, where they shot several of the gliders that had landed the previous day into flames. "It was just like shooting clay pigeons", Karl-Heinz Sundermeier thought. At 1126 hrs, he landed at Gütersloh again, on the last drops of synthetic aviation fuel. The planned effort by German fighters aiming at causing a massacre of the transport planes only became a blow in the air. What had happened?

Over in England, dense ground fog had forced a postponement of the second landing. But the Germans knew just as little about this as the men in the 1st Airborne Division, who did not have any radio contact with the aviation in England. Meanwhile, the battle for the Ginkel Heath was raging in the north, and for the village of Renkum in the south. In the latter place, German frustration was growing as Korvettenkapitän Zaubzer's Schiffstamm-Abteilung 10 was being held back by the British at the brickworks – "B" Company of the 1st Battalion, The Border Regiment.

But during the morning, the men from the SS NCO school's I. Bataillon under SS-Hauptsturmführer Schulz started penetrating the northern parts of Renkum, where there was a gap between Major Armstrong's "B" Company and the remainder of 1st Battalion, The Border Regiment. On the advice by the SS NCO school's commander, Lippert, Zaubzer seconded three of his seaman companies from the road in the south which there had been so much fighting over, and instead let them enter side streets among the houses up to the left in order to proceed up towards Heelsum, the neighbouring village between Renkum and Wolfheze to the north.

Lippert was despairing over Zaubzer's failures. He was forced to supply Zaubzer with some of his own anti-aircraft guns, manned by soldiers from the SS NCO school, and it was only then – at around two o'clock in the afternoon – that the stubborn resistance by the British began to falter. One of those who were there, Second Lieutenant Arthur Royall, remembers, "Then Jerry opened up with his mortars and self-propelled guns (a deadly weapon) and he pinned us down right up until tea time. He blew up our ammunition with one shot and we were left with what ammunition we had in our pouches." Almost completely without ammunition, and with the brickworks and the surrounding houses in flames, Royall and his comrades sneaked out behind the factory – the side facing the Rhine – and ran away crouching along the riverbank. "We left practically everything behind, what remained of our rations, and much of our gear. I lost all mine", Royall recounted – adding, with an instance of British humour: "And we could have neither a shave nor a wash".

The exhausted Germans captured both of the British 6-pound guns, four jeeps, and some other equipment that Armstrong's men had been forced to leave behind, but had destroyed – and took a few wounded British men captive as well. SS-Obersturmführer Erwin

Heck, ordonnance officer at Lippert's SS NCO school, describes the continued development of the fighting: "We made good progress and formed headquarters for Colonel Lippert in a doctors house at Heelsum where we also assembled the first prisoners. From there we fought our way into Kievietsdel and Wolfheze." [399] But it was a temporary success. Lippert had only taken advantage of the gap in the British defence. In the forests south of Wolfheze, the Germans were halted, as we shall see later.

Further north, the German officers in the SS-Wachbataillon had a growing problem with the morale among its Dutch men. A group of British glider pilots had been warned that about 200 Germans were on their way through the woods against their position. The British lay in firing positions, ready for battle, when suddenly a figure appeared through the foliage with his hands above his head. Staff Sergeant Victor Miller thought it looked like a boy, and when the person came closer, he saw that it was an adolescent in civilian clothes. A Dutchman who was with Miller's group stood up and called out to the boy in his language. He came running, panting with his efforts, lowering his hands. Breathing heavily, he started talking with the Dutchman, who explained that the boy had been sent forward on behalf of a large group of German soldiers in the woods. They were ready to surrender, and just wanted to make sure that they would not be shot when showing themselves. The British commander in place asked the youngster to return to the Germans and tell them that if they only came out of the woods slowly and with their hands above their heads, nothing bad would happen to them. The adolescent disappeared into the forest again. When he returned some time later, he was looking dismayed. He explained, "The Germans have gone. It looks as though they have changed their minds". [400]

SCOTS AGAINST DUTCH SS

It was about two o'clock in the afternoon on 18 September. Inside Café Pension J. Kramer on the north-eastern corner of the Ginkel Heath, it was calm. When the fighting had subsided, Helle, the commander of the SS-Wachbataillon, had sat down to sleep in a chair in the pantry. He had handed over his command of the battalion to the commander of the 4. Kompanie, Bartsch.[401] The batman, Bayer, was sitting and filling out forms with the help of his assistant, Oudheusden. Helle's adjutant, SS-Untersturmführer Naumann, was standing by the window when he suddenly heard a rising rumble of engines. And then he saw them: wave after wave of twin-engined aeroplanes coming in at low altitude over the heath.[402]

The aircraft bringing the 4th Parachute Brigade came in from the north, surrounded by tracers from the anti-aircraft defence – this just as most German fighters had returned to their bases to fill up with fuel and ammunition after that day's second or third fruitless hunt for transport planes over the landing zones! The transport planes still had to take some fire from the ground. The Germans had positioned their flak right along the approach. Brigadier John Winthrop "Shan"

Hackett, the barely 34-year-old Irish-Australian commander of the 4th Parachute Brigade, peered out through the window of the C-47 he was traveling in. The sky outside was stained black with clouds

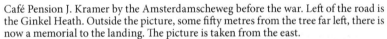

Café Pension J. Kramer by the Amsterdamscheweg before the war. Left of the road is the Ginkel Heath. Outside the picture, some fifty metres from the tree far left, there is now a memorial to the landing. The picture is taken from the east.

from anti-aircraft explosions, and in between, rows of tracers scurried through like furious hornets. In spite of the flak, losses were limited to four aircraft during approach. A fifth one took a direct hit just before Drop Zone "Y", the Ginkel Heath, and went down in flames.

As he stood in the doorway of the C-47, hooked and ready to jump, Hackett could see the rivers Maas, Waal, and Rhine clearly. He and the other men had to hold on tightly since the aircraft was now swaying violently to the sides in the increasing flak fire. Hackett was surprised by this. Indeed, he had been saying earlier that he should be happy if 50 per cent of his men were alive a few days after the landing, but he had thought that the entire landing area was cleared of enemies. The aircraft's swaying made the sunrays blind the paratroopers intermittently, so that they could not see when the red light went out and the green light went on, the signal to jump. With a sound as if someone had poured out a bucket of pebbles onto a barrel, machine gun bullets rattled into the aircraft's aluminium shell, and when something more powerful slammed into the fuselage just behind the door, Hackett and the whole group jumped out.

By then, most of his brigade had already jumped. Private Leonard Derek Moss remembers it all, "Bullets whizzed past from the ground and anti-aircraft shells continued to explode all around. The ground was rushing upwards quickly. 400 feet ... It was chaos below. Men ran all over the place avoiding enemy fire. Mortar shells exploded throwing up clouds of smoke and dirt while fires burned out of control ... Paratroopers were landing all around. It was chaos as heavy machine gun fire raked the area from concealed German positions in the woods. Men were being hit, wounded, killed. Gunfire exploded nearby, ripping into the ground, throwing up puffs of dirt. The air was alive with flying lead."

William Carr from the signals unit of the 4th Parachute Brigade recounted, "When my parachute opened I could see the men who had already landed lying on the ground firing at German troops who were surrounding the drop zone. They were shootimg at us, but the strong wind made for a fast descent and made us difficult targets to hit." [403]

The SS soldiers' fire had soon set the dry heather and the bushes growing on the moor on fire in several places, and the smoke obscured a large part of the ground. A film team from German Propaganda-kompanie 698 was on location at SS-Obersturmführer Wilhelm Fernau's 6. Kompanie of the SS-Wachbataillon at the edge of the forest that marks the eastern edge of the Ginkel Heath, and parts of what it filmed was shown in a German propaganda newsreel in November 1944. This film, which has been preserved, begins with the first C-47 planes coming in in nice three-plane V formations at an altitude of between 250 and 300 metres, and how rows of paratroopers are raining out. After that, the film shows the eastern edge of the Ginkel Heath. Some twenty SS soldiers are emerging, with what seems to be some hesitation, from among the beeches in the avenue that lines the narrow road marking the end of the heath. Most of them are aiming their rifles upwards, firing at the paratroopers who are on their way down through the air a bit further down the heath, but some of them are returning in among the trees to take cover without showing any signs of wanting to shoot at the large multitudes of enemy soldiers that will be down on the ground in a few seconds to attack them.

Some ten metres in front of the bicycle path, there is a Flakpanzer IV with its four-barrel 20 mm anti-aircraft automatic gun mounted on the chassis of a Panzer IV. You can see it firing a remarkably short salvo – only a second or so – and then going silent again. It is definitely not a question of any massive firing. The soldiers are firing their repeating rifles and it then often takes them five, six seconds to reload with the cylinder mechanism and fire again (the normal speed for a trained soldier was four seconds with a Mauser Karabiner 98k). During a five-second sequence of the film, four shots are being heard. After that, the camera pans across the sky, and then focuses on a vehicle-mounted 20 mm automatic gun pounding out a considerably longer shower of fire up towards the sky. Now, the Flakpanzer IV has also been started properly, but it is ground targets it is aiming its weapons against, horizontally. At the other end of the heath, a burning airplane crashes, exploding in a mushroom cloud of smoke and fire.

However, the film is heavily edited and cut. The sequence which then shows two soldiers, one of them bareheaded, in firing position with a machine gun each, for which they are using propped-up British ammunition boxes for support, seems to be shot elsewhere; most likely, the soldiers in the film are former ground crews from the Luftwaffe in Kampfgruppe Bruhn on 19 September. In that case, this explains the British ammunition boxes; several of those ended up in German hands when they were dropped in the wrong place on 18 September. After that, an 88 mm anti-aircraft gun is being shown, firing with a mighty rumble at quite a low angle against the aircraft, and one seemingly downed Short Stirling, which also corresponds better with the events on the 19th rather than the 18th.

This German propaganda film is a good example of how to use editing and cutting to present defeat as success. The film material from the battle at the Ginkel Heath itself does not seem to be more than a minute, which can be explained by the Germans quickly having to take to their heels.

The thing was, the arrival of the transport planes was the signal that Lieutenant-Colonel Payton-Reid had been waiting for. To the mighty sound of the bagpiper's "Blue Bonnets O'er the Border",* which made the blood boil in the highland soldiers' veins, he personally led his Headquarters Company in a furious, screaming bayonet charge against the eastern side of the Ginkel Heath.[404] The SS soldiers and the film crew rushed away in terror and disappeared into the woods. Those who failed to get away quickly enough were captured by the Scots and the newly-landed 10th Parachute Battalion, which arrived at its rallying-point with eighty prisoners of war, including the two company commanders Bartsch and Fernau.

* QR27: MUSIC
The 7th KOSB's regimental march, played on the Ginkel Heath on 18 September 1944 by Lance Corporal Willie Ford from Selkirk.

Inside Café Pension J. Kramer, 300 metres further to the northwest, Naumann hurried to shake Helle awake. It took him some time to come to. Then, when he had come round, the Germans spotted an enemy soldier peering in through the window of the guest room.[405] All Germans rushed out headlong through the back door and fled through the garden. Helle and Naumann ran so fast that they did not see the barbed wire fence on the back, and got stuck in it. But they managed to free themselves before being discovered by the Scots. Payton-Reid and his men had barely met any resistance, and captured ten SS men in the café.

In fact, most of the Dutch SS soldiers abandoned their positions and fled rather than being entangled in close combat with "the Red Devils" which were now coming down against them in what seemed to be never-ending rows of parachutes. That also went for the recruit units that had arrived from Ede. The German city commandant in Ede, SS-Obersturmführer Labahn, wrote, "The largest part of the Luftwaffe members that we have taken over have, without orders, withdrawn to the rear. This unfortunately also includes some Unterführers and men from the Waffen-SS." [406]

In the course of nine minutes, more than two thousand Britons were dropped by parachute. One group came down among the trees in the forest north of the heath, seeing a larger group of SS soldiers bolt. The surprised paratroopers found that the enemy had abandoned a lorry fully loaded with weapons and ammunition, and were able to drive it to the rallying point.

The brigade commander Hackett was among the last ones to jump, and he saw the battles continuing somewhat to the southwest. He had promised the pilot of the C-47, Lieutenant Cecil H. Dawkins of the 310th Troop Carrier Squadron, a bottle of whisky if he dropped them at the exact location. In spite of the fire from the ground, Dawkins dropped them within 300 metres from the designated spot.* When Hackett touched down on the heath, the kind of chaos reigned that is normal during a major parachute landing in combat. During his jump, he had lost the walking stick that he had taken with him, and

---

* When they met again many years later, in 1989, Hackett was able to fulfil his promise and give Dawkins the well-earned bottle of whisky.

4th Parachute Brigade on 18 September 1944

HEADQUARTERS
Commander: Brigadier John Hackett
86 men

10TH PARACHUTE BATTALION
Commander: Lieutenant-Colonel Ken Smyth
582 men

11TH PARACHUTE BATTALION
Commander: Lieutenant-Colonel George Lea
571 men

156 PARACHUTE BATTALION
Commander: Lieutenant-Colonel Sir Richard Des Voeux
621 men

2ND AIRLANDING ANTI-TANK BATTERY, ROYAL ARTILLERY
Commander: Major Annesley Freeman
168 men

4TH PARACHUTE SQUADRON, ROYAL ENGINEERS
Commander: Major Æneas Perkins
155 men

133 PARACHUTE FIELD AMBULANCE
Commander: Lieutenant-Colonel William Carson Alford
129 men

the first thing he did down on the ground was to try to find it – by then, the fire from the enemy was not stronger than that. After a few minutes, he came across two SS soldiers who immediately raised their hands. Hackett made signs to them to "wait here" and continued his search for his stick. Before he had found it, another four SS soldiers had surrendered to him.

50 minutes after the paratroopers, the next air formations arrived, consisting of 296 British aircraft – twin-engined Douglas C-47 Dakotas and Armstrong Whitworth A.W.41 Albemarles as well as four-engined Short Stirlings and Handley Page Halifaxes. They dropped

Horsa and Hamilcar gliders bringing yet more troop units both from the 4th Parachute Brigade and the 1st Airlanding Brigade as well as artillery and 14 tons of supplies at Landing Zones "S" and "X". One aircraft had been shot down, but the pilot of the glider that it brought along managed to carry out a safe landing behind enemy lines and the soldiers were able to make it to the landing zone on foot. Thirteen other gliders were released before arrival at their targets – mostly as a result of firing from the ground – but out of 297 gliders that had taken off, 272 came down in the landing area.

Immediately afterwards – at around three o'clock in the afternoon on this 18 September – 34 Short Stirling-bombers came in, dropping their 803 parachute canisters and baskets with supplies over Drop Zone "L" northwest of Oosterbeek. However, the thick smoke that was billowing up from the landing zones and the anti-aircraft fire by then was disturbing the pilots enough for the cargo to be spread across a large area. Out of 88 tons of supplies, only 12 tons reached the British on the ground.

But the drop of the paratroopers had been carried out with great precision. About 90 percent of Hackett's brigade had been landed where it was supposed to, and already at 1530 hrs, 75-80 per cent of the unit had assembled.[407] Since several aircraft had been shot down, and because of the fire they had been subject to when jumping as well, the 4th Brigade's losses, however, were quite considerable – more than 200 men. This number, however, included both killed and wounded in action as well as those who had been injured when landing by parachute and those who had ended up so far from the assembling point that they had not arrived.

Soon after the assembling was complete, Lieutenant-Colonel Charles Mackenzie, chief of staff at the 1st Airborne Division, arrived to inform Hackett that Hicks had taken command of the division in Urquhart's absence, and that he had ordered one of Hackett's battalions, the 11th Parachute Battalion, to be subordinate to the 1st Airlanding Brigade and advance towards Arnhem.

The short "Shan" Hackett was a real fighter. He had been in action since the beginning of the war and had been wounded twice – when fighting the Vichy French in Syria in 1941 and when his tank had been shot into flames when fighting Rommel's Africakorps in 1942. But Hackett was in no way waiting and seeing just because his burns required long-term hospital treatment; in the meantime, he played a driving role in forming elite units such as the Special Air Service (SAS) and the Long Range Desert Group. He had the unusual combination of toughness as a soldier, aptitude as a commander, and a brilliant intellect. Hackett has even been called "the cleverest soldier of his generation".[408] Only 31 years old, he was entrusted the task to form the 4th Parachute Brigade, which shows his great military talent. In 1943, he fought with his brigade in Italy. As opposed to many other officers, he shared the tribulations of his men – he ate the same food as they did, and when no rations were available for the soldiers under his command, he did not eat either. Therefore, he was very popular with the soldiers, but he was also known for his strong will and his grumpy temper.

According to Cornelius Ryan, Hackett was allegedly upset by Hicks assuming command of the division, but this is something that Hackett himself has denied. He calls Ryan's account "a travesty", and continues: "A great deal has been made of a 'dispute' between Brigadier Hicks and myself over command of the division. There was no such dispute. Pip Hicks was an honest, likeable, dependable person, from whom I could certainly take orders. I had seen no better battlefield commander in any previous campaign and I have seen none since."[409] On the other hand, he did react strongly to the order that the 11th Battalion would be transferred to Hick's brigade and advance on Arnhem. Since his 10th Battalion had been forced to stay at the landing area and protect the medical detail that was busy with rounding up and giving medical care to all the wounded in the Ginkel Heath, only one of Hackett's battalions, 156 Battalion, was thus available for carrying out the original task of the parachute brigade – to take the northern and western parts of Arnhem.[410] Moreover, this was the battalion that had sustained the greatest losses during the landing, more than 100 men out of its force of 625.[411]

Yet another problem appeared for the 1st Battalion, The Border Regiment, which was covering Landing Zone "Z" in the Renkum Heath to the south. Its commander, Lieutenant-Colonel Haddon, continued being dogged by bad luck. After his glider had made an emergency landing in England during the approach flight on 17 September, he had taken a seat in a new glider in this other flight. This time, things went even worse; Haddon made it across the English Channel, but when they came in over the Scheldt Estuary, the glider was hit by flak. The pilot managed to perform an emergency landing, but it was behind the German lines. Even if Haddon managed to avoid being detected by the Germans, and eventually made it back to his own lines, he would continue to be hounded by bad luck – more on this in Volume 2. Major Stuart Cousens would continue to lead the battalion during most of the remainder of the battle.

But to SS-Standartenführer Helle and his unit, the situation was incomparably worse. SS-Wachbataillon 3 was virtually annihilated in this its first battle. According to the adjutant Naumann, it lost about 500 men – 80 per cent of the entire force! Out of these, 150 men allegedly deserted.[412] The former concentration camp guard from Lichtenburg and Sachsenhausen, SS-Obersturmbannführer Hermann Kühne, the "tough guy" who led the 5. Kompanie, had a nervous breakdown and stayed hidden in a house in the countryside for several days after fleeing north together with his panicking men.[413] A few days later, SS-Wachbataillon 3 was formally dissolved.

By defeating the SS-Wachbataillon, Lieutenant-Colonel Payton-Reid and his proud Scottish soldiers had thwarted von Tettau's plans of surrounding and annihilating the 4th Parachute Battalion. Now that the 4th Parachute Battalion was employed, such large German units became tied down at Oosterbeek that Frost's paratroop battalion should have been able to hold out at the road bridge long enough for the XXX Corps to reach it and crown Operation "Market Garden" with complete success. The fact that this was not the case depends on a number of circumstances that will be discussed in Volume 2. The swift and resolute annihilation of SS-Wachbataillon 3, however, shows that the men who planned "Market Garden" were not as wrong in their assessment of the German units' combat value as has so often been claimed.

Had not the Germans been so weak at the sector north of Oosterbeek, between the railway and the Amsterdamscheweg, they would have been able to carry out a swift push from there to attack the 1st Airlanding Brigade from the east, which could have decided the outcome of the battle much quicker. This sector lay wide open during most of 18 September, after the 1st Battalion of the British 1st Parachute Brigade had been ordered to regroup from there to southwestern Arnhem already at half past five in the morning.[414] But all that the Germans had available in this sector was Kampfgruppe Allwörden and Krafft's SS-Panzergrenadier-Ausbildungs- und Ersatz-Bataillon 16. The latter – which had employed three companies to offer the British the first resistance on 17 September – had, in a state of complete demoralisation, withdrawn with its 4. and 9. companies after the 2. Kompanie had been annihilated by the "Red Devils". It was now located in Schaarsbergen on the southern outskirts of Deelen's airfield, about five kilometres north of Oosterbeek, to lick its wounds, and stayed there, far away from the fighting throughout 18 September. Meanwhile Krafft was working on more or less reforming the battalion again with new men consisting of scrambled-together marines and police officers. The fact that his unit was not sent in against the landings on 18 September is quite telling.

Due to the unexpectedly large amount of wounded and injured during the landing, it took longer than expected for the British medical orderlies to fulfil their tasks at the Ginkel Heath. The 10th Parachute Battalion was therefore forced to tarry at the landing zone to protect the medical unit. With the 11th Parachute Battalion seconded to Lathbury's paratrooper brigade in Arnhem, 156 Parachute Battalion thus became the only unit in the 4th Brigade that could be set in to secure Drop Point "V", the fields on both sides of the Amsterdamscheweg at the north-western approaches to Arnhem. The different units in this battalion decamped from the landing area at 1700 hrs on

QR28: VIDEO
Veteran Private Ken Fleet of 156 Battalion recounts the battle.

18 September and assembled at Wolfheze. There, they were ordered by brigade commander Hackett to "halt at dusk, reorganize and then push on before first light". The 10th Parachute Battalion never really "got going" after the unit had completed its mission at the Ginkel Heath, but also received "orders to rest" at Wolfheze![415]

Nevertheless, the commander of 156 Parachute Battalion, Lieutenant-Colonel Sir Richard de Bacquencourt Des Voeux, did not agree at all that it was time to halt and rest – only a few hours after the landing. Des Voeux was a veteran from the fighting in North Africa and Italy. Indeed, the unit had lost more than a hundred men, half of the brigade's losses in connection with the landing, but about 500 men remained, and Des Voeux was determined to use his momentum – after all, he had seen for himself the wretched quality of the German units he had met, and after the battle at the Ginkel Heath, no further resistance had been encountered.

The first German units were three kilometres further to the east, where Kampfgruppe Allwörden had established defensive positions only a few hundred metres west of Drop Point "V". Here, on the heights along the Dreijenscheweg, which climbs the deciduous forest-clad heights north of Oosterbeek from the Oosterbeek Hoog railway station, SS-Hauptsturmführer Klaus von Allwörden had positioned his little force in well-camouflaged and protected positions, based on armoured fighting vehicles. His men made good use of the ammunition and other supplies that had just previously been dropped against Drop/Landing Zone "L".

All was completely dark as von Allwörden's men by the railway station discovered the British advance guard. It was marching along the Johannahoeverweg which runs in parallel with the railway on the northern side – the road where Lieutenant Peter Bucknall from the reconnaissance force's "C" Troop had been subjected to an ambush the previous day. The 10th Platoon of the "C" Company, which was at the vanguard, was met with heavy fire. The soldiers threw themselves down for cover and returned the fire. Germans and Britons fired at each other in pitch-darkness for quite a while, but the former had considerable superiority in firepower with their 20 mm automatic guns mounted on armoured fighting vehicles.

As an attempt to circumvent the German positions to the north with No. 9 Platoon failed – here, too, halfway between the railway and the Amsterdamscheweg, von Allwörden had positioned combat vehicles in the forest – Des Voeux decided to follow Hackett's instructions. He withdrew the battalion a few kilometres and let the men set up camp, joining the 10th Battalion.

With infantry against armoured vehicles in wooded terrain, taking up night-fighting would have been more beneficial to the British than awaiting daylight – it would have given them an opportunity to infiltrate the German positions under cover of darkness and shrubberies. In addition, they had considerable superiority in numbers, at perhaps ten to one. Considering how important their objective was to the entire operation – it would have enabled a whole British infantry division to operate north of the Rhine – one needs to question the decision to let the troops halt for the night.

However, late in the afternoon on 18 September, things still looked very sombre for the Germans. The Allies had been able to carry out their second landing – with a total of more than 6,000 men – at Eindhoven, Nijmegen, and west of Arnhem, without the Luftwaffe intervening. With that, the Allies had landed almost 25,000 paratroopers in two days, and this already was a force that was 70% larger than what the Germans had at their disposal (about 4,500 men against the British 1st Airborne Division, about 4,500 men in the Nijmegen sector, and about 5,000 men in the Eindhoven-Veghel sector). In addition, the Allies also had the British XXX Corps with about 40,000 men and 400 tanks.

In eastern Arnhem, Frost's British paratroopers blocked the road bridge across the Rhine, and thus the road to Nijmegen, and had caused the German forces serious losses. In western Arnhem, SS-Kampfgruppe Spindler had only barely been able to resist two British paratroop battalions. The sight of the second wave of landings was disheartening to these SS soldiers. "We had to watch idly", SS-Hauptsturmführer Möller commented, "once again, wave after wave, thousands of parachutes – fifteen kilometres away from us, the enemy was receiving new reinforcements. What would then happen to us?" [416] At 1540 hrs on 18 September, Bittrich, commander of the

II. SS-Panzerkorps, called the headquarters of the army group and spoke with the chief of staff, General Krebs. "The enemy is steadily reinforcing in the area west of Arnhem", he reported worryingly. "We're also short of petrol." [417]

Moreover, the British tanks had achieved a decisive breakthrough in the south. Between Eindhoven and Nijmegen, there were virtually no German units to send in against the British amour. Further southwest, things were looking, if possible, even darker. The situation report from the LXXXVIII. Armeekorps for 18 September sums up the German fears: "It is still to be expected that the enemy will push north-westwards by transferring forces, in order to roll up the entire canal front [the Albert Canal/the Maas-Scheldt Canal]. In the meantime, because of the withdrawing of forces for the protection of the left flank of the General Command, for the building of a new defence front, and for the combat of the enemy paratroopers in the area Son – St. Oedenroede – Best, this [front] has become so weak that it can only function as a backup line, and cannot fend off a serious attack for long. In particular, the developing backup line from Hapert to Best, section Zuber,* which is only under construction, is so thin, that it performs more like an observation rather than a defence front. At a width of 19 km, only 2 battalions could be used."

On top of that, it was reported that the 1. Fallschirmarmee had received no fuel at all during 18 September. As far as the vehicles were concerned, it was stated: "Motor vehicles of the division utilised to their absolute maximum capacity. Breakdowns through fighter-bomber attacks, wear of engines and tyres very frequent." [418] In the evening of 18 September, Bittrich came back with a report about the situation in Nijmegen: "Own forces not up to enemy pressure in the long run." [419]

Everything seemed to point in the direction of a decisive German defeat.

---

* On 18–19 September, a defence line was set up behind Kampfgruppe Chill by Kampfgruppe Zuber under Oberst Wilhelm Zuber, the artillery commander of the LXXXVIII. Armeekorps.

↑ British paratroopers from the 1st Airborne Division with German prisoners of war from SS-Kampfgruppe Krafft at Wolfheze.
↓ Lieutenant-Colonel John Frost (middle) with some of his men.

German Panzer at Arnhem:
↑   A Panzer IV training tank from Panzerkompanie Mielke of Kampfgruppe Knaust.
↓   A Flammwagen auf Panzerkampfwagen B-2(f), originally a French Char B-1.

↑ Dutch civilians greet paratroopers of U.S. 82nd Airborne Division.

↓ German soldiers being allotted ammunition.

American 82nd Airborne Division is being dropped beneath the Groesbeek Heights.

↑　German soldiers with a 20 mm anti-aircraft automatic gun. Via Daniel Johansson.

↓　Fallen American paratroopers at the Karel Keizerplein in Nijmegen.

↑ British paratroopers from the 1st Airborne Division.
↓ A destroyed German Panzer IV near the road bridge in Arnhem. Inset: SS-Rottenführer Rudolf Trapp (1925–1990) from 3. Kompanie/SS-Panzergrenadier-Regiment 21 in 10. SS-Panzer-Division.

↑   82nd U.S. Airborne Division in Nijmegen.
↓   SS-Hauptsturmführer Karl-Heinz Euling (left), Major-General Allan Adair, commander of the
    British Guards Armoured Division (right).

The armour breaks through to Nijmegen 18–19 September 1944

THE VULNERABLE FLANK

With the right concentration of forces on the Allied side, the battle would no doubt have been won before the end of September. This could perhaps have been true for the entire war as well. Even though the Allies had massive superiority in numbers during "Market Garden", they also had two considerable weaknesses – their often indecisive leadership and the vulnerable flanks of the XXX Corps. "Our corps will advance and be supplied along one single road – there is no other", Lieutenant-General Brian Horrocks, commander of the XXX Corps, had said as he briefed his unit commanders about the ground operation, Operation "Garden". This road had been given the name "Club Route" and stretched from "Joe's Bridge" all the way up to Arnhem to the north. Here, about 20,000 vehicles were supposed to advance along 120 kilometres of enemy-controlled territory. Now, the first thirty kilometres, the bridgehead between "Joe's Bridge" and Eindhoven, were held by the British 50th Infantry Division, and the remaining 75 kilometres up to Nijmegen were secured by the two American paratrooper divisions. But these basically only held the fields on either side of the road. There were, on 18 September, no ground forces that could prevent the Germans from building up forces against this long flank.

As we have seen, the inability of the Allied Supreme Command to prioritise the allocation of supplies had resulted in the XXX Corps not receiving the necessary protection of its flanks. Lieutenant General Courtney Hodges' First U.S. Army to the southeast had a great potential that had been made unavailable to Montgomery's offensive by the circumstances. In early September 1944, this army disposed of a quarter of a million men with about 850 tanks.[420] It was a considerable force – especially compared with its opponent, German Heeresgruppe B, whose headquarters on 11 September summarised the situation in a single sentence: "Continued reduction in combat strength and lack of ammunition have the direst effects on our defensive capacity." [421]

However, because of the Allied supply crisis, Hodges could not maintain the advance to the east that was begun on a wide front a few days before the commencement of Operation "Market Garden". For example, in his 28th Infantry Division, the shortage of artillery shells was so great that an order was sent out to limit the artillery's firing to 25 shells per gun and day.[422] American military historian Charles B. MacDonald observes that the U.S. divisions were often forced to use their own valuable transport vehicles to search for ammunition caches in the rear. For instance, lorries from the 1st Infantry Division made two return runs at 1,100 kilometres each.[423]

On top of this, the commander of the American 12th Army Group, Lieutenant General Omar Bradley, had pushed the First Army southwards, away from British Second Army and the XXX Corps. According to Montgomery's suggestion, Hodges' First Army would have taken up positions in the Brussels-Maastricht-Liège-Namur-Charleroi sector to make a joint attack northward together with the British Second Army, into the south-eastern tip of Holland. But Bradley decided to "hand over" Brussels to the British, and Hodges' army attack instead ended up being aimed eastwards, on a wide front against the Aachen sector, seventy kilometres southeast of the XXX Corps, as well as along the German western border at the rolling Ardennes further south. In that way, there were two separate attacks instead of one collective one. Moreover, instead of marching into flat ground without any major defences – which would have been the case had Hodges been able to follow Montgomerys proposal – the Americans on the southern flank ran straight into heavily broken ground with steep ravines and dense forests along the border between Germany and Luxemburg, going, on the northern flank, straight against the doubtlessly strongest fortifications of the German West Wall. At Aachen, the West Wall had been extended to a depth of about fifteen kilometres, with several belts of linked bunkers, fortifications, "dragons' teeth" and other tank obstacles, vast minefields and barbed-wire barriers. American historian Stephen Ambrose calls this section "undoubtedly the most formidable man-made defence ever contrived".[424] In this sector, the outcome could only be one: "a miserable siege of deliberate, close-in fighting which brought few advantages to either side".[425] Contributing to this in a crucial way was, of course, the shortage of artillery ammunition within the 1st Army.

Further south, on the border between Germany and Luxemburg, the First U.S. Army's V Corps had slightly bigger success. But on 16 September, the corps was ordered to immediately cancel its advance – to the great amazement, and, in many cases, frustration of the front-line soldiers. "That the Germans had not stopped the V Corps armour was plain", Charles B. MacDonald writes. "The first real adversities to come in the Wallendorf sector hit after the issuance of this order. The explanation for the halt appeared to lie instead in the decisions that had emerged from the meeting of General Eisenhower and his top commanders on 2 September at Chartres and in a critical over-all logistical situation." [426] In fact, the V Corps had carried out its advance "on borrowed time and borrowed supplies", since Hodges had given it temporary access to fuel that actually was not intended for it.[427]

This was the situation for the American First Army as Operation "Market Garden" began. "It is not improbable", noted General Hodges' adjutant in the General's diary on 17 September 1944, "that we shall have to slow up, even altogether halt, our drive into Germany and this in the very near future." [428]

The two other corps in Lieutenant-General Miles Dempsey's British Second Army were also in a difficult position when it came to supplies. As we have seen previously, this had forced Dempsey to leave both most of his artillery and all of the VIII Corps under Lieutenant-General Richard O'Connor behind by the river Seine in France, so that fuel and transportation could be freed up for a lightning-speed advance by Horrocks' XXX Corps. Only through the general halt of all advance by the army on 4–6 September (see Chapter 1) was it possible to eventually get the entire Second Army moving towards the Netherlands. Wisely enough, the XXX Corps was given top priority in the allocation of supplies, with considerably lower priority for the

XII Corps on its western flank and the lowest priority for the VIII Corps. The consequence was that the latter corps, which, according to the operation plan was supposed to cover the XXX Corps' eastern flank during Operation "Garden", was left almost without fuel over at the river Seine for several days.[429] The fuel situation was so severe that the corps was only able to regroup minor units at a time from the Seine sector and to Belgium. When "Market Garden" was begun on 17 September, the corps' units were spread out along 300 kilometres from west to east, and it would take 36 hours before its infantry had reached the starting point for attack, which was why there was no eastern flank protection at all as the XXX Corps begun its attack.[430]

The XII Corps under Lieutenant-General Neil Ritchie – with the Scottish 15th Infantry Division, the 53rd (Welsh) Infantry Division, and the 7th Armoured Division, the famous "Desert Rats" – was not in quite as dire straits, but was also severely hampered by a shortage of supplies. Even on 17 September, the 7th Armoured Division had only been able to bring one of its three regiments to the combat area.[431] This corps had a mission to advance in parallel with the XXX Corps towards Tournhout and further north towards the river Maas, at a distance of about 25 kilometres west of the XXX Corps. Thus, it was necessary to cross the Maas-Scheldt Canal, which cuts off northern Belgium from east to west. As we have seen in Chapter 1, the XII Corps had only been able to move two battalions from the Scottish division's 44th Brigade to a small bridgehead on the northern side of the canal at Ten Aard, 25 kilometres west of "Joe's Bridge" at Neerpelt. This bridgehead, established on 13 September, was immediately subject to intense German artillery fire and counterattacks, which stopped all attempts at breaking out efficiently. This deadlock also lasted throughout 17 September, when Operation "Garden" was begun. While the XXX Corps was advancing, the XII Corps' flank support remained limited to this bridgehead across the Maas-Scheldt canal no bigger than 600 x 700 metres. But the following night, XII Corps crossed the canal at Lommel, only a few kilometres west of "Joe's Bridge", taking the Germans completely by surprise. At around five o'clock, engineers from XII Corps started rafting heavy equipment across the canal. Meanwhile, at 0530 hrs in the morning of 18 September, the Guards Armoured

Division – the vanguard of the XXX Corps – resumed its advance from Valkenswaard, where it had been pausing all night under orders from the divisional commander Adair.

STANDSTILL AT EINDHOVEN

In the morning of 18 September, the Guards Armoured Division stood at Valkenswaard, 15 kilometres north of "Joe's Bridge". It had been a night with heavy rain, and dense fog had descended over the area, meaning that the Allies had to manage mainly without air support on this day. The reconnaissance force, consisting of some twenty vehicles from the battalion 2/Household Cavalry Regiment (2 HCR) headed off down the Rijksweg 69 – the "Club Route" according to the Allied designation – towards Eindhoven, twelve kilometres further northeast.

At the front were three Daimler Dingo armoured reconnaissance cars in a Troop under the barely 22-year-old Lieutenant David Tabor. The small BSA Daimler Dingo had a crew of two men, driver and observer/gunner. With a length of 3.18 metres, it was shorter

Daimler Dingo.

than today's ordinary private cars, and of about the same height and width. Armament consisted of one 7.7 mm machine gun. It was not for nothing that the Dingo was considered one of the best armoured reconnaissance vehicles of the Second World War. The 30-mm frontal armour could resist even 37 mm anti-tank guns at a distance of 400 metres or more, and the 6-cylinder, 55-hp, 2.5-litre engine gave a top speed at almost 90 km/h, with five gears in each direction.

The three-ton vehicles rolled along the dead straight concrete road while the crews were carefully looking out in all directions, and especially into the deciduous forest lining the road – which however was made more difficult by the fog that reduced visibility to 500 metres. The nearest town was Aalst, halfway to Eindhoven, eight kilometres north of Valkenswaard.

So far, there was nothing of the enemy to be seen, other than abandoned equipment laying strewn across the road. It was obvious that the Germans had been seriously pummelled by the previous day's attack. This was really true. The paratroop general Kurt Student had been ordered to take command over the defensive battle against British XXX Corps and the American 101st Airborne Division to the south, and had been supplied with reinforcements made up of the 59. Infanterie-Division west of the XXX Corps and the Panzer-Brigade 107* east of the British. Since the opponent did not have any flank protection, the theoretical possibility opened for a pincer movement to isolate the American forces. But the former unit was a division only in name. The commander, Generalleutnant Walter Poppe, reported: "After the battles, involving heavy losses up till then, south of the Scheldt the Division disposed of five field battalions with an average strength of 150-180 men, and the Replacement Training Battalion, pioneer battalion – two weak companies; artillery – two light, one medium battalion, about 30 gun barrels. Antitank defence – about 18 guns. The ammunition supply was meagre. Most of the ammunition had to be left behind for the bridgehead south of the Scheldt." [432]

In addition, the fuel supply was even worse on the German than on the British side. The war diary for German LXXXVIII. Armee-

---

* It would, however, take almost 48 hours before it could be sent into battle.

korps noted: "Supply of engine fuel could no longer take place already on 18 September, since the Army no longer disposed of any fuel." [433]

For this reason, only minor parts of the division had arrived in the morning of 18 September. "The 59 Infantry Division was brought up rapidly to Boxtel, via Tilburg on, mostly on foot", Poppe wrote. "The infantry and pioneer soldiers were transported by rail. The artillery came up partly on foot but with spells of riding in horsedrawn trucks. Rear guards of the Division were still being brought across the Scheldt." [434]

Oberstleutnant Freiherr von der Heydte, the commander of Fallschirmjäger-Regiment 6, describes the sheer panic prevalent on the German side: "The effect of the enemy air landings on 17 September combined with the penetration by the Guards Armoured Division seemed to have panicked higher headquarters right through to Army headquarters. For the first few days following 17 September no intelligence reports could be obtained from Corps or from Army. The only order that was constantly reiterated was that we were not to retreat a single step." [435]

Von der Heydte's regiment was subordinate to Kampfgruppe Walther, but all contact with its commander, Oberst Erich Walther, had been severed during the afternoon of 17 September and had not been re-established since. "Messengers reported that Kampfgruppe Walther had shifted its command post and that the command post could not be found anywhere", von der Heydte recounted.[436] In von der Heydte's own regiment, the companies had been reduced to an average strength of 40 men each.[437] As a compensation, he was supplied with the II. Bataillon from the Fallschirmjäger-Regiment 18 and the penal battalion Luftwaffen-Jäger-Bataillon z.b.V.6. Von der Heydte made sure that "the incompetent commanders of these two battalions were sent to the rear and replaced by officers of 6th Fallschirmjäger Regiment".*

But at the same time, Heydte's regiment was subordinated to the 85. Infanterie-Division (Kampfgruppe Chill), and the commander of the LXXXVIII. Armeekorps, General Hans Wolfgang Reinhard,

---

* Oberstleutnant Stephan, commander of the II./FJR 18, was not only fired, but also demoted to command a guard unit at a bridge. According to the war diary for the LXXXVIII. Armeekorps, however, this took place on 24 September 1944.

urged Generalleutnant Chill to keep a watchful eye on Regiment von der Heydte, especially emphasising that "von der Heydte must not be allowed to take an independent decision of withdrawal".[438]

Kampfgruppe Walther – which was responsible for the section of the front south of Eindhoven – had been scattered to the wind; von der Heydte's regiment and the units that it was supplied with on 18 September had been flung far west, and were drawn into the battle against the XII Corps. The I. Bataillon of Fallschirmjäger-Regiment 18 with a few hundred men commanded by Major Hellmut Kerutt had taken refuge in Heeze, six kilometres east of Valkenswaard, on the other side of the motorway along which the XXX Corps was advancing.[439] All anti-tank guns of the 14. Panzerjäger-Kompanie had been destroyed. Virtually all that stood between the XXX Corps and Eindhoven in the morning of 18 September was what was left of schwere Heeres-Panzerjäger-Abteilung 559 – two Jagdpanthers and two StuG IIIs which had been ordered to Aalst.[440] Led by Oberleutnant Erwin Seitz, these were positioned on the road from Valkenswaard. Soon, Lieutenant Tabor's Daimler Dingos appeared on the road from the south.

The British armoured cars had covered about one kilometre and were halfway to Aalst when their crews spotted the contours of a few vehicles outlined in the fog further ahead. They stopped, and could pick out three assault guns. Tabor called in the Irish tanks by radio, but the infantry reached the spot first. When Seitz saw the infantrymen marching up, he decided to retreat, as he lacked any infantry support himself. With roaring engines, the German armoured vehicles fled into the forest left of the road. One StuG III snapped a track in the process and had to be abandoned. When Tabor arrived soon afterwards, and spotted the German vehicle, he stopped again and called in the tanks. Lance-Serjeant Bertie Cowan had knocked out a StuG with his Sherman Firefly the previous day, forcing the German crew to climb up onto his tank and point out the German positions. This had made him taste blood, so now, he came clanking in his Firefly. He enthusiastically put five shells from his 17-pounder into the StuG.[441] After that, Tabor drove forward, and could verify that the assault gun was abandoned.

All seemed calm, and Lieutenant Tabor was just about to move on, when a Dutch civilian approached on the left side of the road. His name was Cornelius Los, and he was an engineer at the Philips works in Eindhoven. He had drawn the German positions himself onto a town map that he wanted to hand over to Tabor, who proposed that the man hand over his map to the following forces, setting off now again on his reconnaissance mission. He drove through Aalst without anything happening. The little town had been quite badly battered by British artillery fire.

Meanwhile, Oberleutnant Seitz decided to get across the road again to get in touch with Major Kerutt in Heeze. But he had not expected the British to advance as quickly as they did. The two last assault guns were in the open fields at the country road just north of Aalst when the British came driving out of the town. Tabor called forth the tanks again, and before the Germans had made it into the cover of the trees 400 metres east of the road, one assault gun had been hit and damaged. After that, the British would not be disturbed anymore by the schwere Heeres-Panzerjäger-Abteilung 559 that day.[442] The damaged assault gun did not make it far, and was later found abandoned by British soldiers a bit to the east.

However, the Germans were not called masters of improvisation for nothing. Eindhoven, with its industries that were so important to the German war effort, had been equipped with quite extensive flak forces – no less than fifty-four 88 mm guns. These were now put together into the ad hoc unit Kampfgruppe Köppel for the defence of Eindhoven. At the large boarding school Eikenburg at the southern approach to the city, two 88 mm anti-aircraft guns, eleven 75 mm anti-tank guns, and a few 20 mm guns had been positioned. It was about 10 o'clock in the morning when they opened fire against the British reconnaissance vehicles on the road towards Eindhoven. The reconnaissance group was only lucky that their first shots missed. The commander of the first Dingo, Lance-Corporal Sparrow, fired smoke grenades and managed to withdraw, covered by them, by reversing at top speed.

Tanks and artillery were called forward, but from their well-protected positions at the large brick complex, the German soldiers managed to hold back the entire Irish advance. Neither could the British expect any support from the XII Corps; through skilfully planned disturbing fire, the Germans were able to prevent this corps from setting up a Bailey bridge across the new bridgehead at Lommel until late in the day of 18 September, and after that, the corps commander Ritchie decided to wait with starting the advance until the next day.

The situation was highly remarkable – the Americans of the 101st Airborne Division were, by then, behind the Germans at Eikenburg, in central Eindhoven, less than a thousand metres further north. In between, there were hardly any German forces available, and yet the British could not expect any help from the Americans. "Colonel Joe" Vandeleur called the air force requesting an air attack, but received the reply that the weather conditions did not allow for such an effort. Because of ground fog at the airfields in Belgium, the British tactical air force 2nd TAF could only carry out 73 sorties during all of 18 September – which could be compared with 550 the previous afternoon.[443]

As we have seen, the American 506th Parachute Infantry Regiment under Colonel Robert F. Sink had decided to pause for the night when reaching Bokt, the northernmost part of Eindhoven, in the evening of 17 September. Sink ordered his men to start advancing into the city at half past seven in the morning of the 18th – three hours after the XXX Corps had resumed its advance to the north from Valkenswaard, about fifteen kilometres further south.

Inside Eindhoven, there were no more than a couple of hundred German soldiers – mainly staff personnel, anti-aircraft, or baggage soldiers – who turned out to be quite demoralised. "Resistance was so weak and irresolute that it had hardly more than nuisance and delaying effect", the American report observed.[444] First Lieutenant Charley "Sandy" Santasiero, an experienced platoon commander of "I" Company, recounted: "I saw Krauts leave their fox holes and run for the buildings. We fought a running battle, not giving them time to organize or use their 88mm guns."[445] The American paratroopers rather chased than fought the Germans along the streets of the city on their way south. "If you see any Germans just let them filter through you and I guess the 'Ducks' [the nickname for the 502nd Parachute

Infantry Regiment] will take care of them", were the instructions that Colonel Sink gave his men.

It went fast. Townspeople were standing by their windows, pointing out to the Americans where there were Germans, and then, it was mostly only a matter of rounding them up and sending them backwards. Only in Woenselsestraat near Kloosterdreef in the northern part of the town centre did the Americans come across any serious resistance, from two 88 mm anti-aircraft guns.*

However, led by a group of townspeople, a platoon of paratroopers was able to circumvent them and attack the Germans from the rear. The two antiaircraft guns were quickly neutralised. With thirteen of their comrades lying dead on the ground, forty-one Germans surrendered. The American losses amounted to two wounded, one of them by one of his own bullets that had caused his machine gun barrel to explode.

When these two flak guns had been captured, the German resistance in Eindhoven collapsed. As at a given signal, townspeople and American paratroopers filled the streets in the city centre, and exhilarated celebration followed.[446] By noon, there was a carnival mood in town. The American paratroopers were completely absorbed by the wild celebrations.**

"They posed for pictures, signed autographs (some signing 'Monty,' others 'Eisenhower'), drank a shot or two of cognac, ate marvellous meals of fresh vegetables, roast veal, applesauce and milk", Stephen E. Ambrose wrote in *Band of Brothers*.[447]

In the midst of this celebrating – it was by then a quarter past eleven in the morning – the XXX Corps managed to establish radio contact with the 101st Airborne Division and report that its vanguard had been stopped a thousand metres further south. American officers desperately tried to get their partying men out of the Dutch homes

---

* Today, this part of Eindhoven is completely rebuilt. Nowadays, the Kloosterdreef runs from north to south. In 1944, it went westwards from Woenselsestraat, which, in those days, ran northwards just west of the current new Doctor Cuyperslaan. One of the 88 mm guns was positioned where the residential houses are located today on the west side of Doctor Cuyperslaan, only a stone's throw north of Europalaan. The other was where Europalaan today passes Kloosterdreef 2.
** To this day, there are celebrations in the streets of Eindhoven every year on 18 September in remembrance of the liberation in 1944.

and assemble them in combat formations, but without much success, according to T/4 George E. Koskimaki of the divisional headquarters.[448]

One hour later, two armoured Humber reconnaissance cars* led
by Lieutenant Michael Palmer from "B" Squadron, 2nd Household
Cavalry, arrived at the Woensel district. They had made an outflanking movement from Aalst, south and west of Eindhoven, and made it
to the Americans without encountering any resistance. Palmer confirmed that the XXX Corps was being held up by a large German
force to the south, but this did not have any effect either. The American historiography is quite remarkable: "It did not matter; the British tankers did not show up until late that afternoon. They promptly
stopped, set up housekeeping, *and proceeded to make tea.*"[449] [Italics
by the author.]

In general, the 101st Airborne's operations on 18 September give
the impression of being quite uncoordinated. Colonel Sink's 506th
Parachute Infantry Regiment did not coordinate its operations with
the 502nd Parachute Infantry Regiment, which was stuck at Best,
northwest of Eindhoven. It might seem as though this would otherwise have been quite urgent, considering that the important bridge
across the Wilhelmina Canal at Best was still intact – as opposed
to the one that the 506th had reached at Son, about five kilometres
further east. While the 506th Parachute Infantry Regiment was penetrating and liberating Eindhoven, the Germans were able to hold
back both the XXX Corps to the south and the 502nd Parachute
Infantry Regiment to the northwest. A quick push westwards south
of the Wilhelmina canal could have resulted in taking the bridge at
Best, and would definitely have saved the 502nd Parachute Infantry
Regiment several days of bloody battles at Best – which have gone
down in the American airborne division's history as "the unnecessary battle". After all, the capture of these and other bridges was the
main task for the airborne forces.

---

* The Humber was larger than the little Daimler Dingo – especially taller, as it
was fitted with a small retractable armoured turret with a 7.7 mm machine gun.
But, since it was not as fast, and, in addition, had weaker armour, it was not as
popular as the Dingo.

The 502nd Parachute Infantry Regiment had initially positioned most of its forces in order to defend the landing zones. This was because a new landing would take place on this spot on 18 September, but the consequence was also that the reinforced company marching towards the important bridge at Best failed to achieve its task. In that way, the Germans gained some time, and during the night of the 17th, the I. Bataillon from Grenadier-Regiment 723 of the 719. Infanterie-Division and Feld-Ersatz-Bataillon 347 arrived at Best to reinforce the positions that were already held by police forces and flak soldiers. There, they were assembled into Kampfgruppe Rink under the regimental commander Oberstleutnant Berthold Rink and were subordinated to the 59. Infanterie-Division.

With all of the 3rd Battalion eventually sent in at Best to the southwest and the 1st Battalion in Sint-Oedenrode, seven kilometres further northeast, the divisional commander Maxwell Taylor regrouped the 502nd Parachute Infantry Regiment's 2nd Battalion to Son in the southeast to support the 506th PIR on 18 September when it made it across the canal to enter Eindhoven. However, under impression of the failure by Colonel Cole's 3rd Battalion in Best, the commander of the 502nd PIR, Colonel John H. Michaelis, ordered his second battalion to support Cole instead. It was a rational decision, but the procedure might be questioned. The 2nd Battalion could have made it across the Wilhelmina Canal at Son on the provisional ferry that the Americans had made operative, and which was now shuttling across the watercourse which was not very wide, in order to attack the Germans at Best in the rear. But instead, this battalion marched off northbound, and then turned left, across the fields towards Best – only to take up fighting positions side by side with Cole's battalion, just where the Germans had turned out to be strongest.[450] (See map page 130.)

Out in the open fields, the men of the 2nd Battalion were observed by the Germans, and soon, artillery shells started raining over them. But they continued ahead, in spite of paratroopers continuously being killed or wounded by the artillery. There was certainly nothing wrong with the paratroopers' courage! They went straight from their march to frontal attack against Best – across a completely flat grassy field where a couple of haystacks constituted their only opportunity to hide from the Germans.[451] These, in turn, hardly believed their eyes where they were lying well sheltered behind machine guns and mortars.

However, neither the quality nor the morale of the scantily scrambled-together German units at Best was the best. Major Klauck, the commander of Feld-Ersatz-Bataillon 347, had to send in a non-commissioned officer to force his terrified men not to throw their weapons and flee. When the Germans had composed themselves, they opened raging fire on the completely unprotected American paratroopers. In addition, several German Messerschmitt and Focke-Wulf fighters dived down on the Americans with rattling machine guns. American military historian S.L.A. Marshall describes the incredibly brave but foolish American attack:

"From left to right the line rippled forward in perfect order and well-timed discipline, each group of two or three men running on to the next hay pile as it came their turn. Machine gun fire cut into the hay piles, sometimes setting the cover afire, sometimes wounding or killing the men who lay behind it. That stopped only the dead and the wounded. The squad leaders kept leading and the platoon leaders kept shouting to each group when to make a dash for it." [452]

Eventually, the battalion commander was forced to call off the attack, "not because his men were unwilling, but because he realized that his mortal losses were beating him".[453]

The attack, which was not coordinated at all with Cole's 3rd Battalion – which lay in position in the Sonsche Forest a bit further south – and was carried out without any supporting fire, cost the 2nd Battalion a loss of one fifth of all of its men, in killed and wounded.[454] Meanwhile – in parallel with and independently of this – the 506th Parachute Infantry Regiment penetrated and captured central Eindhoven, and at 1300 hrs, the German soldiers at Best were given orders to blow up both the road bridge and the railway bridge – which also happened.[455] Meanwhile, a telephone report came in about the situation for the battle group at Best, which had now been cut off, to the headquarters of LXXXVIII. Armeekorps: "Enemy has penetrated north of Eindhoven. Street fighting. Unit can no longer be contacted, bringing up infantry reinforcements ruled out. Anti-tank battalion Grünewald requesting further orders from the army..." – then, the telephone line was cut.[456] In the midst of all this, scores of American aircraft appeared. First of all came swarms of fighters. Almost 400 Mustang and Thunderbolt planes from the Eighth Air Force in England had been sent off to protect the arrival of 450 transport aircraft which brought in reinforcements for the 101st Airborne Division in Waco gliders. Several P-47 Thunderbolts broke free from the formations high up in the sky and came sweeping downwards – and opened fire, by mistake, against the 3rd Battalion's positions![457] The battalion commander, the experienced and hot-headed Texan Lieutenant Colonel Robert Cole, was hit by a bullet and dropped dead. According to the American report, he fell victim to a German sniper, but it is interesting to note that he was killed at about the same time that his battalion was unexpectedly subject to "friendly fire" from fighter pilots. A memorial stands to this day on the spot of his death by the roadside in the Sonsche Forest.*

Then hundreds of transport planes roared in over the area and disconnected their gliders. The American airmen only met light and poorly aimed fire from the ground. A total of 428 gliders touched ground on or close to Drop Zone "W" between 1430 and 1620 hrs, carrying another 2,579 soldiers, 151 jeeps, and 109 trailers – mainly the 101st Airborne Division's fourth regiment, the 327th Glider Infantry Regiment (apart from the 1st Battalion), as well as the remains of the engineer and the medical units which partly had been landed the previous day, the 326th Airborne Engineer Battalion, and the 326th Airborne Medical Company. "The arrival of the enemy glider planes", Major Klauck recounted, "was a blow to the mind. It hit all of us. From knowing that we were to win this battle, in a moment we were destined to be the losers."[458] Under apparent impression of this, the Germans abandoned the positions that they were holding against the XXX Corps at Eikenburg on the southern outskirts of Eindhoven.

Now, the hilarity ensued that the XXX Corps lay still south of Eindhoven, while the American 101st Airborne Division was celebrating the victory in the city – without any German units whatsoever left in the one thousand metres wide area that separated the Allies. For one and a half hours, this deadlock remained. Only at around five o'clock in the afternoon, when Lieutenant Tabor and his force from the 2nd Household Cavalry Regiment had made it on foot around to the rear of the German position, was it discovered that the Germans were gone. All ᾽88s and anti-tank guns had been abandoned since the Germans had not had any traction vehicles.

With the 2nd Irish Guards Battalion still at the lead, the Guards Armoured Division roared ahead, passing half a dozen abandoned 88 mm anti-aircraft guns, running straight into the crowds of celebrating Dutchmen and American paratroopers. Captain John Gorman, tank commander at the No. 2 Squadron, recounts his first meeting with the men of the 101st Airborne in Eindhoven: "These soldiers created a great impression. They were tall, fit, well turned out, extremely friendly and obviously interested in the famous Guards. Many of them had Irish ancestors and were astonished to meet the Irish Guards." [459]

While the Irish were making their way through the crowds in Eindhoven on their way towards the northeast and the bridge at Son – which they now knew was demolished – the 502nd Parachute Infantry Regiment in the northwest made a last effort at around 1700 hrs in the afternoon to do, as S.L.A. Marshall sarcastically puts it, "one more try toward capturing the bridge [at Best] which was no longer there". [460] This attack, too, was repelled.

At around 1900 hrs in the evening of 18 September, the Irish Guards reached the southern bank of the Wilhelmina Canal at Son, where the Germans had blown up the bridge right in front of the eyes of the American airborne major James LaPrade the previous day. "Colonel Joe" Vandeleur, commander of the Irish Guards, made his way across the shallow canal in a rowing boat and met Colonel Michaelis, commander of the 502nd PIR, on the other side. Engineers from the Guards Armoured Division were soon busy with constructing a Bailey bridge across the canal. Here, the 32nd Guards Brigade lost a tank

---

* Today, Cole is buried in the American military cemetery in Margraten, Plot B, Row 15, Grave 27.

battalion, 15/19 The King's Royal Hussars, as it was subordinated to the 101st Airborne Division and positioned east of the bridge at Son.[461] This was the consequence of the VIII Corps not yet having got started with its advance to cover the eastern flank. Meanwhile, however, the 101st Airborne Division was transferred from the airborne corps to Dempsey's British Second Army.

A couple of armoured cars were also sent west along the canal to aid Colonel Michaelis' troops at Best. An American officer on the other side of the canal shouted out an explanation of the situation to them. The Irish armoured cars fired away at full force with their machine guns against the German positions just north of the canal. "The effect was surprising", Marshall writes: "The German force on the far bank quit their foxholes and withdrew westward."[462] However, this did not mean that the "unnecessary battle" for Best was over.

The German situation was now even more desperate. Morale within Kampfgruppe Rink at Best was at breaking point, not least since the unit commander, Oberstleutnant Berthold Rink, had disappeared.*

His successor, Oberstleutnant Lentz, received a sharp warning from the commander of the LXXXVIII. Armeekorps, General Reinhard, "I will take court martial action against every commander even considering retreat."[463]

The total lack of fuel reserves delayed the transport of the German reinforcements considerably. In addition, the Dutch railway workers had gone on almost all-out strike, complicating the situation even further. When Major Berndt-Joachim Freiherr von Maltzahn, the commander of Panzer-Brigade 107, arrived on 18 September by train

QR29: VIDEO
Authentic wartime footage.
The Guards Armoured Division
passing through Eindhoven.

---

* Rink had ended up, badly wounded, in American captivity, and died there two months later. (Didden & Swarts, *Autumn Gale*, p. 215.)

to Venlo, sixty kilometres east of Eindhoven, he found to his surprise that the railway station was completely unmanned. Von Maltzahn recounted: "In the early morning hours, that is, in the night between 18/19 September, the first transport train, which contained the staff unit of the brigade as well as some officers' vehicles, arrived in Venlo (Holland). At the railway station, there was nobody except for a few railway officials. There was no information about the situation. As for the units that were to be sent in to build fortifications in and around Venlo, there was no information about where the brigade was supposed to be sent in. Eventually, I got in touch by telephone with the staff of Gen. Oberst Student, and received orders to report to the LXXXVI. AK [Armeekorps], which the brigade had been subordinated to, at the Hillenraad castle east of Roermond." [464]

The Dutch railway strike

The Dutch railway strike that was begun on 17 September 1944 and actually lasted for the remainder of the war, was coordinated with Operation "Market Garden" and was ordered by the country's national resistance council RVV (Raad Van Verzet) via Radio Oranje from London. In the dawn of 17 September, the coded message was broadcast that initiated the strike: *"De kinderen van Versteeg moeten onder de wol"* ("The Versteeg children must go to bed"). The appeal had a broad response. 30,000 railway workers immediately went underground.

This forced the Germans to deploy their own men and their own railway workers to maintain rail traffic, which initially created great difficulties.

QR30: SOUND
Listen to Radio Oranje's broadcast
on 17 September 1944.

The mass effort by the Luftwaffe ordered by Hitler became a huge failure as well. An estimated 500 fighters from the Luftwaffe's 3. Jag-ddivision and II. Jagdkorps were instructed in the evening of 17 September to transfer to airfields close to the landing areas in order to be sent in against the Allied airborne forces. Among the documents that had been captured in a downed glider (see page 138), there were times for the new landings at Eindhoven and Arnhem on 18 September. In the evening of 17 September, the headquarters of the 3. Jagddivision issued an order to its units, "Enemy transport and bomber units in the Dutch airspace are to be fought in closest possible collaboration with the headquarters of the II. Jagdkorps. In this, the main emphasis lies in the annihilation of enemy transport gliders and transport aircraft as well as armed action against landed paratroopers."[465]

But this aerial effort was an empty gesture. In the morning of 18 September, the German fighters took off, flying expectantly towards the Eindhoven and Arnhem areas. For one hour – between nine and ten in the morning – they were circling in vain over the landing zones, without any Allied aircraft appearing. What they did not know was that the Allies had decided the previous night to postpone the second wave of landed reinforcements from 1000 to 1400 hrs because of the weather forecast that predicted dense fog on the ground in the morning of the 18th. When the transport planes turned up in the afternoon, there were barely any German fighters nearby – and those that were there were efficiently disposed of by the American fighter escort.

Hitler was absolutely furious about what he perceived as "trea-son" by the air force. When the chief of the Luftwaffe's staff, General Werner Kreipe, tried to explain the reason, Hitler turned his anger against him and banned him from being present at any more situation conferences at the Führer Headquarters.[466]

The Luftwaffe retaliated twofold during the following night. The bomber air corps, IX. Fliegerkorps, deployed a total of 78 twin-engined Junkers 88s, Junkers 188s, and Dornier Do 217s against Eind-hoven.* All except three reached their targets, dropping their bombs

---

* The aircraft came from Stab, I. and II./KG 2, Stab, I., II. and III./KG 6, Stab, I. and II./KG 30, I., 4. and 5./KG 66, as well as Stab, I. and II./LG 1. These had an assigned force of 472 aircraft, but in early September 1944, they only had 143 at their disposal, which illustrates the miserable condition of the German bomber command at this late stage of the war.

within 40 minutes in a concentrated fashion over the thoroughfares in the city – Aalsterweg, Stratumsedijk, Stratumseind, Rechtestraat, Wal, Emmasingel, Hertogstraat, and surrounding areas. In these streets, British vehicles were densely packed together, and enormous devastation was achieved – not least when lorries loaded with ammunition blew up. The Guards Armoured Division alone lost sixteen ammunition lorries and seven fuel vehicles in this bomb attack.[467] The German airmen could see the glare from the fires in Eindhoven for a long time during their return flight. The losses in human lives were extensive. Among the civilians, 227 people were killed and 88 were wounded. 230 houses were destroyed and many more were damaged.

Regardless of this, the Royal Engineers continued working on the Bailey bridge at Son all through the night, and at six o'clock in the morning on 19 September, it was completed.*

THE BRITISH REACH NIJMEGEN

The British combat vehicles quickly roared across the bridge. This time, it was Gwatkin's 5th Guards Armoured Brigade – with the 2nd (Armoured) Battalion, Grenadier Guards at the lead – that followed straight after the armoured reconnaissance vehicles of 2/Household Cavalry.[468]

The 45-year-old Gwatkin was a known "pusher" and very popular among his men. Lieutenant David Fraser, commander of a tank Troop in his brigade, describes him as "a man of enormous character; a Coldstreamer, with a high colour, a choleric expression, a loud, infectious laugh, he was loved by our Grenadiers and known as were

---

* A note in the 153rd Field Artillery Regiment's war diary perhaps illustrates the low motivation of many German soldiers to keep fighting. The diary note reads: "The REs worked flat out all through the night an did very well to get it completed by first light. An amusing incident happened that night when a certain Gunner officer walked on to the bridge to see how it was progressing, when a German POW who was helping in the job turned and spoke to him in perfect English and told him to move off as he was 'bloody well getting in everybody's way and holding up the work!'"

few senior officers. 'There, the Brigadier!' they would say, chuckling, and I remember one Serjeant adding, 'and he's an inspiration to the men!' – a rare, articulate expression. He cheered all men, wherever they were and whatever the circumstances: and when an advance was held up by German defensive posts and the situation was obscure the column would generally be passed by the Brigadier, driving himself in a jeep, small pennant flying, pipe in mouth, heading for the front, for the tip of the spear, to see what was up." [469]

Rijksweg 69 was lined for several kilometres north by cheering American paratroopers who flung their helmets far into the air. Some did not even satisfy with that. Private First Class Mario Petruno from "F" Company, 506 PIR, recounted: "My buddy and I said, Let's get on the tanks and be among the first to get into Berlin. So we got on and we rode the tanks up Hell's Highway. It took us seven hours to go 30 miles."*

The British tanks were driven at top speed through an area that had already been liberated by the Americans. At a quarter to seven in the morning of 19 September, the armoured reconnaissance vehicles reached Veghel. Half an hour later, the Sherman tanks followed. At Uden, some five kilometres north of Veghel, the British left the motorway and turned to the right to take the nearest road up to Nijmegen. In the town, happily surprised Dutchmen rushed out of their houses, waving at the quickly passing vehicles. The 15 kilometres of countryside between Uden and Grave to the north were not held by the Americans, but had been abandoned by fleeing Germans, so that the British could drive undisturbedly through no-man's land. The sun was shining from an almost cloudless sky – here, the weather was completely different than over the Allied air bases in Belgium – and it felt as though the last German resistance had finally col-

*QR31: VIDEO
4:39: The American veteran Private First Class Mario Petruno from the 101st Abn.Div., 506 PIR, Company F.

lapsed. A British account gives a clear picture of the weakness among the German units, who could not offer any resistance in spite of the good conditions that the terrain offered, "The road was not a good one, narrow and embanked most of the way, and running through flat, sandy fields, interspersed by considerable stretches of birch and pine-forests, which, in addition to the inevitable dykes, afforded ample cover for small parties of enemy infantry. The population was confined mainly to the neat modern villages, with small isolated farms in the cultivated areas." [470]

At twenty past eight in the morning, the reconnaissance vehicles crossed the bridge on the river Maas at Grave, thirty kilometres further north. There, they made a short stop for a conference with the American commander on site. Unfortunately, he was misinformed and said that the important bridge at Nijmegen was secured, which meant that the British got the impression that there was no particular hurry. This report was passed on backwards.

The men of"B" Company in 2/Household Cavalry continued optimistically along the main road up towards Nijmegen. It was only when they reached the Maas-Waal Canal at Neerbosch* in the morning of 19 September – having covered almost two thirds of the 17 kilometres between Grave and the important bridge across the Waal in the northern part of Nijmegen – that they became aware that the Americans had not managed to achieve all of their objectives. They saw clear signs of fighting already as they were approaching the road bridge.

As we have seen (Chapter 6), the commander of the 82nd Airborne Division, Gavin, had settled for controlling the sluice bridge at Heumen across the Maas-Waal Canal a little more than five kilometres further south on 17 September, and assembled most of his troops for defence. This gave the Germans the opportunity to concentrate their defence to the road and railway bridges at Neerbosch. Only at half past three in the morning of 18 September had a platoon under First Lieutenant Lloyd L. Polette from 508th PIR's "E" Company on the eastern side of the canal been ordered to take these crossings.

* In American accounts, the place is usually called Honinghutje.

By then, Hauptmann Max Runge – a company commander of the Fallschirm-Panzer-Ersatz- und Ausbildungs-Regiment "Hermann Göring" – had taken command of the German forces in the area, organising them into a Kampfgruppe.*

Even though Kampfgruppe Runge did not have more than second-class soldiers at its disposal, it could, thanks to cunning positioning in quickly organised defences, offer strong resistance. The Germans discovered Polette's men when they were approaching in the darkness, and opened fire at a distance of 300 metres. The Americans immediately threw themselves down for cover in the surrounding ditches and continued advancing by crawling forward. At around seven o'clock in the morning of 18 September, when it had started dawning on the horizon, Polette ordered his machine guns to take up positions. But they were not able to fire many rounds before grenades were raining down from German mortars, knocking out the machine guns.

With eight men dead and four wounded, Polette withdrew his force to an adjacent building, and dispatched two runners to request reinforcements. Soon, yet another dozen of paratroopers arrived, and, covered by fierce fire from machine guns and mortars, Polette led a new charge – but in vain. As the Americans had experienced on several locations on 17 September, one of the bridges at Neerbosch – the railway bridge – was blown up by a German explosive charge. American fire had caused the wires to the charges that were primed on the road bridge to be cut, so that they could not be detonated, but the damages that were inflicted on this bridge when the adjacent railway bridge was blown up were sufficient to make the Americans doubt whether it could carry the heavy Sherman tanks.

When"B" Company of 2/Household Cavalry arrived at Neerbosch twenty-four hours later, Kampfgruppe Runge had already withdrawn north-eastwards to Nijmegen – it did so in stages during 18 September – and the Americans controlled what was left of the

---

* The core of this motley battle group consisted of a non-commissioned officers' training company in the Fallschirm-Panzer-Ersatz- und Ausbildungs-Regiment "Hermann Göring" under Oberleutnant Böhme. On the night of 17 September, it was joined by Hauptmann Ernst Sieger's 4. Kompanie from the home guard battalion Landesschützen-Bataillon II/6, which was retreating from the canal bridge at Hatert a few kilometres south, as well as the seamen of the 4. and 5. Kompanies from Schiffstamm-Abteilung 14 from Betuwe. To them were added the pioneers of Pionier-Kompanie 454.

two bridges. But the British, too, estimated that the damages on the road bridge meant that it could not be used by the tanks. The 2nd Battalion, Grenadier Guards Regiment, was informed about this over the radio sufficiently in advance and turned right without delay over at Grave, crossing the Maas-Waal Canal on the sluice bridge at Heumen.[471] They turned north, passing the little village of Malden, which bore clear traces of the previous day's fighting, advancing further up towards Nijmegen along the main route that ran through a dense forest.

At noon on 19 September, the tanks started gathering at the Mariënbosch monastery just on the outskirts of Nijmegen's south-eastern parts.[472] "We must reach Arnhem, if possible, in 48 hours", Horrocks had said. Now, it was exactly 45 hours since Lieutenant Keith Heathcote in the first Sherman tank of the Guards Armoured Division had given his brief order at "Joe's Bridge" – "Forward!" – setting the entire XXX Corps in motion towards Arnhem. During the last five hours, the British tanks had covered 60 kilometres, and there were only 25 kilometres left to Arnhem. In spite of the pause in Valkenswaard in the evening of 17 September, and the stop south of Eindhoven on the 18th, the schedule seemed to hold.

In Mariënbosch, the British were met by a liaison officer, who announced that Lieutenant-General "Boy" Browning, commander of the I Airborne Corps, had his headquarters in a forest not far from there, and that he would like to meet the commanders for a situation report. What Horrocks, Adair, and Gwatkin (the commanders of the XXX Corps, the Guards Armoured Division, and the 5th Guards Armoured Brigade respectively) heard from Browning came as an equally unexpected and unpleasant surprise.

XI.

Nijmegen
19 September 1944

When the British tanks reached Grave, and then eventually also Mariënbosch during the morning of 19 September, they found Gavin's 82nd Airborne Division scattered everywhere south, west, and east of Nijmegen, but not, as had been its task, with the bridges across the Waal under control. Most of the almost 9,000 paratroopers of the 82nd Airborne were in rather quiet sectors, having left Nijmegen entirely to the Germans.

The 504th Parachute Infantry Regiment under Colonel Reuben H. Tucker stood in the area in the triangle between the Maas-Waal Canal, Grave, and Maas, southwest of Nijmegen. Of course, the bridges at these places needed to be secured, and with a force of 2,000 men, at least half of them could and should have entered Nijmegen to secure those bridges too. Ever since they had been landed in this sector, Tucker's men had been able to note that there were virtually no German units to the west, and in the east, the Germans who had been there had already been chased away. The commander of "H" Company in this regiment, Captain Carl Kappel, concluded in a report: "Action on D Plus One was very light. All units of the battalion maintained their positions and patrolled vigorously in all directions from the bridgehead." [473] A patrol consisting of two squads – that is, about twenty men – was dispatched on 18 September to the town of Hernen, six kilometres northwest of Grave. "The patrol encountered no enemy and consequently no prisoners or vehicles were taken", Kappel noted. [474]

About eighteen hundred men from the 505th PIR under Colonel William Ekman were present in the area south of Nijmegen, where they had beaten a few weak German units to smithereens the previous day, and were now enjoying a day of relative calm. From here,

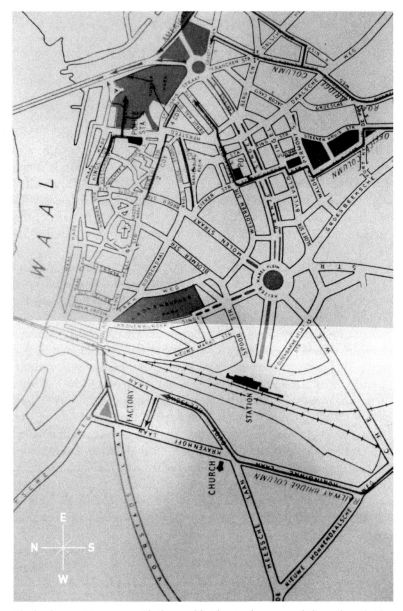

The bridges in Nijmegen with the road bridge to the east and the railway bridge to the west.

350

too, it would have been possible to deploy units against the Nijmegen bridges.

The only one of the three landed regiments in Gavin's division that was involved in any fighting was the 508th PIR under Colonel Roy Lindquist, in position among the forested heights southeast of Nijmegen. It was from this regiment that the 1st Battalion had been sent into Nijmegen. But just as it was approaching the coveted road bridge, it was called back to the sector to the southeast to meet General Feldt's utterly weak counterattack on 18 September.

In spite of the failed German counterattack on 18 September having proven to be considerably weaker than the Americans had feared, it seemed to have frightened them enough to momentarily completely abandon the attempts to occupy the bridges across the Waal in Nijmegen. Instead, Gavin deployed Lindquist's 1st and 3rd battalions in the morning of 19 September, with a total of about twelve hundred men, to take a few square kilometres of terrain out in the countryside southeast of Nijmegen. Had Gavin and Browning given the conquest of the Nijmegen bridges higher priority, they could have given one of those battalions this task, but now, they chose instead to deploy most of the 508th Parachute Infantry Regiment, supported by the 319th Glider Field Artillery Battalion, to occupy Wyler – a little village with less than 200 inhabitants just inside the border with Germany, a little more than five kilometres southeast of Nijmegen – and the northern part of the Groesbeek Ridge, the 70 to 90 metres high, forested massif, towering just northwest of Wyler.

Following initial skirmishes with losses on both sides, the German resistance collapsed. One of the American paratroopers, Technician Fifth Grade John E. Brickley, recounted, "The Germans jumped out of their foxholes and we kept after them. Sergeant Bob White of 3rd Platoon attacked on the run over the hill and down the north-east side of the hill. The Germans on that side of the hill had their backs on us. The ones we did not kill ran down the hill to the woods." When the fighting was over, the Americans counted 40 dead Germans and two prisoners of war.

These skirmishes still continued – while the 2nd Battalion of the 508th PIR remained waiting for its passive opponent on the regiment's right flank – when the British commanders at noon on 19 September received a situation report by Lieutenant-General "Boy" Browning. "We now learned", Lieutenant-Colonel Edward Roderick Hill* wrote, "that the 82nd U.S. Airborne Division held only a part of Nijmegen and had not been able to approach the bridges owing to its very considerable other commitments."[475] The British could hardly believe it to be true. "Like the British 1st Airborne Division at Arnhem they had been waiting for two days and nights for the relieving force of the British Second Army, led by ourselves. Meanwhile Nijmegen was in German hands", Lieutenant David Fraser, commander of a tank Troop of the 2nd (Armoured) Battalion Grenadier Guards, remarked caustically.[476]

From Nijmegen, large, black clouds of smoke rose towards the sky. It was the SS soldiers setting buildings on fire all around the road bridge to make it more difficult for the Americans to reach the bridge. At two o'clock in the afternoon, Lieutenant-General Browning was reached by a message from the 1st Airborne Division conveyed by a Dutch civilian that German tanks were on their way into Arnhem.[477] An attack plan was quickly drawn up from the information that the British had received both from Americans and Dutch resistance men. Hill recounted, "The approaches to both bridges were difficult and favoured the defence, but we were told that they were not as yet strongly held. Accordingly a mixed force of tanks and infantry was to pass through the American positions on the outskirts of the town and attempt to rush the bridges before reinforcements arrived."[478]

But this information turned out to be outdated. In the absence of any serious American attack against the bridges – "on 18 September, the expected attack on the bridges failed to take place", wrote Wilhelm Tieke, a soldier in the 9. SS-Panzer-Division[479] – the Germans were able to consolidate their positions for the defence of the bridges. As we have seen, Oberst Fritz Hencke, commander of the paratroop training staff Fallschirm-Lehrstab 1, had taken command of the defence of the Nijmegen bridges, organised into Kampfgruppe Hencke. This had received considerable reinforcements, mainly through the ferry

* Commander of the 5th Battalion, Coldstream Guards.

that was now shuttling SS soldiers and equipment at Pannerden to the northeast. When the Allied attack on Nijmegen was deployed on 19 September, Hencke had at his disposal about fifteen hundred men, a handful of tanks and anti-tank guns, as well as fire support from a flak company and two artillery batteries – a considerably bigger force than what the Americans had met twenty-four hours earlier.

But the German officers were not always the most suited here at the Nijmegen bridges. SS-Hauptsturmführer Karl-Heinz Euling, who led the force in the Hunner Park closest to the southern ramp of the road bridge, lacked experience of combat in built-up areas. His closest commander, SS-Sturmbannführer Leo-Hermann Reinhold, was considered by many as directly unfit for command. Reinhold's adjutant, SS-Hauptsturmführer Gernot Traupel,* recounted after the war: "In the battalion, Reinhold was in no way perceived as any brave or resolute officer. During the fighting at the Nijmegen bridge, I personally experienced how Reinhold practically did not take any crucial decisions, and neither could he be reached when the situation became critical. I was constantly in touch by telephone with the division's chief of staff, Sturmbannführer Hans-Joachim Stolley, and together with him and the subordinate unit commanders, I took the decisions on necessary measures."[480]

On the Allied side, there was much confidence, as Lieutenant Fraser of the 2nd Battalion Grenadier Guards, writes: "[At] a Dutch café in the outskirts of Nijmegen,** a few miles up the road north of Grave, a quick conference was being held at midday on 19th September and orders were being given out. Beside our own people American uniforms were everywhere. Members of the Dutch Resistance were buzzing around us like bees, with information (we hoped) of where the Germans were. Our task and our hope was that an armoured column could smash their way through the town, using the main road to the Waal, and cross the enormous bridge – Nijmegen lies entirely on the south bank. That would mean the southern arm of the Rhine in Allied hands, and a short drive – about thirteen miles, no more – up

---

* Towards the end of the war, Traupel was the future German author Günther Grass's closest commander.
** Hotel-Restaurant Sionshof at Nijmeegsebaan 53. The hotel is still open.

German units at Nijmegen on 19 September 1944
KAMPFGRUPPE HENCKE
  Commander: Oberst Fritz Hencke
  4. Kompanie/ schwere Flak-Abteilung 572/ Flakbrigade 18
  four 88 mm and eight 20 mm anti-aircraft guns

The road bridge across the Waal
SS-KAMPFGRUPPE REINHOLD
Commander: SS-Sturmbannführer Leo-Hermann Reinhold
- SS-Kampfgruppe Euling (the remains of the II. Bataillon of the SS-Panzer-
  grenadier- Regiment 19 of the 9. SS-Panzer-Division – reorganised into
  I. Bataillon of the 10. SS-Panzer-Division's SS-Panzergrenadier-Regiment 22 –
  under SS-Hauptsturmführer Karl-Heinz Euling) 400 men and two Jagdpanzer IV
  tank destroyers, four armoured personnel carriers (two of which with one
  75 mm gun each), four 20 mm anti-tank guns, one 75 mm light infantry gun
  and one 120 mm mortar.
- 1. Kompanie/SS-Panzer-Pionier-Abteilung 10
  (the remains of the 10. SS-Pionier-Abteilung and the SS-Ersatz-Abteilung,
  commander: SS-Unterstürmführer Werner Baumgärtel)
  200 men (part of SS-Kampfgruppe Reinhold)

In front of (south of) the road bridge across the Waal
- III. Abteilung/Fallschirm-Panzer-Ersatz- und Ausbildungs-Regiment
  "Hermann Göring" (Commander: Major Bodo Ahlborn) – about 200 men with
  five Panzer IIIs and two Panzer IVs (training tanks).

North of the road bridge at Nijmegen
- II. Abteilung / SS-Panzer-Regiment 10 200 men, probably without tanks

At the Pannerden ferry berth across the Rhine to the north
- SS-Flak-Abteilung 10 (part of SS-Kampfgruppe Reinhold) – 16 88 mm and
  9 37 mm anti-aircraft guns

The railway bridge across the Waal
KAMPFGRUPPE RUNGE
Commander: Hauptmann Max Runge
- 21. Unterführer-Lehrkommando/ Fallschirm-Panzer-Ersatz- und Ausbildungs-
  Regiment "Hermann Göring" (commander: Oberleutnant Böhme).
- 4. Kompanie/Landesschützen-Bataillon II/6
  (commander: Hauptmann Ernst Sieger).
- 4. and 5. Kompanie/Schiffstamm-Abteilung 14.
- Pionier-Kompanie 434
  In total about 600 men.

South of the Waal, between the country road and railway bridges
KAMPFGRUPPE MELITZ
Commander: Major Engelbert Melitz
- Two provisional companies consisting of the remains of Nijmegen's garrison, military police, and guard soldiers – about 200 men

At Betuwe (north of the Waal)
- V. Abteilung/SS-Artillerie-Ausbildungs-und-Ersatz-Regiment
  (commander: SS-Sturmbannführer Oskar Schwappacher)
- Stabsbatterie V./SS-Artillerie-Ausbildungs-und-Ersatz-Regiment
  (commander: SS-Sturmbannführer Oskar Schwappacher).
- 21. (schwere) Batterie V./SS-Artillerie-Ausbildungs-und-Ersatz-Regiment
  (commander: SS-Hauptsturmführer Horst Krüger)
- 19. (leichte) Batterie V./SS-Artillerie-Ausbildungs-und-Ersatz-Regiment
  (arrived on 19–20 September)

a broad, hard-surfaced, raised road to the northern arm of the river, the Neder Rijn, at Arnhem thereafter. Then the Allies would be across the Rhine."[481]

The forces from the Guards Armoured Division which had made it to the southern outskirts of Nijmegen in the afternoon on 19 September, were made up of two companies each from the 1st and 2nd Battalion, Grenadier Guards with tanks and motorised infantry respectively, from Brigadier Gwatkin's 5th Guards Armoured Brigade. In order to get started quickly with the attack without having to await more supporting infantry, Gwatkin took command of Lieutenant Colonel Benjamin "Vandy" Vandervoort's 2nd Battalion of the 505th PIR. (In return, several units were transferred from the Guards Armoured Division to Gavin.*)

The attack force was put under the command of Lieutenant-Colonel Edward "Eddie" Goulburn, commander of the 1st (Motor) Battalion, Grenadier Guards. Even though the 41-year-old Goulburn

---

* 1st (Motor) Battalion Grenadier Guards, 5th Battalion Coldstream Guards, 2nd (Armoured) Battalion Irish Guards, Reconnaissance Troop from the Nottinghamshire Yeomanry (Sherwood Rangers) Regiment, and the 1st Royal Dragoon.

had "a brusque exterior", he was, according to David Fraser of the Grenadier Guards, "trusted absolutely by his entire battalion, and, indeed, by the whole Grenadier Group". Fraser adds that "his care for them was exemplary".[482] Later, when Goulburn had been promoted to general, he was referred to by his men simply as "The General".

Goulburn's care for his soldiers was possibly, as we shall see further on (in Volume 2), a little too strongly influenced by the bitter fighting for Drouet in Normandy in early August 1944, when his battalion had been caused terrible losses by SS units.*

Vandervoort and Colonel Ekman, commanding the 505th PIR, were to come along as well. Vandervoort felt honoured by being able to fight side by side with the famous Guards Armoured Division.

The attack was to be aimed against both the road bridge and the railway bridge, located a little over a kilometre from each other. Against the road bridge to the east – the most important target – three of the four Troops (with four tanks in each) of No. 3 Squadron, 2nd Battalion Grenadier Guards, as well as three of the four platoons of No. 2 Company, 1st Battalion Grenadier Guards and the "E" and "F" companies of the American airborne battalion were aimed. Against the railway bridge, one Troop from No. 3 Squadron, 2nd Battalion Grenadier Guards, as well as one platoon from No. 2 Company, 1st Battalion Grenadier Guards, and the American "D" Company were deployed.[483]

With Dutch guides in the turrets of the leading tanks and American paratroopers mounted, the two columns drove into town just after 1530 hrs on 19 September. "The clanking steel monsters were a comfort to the foot-slogging paratroopers", Vandervoort recounted. "Morale was high. We were 600 strong, slightly over T/O strength."[484] Between each Sherman, one small Bren Gun Carrier or Humber armoured reconnaissance car with Grenadier Guards infantry was rolling. Fire support was given by the 86th (East Anglian) (Herts Yeo)

---

* This was during the failed Operation "Bluecoat", which cost the British heavy losses without gaining any success. It was as a result of this that Horrocks was given command over the XXX Corps, since its previous commander, Lieutenant-General Gerard Bucknall, had been fired for the setback. Besides, that also happened to Major General George Erskine, commander of the 7th Armoured Division.

Field Regiment, Royal Artillery under Lieutenant-Colonel George Fanshawe.[485]

The eastern force was guided by Gert van Hees, the Dutch resistance man who had been showing other American paratroopers the way to the road bridge twice in the evening of 17 September. One has to assume that van Hees was now hoping that they would be "third time lucky". The column worked its way ahead along the Groesebeekscheweg and adjacent smaller parallel streets while cheering Nijmegenians kept coming flocking, increasing in numbers by the minute. The streets of the city were bathing in the evening sun when the Allied force came to the point where the Groesebeekscheweg forks. Here, the road was packed with Dutch civilians. One of them, Cor Kleijwegt, recounted, "I will never forget the emotion that ran like a flame through me when a helmeted paratrooper – gun at the ready – walked past us and apparently unmoved said: 'You are free!' As I walked back almost drunk-like, I kept repeating 'you are free' as if I wanted to keep his softly spoken words like a relic."[486]

But the Germans were well-informed and ready in their positions on the northern outskirts of the town.

Bren Carrier.

"Shortly before noon we learned that the enemy had moved about 15 tanks and armoured vehicles to reinforce his forces in Nijmegen", Hauptmann Ernst Sieger said. Soon, a couple of guns from SS-Sturmbannführer Schwappacher's both batteries on the other side of the Waal opened fire, and shells struck, causing the Allied column its first losses.

Soon after passing the Krayenhoff Barracks, after about 10 kilometres' calm journey along the Groesebeekscheweg, the first force was divided as the main part, the "A Column", turned right onto the smaller Groesbeekschedaarsweg. The smaller part of the eastern force, the "C Column" with four tanks and three rifle platoons (two British and one American) under the British major George Thorne, took the next exit right, towards the post office at Van Schevichavenstraat 1 – five hundred metres further up, right between the Kreizer Karelplein and the Lodewijkplein. The Dutch resistance believed that the detonators for the explosives on the bridges were located there. The school building where the Germans had had a command post only two days earlier was now seized, and a few shells were blasted away against the post house on the other side of the street. But when it was taken at around half past five, it turned out that there were no detonators there.

The main force, the "A Column" with eight Sherman tanks, armoured cars, and the main part of Vandervoort's battalion – including one motorcycle platoon[487] – continued along the Groesbeekschedaarsweg until arriving at the crossroads 300 metres further ahead. There, they turned right into the Daalsedarsweg towards the road bridge, about one and a half kilometres further ahead. In the Dominicanenstraat, the extension of the Daalsedarsweg, there was smoke from fires in the air from the buildings that the Germans had previously set fire to. When they made it across the Mariaplein, with two hundred metres left to the Lodewijkplein roundabout at the road bridge, they were discovered by the Germans in II. Abteilung/Fallschirm-Panzer-Ersatz- und Ausbildungs-Regiment "Hermann Göring" under Major Bodo Ahlborn. Supported by a few 88 mm guns, these were positioned around Villa Belvoir, a large building complex on a small hill on the eastern side of the Lodewijkplein (currently the site of Hotel Belvoir that was erected after the war).

The three leading Shermans – named "d'Artagnan", "Portos", and "Aramis" – raced across the Mariaplein and went into cover from the two- and three-storey buildings in Doctor Claas Noorduijnstraat. Here, the tank soldiers could see defiant mottos that the SS soldiers had just recently been painting in metre-high letters on the façades: "Death over tyranny!", "Our glory is faithfulness!", "We believe in Adolf Hitler and victory!"[488]

The leading Sherman tank, commanded by Lieutenant John Moller, made it to the Graadt van Roggenstraat below Villa Belvoir and opened fire up against the Lodewijkplein, and, behind it, the Hunner Park. Moller managed to knock out a German anti-tank gun, but the next moment, his own tank was hit by an 88 mm gun in the Lodewijk-plein and caught fire.[489] The entire crew was killed in the flames.*

Immediately afterwards, the next two tanks were hit as well. One of them was soon in flames. But the British tank soldiers' courage

* Today, they rest, together with many other Guardsmen, in the Jonkerbos war cemetery in southeastern Nijmegen, Moller in Grave 22.F.1.

made an impression on the Americans. The paratrooper Private Don Lassen never forgot seeing "one English tanker bail out of his tank with a teacup in his hand". According to Vandervoort, the British tank crews were a little too eager to attack. "In order not to lose tanks", he wrote, "the armour had to wait until the troopers worked ahead and solved the problem from the flanks." [490]

American paratroopers and British infantry now went into battle to outflank the Germans. The Americans worked their way forward in squads of 13 men, which had been trained to divide into three assault teams of four or five men, each equipped with a light machine gun. The squad commanders moved these teams forward in such a way that they supported each other to circumvent and attack enemy positions.

The SS soldiers offered stiff resistance, but it was obvious that the Americans were better trained. Using Bazookas, they blasted holes in house walls to enter buildings that the Germans held, they threw hand grenades through windows, they fired fiercely when they stormed into buildings, and inside, they threw themselves over the Germans with bayonets and trench knives. "The cooperation between the tough American paratroopers and the phlegmatic British guardsmen went remarkably smoothly, both units regarding the others as elite fighters." [491]

A group of Guardsmen under Lieutenant Martin Dawson made their way to the two-storey house at Graadt van Roggenstraat 2, just next to the Lodewijkplein. They hurried to fetch all available automatic weapons and then opened devastating fire on the surprised Germans. Several German soldiers were killed or wounded, but soon, the 88 mm gun in the roundabout aimed and put a shell in the house, forcing the British into quick retreat. [492]

"In the labyrinth of houses and brick-walled gardens, the fighting deteriorated into confusing face-to-face, kill-or-be-killed show-downs between small momentarily isolated groups and individuals", Vandervoort recounted. [493] But in spite of the embittered fighting, the Allies held their fire on one occasion when the Germans sent out medical orderlies to take care of the wounded in no man's land. [494]

Meanwhile, the western attack force, the "B Column", led by Captain John Neville from the Grenadier Guards, was advancing against the railway bridge. Led by another Dutch resistance man, Neville's men made it north through the town along Wezenlaan, a few kilometres west of "Column A" in Groesebeekscheweg. This column, too, initially met nothing but cheering Dutchmen. Where Wezenlaan ends in a four-way crossing, the column turned left, and made it up through Groenestraat onto the main road Graafscheweg. This was the wide road leading from Neerbosch (where Germans and Americans had been fighting for Bridge No. 10 at the Maas-Waal Canal the previous day) to the Keizer Karelplein, and from there further ahead straight towards the large road bridge across the Waal. Captain Neville's force followed Graafscheweg to the right, until reaching the railway five hundred metres further ahead. There, they turned left into Nieuwe Nonnendaalscheweg, which took them to Koninginnelaan, which runs in parallel with the railway. Now, it was only little over a kilometre left to the railway bridge to the northeast.

Hauptmann Max Runge had positioned his Kampfgruppe into defence positions in and around the houses surrounding the southern abutment of the railway bridge. As far as can be judged, he also had support from at least one assault gun – probably a Jagdpanzer IV seconded from SS-Kampfgruppe Euling at the road bridge. When Neville's vanguard drove out onto Oude Heeslaan, which crosses the Koninginnelaan, which in turn then segues into Krayenhofflaan, what was reported as being a German tank was discovered at the next crossing. The German vehicle quickly disappeared behind a few houses, but Neville ordered full speed ahead towards the bridge along the Oude Heeslaan, which turns to the left and runs just next to the railway bank. His plan was to take the bridge through a coup de main, and therefore, three tanks were detailed for storming the bridge, while the other two took up positions to provide fire support. A small infantry force followed in three Bren Carriers, while the infantry on foot was left behind.

Hauptmann Sieger, who had retreated from the Neerbosch bridge with his German home guard company, remembered: "Heavy fire rained down on the Company CP and harbour. Our line received extraordinary heavy, relentless fire from a Sherman tank, killing or wounding several men in our group."[495]

Hauptmann Runge did not have much artillery at his disposal – only a captured Soviet 45 mm 53-K-type anti-tank gun and two 20 mm automatic guns – but when Neville's vanguard arrived at the railway viaduct down by the harbour, he summoned artillery fire from SS-Sturmbannführer Schwappacher's batteries on the other side of the river. The German guns had already been aimed carefully, and the first round was a bull's-eye hit. SS-Oberscharführer Gerhard Hotop destroyed the leading tank with a Panzerfaust.[496] The entire crew, save for one man, was killed. The remaining Sherman tanks reversed into cover behind buildings, and instead, Neville ordered the infantry to attack up the railway bank. Shooting from the hip, they made it across the railway tracks, and down into the Kronenburger Park between the railway station and the bridge. Hence, Hauptmann Sieger found himself cut off.

But the Germans immediately – true to their usual habit – started a counterattack from the north. Sieger recounted, "As the enemy approached, parts of Pionier-Kompanie 434 on the west side of the city headed towards the Waal, intending to cross. There Leutnant Königsmann gathered part of the Pionier Einheit and both 20mm Flak guns, and immediately sent them into action, while Hauptmann Runge launched a counterattack from the Company CP area."[497]

The American airborne Staff Sergeant Paul D. Nunan saw how the Kronenburger Park was illuminated in the twilight by "tracer slugs, three colours of tracer, red, orange, and light greenish colors". He spotted a German who had gone into position with a 20 mm automatic gun behind a telephone pole, and opened fire against him with his Thompson submachine gun. Meanwhile, another soldier was blazing away full force from the hip with his .30-calibre (7.62 mm) Browning machine gun. Aiming this with any precision, however, was more than one man could manage. The bullets from the 14-kilo machine gun flew in all directions because of the heavy recoil, but Nunan saw five Germans fall – uncertain, however, whether they had been hit or just threw themselves down for cover. A Bazooka grenade exploded next to the German automatic gun and Nunan dispatched it conclusively with a Gammon grenade.*

"It exploded on the gun with a roar", Nunan recounted. "I turned to rejoin my platoon and felt a blow at the back of my left knee as though I had been struck with a club. I went down on the sidewalk and quickly got up." Nunan had been hit by a bullet. While a medic gave him first aid, he started shaking with spasms because of the severe shock.

Both sides now withdrew. "Because of strong enemy fire", Hauptmann Sieger recalled, "increasing casualties and the fall of darkness, the counterattack did not achieve its goal, which meant enemy fire from the houses, and a breakthrough to the southeast was impossible. In view of the situation, we could also expect an enemy attack from the west, so Leutnant Königsmann gathered the remnants of the company, about 80 men, at the electricity works approximately two kilometers northwest of the railway bridge."

From the British side, Captain Neville recounted, "There were about six seriously wounded men who probably would not have survived without medical treatment whom I decided to send back in the carrier. The Americans, despite the reverse and a few casualties, were still quite unmoved. We placed our three remaining tanks in strategic places and everyone else took cover in the adjoining houses. The American commander, who was otherwise a most-cooperative man, refused at this stage to have anything to do with sentries, on the grounds that his men needed 'a good night's sleep'. Despite some forceful words from me, he remained adamant. To protect themselves against surprise attack, their so-called 'sentries' slept behind the doors, so that any intruder would have to wake them up before getting in."

But while Neville's western "Column B" camped for the night, "Column A" at the road bridge slowly started breaking through. The tanks were now used to smash down garden walls and house walls, and the British and American infantrymen focused on taking the attics in the two- and three-storey houses, from where they could fire

* A British-made grenade in the shape of a canvas bag, also known as a "bean bag".

at German anti-tank guns below. The American battalion commander Vandervoort reported, "The Jerries fought hard and courageously, but the relentless closing tanks and troopers forced them to scramble to alternate positions and fall back to continue the fight. To do so, they had to abandon their heavy weapons and ammunition."[498]

The intense artillery fire from the 86th (East Anglian) Field Regiment also made it impossible for the Germans to send forward any reinforcements across the bridge.[499] Contributing to that were also the Allied infantry's mortar fire. Vandervoort remembered how a German soldier on one occasion tried to make it across the bridge running: "Our mortar observer fired one round that knocked him flat. He got up and began running away without his rifle. Then he stopped, turned around, came back, picked up his piece and started away again at a full jog – weapon in hand. The mortar platoon leader ordered 'Cease fire' and watched the good soldier run away." This corresponds well with an account from the German side in the Hunner Park: "A Sturmmann took on the task of trying to get through to the command post on the northern side of the bridge. Three times during the course of one day did he set off on this dangerous double-up, and three times did he escape the ceaseless machine gun fire as by a miracle."[500]

The Valkhof Park, the Hunner Park, the Keizer Lodewijkplein, and the south abutment, were a cauldron of exploding grenades. The incessant explosions and blasts from automatic weapons and rifles were woven together into a completely ear-splitting cacophony. Smoke from gunpowder and fires made the eyes water on friend and foe alike. The whole area was engulfed in smoke from fires, which condensed the darkness as the sun set at around eight o'clock in the evening. The German defenders were quite exhausted when suddenly a British tank appeared on the flank – in the Gerard Noodtstraat just at the southwest corner of the Hunner Park. The next minute, a shell from the tank's 17-pound gun slammed into one of the assault guns in the Hunner Park, with devastating effect.

Major George Thorne, commander of "Column C", had personally led a patrol of 18 men with two Sherman tanks from the post office, 500 metres further down southwest, along the small streets of

Van Broekhuysenstraat and Hertogplein and managed to sneak up on the Germans in that way. The moustachioed 31-year-old former heavyweight boxer Thorne was a veteran from Dunkirk in 1940 and was described as "a man of tremendous physical strength and endurance". When he was later awarded the Military Cross – especially for his efforts during the battle of Nijmegen – his "undaunted courage" was emphasised. While the British infantry spread out to the houses on both sides of the street, the Sherman's mighty gun rumbled again. This time, its high-explosive shell scattered the roadblock that the Germans had set up at the end of Gerard Noodtstraat.

Now, the Germans were attacked across a semicircle. "Van" Vandervoort describes the continued development of the battle while darkness descended: "With the overwhelming preponderance of armoured fire-power, the foot soldiers and tanks moved methodically the last few blocks toward our objective. At some point we worked through the German main line of resistance, but didn't know it at the time. We did know we had taken out most of their anti-tank guns with the exception of a few near the bridge. After three-plus hours of give and take, we forecably occupied the residential row of houses facing the Hunner Park at the south end of the highway bridge. Hunner Park was congested with Germans. [...] [They] had to be dislodged to give the tanks unmolested access to the bridge. From second-storey windows we looked down their throats. Time was running out for them unless they got help. Whatever their number, we had them outmanoeuvred, outgunned, and, believed in our bones, outclassed. Why not? We had driven them back for blocks."

One of the SS soldiers in the Hunner Park had previously stood against Frost's British paratroopers in Arnhem, during fighting that he described as "extremely tough", but to him, Nijmegen was "more unpleasant still, owing to fire from artillery and mortars". Out of twelve men in his group, eight were killed by artillery fire. He recounted that the effect of this artillery barrage "was increased by the hard ground in the town into which it was almost impossible to dig". He experienced the artillery fire as "almost unendurable", and suddenly – in the evening of 19 September – morale collapsed among many of the defenders: "A large number of the garrison rushed towards the bridge in an attempt to get away, only to be met at the other side by an SS Captain with a revolver who ordered them back saying that 300 SS were being sent up as reinforcements next day." [501]

But the SS soldiers realised that this was a bluff. The intense artillery fire had by then efficiently cut off the bridge from all German traffic. On the south side of the river, the Germans anxiously counted their last remaining cartridges and shells. [502]

In the evening of 19 September, the Allies doubtlessly had victory within reach. The Germans had brought forward their last reinforcements to the Nijmegen bridge, and these now went to their doom. There was not much more available – all of the 9. SS-Panzer-Division (or, rather, what was left of it) was tied down in Arnhem by the British 1st Airborne Division, whose 2nd Battalion under Lieutenant-Colonel Frost in addition had cut off the bridge across the Rhine, so that the Germans in any case would not be able to bring forward any major reinforcements to Nijmegen. From the Nijmegen bridge, it was about fifteen kilometres of flat terrain to the bridge in Arnhem.

QR32: VIDEO
0.00-6.27: Authentic wartime footage. The advance through Nijmegen and the fighting south of the bridge.

ARNHEM 1944 – AN EPIC BATTLE REVISITED 2: THE LOST VICTORY. SEPTEMBER–OCTOBER 1944

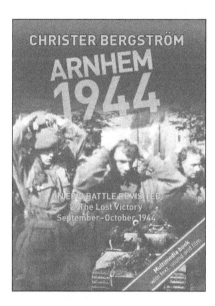

To be published in September 2019, in connection with the 75th Anniversary of "Market Garden".

Christer Bergström
ISBN: 978-91-88441-49-2
440 pages

All previous published accounts of Operation "Market Garden" end the main story with the evacuation of the British airborne troops from Oosterbeek – which obscures the fact that Operation Market Garden at that time was still regarded as, essentially, a great success. It was only because of the following development of events (including the battle at Overloon in October 1944) that the strategic success of Operation Market Garden could not be utilised to end the war before the turn of the year 1944–45. This is a story that has never been told before, and which is described and analysed in detail in the concluding Volume 2 of Christer Bergström's "Arnhem 1944".

ORGANISATIONAL STRUCTURE
OF MILITARY UNITS ON BOTH SIDES

The German, British, and American armies were based on the same organisational structure:

A Platoon was called a *Zug* in the German Army.

The nominal strength of a *Zug* was usually 48–50 men, divided into different *Gruppe* (sections) of ten men each on average, and one command *Trupp* (platoon staff) consisting of a platoon commander (*Zugführer*), deputy platoon commander, a runner, and sometimes a radio operator.

A British platoon consisted of three sections of 10 men each.

The nominal strength of an American platoon was usually 41 men, divided into three squads (sections).

A Company was called *Kompanie* in the German Army. A German *Kompanie* usually consisted of up to 200 men, divided into three rifle platoons, three anti-tank sections, and one company staff, as well as support units.

A British company consisted of three platoons.

An American company usually consisted of 193 men, divided into four platoons – three rifle platoons and one Weapons Platoon (support platoon) consisting of Platoon Headquarters, each with one Squad for mortars and machine guns (12 men).

A Battalion was called *Bataillon* or *Abteilung* in the German army. (In the German army and in the Waffen-SS, the battalion was called *Abteilung* in the cavalry, the Panzer troops, the anti-tank units, the artillery, and the liaison units.)

A *Bataillon* in the German infantry usually consisted of 860 men, divided into three rifle companies (numbered 1–3), one battalion staff, and various support and auxiliary units.

A battalion in the British infantry or airborne forces consisted of four Rifle Companies and one Headquarters Company, as well as a support company with a medical platoon, one mortar platoon, one anti-tank platoon, and one sapper platoon, with a nominal strength of a total of 821 men.

A battalion in the American infantry or the airborne forces nominally consisted of 860 men, divided into Battalion Headquarters with four officers, Headquarters Company with about 120 men, Heavy Weapons Company with about 160 men, and three rifle companies. The three rifle companies in U.S. battalions were "numbered" in the following way: 1st Battalion: A, B, and C, as well as D, which was the Heavy Weapons Company; 2nd Battalion: E, F, and G, as well as H, which was the Heavy Weapons Company; 3rd Battalion: I, K, and L, as well as M, which was the Heavy Weapons Company. (It is worth noting that there was no J company because of the risk of misreading a hand-written "I" as a "J".)

A **Regiment** was called *Regiment* (or *Volksgrenadier-Regiment* or *Grenadier-Regiment*) in the German Army.

A *Regiment* in the German infantry usually consisted of about 3,000 men, divided into three battalions, one regimental staff, and various support troops.

A regiment in the American infantry had a nominal strength of 3,118 man, divided into the Regimental Headquarters and Headquarters Company, three battalions (numbered 1–3), and various support and auxiliary units.

In the British Army, a battalion was the basic unit, and three battalions formed a brigade, which could be compared with a regiment.*

---

* The British Army also had regiments, but these were in certain cases the same size as a Battalion, and in that case, three regiments formed a brigade; in other cases, a regiment could also consist of an unspecified number of battalions. For example, the 7th KOSB was a battalion that was part of the regiment The King's Own Scottish Borderers. However, the 7th KOSB was part of the 4th Parachute Brigade (in the Arnhem sector) together with two other battalions from other regiments, while, for instance, the 2nd Battalion, KOSB was stationed in Burma. As for the artillery, the basic unit was the regiment, consisting of 580 men with 24 artillery guns.

However, e.g. the 5th Guards Armoured Brigade of the Guards Armoured Division had four battalions. In certain cases, a *Group* was formed by two battalions, such as The Irish Guards Group, which consisted of the 2nd Armoured Battalion and the 3rd Infantry Battalion from The Irish Guards.

A Division was called "division" in both the German, British, and American armies.

A German *Infanterie-Division* had a nominal strength of more than 12,352 men, divided into two infantry regiments (*Regiment*), one artillery regiment, one pioneer (engineer) battalion, one anti-tank battalion, one signals battalion, and one *Füsilier-Bataillon* with ten mortars, as well as various support and auxiliary units.

A British infantry division had a nominal strength of 18,347 men, divided into three brigades, three field artillery regiments, one machine gun battalion, and several various support units. A British airborne division consisted of two Parachute Brigades, one Airlanding Brigade (gliders) and one (Airlanding) artillery regiment, as well as various support units.

An American infantry division had a nominal strength of 14,253 men, divided into the headquarters and headquarters company, three infantry regiments, four field artillery battalions, one engineer battalion, one tank destroyer battalion, one Anti-Aircraft Automatic Weapons Battalion, various support and auxiliary units, and often one tank battalion.

An American airborne division consisted of four regiments – two parachute infantry regiments and one Glider Infantry Regiment as well as three artillery battalions, one anti-aircraft battalion, and various support units.

A Corps was called *Korps* in the German Army.

A German *Korps* and a British or American Corps usually consisted of two to five divisions. All were numbered with Roman numerals.

371

Army was called *Armee* in the German Army.

A German *Armee* and a British or American Army usually consisted of two to six corps. All were numbered with Arabic numerals.

An Army Group was called *Heeresgruppe* (or *Armeegruppe*) in the German Army.

A German *Heeresgruppe* and the British and American Army groups usually consisted of two to four armies. The German *Heeresgruppe* were usually "numbered" with letters. The Allied Army groups were numbered with Arabic numerals.

ARMOURED UNITS

The Germans armoured divisions (*Panzer-Division*) in those days consisted of one armoured regiment (*Panzer-Regiment*), two Panzer grenadier regiments (*Panzergrenadier-Regiment*), one artillery regiment (*Panzer-Artillerie-Regiment*), and one pioneer battalion (*Panzer-Pionier-Bataillon*), one anti-tank battalion (*Panzerjäger-Abteilung*), one anti-aircraft battalion (*Flak-Artillerie-Abteilung*), and one reconnaissance battalion (*Panzer-Aufklärungs-Abteilung*).

A German Panzer regiment was divided into one staff platoon (*Stabs-Zug*) and two battalions (*Panzer-Abteilung*), each having one staff platoon (*Stabs-Zug*) and four companies (company No. 1–4 in *I. Panzer-Abteilung*; company No. 5–8 in *II. Panzer-Abteilung*). The Panther tanks and the Panzer IV tanks were usually grouped into one regiment each.

The nominal force of German Panzer units was: Tank platoon (*Zug*) five tanks; company (*Kompanie*, consisting of four platoons and two command tanks) 22 tanks; battalion (*Abteilung*) 88 tanks; regiment (*Regiment*) 176 tanks.

British pure tank units were divided into:
• Troop (platoon) of four tanks.
• Squadron (company) of four Troops and one Squadron Fighting Headquarters (staff) of three tanks.

- Battalion* consisting of one staff company (Headquarters Squadron) and three companies (Squadrons), designated A, B, and C respectively.

A British armoured division consisted of two to three compound brigades of tank battalions, infantry, and motorised infantry, as well as two artillery regiments and several other supporting units. The nominal strength was 14,964 men, 290 tanks, 100 armoured cars, 261 armoured personnel carriers, forty-eight 25-pound field guns, 160 mortars, 78 anti-tank guns, and 141 anti-aircraft guns.

An American armoured division normally consisted of three Tank Battalions, three Armored Infantry Battalions, four Armored Field Artillery Battalions, one Armored Engineer Battalion, one Tank Destroyer Battalion and one AAA AW, Anti-Aircraft Artillery – Automatic Weapons Battalion as well as one Cavalry Squadron (reconnaissance battalion).

An American tank battalion was divided into one Headquarters Company with two medium-sized Sherman tanks and three 105 mm Sherman self-propelled guns, three companies each consisting of 17 Sherman medium tanks and one 105 mm Sherman self-propelled gun, one company of 17 light tanks (usually Stuarts), and one Service Company. The nominal strength of an American tank division was thus 59 Sherman medium tanks and 17 light tanks. Including the light tanks of the division's reconnaissance battalion, an American armoured division had a nominal strength of 10,500 men and 263 tanks (177 Shermans and 86 Stuarts).

Some American armoured divisions were so-called Heavy Armored Divisions – each consisting of two Armored Regiments with three tank battalions each – and one infantry regiment. The nominal strength of a Heavy Armored Division was 14,000 men and 390 tanks (252 of which were Shermans).

The American armoured divisions that were not Heavy Armored Divisions were normally divided for battle into three battle groups –

---

* Here, a Regiment was the exact same size as a Battalion. This had to do with British cavalry regiments in the interwar period being mechanised into tank units the size of a battalion.

Combat Command A, Combat Command B, and Combat Command Reserve (CCA, CCB, and CCR), each usually consisting of one tank battalion, one Armored Infantry Battalion, one artillery battalion, and one platoon of tank destroyers.

ARTILLERY

A German artillery regiment (*Artillerie-Regiment*) consisted of three light (*leichte*; with light guns) battalions (*Abteilung*) and one heavy (*schwere*; with heavy guns) battalion, each of which consisted of three batteries (*Batterie*) with four guns (cannon or rocket artillery) each.
A British artillery regiment consisted of three batteries, each with two troops of four artillery pieces each.

The American artillery battalion usually consisted of three batteries with four guns in each. Exceptions were the armoured units' Armored Field Artillery Battalions which each had a total of 18 guns, as well as a 240mm Howitzer Battalions, and the battalions that were equipped with 203 mm 8 inch Gun M-1; these battalions consisted of six guns each.

WRITTEN SOURCES

Primary sources – Archives

Airborne Assault Archive, Duxford.
Airborne Museum Oosterbeek Archive.
Archief Bevrijdingsmuseum in Groesbeek.
Archief Nederlandse Provincie van de Congregatie der Redemptoristen.
Bund Deutscher Fallschirmjäger e.V.
Bundesarchiv/Militärarchiv.
Combined Arms Research Library (CARL), Fort Leavenworth, Kansas.
Cumbria's Museum of Military Life, Carlisle.
Gelders Archief, Arnhem.
Gemeentearchiv Ede, Ede.
Imperial War Museum Archive.
King's College London. Liddell Hart Centre for Military Archives.
Krigsarkivet, Stockholm.
Mahn Center for Archives and Special Collec- tions, Ohio University Libraries.
Maneuver Center of Excellence Libraries, Fort Benning.
National Army Museum London.
National Collection of Aerial Photography, Edinburgh.
National Archives, Kew.
National Archives and Records Administration (NARA).
National Collection of Aerial Photography HES, Edinburgh.
Nederlands Instituut voor Militaire Historie, Haag.
Royal Artillery Museum Archive, Larkhill.
Royal Engineers Museum, Chatham.
Tank Museum Bovington Archive.

Foreign Military Studies, US Historical Division.

B-044. Mattenklott, Lt Gen of Inf. *Rhineland 15 Sep 44–21 Mar 45.*
B-149. Generalleutnant Walter Poppe. *Commitment of 59th Infantry Division in the Netherlands 18 September to 25 November 1944.*
B-262. Blauensteiner, Ernst. *Employment of the*

II Fallschirm Korps between the Maas and the Rhine Rivers 19 September 1944 to 10 March 1944.
B-343. Gen Inf Reinhard. *LXXXVIII. Inf. Corps.*
C-001. von der Heydte, *6th Fallschirm Jaeger Regiment in Action against US Paratroopers in the Netherlands in September 1944.*
C-085. Franz Halder i Reinhardt, Generalmajor Hellmuth, *The Commitment of the 406th Division against the Allied Air Landing at Nijmegen in September 1944.*
P-155. General der Waffen-SS Wilhelm Bittrich, *Das II.SS-Pz.A.K. Sept/Okt 1944.*
P-187. H. von Tettau. *Einsatz des Stabes von Tettau in Holland Sept.–Okt. 1944.*
P-188. *Erster Teil: Die Kämpfe der Gruppe "Walther" vom 13.9.1944 bis zum 12.10.1944 in Südholland,* Gerhard Schacht, Major i.G. a.D.
P-189. Sixt, Generalleutnant Friedrich. *Die Kaempfe der Panzerbrigade 107 im September und Oktober 1944, nach einer Ausarbeitung von Oberstleutnant a.D. Bendt-Joachim Frhr.v. Maltzahn mit Ergänzungen gemäss dem Kriegstagebuch des O.B. West. 1954. Anhang B: Schilderung des Oberstlt. v. Maltzahn v. Mai 1954 über den Verlauf des 18.9.*

Secondary sources – Bibliography

This bibliography only lists works that are referred to in the notes. Some titles considered standard works on the subject are not included, since most of this book is based on primary sources.

Ambrose, Stephen E. *Citizen Soldiers: The U.S. Army From the Normandy Beaches to the Bulge to the Surrender of Germany.* Easton Press, 1997.
Ambrose, Stephen E. *Band of Brothers.* Simon & Schuster, New York 2001.
Barnett, Correlli (ed.). *Hitler's Generals.* Grove Press, New York 2003.
Bauer, Cornelis & Theodoor Alexander Boeree. *The Battle of Arnhem.* Fonthill, 2012.
Baynes, John. *The Forgotten Victor: General Sir Richard O'Connor.* Brassey's, London 1989.
Bennett, David. *A Magnificent Disaster.* Casemate, Havertown 2011.

Bergström, Christer. *The Ardennes 1944–1945: Hitler's Winter Offensive*. Vaktel förlag, Eskilstuna and Casemate, 2014

Blumenson, Martin. *Breakout and Pursuit*. *United States Army in World War II European Theater of Operations*. Center of Military History, United States Army, Washington, D.C. 1961.

Boroughs, Zig, *The 508th Connection*. Xlibris, 2013.

Bradley, Omar. *A Soldier's Story*. Henry Holt, New York 1951.

Brown, Chris. *Arnhem: Nine Days of Battle*. Spellmount, Stroud 2014.

Buckingham, William F. *Arnhem 1944*. Tempus, Stroud 2004.

Burgett, Donald R. *The Road to Arnhem*. Presidio, Novata, CA, 1999.

Courage, Major G. *15/19 The King's Royal Hussars 1939–1945*. Gale & Polden Ltd., Aldershot 1949.

Daglish, Ian. *Operation Bluecoat: Breakout from Normandy*. Pen & Sword, Barnsley 2009.

Delaforce, Patrick. *The Black Bull: From Normandy to the Baltic with the 11th Armoured Division*. Pen & Sword, Barnsley 2010.

Didden, Jack & Maarten Swarts. *Autumn Gale/ Herbststurm*. De Zwaardvisch, 2013.

------ *Kampfgruppe Walther and Panzerbrigade 107*. De Zwaardvisch, 2016.

Dover, Victor. *The Silken Canopy*. Littlehampton Book Service, Littlehampton 1979.

Dugdale, Jeff. *Panzer Divisions, Panzergrenadier Divisions, Panzer Brigades of the Army and the Waffen SS in the West. Autumn 1944–February 1945. Their Detailed and Precise Strengths. Vol. I, Part 1. Refitting and Re-Equipment*. The Military Press, Milton Keynes 2000.

Fairley, John. *Remember Arnhem: Story of the First Airborne Reconnaissance Squadron at Arnhem*. Pegasus Press, Aldershot 1978.

Fitzgerald, Major Desmond J. L. *History of the Irish Guards in the Second World War*. Gale & Polden Ltd., Aldershot 1952.

Fraser, Sir David. *War and Shadows*. Allen Lane, London 2002.

Frost, John. *A Drop Too Many*. Pen & Sword, Barnsley 2014.

Furbringer, Herbert. *9. S.S. Panzer-Division. 1944: Normandie - Tarnopol - Arnhem*. Editions Heimdal 1994.

Gavin, General James M. *On To Berlin*. Bantam Books, New York 1985.

------ *Airborne Warfare*, Pickle Partners Publishing, 2014.

Gerritsen, Bob & Scott Revell. *"Retake Arnhem Bridge"*. Sigmond, Renkum 2014.

Gibson, Ronald, *Nine Days*. Upfront Publishing, 2012.

Golden, Lewis, *Echoes From Arnhem*. William Kimber, London 1984.

Gorman, Sir John. *The Time of My Life*. Leo Cooper, Barnsley 2002.

Horrocks, Sir Brian. *Corps Commander*. Sidgwick & Jackson, London 1977.

de Jong, Lou, *Het Koninkrijk der Nederlanden in de Tweede Wereldoorlog*. Amsterdam 1982.

Jung, Hermann. *Die Ardennen-Offensive 1944/45: Ein Beispiel für die Kriegführung Hitlers*. Ur *Studien und Dokumente zur Geschichte des zweiten Weltkrieges*. *Band 12*. Arbeitskreis für Wehrforschung in Stuttgart, Musterschmidt, Göttingen 1971.

Kammann Willi. *Die Geschichte des Fallschirmjäger-Regiment 2 1939 bis 1945*. Herausgegeben von Werner Ewald und Arnold von Roon. 1987.

Kershaw, Robert. *It Never Snows in September*. Ian Allan, Hersham 2013.

------ *A Street in Arnhem*. Ian Allan, Hersham 2014.

Kopka, Franz M. *Missbraucht und Gebeutelt 1939–1945 : Schicksal einer selbständigen Einheit schwerer Panzerjäger als Heerestruppe, Feldpostnummer 10 509 : Militärhistorischer Dokumentarbereicht*. Eigenverlag, Brühl/Köln 1999.

Koskimaki, George E. *Hell's Highway*. Ballantine Books, New York 2007.

LoFaro, Guy. *The Sword of St. Michael*. Da Capo Press, Cambridge, MA, 2011.

Liddell Hart, Basil. *Andra världskrigets historia, del 2*. Natur & Kultur, Stockholm 1985.

Longson, Jim & Christine Taylor. *An Arnhem Odyssey: "Market Garden" To Stalag IVB*. Pen & Sword, Barnsley 1991.

van Lunteren, Frank. *The Battle for the Bridges*. Casemate, Havertown 2014.

MacDonald, Charles B. *United States Army in World War II European Theater of Operations: The Siegfried Line Campaign*. Washington, D.C: Center of Military History United States Army, 1990.

Magry, Karel (ed.). *Operation Market-Garden Then and Now*. After the Battle, Old Harlow 2013 & 2014.

Marshall, S.L.A. *Battle at Best*. Jove Books, New York 1989.

McKee, Alexander. *The Race for the Rhine Bridges*. Souvenir Press, 1971.

McManus, John C. *September Hope*. Nal Caliber, New York 2013.

Middlebrook, Martin. *Arnhem 1944: The Airborne Battle*. Stackpole, Mechanicsburg 2011.

Miller, Victor, *Nothing is Impossible: A Glider Pilot's Story of Sicily, Arnhem and the Rhine Crossing*. Pen & Sword Aviation 2015.

Montgomery, Bernard Law. *The Memoirs of Field-Marshal Montgomery*. Fontana Monarchs, 1961.

Neillands, Robin. *The Battle for the Rhine 1944*. Cassell, London 2005.

Nordyke, Phil. *All American, All the Way*. Zenith Press, Minneapolis, MN, 2005.

Patton, *War As I Knew* It. Houghton Mifflin, New York 1947

Piekalkiewicz, Janusz. *Arnheim 1944: Deutschlands letzter Sieg*. Stalling, Oldenburg 1976.

Pitt, Barrie. *Churchill and the Generals*. Pen & Sword, Barnsley 2004.

Powell, Geoffrey. *The Devil's Birthday*. Papermac, London 1985.

Retallack, John. *The Welsh Guards*. Frederick Warne Ltd, 1981.

Revell, Scott, Niall Cherry & Bob Gerritsen. *Arnhem: A Few Vital Hours*. Sigmond, Renkum 2013.

Ritchie, Sebastian. *Arnhem, Myth and Reality*. Robert Hale, 2011.

Rosendaal, Jost. *The Destruction of Nijmegen, 1944*. Vantilt Publishers, Nijmegen 2014.

Rosse, Captain the Earl of (Brendan Parsons) & E.R. Hill. *The Story of the Guards Armoured Division*. Geoffrey Bles, London 1956.

Ryan, Cornelius. *A Bridge Too Far*. Simon & Schuster, New York 1974.

Saunders, Tim. *Hell's Highway: US 101st Airborne & Guards Armoured Division*. Pen & Sword, Barnsley 2001.

Sims, James. *Arnhem Spearhead*. Arrow Books, London 1989.

Sliz, John. *Engineers at the Bridge*. Stormboat Kings, 2010.

SS-Kriegsberichterzug 10. SS-Panzer-Division "Frundsberg", *Dran, drauf und durch: Buczacz-Caen-Nimwegen*

Stenger, Dieter. *Panzers East and West: The History of the German 10th SS Panzer Division in World War II*. Stackpole Books, 2017.

Sylvan, Major William C. & Captain Francis G. Smith, Jr., ed. John T. Greenwood. *Normandy to Victory: the War Diary of General Courtney H. Hodges & the First U.S. Army*. University Press of Kentucky, Lexington, Kentucky 2008.

Urquhart, Major-General R.E. *Arnhem*. Pan Books, London 1972.

Tieke, Wilhelm. *Im Feuersturm letzter Kriegsjahre*. Pour le Mérite, Selent 2006.

Verhoef, D.E.H.J. *The Battle for Ginkel Heath near Ede*. Aspekt, Soesterberg 2003.

Wilmot, Chester. *The Struggle for Europe*. Wordsworth, Ware 1998.

Vincx, Jan & Viktor Schotanius. *Nederlandse vrijwilligers in Europese krijgsdienst 1940–1945. Deel 1: De Landstorm*. Herentals: Etnika 1988.

Wuyts, Gerard. *Herfststorm over Hechtel : 6–12 september 1944*. Uitgegeven in eigen beheer door Gerard Wuyts, Hechtel 2004.

Zetterling, Niklas. *Normandy 1944: German Military Organisation, Combat Power and Organizational Effectiveness*. J.J. Fedorowicz, 2000.

Periodicals

Der Deutsche Fallschirmjäger

Die Hellebarde

Die weissen Spiegel

Newsletter, Vereniging Vrienden van het Airborne Museum Oosterbeek

Signal

The Sunday Times

The Times

NOTES

1   National Archives. WO 171/441. War Diary "G" Branch HQ 7 Armd Div. Appendix "A" mto 7 Amd Div Intelligence Summary No. 85.

2   Imperial War Museum Archive. Documents 3856. Private Papers of Lieutenant D Holdsworth. Box No: 83/2/1.

3   Zetterling, *Normandy 1944: German Military Organisation, Combat Power and Organizational Effectiveness*, p. 32.

4   Tieke, *Im Feuersturm letzter Kriegsjahre*, s. 281.

5   Wilmot, *The Struggle for Europe*, p. 434.

6   Bundesarchiv/Militärarchiv. MSG 3/3991. Die Hellebarde No. 18/1996.

7   National Archives. WO 171/441. War Diary "G" Branch HQ 7 Armd Div.

8   Bundesarchiv/Militärarchiv. RH 19-IV/54. Anlagen zum Kriegstagebuch OB West. 21 augusti 1944.

9   MS A-901. Bayerlein, Fritz. *Ergänzende Fragen zur früheren Fragebogen: "Withdrawal from France"*, 1950.

10 Foreign Military Studies B-262. Blauensteiner, Ernst. *Employment of the II Fallschirm Korps between the Maas and the Rhine Rivers 19 September 1944 to 10 March 1944.* US Historical Division. Allendorf 1946, p. 1.

11 Rosse and Hill, *The Guards Armoured Division*, p. 85.

12 Delaforce, *The Black Bull*, p. 120.

13 Ibid., p. 121.

14 National Archives. WO 171/441. War Diary "G" Branch HQ 7 Armd Div.

15 Imperial War Museum Archive. Documents 3856. Private Papers of Lieutenant D Holdsworth. Box No: 83/2/1.

16 National Archives. WO 171/441. War Diary "G" Branch HQ 7 Armd Div.

17 Harmel, Heinz Generalmajor der Waffen-SS. *Die 10.SS-Panzer-Division "Frundsberg" im Einsatz vom Juni bis November 1944.* Überarbeitet von Generalleutnant a.D. Friedrich Sixt. Stenger Historica Publishing Spotsylvania, Virginia. Via Dieter Stenger. , p. 87.

18 King's College London. Liddell Hart Centre for Military Archives. 15/15: Papers of

Reginald William Winchester ('Chester') Wilmot (1911–1954). 15/15/50/1. Notes from official sources and interrogation of Gen Kurt Student, Cdr 1 German Parachute Army on the German tactical response.

19 Foreign Military Studies MS C-001. von der Heydte, *6th Fallschirm Jaeger Regiment in Action against US Paratroopers in the Netherlands in September 1944.* , p. 1.

20 National Archives. WO 171/638. War Diary HQ 32 Guards Brigade.

21 Foreign Military Studies MS C-001. von der Heydte, *6th Fallschirm Jaeger Regiment in Action against US Paratroopers in the Netherlands in September 1944.* , pp. 6–7.

22 Kammann Willi. *Die Geschichte des Fallschirmjäger-Regiment 2 1939 bis 1945.* Herausgegeben von Werner Ewald und Arnold von Roon. 1987. , p. 172.

23 King's College London. Liddell Hart Centre for Military Archives. 15/15: Papers of Reginald William Winchester ('Chester') Wilmot (1911–1954). 15/15/50/1. Notes from official sources and interrogation of Gen Kurt Student, Cdr 1 German Parachute Army on the German tactical response.

24 Swarts & Didden, *Autumn Gale*, p. 40.

25 King's College London. Liddell Hart Centre for Military Archives. 15/15: Papers of Reginald William Winchester ('Chester') Wilmot (1911-1954). 15/15/50/1. Notes from official sources and interrogation of Gen Kurt Student, Cdr 1 German Parachute Army on the German tactical response.

26 Jung, *Die Ardennen-Offensive 1944/45*, p. 33.

27 King's College London. Liddell Hart Centre for Military Archives. 15/15: Papers of Reginald William Winchester ('Chester') Wilmot (1911–1954). 15/15/50/1. Notes from official sources and interrogation of Gen Kurt Student, Cdr 1 German Parachute Army on the German tactical response.

28 Ibid.

29 Ibid.

30 Bundesarchiv/Militärarchiv. RH 24-88. Bestand LXXXVIII. Armeekorps: Ia-KTB mit Anlagen 1.7–31.12.1944.

31 Bundesarchiv/Militärarchiv. RH 19, IX/90.

KTB H.Gr.B. v. 16.09-30.09.44. 22 September 1944.

32 National Archives. WO 219/1923. Weekly Intelligence Summaries: 24–25. 1944 Sept.

33 National Archives. Records of the Cabinet Office. CAB 121/1413.

34 National Archives. WO 171/441. War Diary "G" Branch HQ 7 Armd Div. 1st US Infantry Div Int. Summary No. 79.

35 Bundesarchiv/Militärarchiv. RH 19 IX/89. Kriegstagebuch Heeresgruppe B. 6 September 1944.

36 Montgomery, The Memoirs of Field-Marshal Montgomery, p. 274.

37 Ibid., p. 280.

38 Didden & Swarts, Autumn Gale, p. 61.

39 Bundesarchiv/Militärarchiv. RH 24-88. Bestand LXXXVIII. Armeekorps: Ia-KTB mit Anlagen 1.7–31.12.1944.

40 Ibid.

41 National Archives. WO 171/638. War Diary HQ 32 Guards Brigade. Bde Intelligence Summary No. 40, up to 1800 hrs 7 Sep 44.

42 Retallack, John. The Welsh Guards. Frederick Warne Ltd, 1981. , p. 110.

43 Bundesarchiv/Militärarchiv. RH 24-88. Bestand LXXXVIII. Armeekorps: Ia-KTB mit Anlagen 1.7–31.12.1944. 8 September 1944.

44 Retallack, John. The Welsh Guards. Frederick Warne Ltd, 1981. , p. 110.

45 National Archives. WO 171/1259. War Diary 1 Welsh Guards 1944 Jan.–Dec. 7 September 1944.

46 MS B-717. Student, Kurt. Supplement to Report by Oberst i.G. Geyer (Concerning First Parachute Army). , pp. 6–7.

47 Rosse & Hill, p. 107.

48 Didden & Swarts, Kampfgruppe Walther and Panzerbrigade 107, p. 38.

49 Kopka, Franz M. Missbraucht und Gebeutelt 1939–1945 : Schicksal einer selbständigen Einheit schwerer Panzerjäger als Heerestruppe, Feldpostnummer 10 509: Militärhistorischer Dokumentarbereicht. Eigenverlag, Brühl/Köln 1999. , p. 152.

50 National Archives. WO 171/1252. 5 Coldstream Guards War Diary 1944 Jan–Dec.

51 National Archives. WO 171/1252. 5 Coldstream Guards War Diary 1944 Jan–Dec.

52 Rosse & Hill, p. 109.

53 Kopka, p. 157.

54 Bundesarchiv/Militärarchiv. RH 24-88. Bestand LXXXVIII. Armeekorps: Ia-KTB mit Anlagen 1.7–31.12.1944. 9 September 1944.

55 Archive Tank Museum Bovington. MH.5. RH.4. 1st & 2nd Fife & Forfar Yeomanry.

56 Wuyts, Gerard. Herfststorm over Hechtel: 6–12 September 1944. Uitgegeven in eigen beheer door Gerard Wuyts, Hechtel 2004. , p. 238.

57 National Archives. WO 171/1256. War Diary of 2nd Guards Bn Irish Guards from 1st September 1944 to 30th September 1944. Appendix B. 10 September 1944.

58 National Archives. WO 373/53/222. Recommendation for Award for McGurren, Thomas Edward. Rank: Corporal. Service No: 6977185. Regiment: 2 Armoured Irish Guards.

59 National Archives. WO 373/51/195. Recommendation for Award for Stanley-Clarke, John Oliver. Rank: Lieutenant, Acting Captain. Service No: 237623. Regiment: 3 Battalion Irish Guards.

60 National Archives. WO 373/51/166. Recommendation for Award for Hutton, Ronald David. Rank: Lieutenant, Service No: 269055.Regiment: 615 Field Squadron Royal Engineers.

61 National Archives. WO 171/638. War Diary HQ 32 Guards Brigade. Bde Intelligence Summary No. 42, up to 1800 hrs 11 Sep 44.

62 Horrocks, Sir Brian. Corps Commander, p. 89.

63 National Archives. WO 171/837. War Diary 2 Household Cavalry 1st September 1944 to 30th September 1944.

64 Bundesarchiv/Militärarchiv. MSG 2/1948. Tagebuch Oberst Fullriede.

65 National Archives. WO 171/638. War Diary HQ 32 Guards Brigade.

66 Didden and Swarts, Autumn Gale, p. 135.

67 National Archives. WO 171/1259. War Diary 1 Welsh Guards 1944 Jan.–Dec. 7 September 1944.

68 Blumenson, Martin. Breakout and Pursuit. United States Army in World War II European Theater of Operations. Center of Military History, United States Army, Washington, D.C. 1961. , p. 690.

69 King's College London. Liddell Hart Centre for Military Archives. 15/15/130.

Dempsey, Gen Sir Miles Christopher. Notes of interview with Dempsey, 1946, on SHAEF strategy and operations in North West Europe, 1944.

70 Montgomery, p. 300.

71 Bradley, Omar. *A Soldier's Story*. Henry Holt, New York 1951. , p. 416.

72 According to John Hackett, who commanded the British 4th Parachute Brigade during "Market Garden". Middlebrook, Arnhem 1944, p. 8.

73 Montgomery, p. 284.

74 Imperial War Museum Archive. Documents 9487. Private Papers of Brigadier A. G. Walch O.B.E.

75 Powell, *The Devil's Birthday*, p. 33.

76 King's College London. Liddell Hart Centre for Military Archives. 15/15: Papers of Reginald William Winchester ('Chester') Wilmot (1911-1954). 15/15/50/1. Notes from official sources and interrogation of Gen Kurt Student, Cdr 1 German Parachute Army on the German tactical response.

77 Montgomery, p. 285.

78 National Archives. WO 205/972B. An account of the operations of Second Army in Europe: Volume I.

79 Montgomery, pp. 285–286.

80 Wilmot, p. 493.

81 Patton, *War As I Knew* It. Houghton Mifflin, NewYork 1947. , p. 125.

82 Bennett, *A Magnificent Disaster*, p. 24.

83 Liddell Hart, *Andra världskrigets historia, del 2*, p. 228.

84 Montgomery, p. 70.

85 Pitt, Barrie. *Churchill and the Generals*. Pen & Sword, Barnsley 2004.

86 Bennett, p. 14.

87 Daglish, Ian. *Operation Bluecoat: Breakout from Normandy*. Pen & Sword, Barnsley 2009. , p. 317.

88 Gavin, *On To Berlin*, p. 83.

89 Magry, *Operation Market-Garden Then and Now*, vol. 1, p. 37.

90 Frost, *A Drop Too Many*, p. 242.

91 Airborne Assault: ParaData. "Lieutenant-General Sir Ernest Down". paradata.org.uk/people/ernest-down.

92 Buckingham, William F. *Arnhem 1944*, p. 32.

93 Frost, p. 194.

94 King's College London. Liddell Hart Centre for Military Archives. 15/15: Papers of Reginald William Winchester ('Chester') Wilmot (1911–1954). 15/15/50/58. Letter from Major General G.W. Lathbury, 2 March 1951.

95 The Cornelius Ryan Collection of World War II Papers, Mahn Center for Archives and Special Collections, Ohio University Libraries. Box 108. Folder 6. Urquhart, Maj Brian, Interview.

96 National Collection of Aerial Photography. Allied Central Interpretation Unit (ACIU). 106G/2872.

97 National Archives, WO 171/397. Annexure 'D'. Operation "MARKET". 1 Para Bde Intelligence Summary No.1, 13 Sep 44.

98 National Archives, WO 171/397. 1 Airborne Division Planning Intelligence Summary No 2 dated 14th Sep 1944.

99 Harmel, Heinz Generalmajor der Waffen-SS. *Die 10.SS-Panzer-Division "Frundsberg" im Einsatz vom Juni bis November 1944*, p. 91; Tieke, p. 313.

100 Ryan, p. 150.

101 Harmel, Heinz Generalmajor der Waffen-SS. *Die 10.SS-Panzer-Division "Frundsberg" im Einsatz vom Juni bis November 1944*, p. 92.

102 Tieke, p. 313.

103 Gelders Archief. Archiefblok 2867. Collectie L.P.J. Vroemen. Doos nr. 54. Walter Harzer. Leserbriefe zum "Verrat von Arnheim".

104 Generalfeldmarschall Walter Model, Rapport. OMR. Dr. Egon Skalka. Gelders Archief. Archiefblok 2867. Collectie L.P.J. Vroemen. Doos nr. 45.

105 Bundesarchiv/Militärarchiv. RH 2-2/32. Zusammengefasster Bericht des II. SS-Pz. Korps über die Kämpfe im Raume Arnheim 10.9.–15.10. 1944.

106 Barnett, Correlli (red.). *Hitler's Generals*. Grove Press, New York 2003. , pp. 463–464.

107 Bundesarchiv/Militärarchiv, RH 24-88. Bestand LXXXVIII. Armeekorps: Ia-KTB mit Anlagen 1.7–31.12.1944.

108 Bundesarchiv/Militärarchiv, RH 24-88. Bestand LXXXVIII. Armeekorps: Ia-KTB mit Anlagen 1.7–31.12.1944.

109 Bundesarchiv/Militärarchiv, RH 24-88. Bestand LXXXVIII. Armeekorps: Ia-KTB mit Anlagen 1.7–31.12.1944.

NOTES

110 Mckee, *The Race for the Rhine Bridges*, s. 126.

111 National Archives. WO 171/638. War Diary HQ 32 Guards Brigade. Bde Intelligence Summary No. 43, up to 1800 hrs 13 Sep 44.

112 Bundesarchiv/Militärarchiv. RH 24-88. Bestand LXXXVIII. Armeekorps: Ia-KTB mit Anlagen 1.7-31.12.1944.

113 National Archives. WO 171/638. War Diary HQ 32 Guards Brigade.

114 National Archives. WO 373/52. Recommendations for Honours and Awards for Gallant and Distinguished Service (Army).

115 Foreign Military Studies. MS P-188. *Erster Teil: Die Kämpfe der Gruppe "Walther" vom 13.9.1944 bis zum 12.10.1944 in Südholland*, Gerhard Schacht, Major i.G. a.D., München, 7 May 1954.

116 Bundesarchiv/Militärarchiv. MSG 3/3991. Bericht Friedrich Richter, SS-Hstuf./SS-Pz. Gren.Rgt. 22 / "KG-Richter". Die Hellebarde No. 18/1996.

117 Stenger, Dieter. *Panzers East and West: The History of the German 10th SS Panzer Division in World War II*, pdf page 200.

118 Bundesarchiv/Militärarchiv. MSG 3/3991. Bericht Johannes Rüsing, SS-Rttf., 1.Kp./2. Zug/AA-Pz.AA. 10 "Frundsberg". Die Hellebarde No. 18/1996.

119 National Archives, ULTRA Records. HW 5/587. CX/MSS/T310/76.

120 National Archives. WO 171/441. War Diary "G" Branch HQ 7 Armd Div.

121 National Archives, ULTRA Records. HW 5/587. CX/MSS/T310/68 (c). HP 477.

122 National Archives, WO 171/1256. War Diary of 2nd Guards Bn Irish Guards from 1st September 1944 to 30th September 1944.

123 National Archives. WO 171/638. War Diary HQ 32 Guards Brigade. Bde Intelligence Summary No. 44, up to 1600 hrs 15 Sep 44.

124 National Archives, ULTRA Records. HW 5/587.

125 Horrocks, pp. 96-97.

126 Gorman, *The Time of My Life*, Kindle version, Location 1108.

127 Horrocks, , p. 98.

128 Ibid., p. 99.

129 National Archives. WO 171/376. War Diary "G" Branch Guards Armoured Division.

130 Horrocks, p. 99.

131 Gorman, Location 1109.

132 Bundesarchiv/Militärarchiv. MSG 3/3991. Bericht Heinz Damaske, SS-Ustuf./Btl. Adju. I./II. SS-Pz.Gren.Rgt. 22 "F". Die Hellebarde No. 18/1996.

133 Bundesarchiv/Militärarchiv. MSG 2/1948. Tagebuch Oberst Fullriede.

134 341 Battery, 86th Field Regt RA (Herts Yeomanry): War Diary 3 June 1944 to 9 April 1946" by Benjamin p. Beck. benbeck.co.uk/fh/transcripts/sjb_war_diaries/batterydiary.htm.

135 Gemeentearchiv Ede, Map 258, 2e afd. Documentatue Bevrijding Veluwe (1), "Market Garden". Allied Expeditionary Air Force. Daily Int/Ops Summary No. 242.

136 National Archives. WO 171/837. War Diary 2 Household Cavalry 1st September 1944 to 30th September 1944.

137 Airborne Assault Archive. Box 4F1, 2/10/4. File No. 48, Arnhem. Major Gen G.W. Lathbury. Arnhem Diary September–October 1944.

138 Airborne Assault Archive. Box 4F1, 2/10/4. File 54/61, Arnhem. 14217084 Sgt Cox BE 3 Plt. A' Coy 3 Para. Into Arnhem – Day One by Bruce Cox.

139 Airborne Assault Archive. Box 4F2 2/10/10. Arnhem 1944 Veterans Club. Letter from Mrs. Belinda Brinton 18-2-98.

140 Ibid.

141 Horrocks, p. 101.

142 Rosse & Hill, p. 127.

143 National Archives, WO 171/1256. War Diary of 2nd Guards Bn Irish Guards from 1st September 1944 to 30th September 1944.

144 "Südholland 1944" by SS-Hauptsturmführer Karl Godau. Suchdienst Frundsberg, Die Hellebarde No. 21/2001, pp. 42–43.

145 Bundesarchiv/Militärarchiv. MSG 3/3991. Die Hellebarde No. 11/1988.

146 Courage, Major G. *15/19 The King's Royal Hussars 1939-1945*. Gale & Polden Ltd., Aldershot 1949. , p. 117.

147 National Archives. WO 171/837. War Diary 2 Household Cavalry 1st September 1944 to 30th September 1944.

148 Bundesarchiv/Militärarchiv. MSG 3/3991. Bericht Johannes Rüsing, SS-Rttf., 1.Kp./2. Zug/AA-Pz.AA. 10 "Frundsberg". Die Hellebarde No. 18/1996.

149 Fitzgerald, Major Desmond J. L. *History of*

the Irish Guards in the Second World War. Gale & Polden Ltd., Aldershot 1952. , p. 492.

150 King's College London. Liddell Hart Centre for Military Archives. 15/15: Papers of Reginald William Winchester ('Chester') Wilmot (1911–1954). 15/15/50/31. "Holland's Liberation."

151 Fitzgerald, p. 492.

152 National Archives, WO 171/1256. War Diary of 2nd Guards Bn Irish Guards from 1st September 1944 to 30th September 1944.

153 Bundesarchiv/Militärarchiv. MSG 3/3991. Bericht Johannes Rüsing, SS-Rttf., 1.Kp./2. Zug/AA-Pz.AA. 10 "Frundsberg". Die Hellebarde No. 18/1996.

154 National Archives, WO 171/1256. War Diary of 2nd Guards Bn Irish Guards from 1st September 1944 to 30th September 1944.

155 Ibid.

156 Griesser, Die Löwen von Carentan, p. 190.

157 Courage, p. 118.

158 Kopka, p. 207.

159 National Archives, WO 171/1256. War Diary of 2nd Guards Bn Irish Guards from 1st September 1944 to 30th September 1944.

160 Saunders, Hell's Highway: US 101st Airborne & Guards Armoured Division, p. 59.

161 War Diary HQ Royal Artillery of 43rd (W) Division.

162 King's College London. Liddell Hart Centre for Military Archives. 15/15: Papers of Reginald William Winchester ('Chester') Wilmot (1911–1954). 15/15/50/29. Airborne Invasion and the Battle for the Bridges.

163 Ibid.

164 National Archives, WO 171/1256. War Diary of 2nd Guards Bn Irish Guards from 1st September 1944 to 30th September 1944.

165 Koskimaki, Hell's Highway, p. 61.

166 Foreign Military Studies. MS B-343. Gen Inf Reinhard. LXXXVIII. Inf. Corps. US Historical Division. Allendorf 1951. , p. 27.

167 Burgett, The Road to Arnhem, p. 29.

168 Granaatweken Schijndel 1944 versie 2014 Geschreven door de Schijndelaren Ben Peters en Louis van Dijk. granaatweken.nl/author/de-granaatweken.

169 Battalion and small unit study #1, Holland.

170 King's College London. Liddell Hart Centre for Military Archives. 15/15: Papers of Reginald William Winchester ('Chester')

Wilmot (1911–1954). 15/15/50/1. Notes from official sources and interrogation of Gen Kurt Student, Cdr 1 German Parachute Army on the German tactical response.

171 Ibid.

172 Ibid.

173 Ritchie, Arnhem, Myth and Reality, p. 175.

174 Kurt Student, "Arnheim: Letzter deutscher Erfolg" in Der deutsche Fallschirmjäger, nr 9/1964.

175 Kriegstagebuch Oberst Dewald.

176 Ibid.

177 Battalion and small unit study #1, Holland.

178 Kriegstagebuch Oberst Dewald.

179 Peters, Ben and Louis van Dijk, Granaatweken Schijndel 1944 (2014). granaatweken.nl/author/de-granaatweken; tvschijndel.nl/index.php/laatste-nieuws/5193-boekpresentatie-granaatweken-schijndel-1944.

180 Kriegstagebuch Oberst Dewald.

181 Ibid.

182 Foreign Military Studies. MS B-343. Gen Inf Reinhard. LXXXVIII. Inf. Corps. US Historical Division. Allendorf 1951. , p. 27.

183 ZStL 107 AR 294/67 Bd. V, Bl.873 = StAw Bremen 29 a Js 306/64, Schlussbericht LKA, 8.2.1968, Bl. 32. Georg-Elser-Initiative Bremen e.V. geibev.de.

184 Didden and Swarts, Autumn Gale, p. 200.

185 Foreign Military Studies. MS B-343. Gen Inf Reinhard. LXXXVIII. Inf. Corps. US Historical Division. Allendorf 1951. , p. 27.

186 Bundesarchiv/Militärarchiv, RH 24-88. Bestand LXXXVIII. Armeekorps: Ia-KTB mit Anlagen 1.7–31.12.1944. Korpsbefehl Nr. 12. p. 733.

187 Koskimaki, p. 157.

188 Bundesarchiv/Militärarchiv, RH 24-88. Bestand LXXXVIII. Armeekorps: Ia-KTB mit Anlagen 1.7–31.12.1944.

189 Ibid.

190 Foreign Military Studies. MS B-343. Gen Inf Reinhard. LXXXVIII. Inf. Corps. US Historical Division. Allendorf 1951. , p. 28.

191 Combined Arms Research Library. Battalion and Small Unit Study No. 6: Parachute Infantry at Best, 1945.

192 Bundesarchiv/Militärarchiv, RH 24-88. Bestand LXXXVIII. Armeekorps: Ia-KTB mit Anlagen 1.7-31.12.1944.

193 Combined Arms Research Library. Battalion
and Small Unit Study No. 6: *Parachute
Infantry at Best*, 1945.

194 Saunders, p. 108.

195 Bundesarchiv/Militärarchiv, RH 24-88.
Bestand LXXXVIII. Armeekorps: Ia-KTB
mit Anlagen 1.7–31.12.1944.

196 Ibid.

197 McManus, *September Hope*, p. 145.

198 Koskimaki, p. 122.

199 Airborne Assault Archive. Box 4F1, 2/10/4.
File 54/61, Arnhem. 14217084 Sgt Cox BE 3
Plt. A' Coy 3 Para. Into Arnhem – Day One
by Bruce Cox.

200 Gibson, Ronald, *Nine Days*. Upfront
Publishing, 2012, p. 22.

201 King's College London. Liddell Hart Cen-
tre for Military Archives. 15/15: Papers of
Reginald William Winchester ('Chester')
Wilmot (1911–1954). 15/15/50/1. Notes from
official sources and interrogation of Gen
Kurt Student, Cdr 1 German Parachute
Army on the German tactical response.

202 Revell et al, *Arnhem: A Few Vital Hours*, p. 38.

203 Gefechtsbericht SS.Pz.Gren.A.u.E.Btn. 16
in den Kämpfen bei Arnheim. 17-9-44 zum
7-10-44 von SS-Sturmbannführer Josef
Krafft. Gelders Archief. Dokument 2171.
Collectie Boeree. 1. De Slag om Arnhem.
1.3. De Duitsers. 24, p. 3.

204 Ibid., p. 11.

205 SS-Sturmmann K. H. Bangard. "Erlebnis-
bericht über die Landung der 1. engl.
Luftlandedivision am 17. September 1944
bei Arnhem". Gelders Archief. Archiefblok
2867. Collectie L.P.J. Vroemen. Doos nr. 45.

206 Gefechtsbericht SS.Pz.Gren.A.u.E.Btn. 16
in den Kämpfen bei Arnheim. 17-9-44 zum
7-10-44 von SS-Sturmbannführer Josef
Krafft. Gelders Archief. Dokument 2171.
Collectie Boeree. 1. De Slag om Arnhem.
1.3. De Duitsers. 24, p. 6.

207 SS-Sturmmann K. H. Bangard. "Erlebnis-
bericht über die Landung der 1. engl.
Luftlandedivision am 17. September 1944
bei Arnhem". Gelders Archief. Archiefblok
2867. Collectie L.P.J. Vroemen. Doos nr. 45.

208 Revell et al, *Arnhem: A Few Vital Hours*, p. 59.

209 Gefechtsbericht SS.Pz.Gren.A.u.E.Btn. 16
in den Kämpfen bei Arnheim. 17-9-44 zum
7-10-44 von SS-Sturmbannführer Josef
Krafft. Gelders Archief. Dokument 2171.

210 Airborne Assault Archive. Box 4F1, 2/10/4.
File 54/61, Arnhem. 14217084 Sgt Cox BE 3
Plt. A' Coy 3 Para. Into Arnhem - Day One
by Bruce Cox.

211 Nederlands Instituut voor Oorlogs-
documentatie (NIOD), Amsterdam.
Identificatiecode 001. Wehrmachtbefehlshaber in den Niederlanden.

212 Gelders Archief. Dokument 2171. Collectie
Boeree. 1. 11. "The History of 7 Battalion
K.O.S.B. in the Battle of Arnhem by Th.A.
Boeree", 1954. Eén band, 103 genummerde
bladen, afbeeldingen, kaarten, p. 26.

213 King's College London. Liddell Hart Centre for Military Archives. 15/15: Papers of
Reginald William Winchester ('Chester')
Wilmot (1911–1954). 15/15/50/81. Operation
"Market Garden". Events in Arnhem town
as seen by the Dutch. Notes of Interviews
with members of the Arnhem Police and
others in Arnhem, July 1947.

214 The Cornelius Ryan Collection of World
War II Papers, Mahn Center for Archives
and Special Collections, Ohio University
Libraries. Box 131, Folder 5. Jupe, Pvt Horst,
Questionnaire.

215 Gelders Archief. Dokument 2171. Collectie
Boeree. 1. 11. "The History of 7 Battalion
K.O.S.B. in the Battle of Arnhem by Th.A.
Boeree", 1954. Eén band, 103 genummerde
bladen, afbeeldingen, kaarten, p. 26.

216 Gefechtsbericht SS.Pz.Gren.A.u.E.Btn. 16
in den Kämpfen bei Arnheim. 17-9-44 zum
7-10-44 von SS-Sturmbannführer Josef
Krafft. Gelders Archief. Dokument 2171.
Collectie Boeree. 1. De Slag om Arnhem.
1.3. De Duitsers. 24, p. 8.

217 Ryan, *A Bridge Too Far*, p. 227.

218 Powell, *The Devil's Birthday*, p. 62.

219 Golden, Lewis, *Echoes From Arnhem*,
pp. 148–149.

220 Brown, *Arnhem: Nine Days of Battle*, p. 112.

221 National Archives. WO 171/397. Report of
Activities 9 Field Company RE.

222 Fairley, John. *Remember Arnhem:
Story of the First Airborne Reconnaissance
Squadron at Arnhem*. Pegasus Press,
Aldershot 1978, pp. 69–70.

223 Gefechtsbericht SS.Pz.Gren.A.u.E.Btn. 16
in den Kämpfen bei Arnheim. 17-9-44 zum
7-10-44 von SS-Sturmbannführer Josef

Krafft. Gelders Archief. Dokument 2171.
Collectie Boeree. 1. De Slag om Arnhem.
1.3. De Duitsers. 24, pp. 11–12.

224 Ibid., p. 12.

225 SS-Obersturmbannführer Walter Harzer.
"Arnhem Interview."Gelders Archief.
Archiefblok 2867. Collectie L.P.J. Vroemen.
Doos nr. 30, p. 2.

226 Gelders Archief. Dokument 2171. Collectie
Boeree. 1. De Slag om Arnhem. 1.3. De
Duitsers. Brieven van Walter Harzer, voormalig commandant van 9de SS-pantserdivisie "Hohenstaufen", aan Boeree, 9.9.56.

227 SS-Obersturmbannführer Walter Harzer.
"Arnhem Interview."Gelders Archief.
Archiefblok 2867. Collectie L.P.J. Vroemen.
Doos nr. 30, p. 5.

228 Ibid., p. 2.

229 Dugdale, Jeff. *Panzer Divisions, Panzergrenadier Divisions, Panzer Brigades of
the Army and the Waffen SS in the West.
Autumn 1944–February 1945. Their Detailed
and Precise Strengths. Vol. I, Part 1. Refitting and Re-Equipment.* The Military Press,
Milton Keynes 2000.

230 Gelders Archief. Dokument 2171. Collectie
Boeree. 1. De Slag om Arnhem. 1.3. De
Duitsers. Brieven van Walter Harzer, voormalig commandant van 9de SS-pantserdivisie "Hohenstaufen", aan Boeree, 9.9.56.

231 Gelders Archief. Archiefblok 2867. Collectie
L.P.J. Vroemen. Doos nr. 54. 140/145. Kriegserleben: "Fallschirme über Arnheim."

232 Ibid.

233 Bundesarchiv/Militärarchiv. RH 2-2/32.
Zusammengefasster Bericht des II. SS-Pz.
Korps über die Kämpfe im Raume Arn-
heim 10.9.–15.10. 1944.

234 Bundesarchiv/Militärarchiv. MSG 3/3991.
Bericht H.G. Sonnenstuhl, SS-Stubaf.Rgt.
Kdr.SS-Pz.Art.Rgt.10 "Frundsberg". Die
Hellebarde No. 18/1996.

235 Ibid.

236 Ibid.

237 Gerritsen and Revell, *"Retake Arnhem
Bridge"*, p. 25.

238 King's College London. Liddell Hart Cen-
tre for Military Archives. 15/15: Papers of
Reginald William Winchester ('Chester')
Wilmot (1911–1954). 15/15/50/55. Arnhem:
The German Side of the Story. Letter from
Hans Peter [sic], of Kevelaer in the Lower

Rhineland, who commanded a Panzer
Battlegroup at Arnhem.

239 The Cornelius Ryan Collection of World
War II Papers, Mahn Center for Archives
and Special Collections, Ohio University
Libraries. Box 130. 10th SS Panzer Division
(Frundsberg). Folder 14. Ringsdorf, Pvt
Alfred, Interview, 28 November 1967.

240 Bundesarchiv/Militärarchiv. RH 2-2/32.
Zusammengefasster Bericht des II. SS-Pz.
Korps über die Kämpfe im Raume Arn-
heim 10.9.–15.10. 1944.

241 Gelders Archief. Dokument 2171. Collectie
Boeree. 1. De Slag om Arnhem. 1.3. De
Duitsers. Rapport van Harzer, pp. 57–58.

242 Gelders Archief. Archiefblok 2867.
Collectie L.P.J. Vroemen. Doos nr. 30.

243 SS-Sturmbannführer Hans Möller, "Die
Schlacht um Arnheim und in Osterbeck."
[sic]. Gelders Archief. Archiefblok 2867.
Collectie L.P.J. Vroemen. Doos nr. 54. , p. 22.

244 Gefechstbericht der 7. (Stamm) Kompanie
für die Zeit vom 17.9. bis 26.9.44 von
SS-Obersturmführer Karl Labahn.
2 Oktober 1944, p. 1. Gemeentearchiv Ede.
Map 258, 2e afd. Documentatie Bevrijding
Veluwe.

245 Gelders Archief. Dokument 2171. Collectie
Boeree. 1. 11. "The History of 7 Battalion
K.O.S.B. in the Battle of Arnhem by Th.A.
Boeree", 1954. Eén band, 103 genummerde
bladen, afbeeldingen, kaarten, p. 26.

246 Gefechtsbericht SS.Pz.Gren.A.u.E.Btn. 16
in den Kämpfen bei Arnheim. 19-9-44 zum
7-10-44 von SS-Sturmbannführer Josef
Krafft. Gelders Archief. Dokument 2171.
Collectie Boeree. 1. De Slag om Arnhem.
1.3. De Duitsers. 24, p. 14.

247 Bundesarchiv/Militärarchiv. MSG 3/3991.
Bericht Helmut Buttlar, SS-Strn./4. Bttr./
SS-Flak-Abt. 10, "Frundsberg". Die Helle-
barde No. 18/1996.

248 SS-Sturmbannführer Hans Möller, "Die
Schlacht um Arnheim und in Osterbeck."
[sic]. Gelders Archief. Archiefblok 2867.
Collectie L.P.J. Vroemen. Doos nr. 54. ,
p. 20.

249 Urquhart, *Arnhem*, p. 57.

250 Middlebrook, *Arnhem 1944*, p. 136.

251 National Archives, WO 171/123. 1st
Parachute Battalion War Diary.

252 Kershaw, *It Never Snows in September*, p. 124.

253 IWM LBY 09/112. Grenville, Harvey. "Tim's tale: a wartime biography of Major John Timothy winner of 3 Military Crosses."

254 Jeanne Meeter Endt, diary.

255 National Archives, WO 171/1237. 2nd Bn The Parachute Regiment - O.O. No.1.

256 Jeanne Meeter Endt, diary.

257 National Archives, WO 171/1237. 2nd Bn The Parachute Regiment - O.O. No.1.

258 Truppenführung: Heeresdienstvorschrift 300, p. 1.

259 Bundesarchiv/Militärarchiv. MSG 3/3991. Bericht Helmut Buttlar, SS-Strn./4. Bttr./ SS-Flak-Abt. 10, "Frundsberg". Die Hellebarde No. 18/1996.

260 Urquhart, p. 49.

261 SS-Sturmbannführer Hans Möller, "Die Schlacht um Arnheim und in Osterbeck." [sic]. Gelders Archief. Archiefblok 2867. Collectie L.P.J. Vroemen. Doos nr. 54. , p. 20.

262 National Archives, WO 205/623. Report on Operation "Market": Arnhem 17–26 Sep 1944. Great Britain, Army First Airborne Division.

263 SS-Sturmbannführer Hans Möller, "Die Schlacht um Arnheim und in Osterbeck." [sic]. Gelders Archief. Archiefblok 2867. Collectie L.P.J. Vroemen. Doos nr. 54. , ss. 23–24.

264 Frost, p. 214.

265 SS-Sturmbannführer Hans Möller, "Die Schlacht um Arnheim und in Osterbeck." [sic]. Gelders Archief. Archiefblok 2867. Collectie L.P.J. Vroemen. Doos nr. 54. , p. 25.

266 Foreign Military Studies. MS P-155. General der Waffen-SS Wilhelm Bittrich, Das II.SS-Pz.A.K. Sept/Okt 1944, 1954.

267 Sims, Arnhem Spearhead, p. 64.

268 Tieke, p. 318.

269 Dover, The Silken Canopy.

270 "In Memoriam Private Leslie D Sadler" by Bob Hilton. Paradata: The living history of The Parachute Regiment and Airborne Forces. paradata.org.uk/people/leslie-d-sadler-0.

271 Bundesarchiv/Militärarchiv. MSG 3/3991. Bericht Helmut Buttlar, SS-Strn./4. Bttr./ SS-Flak-Abt. 10, "Frundsberg". Die Hellebarde No. 18/1996.

272 King's College London. Liddell Hart Centre for Military Archives. LH 9/24/223. Part 2: Papers of Reginald William Winchester

('Chester') Wilmot (1911–1954). 15/15/50/81. Operation "Market Garden". Events in Arnhem town as seen by the Dutch.

273 Bundesarchiv/Militärarchiv. MSG 3/3991. Bericht Adolf Lochbrunner, SS-Uscha. 3. Kp., (SPW-Btl.), SS-Pz.Gren.Rgt. 21. Die Hellebarde No. 18/1996.

274 The Cornelius Ryan Collection of World War II Papers, Mahn Center for Archives and Special Collections, Ohio University Libraries. Box 131. Folder 1. Weber, Pvt Horst, Interview.

275 Bundesarchiv/Militärarchiv. MSG 3/3991. Bericht Adolf Lochbrunner, SS-Uscha. 3. Kp., (SPW-Btl.), SS-Pz.Gren.Rgt. 21. Die Hellebarde No. 18/1996.

276 Bundesarchiv/Militärarchiv. MSG 3/3991. Bericht Rudi Trapp, SS-Strm. 3. Kompanie /I. (SPW) Btl./SS-Pz.Gren.Rgt. 21. Die Hellebarde No. 14/1991.

277 Gelders Archief. Dokument 2171. Collectie Boeree. 1. De Slag om Arnhem. 1.3. De Duitsers. Brieven van Walter Harzer, voormalig commandant van 9de SS-pantserdivisie "Hohenstaufen", aan Boeree, 19.1.58.

278 McManus, September Hopes, p. 132.

279 504th Parachute Infantry Regiment, S-3 Journal. September 18, 1944.

280 The Cornelius Ryan Collection of World War II Papers, Mahn Center for Archives and Special Collections, Ohio University Libraries. Box 132, Folder 12. Moll, MSG Jakob, Telephone interview.

281 Ibid.

282 Nordyke, All American, All the Way, p. 454.

283 Boroughs, Zig, The 508th Connection, Kindleversion, p. 233.

284 Rosendaal, The Destruction of Nijmegen, 1944, p. 106.

285 Gelders Archief. Archiefblok 2867. Collectie L.P.J. Vroemen. Doos nr. 31.

286 Rosendaal, p. 107.

287 Kershaw, It Never Snows in September, p. 188.

288 Lofaro, The Sword of St. Michael, p. 330.

289 Archief Nederlandse Provincie der Congregatie der Redemptoristen, Wittem. R-P039: 11588 Dagboek van pater H. van Driel cssr over de laatste dagen van de Tweede Wereldoorlog van 17 September 1944 tot 8 mei 1945, z.j.

290 Intervju med Joseph E. Atkins; Boroughs,

Zig, *The 508th Connection*, Kindleversion, p. 246.

291 Ibid.

292 Newsletter, Vereniging Vrienden van het Airborne Museum Oosterbeek. "SS-Panzer-Aufklärungs-Abteilung 9 and the Arnhem Road Bridge" by Marcel Zwarts. Appendix to Newsletter No. 90, June 2003.

293 Neillands, *The Battle for the Rhine 1944*, s. 104.

294 MacDonald, *The Siegfried Line Campaign*, p. 162.

295 Ibid., p. 163.

296 Gavin, *Airborne Warfare*, Kindleutgåva, position 1324.

297 The Cornelius Ryan Collection of World War II Papers, Mahn Center for Archives and Special Collections, Ohio University Libraries. Box A, Folder 8. Maps: Holland showing disposition of German forces, Sept 17, 1944. Zwischenlage 16.30 17.9.44 Chef WFSt.

298 Bundesarchiv/Militärarchiv. MSG 3/3991. Bericht Adolf Lochbrunner, SS-Uscha. 3. Kp., (SPW-Btl.), SS-Pz.Gren.Rgt. 21. Die Hellebarde No. 18/1996.

299 Ibid.

300 Ibid.

301 Frost, p. 218.

302 Bundesarchiv/Militärarchiv. MSG 3/3991. Bericht Adolf Lochbrunner, SS-Uscha. 3. Kp., (SPW-Btl.), SS-Pz.Gren.Rgt. 21. Die Hellebarde No. 18/1996.

303 Bundesarchiv/Militärarchiv. MSG 3/3991. Bericht Wilhelm Balbach, SS-Strm. 8. Kp. (Schw.) II. Btl./SS-Pz.Gren.Rgt. 22. Die Hellebarde No. 18/1996.

304 Sliz, *Engineers at the Bridge*, p. 19.

305 Bundesarchiv/Militärarchiv. MSG 3/3991. Bericht H.G. Sonnenstuhl, SS-Stubaf.Rgt. Kdr.SS-Pz.Art.Rgt.10 "Frundsberg". Die Hellebarde No. 18/1996.

306 The Cornelius Ryan Collection of World War II Papers, Mahn Center for Archives and Special Collections, Ohio University Libraries. Box 130. 10th SS Panzer Division (Frundsberg). Folder 13. Knaust, Maj Hans-Peter, Interview 2 November 1967, p. 3.

307 Gelders Archief. Archiefblok 2867. Collectie L.P.J. Vroemen. Doos nr. 54. Kriegserleben: "Fallschirme über Arnheim."

308 Bundesarchiv/Militärarchiv. MSG 3/3991. Bericht Rudi Trapp, SS-Strm. 3. Kompanie /I. (SPW) Btl./SS-Pz.Gren.Rgt. 21. Die Hellebarde No. 14/1991.

309 The Cornelius Ryan Collection of World War II Papers, Mahn Center for Archives and Special Collections, Ohio University Libraries. Box 131. Folder 1. Weber, Pvt Horst, Interview.

310 The Cornelius Ryan Collection of World War II Papers, Mahn Center for Archives and Special Collections, Ohio University Libraries. Box Box 113. Folder 48. Crook, LBombardier John W., Questionnaire.

311 Bundesarchiv/Militärarchiv. MSG 3/3991. Bericht Rudi Trapp, SS-Strm. 3. Kompanie /I. (SPW) Btl./SS-Pz.Gren.Rgt. 21. Die Hellebarde No. 14/1991.

312 Harmel, Heinz Generalmajor der Waffen-SS. *Die 10.SS-Panzer-Division "Frundsberg" im Einsatz vom Juni bis November 1944*. Überarbeitet von Generalleutnant a.D. Friedrich Sixt. Stenger Historica Publishing Spotsylvania, Virginia. Via Dieter Stenger. , p. 102.

313 The Cornelius Ryan Collection of World War II Papers, Mahn Center for Archives and Special Collections, Ohio University Libraries. Box 130. 10th SS Panzer Division (Frundsberg). Folder 12. Harmel, Maj Gen Heinz, Interview November 2 and 22, December 1967.

314 The Cornelius Ryan Collection of World War II Papers, Mahn Center for Archives and Special Collections, Ohio University Libraries. Box 130. 10th SS Panzer Division (Frundsberg). Folder 12. Harmel, Maj Gen Heinz, Interview November 2 and 22, December 1967.

315 Gelders Archief. Archiefblok 2867. Collectie L.P.J. Vroemen. Doos nr. 54. Der Freiwillige, december 1955.

316 King's College London. Liddell Hart Centre for Military Archives. 15/15: Papers of Reginald William Winchester ('Chester') Wilmot (1911–1954). 15/15/50/55. Arnhem: The German Side of the Story. Letter from Hans Peter [sic], of Kevelaer in the Lower Rhineland, who commanded a Panzer Battlegroup at Arnhem.

317 Gelders Archief. Archiefblok 2867. Collectie L.P.J. Vroemen. Doos nr. 54. 140/145. Kriegserleben: "Fallschirme über Arnheim."

318 Frost, p. 221.

319 The Cornelius Ryan Collection of World
War II Papers, Mahn Center for Archives
and Special Collections, Ohio University
Libraries. Box 130. 10th SS Panzer Division
(Frundsberg). Folder 12. Harmel, Maj
Gen Heinz, Interview November 2 and 22,
December 1967.
320 Ibid.
321 Frost, p. 224.
322 The Cornelius Ryan Collection of World
War II Papers, Mahn Center for Archives
and Special Collections, Ohio University
Libraries. Box 130. 10th SS Panzer Division
(Frundsberg). Folder 12. Harmel, Maj
Gen Heinz, Interview November 2 and 22,
December 1967.
323 SS-Obersturmbannführer Walter Harzer.
"Arnhem Interview." Gelders Archief.
Archiefblok 2867. Collectie L.P.J. Vroemen.
Doos nr. 30, p. 4.
324 Bundesarchiv/Militärarchiv. RH 2-2/32.
Zusammengefasster Bericht des II. SS-Pz.
Korps über die Kämpfe im Raume Arnheim
10.9.–15.10. 1944.
325 Newsletter, Vereniging Vrienden van
het Airborne Museum Oosterbeek.
"SS-Panzer-Aufklärungs-Abteilung 9
and the Arnhem Road Bridge" by Marcel
Zwarts. Appendix to Newsletter No. 90,
June 2003.
326 Sliz, Engineers at the Bridge, p. 29.
327 Furbringer, Herbert. 9. S.S. Panzer-Division.
1944: Normandie – Tarnopol – Arnhem.
Editions Heimdal 1994. , p. 430.
328 Sims, Arnhem Spearhead, p. 84.
329 Gerritsen and Revell, Retake Arnhem
Bridge, p. 53.
330 Sims, Arnhem Spearhead, p. 84.
331 Gerritsen and Revell, Retake Arnhem
Bridge, p. 54.
332 The Cornelius Ryan Collection of World
War II Papers, Mahn Center for Archives
and Special Collections, Ohio University
Libraries. Box 131. Folder 1. Weber, Pvt
Horst, Interview.
333 The Cornelius Ryan Collection of World
War II Papers, Mahn Center for Archives
and Special Collections, Ohio University
Libraries. Box 130. 10th SS Panzer Division
(Frundsberg). Folder 14. Ringsdorf, Pvt
Alfred, Interview, 28 November 1967.
334 "Operation "Market Garden": Last Stand at
an Arnhem Schoolhouse" by Niall Cherry.
Historynet. historynet.com/operation-
market-garden-last-stand-at-an-anhem-
schoolhouse.htm.
335 Gerritsen and Revell, Retake Arnhem
Bridge, p. 58.
336 "Operation 'Market Garden': Last Stand at
an Arnhem Schoolhouse" by Niall Cherry.
Historynet. historynet.com/operation-
market-garden-last-stand-at-an-anhem-
schoolhouse.htm.
337 Middlebrook, p. 296.
338 Stenger, Dieter. Panzers East and West:
The History of the German 10th SS Panzer
Division in World War II, pdf sidan 210.
339 Boroughs, Zig, The 508th Connection,
Kindleversion, p. 248.
340 Ibid., p. 249.
341 LoFaro, p. 647.
342 Gavin, On to Berlin, p. 165.
343 Gavin, Airborne Warfare, Kindleversion,
position 1785.
344 LoFaro, p. 337.
345 Boroughs, p. 256.
346 NARA. Record Group 242.3.3. A 3343.
Series SSO, Roll 121B. Records of the
Armed SS (Waffen-SS): SS Officer Personnel File. Oskar Schwappacher, Ia., V./
SS-Art.Ausb.u.Ers.Regt., Gef.St., 29.9.44,
Betr.: Einsatz der Abteilung bei den Kämpfen um Nijmegen.
347 Harmel, Heinz Generalmajor der
Waffen-SS. Die 10.SS-Panzer-Division
"Frundsberg" im Einsatz vom Juni bis
November 1944. Überarbeitet von Generalleutnant a.D. Friedrich Sixt. Stenger Historica Publishing Spotsylvania, Virginia. Via
Dieter Stenger., p. 103.
348 Ibid., p. 104.
349 NARA. Record Group 242.3.3. A 3343.
Series SSO, Roll 121B. Records of the
Armed SS (Waffen-SS): SS Officer Personnel File. Oskar Schwappacher, Ia., V./
SS-Art.Ausb.u.Ers.Regt., Gef.St., 29.9.44,
Betr.: Einsatz der Abteilung bei den Kämpfen um Nijmegen.
350 Hauptsturmführer Euling. "Nymwegen."
Gelders Archief. Archiefblok 2867. Collectie L.P.J. Vroemen. Doos nr. 31.
351 Foreign Military Studies. MS B-044. Mattenklott, Lt Gen of Inf. Rhineland 15 Sep
44–21 Mar 45, p. 6.
352 National Archives. WO 208/3649. Prisoner

of War Interrogation Section (Home) London District Cage: interrogation reports, L.D.C. 377–462.

353 Foreign Military Studies. MS C-085. General der Kavallerie Kurt Feldt i Reinhardt, Generalmajor Hellmuth, *The Commitment of the 406th Division against the Allied Air Landing at Nijmegen in September 1944*, p. 16.

354 Foreign Military Studies. MS C-085. Franz Halder i Reinhardt, Generalmajor Hellmuth, *The Commitment of the 406th Division against the Allied Air Landing at Nijmegen in September 1944*, p. 1.

355 Foreign Military Studies. MS C-085. General der Kavallerie Kurt Feldt i Reinhardt, Generalmajor Hellmuth, *The Commitment of the 406th Division against the Allied Air Landing at Nijmegen in September 1944*, p. 17.

356 Ibid.

357 Bundesarchiv/Militärarchiv, RH 19, IX/90. KTB H.Gr.B. v. 16.09–30.09.44. 18 September 1944.

358 Rasch, *Meine eigenen Erlebnisse in den letzten Kaempfen zwischen Maas und Elbe. I. Groesbeek*. Cit. i Kershaw, *It Never Snows in September*, p. 145.

359 Gavin, *On to Berlin*, p. 166.

360 LoFaro, p. 341.

361 Tallerday, "The Operations of the 505th Parachute infantry Regiment (82nd Airborne Division) in the Airborne Landing and Battle of Groesbeek and Nijmegen, Holland, 17–23 September 1944", Course text at Infantry Officer's Course, Ft Benning, Ga 1948.

362 Foreign Military Studies. MS C-085. General der Kavallerie Kurt Feldt i Reinhardt, Generalmajor Hellmuth, *The Commitment of the 406th Division against the Allied Air Landing at Nijmegen in September 1944*, p. 18.

363 Foreign Military Studies. MS B-044. Mattenklott, Lt Gen of Inf. *Rhineland 15 Sep 44–21 Mar 45*, p. 6.

364 Bundesarchiv/Militärarchiv, RH 19, IX/90. Kriegstagebuch Heeresgruppe B. v. 16.09-30.09.44. 19 September 1944.

365 Ibid.

366 Bundesarchiv/Militärarchiv. MSG 3/3991. Bericht Helmut Buttlar, SS-Strn./4. Bttr./ SS-Flak-Abt. 10, "Frundsberg". Die Hellebarde No. 18/1996.

367 SS-Obersturmbannführer Walter Harzer. "Arnhem Interview." Gelders Archief. Archiefblok 2867. Collectie L.P.J. Vroemen. Doos nr. 30, p. 4.

368 SS-Sturmbannführer Hans Möller, "Die Schlacht um Arnheim und in Osterbeck." [sic]. Gelders Archief. Archiefblok 2867. Collectie L.P.J. Vroemen. Doos nr. 54., p. 24.

369 Gelders Archief. Dokument 2171. Collectie Boeree. 1. De Slag om Arnhem. 1.3. De Duitsers. Rapport van Harzer, p. 66.

370 SS-Sturmbannführer Hans Möller, "Die Schlacht um Arnheim und in Osterbeck." [sic]. Gelders Archief. Archiefblok 2867. Collectie L.P.J. Vroemen. Doos nr. 54., p. 24.

371 Middlebrook, p. 183.

372 Urquhart, p. 76.

373 Bauer, Cornelis & Theodoor Alexander Boeree. *De Slag bij Arnhem. De mythe van het verraad weerlegd*. Amsterdam: Elsevier, 1964, p. 57.

374 NARA. Berlin Document Center Series 6400: SS Officers Service Records. Microfilm Publication A3343, Series SSO, Roll 170, Eberwein, Eugen.

375 Kershaw, *A Street in Arnhem*, p. 93.

376 de Jong, Lou, *Het Koninkrijk der Nederlanden in de Tweede Wereldoorlog*. Amsterdam 1982.

377 Janssens, Yvo and Edwin Meinsma. *Janssens Krijgshistorie*. "SS-Wachbataillon 'Nordwest' (later: SS-Wachbataillon 3)". waffen-ss.nl/wachbat.php.

378 Airborne Assault Archive. Box 4F1 2/10/6. File No. 54/8. Lt.-Col. Payton Reid 7th K.O.S.B.

379 Gefechstbericht der 7. (Stamm) Kompanie für die Zeit vom 17.9. bis 26.9.44 von SS-Obersturmführer Karl Labahn. 2 Oktober 1944, p. 2. Gemeentearchiv Ede. Map 258, 2e afd. Documentatie Bevrijding Veluwe.

380 Ibid.

381 Verhoef, *The Battle for Ginkel Heath near Ede*, p. 47.

382 Gefechstbericht der 7. (Stamm) Kompanie für die Zeit vom 17.9. bis 26.9.44 von SS-Obersturmführer Karl Labahn. 2 Oktober 1944, p. 2. Gemeentearchiv Ede. Map 258, 2e afd. Documentatie Bevrijding Veluwe.

383 SS-Obersturmführer Gottlob Ellwanger, "4. Bttr.(3,7cm) SS-Flak-Abt.10", i Die Hellebarde No. 18,/1996, 46–47.

384 Verhoef, p. 51.

385 Gelders Archief. Dokument 2171. Collectie Boeree. 1. De Slag om Arnhem. 1.3. De Duitsers. 22. Th. A. Boeree. "The mystery of the 9th SS Panzer Division (the Hohenstaufen Division) in the Battle of Arnhem". Met bijlagen, krtn, (z.j.). 91 genummerde bladen. Annexes. Annex 3. "The fight at Ginkel heath", p. 15.

386 Airborne Museum Hartenstein Archives, Oosterbeek. MS P-187. H. von Tettau. Einsatz des Stabes von Tettau in Holland Sept.–Okt. 1944, p. 4.

387 Miller, Victor, Nothing is Impossible: A Glider Pilot's Story of Sicily, Arnhem and the Rhine Crossing. Pen & Sword Aviation 2015. , p. 169.

388 National Archives, WO 171/392. War Diary 1st Airborne Division.

389 National Archives. WO 171/1375 War Diary 2 South Staffordshire Regiment Jan.–Dec. 1944.

390 National Archives. WO 171/1375. Appendix to War Diary 2 South Staffordshire Regiment Jan.–Dec. 1944.

391 Longson, Jim, An Arnhem Odyssey: "Market Garden" To Stalag IVB, p. 144.

392 Dokument: SS-Wachbataillon 3, Kommandeur. Beurteilung für den SS-Obersturmführer Kühne, Hermann. Amersfoort, den 1. August 1944. Via Scott Revell.

393 Vincx, Jan & Viktor Schotanius. Nederlandse vrijwilligers in Europese krijgsdienst 1940–1945. Deel 1: De Landstorm. Herentals: Etnika 1988. , p. 210.

394 National Archives, WO 171/1323. War Diary 7 King's Own Scottish Borderers January–December 1944.

395 Karlheinz Sundermeier, loggbok.

396 National Archives. WO 171/1323. War Diary 7 King's Own Scottish Borderers January-December 1944.

397 Miller, p. 175.

398 Piekalkiewicz, Arnheim 1944: Deutschlands letzter Sieg, p. 42.

399 The Cornelius Ryan Collection of World War II Papers, Mahn Center for Archives and Special Collections, Ohio University Libraries. Box 131 Folder 24. Heck, Cpl Erwin.

400 Miller, p. 173.

401 Vincx & Schotanius, p. 209.

402 Gelders Archief. Dokument 2171. Collectie Boeree. 1. De Slag om Arnhem. 1.3. De Duitsers. 22. Th. A. Boeree. "The mystery of the 9th SS Panzer Division (the Hohenstaufen Division) in the Battle of Arnhem". Met bijlagen, krtn, (z.j.). 91 genummerde bladen. Annexes. Annex 3. "The fight at Ginkel heath", p. 17.

403 Airborne Assault Archive. Box 4F1 2/10/5. 4 Para Brigade, Signal Section. Memories of Arnhem. William Carr.

404 Gelders Archief. Dokument 2171. Collectie Boeree. 1. 11. "The History of 7 Battalion K.O.S.B. in the Battle of Arnhem by Th.A. Boeree", 1954. Eén band, 103 genummerde bladen, afbeeldingen, kaarten, p. 32.

405 Gelders Archief. Dokument 2171. Collectie Boeree. 1. De Slag om Arnhem. 1.3. De Duitsers. 22. Th. A. Boeree. "The mystery of the 9th SS Panzer Division (the Hohenstaufen Division) in the Battle of Arnhem". Met bijlagen, krtn, (z.j.). 91 genummerde bladen. Annexes. Annex 3. "The fight at Ginkel heath", p. 18.

406 Gefechstbericht der 7. (Stamm) Kompanie für die Zeit vom 17.9. bis 26.9.44 von SS-Obersturmführer Karl Labahn. 2 Oktober 1944, p. 2. Gemeentearchiv Ede. Map 258, 2e afd. Documentatie Bevrijding Veluwe.

407 National Archives. WO 171/594. War Diary 4 Parachute Brigade. HQ. January–September 1944. Appendix "C". Copy of Diary Kept by Brigadier J.W. Hackett D.S.O., M.B.E., M.C. Commander 4 Parachute Bde.

408 "Hackett obituary". The Times, 10 September 1997. hill107.net/battle-of-arnhem/ john-hackett/hackett-obituary-the-times/

409 John Hackett, The Sunday Times, 15 September 1974.

410 National Archives. WO 171/594. War Diary 4 Parachute Brigade. HQ. January–September 1944. Appendix "C". Copy of Diary Kept by Brigadier J.W. Hackett D.S.O., M.B.E., M.C. Commander 4 Parachute Bde.

411 National Archives. WO 171/1247 156th Parachute Battalion. War Diary March–October 1944.

412 Verhoef, p. 79.

413 Bauer, The Battle of Arnhem, p. 114.

414 National Archives. WO 171/1236. War Diary, 1st Battalion, 1st Parachute Brigade 1944 Jan.–Dec.

415 National Archives. WO 171/594. War Diary 4 Parachute Brigade. HQ. January-September 1944. Appendix "C". Copy of Diary Kept by Brigadier J.W. Hackett D.S.O., M.B.E., M.C. Commander 4 Parachute Bde.

416 SS-Sturmbannführer Hans Möller, "Die Schlacht um Arnheim und in Osterbeck." [sic]. Gelders Archief. Archiefblok 2867. Collectie L.P.J. Vroemen. Doos nr. 54. , p. 25.

417 Bundesarchiv/Militärarchiv, RH 19, IX/90. Kriegstagebuch Heeresgruppe B v. 16.09-30.09.44. 18 September 1944.

418 Bundesarchiv/Militärarchiv, RH 24-88. Bestand LXXXVIII. Armeekorps: Ia-KTB mit Anlagen 1.7-31.12.1944.

419 Bundesarchiv/Militärarchiv, RH 19, IX/90. Kriegstagebuch Heeresgruppe B v. 16.09-30.09.44.

420 MacDonald, p. 20.

421 Bundesarchiv, Militärarchiv. RH 19 IX/10. Heeresgruppe B, Kriegstagebuch, Anlage Tagesmeldungen, 6.VI.-15.X.44.

422 MacDonald, p. 25.

423 Ibid., p. 68.

424 Ambrose, Stephen E. Citizen Soldiers: The U.S. Army From the Normandy Beaches to the Bulge to the Surrender of Germany. 1997, p. 144.

425 MacDonald, p. 68.

426 Ibid., p. 61.

427 Ibid., p. 174.

428 Sylvan, Major William C. and Captain Francis G. Smith, Jr., red. John T. Greenwood. Normandy to victory: the war diary of General Courtney H. Hodges & the First U.S. Army. Lexington, Kentucky: University Press of Kentucky, 2008. , p. 131.

429 Baynes, The Forgotten Victor: General Sir Richard O'Connor, p. 226.

430 Ibid., p. 229.

431 Bennett, p. 24.

432 Foreign Military Studies. MS B-149. Generalleutnant Walter Poppe. Commitment of 59th Infantry Division in the Netherlands 18 September to 25 November 1944, p. 2.

433 Bundesarchiv/Militärarchiv, RH 24-88. Bestand LXXXVIII. Armeekorps: Ia-KTB mit Anlagen 1.7–31.12.1944.

434 Foreign Military Studies. MS B-149. Generalleutnant Walter Poppe. Commitment of 59th Infantry Division in the Netherlands 18 September to 25 November 1944, p. 2.

435 Foreign Military Studies. MS C-001. von der Heydte, 6th Fallschirm Jaeger Regiment in action against US Paratroopers in the Netherlands in September 1944. p. 4.

436 Ibid.

437 Ibid.

438 Bundesarchiv/Militärarchiv, RH 24-88. Bestand LXXXVIII. Armeekorps: Ia-KTB mit Anlagen 1.7-31.12.1944. 18 September 1944.

439 Didden & Swarts, Autumn Gale, p. 222.

440 Kopka, p. 207.

441 National Archives, WO 171/1256. War Diary of 2nd Guards Bn Irish Guards from 1st September 1944 to 30th September 1944.

442 Kopka, p. 211.

443 Fitzgerald, Major Desmond J. L. History of the Irish Guards in the Second World War. Gale & Polden Ltd., Aldershot 1952. , p. 500.

444 Koskimaki, p. 126.

445 Ibid.

446 Ibid., p. 146.

447 Ambrose, Band of Brothers, p. 127.

448 Koskimaki, p. 146.

449 Ambrose, Band of Brothers, p. 127.

450 Marshall, Battle at Best, p. 22.

451 Combined Arms Research Library. Battalion and Small Unit Study No. 6: Parachute Infantry at Best, 1945.

452 Ibid.

453 Marshall, p. 22.

454 Combined Arms Research Library. Battalion and Small Unit Study No. 6: Parachute Infantry at Best, 1945.

455 Bundesarchiv/Militärarchiv, RH 24-88. Bestand LXXXVIII. Armeekorps: Ia-KTB mit Anlagen 1.7–31.12.1944. 18 September 1944.

456 Ibid.

457 Combined Arms Research Library. Battalion and Small Unit Study No. 6: Parachute Infantry at Best, 1945.

458 Saunders, p. 112.

459 Gorman, Location 1140.

460 Marshall, p. 30.

461 Courage, p. 116.

462 Marshall, p. 30.

463 Bundesarchiv/Militärarchiv, RH 24-88. Bestand LXXXVIII. Armeekorps: Ia-KTB mit Anlagen 1.7–31.12.1944. 18 September 1944.

464 Foreign Military Studies. MS P-189. Sixt, Generalleutnant Friedrich. *Die Kaempfe der Panzerbrigade 107 im September und Oktober 1944, nach einer Ausarbeitung von Oberstleutnant a.D. Bendt-Joachim Frhr.v. Maltzahn mit Ergänzungen gemäss dem Kriegstagebuch des O.B. West. 1954. Anhang B: Schilderung des Oberstlt. v. Maltzahn v. Mai 1954 über den Verlauf des 18.9.*

465 Bundesarchiv/Militärarchiv. RL 8/177. Kriegstagebuch 3. Jagddivision. 17 September 1944.

466 Bundesarchiv/Militärarchiv. RL 2-I/31. Persönliche Aufzeichnungen des Generals der Flieger Kreipe: Persönliches Tagebuch, 22. Juli bis 02. Nov. 1944. 18 September 1944.

467 National Archives. WO 171/376. War Diary "G" Branch Guards Armoured Division.

468 National Archives. WO 171/1254. War Diary Grenadier Guards Regiment January–September 1944.

469 Fraser, *War and Shadows*, p. 236.

470 Archive Tank Museum Bovington. MH.5. RH.4. 7th Armoured Division. Box 2: A Short History 7th Armoured Division June 1943–July 1945.

471 National Archives, WO 171/1254. War Diary Grenadier Guards Regiment January-September 1944.

472 Ibid.

473 Maneuver Center of Excellence Libraries – Fort Benning. Academic Department, The Infantry School, Fort Benning, Georgia. Advanced Infantry Officers Course 1948-1949: Kappel, Carl W. CPT, *Operations of Company H, 504th Parachute Infantry (82nd Airborne Division) in the Invasion of Holland 17–21 September 1944 (Rhineland Campaign)*, p. 26.

474 Ibid.

475 Rosse & Hill, *The Guards Armoured Division*, p. 133.

476 Fraser, p. 235.

477 National Archives. WO 171/366. War Diary British Airborne Corps. 17 September 1944–30 September 1944.

478 Rosse and Hill, p. 134.

479 Tieke, 329.

480 Bundesarchiv/Militärarchiv. MSG 3/3991. Informations-Kopie Gernot Traupel, 4. Mai 1981. Die Hellebarde No. 18/1996.

481 Fraser, p. 234.

482 Ibid., p. 206.

483 National Archives, WO 171/1254. War Diary 1st Battalion Grenadier Guards January–September 1944. 18 September 1944.

484 Margry, *Operation Market-Garden Then and Now*, vol. 2, p. 354.

485 National Archives, WO 171/981. War Diary 86th (East Anglian) (Herts Yeo) Field Regiment, Royal Artillery January–December 1944.

486 Margry, vol. 2, p. 352.

487 Rosendaal, *The Destruction of Nijmegen, 1944*, p. 115.

488 McManus, *September Hope*, p. 257.

489 National Archives, WO 171/1254 War Diary Grenadier Guards Regiment January–September 1944.

490 Margry, vol. 2, p. 356.

491 Ibid., p. 353.

492 Rosse & Hill, p. 135.

493 Margry, vol. 2, p. 356.

494 Ryan, p. 431.

495 van Lunteren, *The Battle for the Bridges*, p. 109.

496 Bundesarchiv/Militärarchiv. MSG 3/3991. Die Hellebarde No. 18/1996, p. 140.

497 van Lunteren, p. 110.

498 Margry, vol. 2, p. 355.

499 National Archives, WO 171/981. War Diary 86th (East Anglian) (Herts Yeo) Field Regiment, Royal Artillery January–December 1944.

500 SS-Kriegsberichterzug 10. SS-Panzer-Division "Frundsberg", *Dran, drauf und durch: Buczacz–Caen–Nimwegen*, p. 78.

501 National Archives, WO 171/1254. War Diary Grenadier Guards Regiment January-September 1944. Gds Armd Div Int Summary No 72 - Up to 2359 hrs 20 Sep 44.

502 Heinz Harmel, handwritten notes. Gelders Archief. Archiefblok 2867. Collectie L.P.J. Vroemen. Doos nr. 31.

THE ARDENNES 1944–1945
– HITLER'S WINTER OFFENSIVE

Christer Bergström
ISBN: 978-16-1200-277-4
504 pages
Large format, heavily illustrated

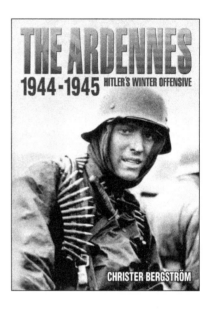

This book has become the main reference work on the Battle of the Bulge. Christer Bergström has interviewed veterans, gone through huge amounts of archive material, and performed on-the-spot research in the area. The result is a large amount of previously unpublished material and new findings and the most accurate picture yet of what really transpired.

"I have never read a more outstanding World War II book."

– Review by Lars Navander, Lieutenant Colonel and former Intelligence Officer at the Swedish Headquarters of the Armed Forces

THE BATTLE OF BRITAIN
– AN EPIC CONFLICT REVISITED

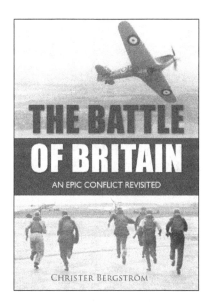

Christer Bergström
ISBN: 978-16-1200-347-4
336 pages
Large format, heavily illustrated

The most thorough, expert examination of the topic ever written. Illustrated throughout with maps and rare photos, plus a colour section closely depicting the aircraft, this work lays out the battle as seldom seen before.

This book contains a large number of dramatic eyewitness accounts, even as it reveals new facts that have altered much of the perception of the battle in the public eye. For example, the twin-engined Messerschmitt Bf 110 was actually a good daytime fighter, and it performed at least as well in this role as the Bf 109 during the battle. The Luftwaffe commander, Hermann Göring, performed far better than his public image has previously indicated.

BLACK CROSS RED STAR
– AIR WAR OVER THE EASTERN FRONT VOLUME 4
STALINGRAD TO KUBAN 1942–1943

Christer Bergström
ISBN: 978-91-8844-121-8
400 pages
Large format, heavily illustrated

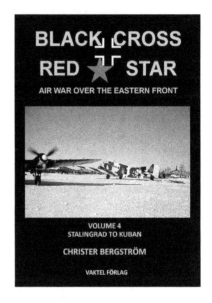

Regarded as the standard work on the air war over the Eastern Front during the Second World War, Christer Bergström's unique Black Cross/Red Star series covers the history of the air war on the Eastern Front in close detail, from the perspectives of both sides. Based on a close study of German and Russian archive material, as well as interviews with a large number of the airmen who participated in this aerial conflict, it has established itself as the main source on the air war on the Eastern Front.

Black Cross/Red Star, Volume 4 covers the air war along the entire Eastern Front during the winter period of 1942–1943 through March 1943, in great detail, with a balance between German and Soviet archive sources etc, and with many first-hand accounts.

INDEX

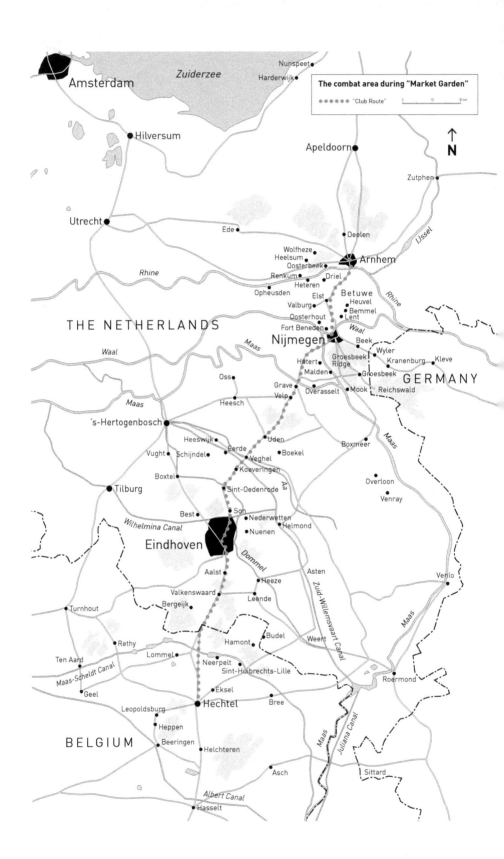

The combat area during "Market Garden"

●●●●●● "Club Route"

0   10   20 km

N

Amsterdam
Zuiderzee
Nunspeet
Harderwijk
Hilversum
Apeldoorn
Zutphen
Utrecht
Ede
Deelen
Wolfheze
Heelsum
Oosterbeek
Renkum
Oosterbeek
Driel
Arnhem
Rhine
Heteren
Elst
Betuwe
Opheusden
Heuvel
Valburg
Bemmel
Oosterhout
Lent
THE NETHERLANDS
Fort Beneden
Waal
Rhine
Waal
Beek
Nijmegen
Wyler
Kranenburg
Kleve
Maas
Hatert
Groesbeek
Ridge
Oss
Malden
Groesbeek
GERMANY
Grave
Overasselt
Mook
Reichswald
Heesch
Velp
's-Hertogenbosch
Maas
Maas
Heeswijk
Uden
Boxmeer
Eerde
Vught
Schijndel
Boekel
Veghel
Boxtel
Koeveringen
Overloon
Tilburg
Sint-Oedenrode
Venray
Best
Son
Wilhelmina Canal
Nederwetten
Helmond
Eindhoven
Nuenen
Dommel
Aalst
Asten
Heeze
Venlo
Valkenswaard
Leende
Turnhout
Bergeijk
Zuid-Willemsvaart Canal
Maas
Rethy
Budel
Ten Aard
Hamont
Weert
Lommel
Maas-Scheldt Canal
Neerpelt
Sint-Huibrechts-Lille
Roermond
Geel
Eksel
Juliana Canal
Leopoldsburg
Hechtel
Bree
Heppen
BELGIUM
Beeringen
Helchteren
Sittard
Asch
Albert Canal
Hasselt

CPSIA information can be obtained
at www.ICGtesting.com
Printed in the USA
BVHW041029180719
553828BV00016B/2082/P